HARRY SMITH

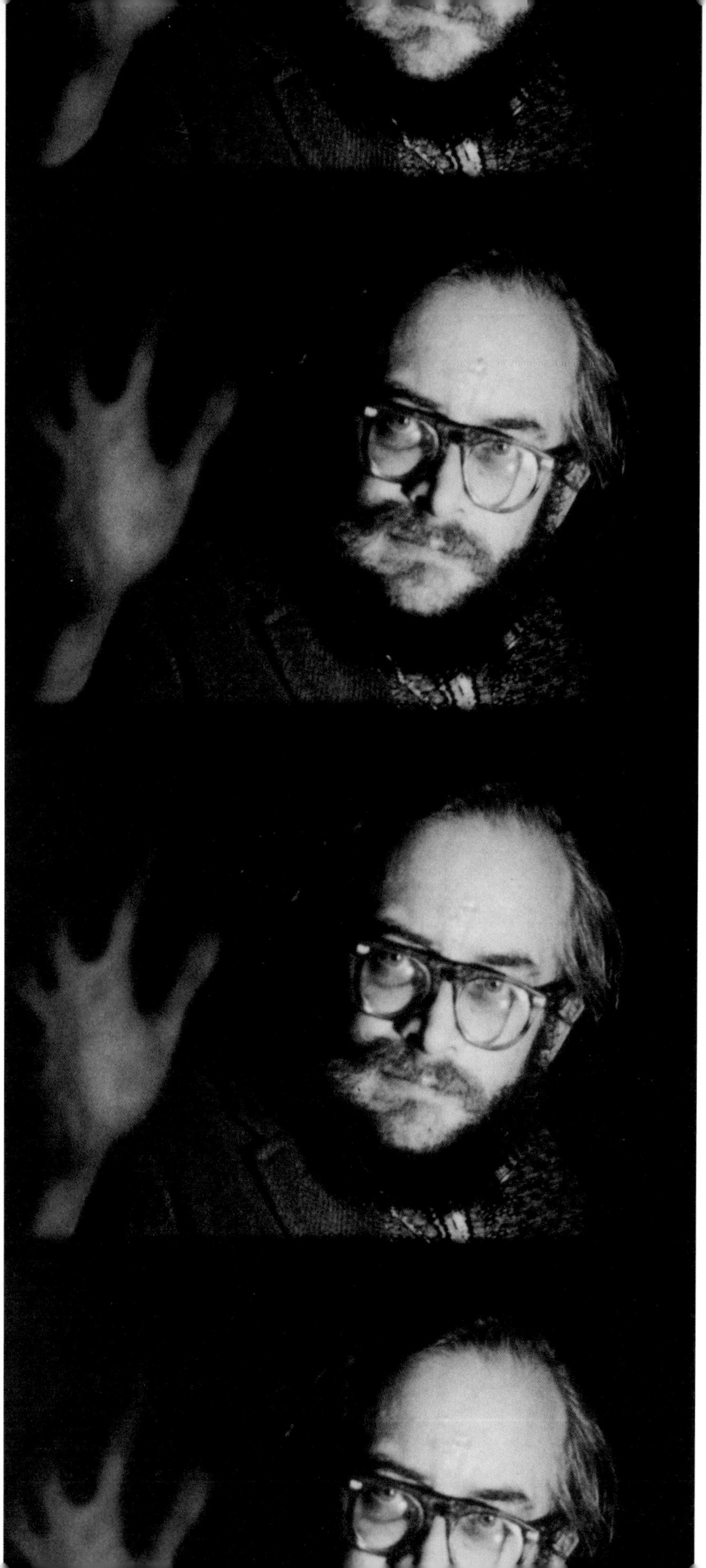

Getty Research Institute
Issues & Debates

HARRY SMITH

THE AVANT-GARDE IN THE AMERICAN VERNACULAR

Edited by
ANDREW PERCHUK
and RANI SINGH

THE GETTY RESEARCH INSTITUTE PUBLICATIONS PROGRAM
Thomas W. Gaehtgens, *Director, Getty Research Institute*
Gail Feigenbaum, *Associate Director, Research and Publications*
Julia Bloomfield, *Head, Publications Program*

ISSUES & DEBATES
Thomas Crow, Jeffrey M. Hurwit, Jacqueline Lichtenstein, Alex Potts, and Mimi Hall Yiengpruksawan, *Publications Committee*

HARRY SMITH: THE AVANT-GARDE IN THE AMERICAN VERNACULAR
Edited by Andrew Perchuk and Rani Singh
Michelle Bonnice, *Manuscript Editor*

This volume, the sixteenth in the series Issues & Debates, evolved from two symposia organized by the Getty Research Institute and held at the Getty Center in Los Angeles: "Harry Smith: The Avant-Garde in the American Vernacular," 20–21 April 2001, and "Investigating *Mahagonny*," 30–31 May 2002

Published by the Getty Research Institute, Los Angeles
Getty Publications
Gregory M. Britton, *Publisher*
1200 Getty Center Drive, Suite 500
Los Angeles, CA 90049-1682
www.getty.edu
14 13 12 11 10 5 4 3 2 1

Back cover: Harry Smith, String figure, 1960s; Hy Hirsh, Harry Smith with his "brain drawings," ca. 1950; Harry Smith, Still from *Film #12: Heaven and Earth Magic*, ca. 1957–62. See pp. 49, 22, 74

Library of Congress Cataloging-in-Publication Data
Harry Smith : the avant-garde in the American vernacular / edited by Andrew Perchuk and Rani Singh.
p. cm. — (Issues & debates)
"This volume, the sixteenth in the series Issues & Debates, evolved from two symposia organized by the Getty Research Institute and held at the Getty Center in Los Angeles: "Harry Smith: The Avant-Garde in the American Vernacular," 20–21 April 2001, and "Investigating 'Mahagonny,'" 30–31 May 2002."
Includes bibliographical references and index.
ISBN 978-0-89236-735-1 (pbk.)
1. Smith, Harry Everett, 1923-1991—Congresses. 2. Avant-garde (Aesthetics)—United States—History—20th century. I. Perchuk, Andrew. II. Singh, Rani. III. Getty Research Institute.
NX512.S65H37 2010
700.92—dc22

2009022201

CONTENTS

ACKNOWLEDGMENTS

A volume such as this is made possible only through the thoughtful assistance of many individuals and organizations. This publication originated from two symposia held at the Getty Center: "Harry Smith: The Avant-Garde in the American Vernacular," 20–21 April 2001, and "Investigating *Mahagonny*," 30–31 May 2002. These symposia provided, for the first time, public forums for interdisciplinary discussion of Harry Smith's endeavors that extended across his myriad interests. We were able to make connections that traversed the varied media in which he worked—including film, music, and the visual arts—bringing into focus the ways in which Smith himself approached and presented his creative output. The result was purely electric, and we hope that this book transmits some of that energy.

We are immensely grateful to Nick Amster, William Breeze, Raymond Foye, Hal Willner, and Peter Lamborn Wilson, whose continual assistance, constructive advice, and profound understanding of Harry Smith have guided us through every step of this venture. Not only have their insights, culled from years of direct experience and dedicated engagement with Smith, kept his work alive but their support helped make the Harry Smith Archives—the backbone of this undertaking—a reality. We wish to thank all the contributors to the two symposia on Harry Smith, and we extend special thanks to the authors of the essays in this book. Their scholarship has greatly expanded our understanding of Smith's life and work. We note the passing of Paul Arthur, Percy Heath, and William Moritz in the interval between the symposia and the appearance of this volume. They are sorely missed.

Our sincere gratitude to Jeff Place and Stephanie Smith, archivists at the Smithsonian Institution's Center for Folklife and Cultural Heritage; Jonas Mekas and the staff of Anthology Film Archives; Peter Hale of the Allen Ginsberg Trust; John Cohen; Peter Cole; Darrin Daniel; Ken Eisenstein; Ernie Gehr; Brian Graham; Peter Kubelka; Martina Kudláček; Bret Lunsford; Kristine McKenna; Jürgen Schebera; Philip Smith; Michael Snow; and Mary and Stacey Wolfe. Each advanced the project by either helping track down images or generously loaning them for publication or by providing editorial suggestions. Many of them have a long history of commitment to the educational mission of Harry Smith, and their contributions have been vital.

This publication could not have happened without the extraordinary backing of two successive directors of the Getty Research Institute. Thomas Crow recognized at the very onset of his tenure at the Research Institute that Harry Smith was worthy of serious study and was largely responsible for us having time as residential scholars at the Research Institute to turn this project into a finished work. Thomas Gaehtgens, the current director, has been equally supportive of contemporary art research and programming and of the Harry Smith project. We also thank Gail Feigenbaum, associate director for programs at the Research Institute, and Julia Bloomfield, head of GRI Publications, for their long and persistent advocacy of this volume.

We are indebted as well to many of the staff of the Research Institute, far more than the few we mention here. David Brafman, curator of rare books, located various images in the Research Library's collections. John Kiffe and the personnel of Visual Media Services meticulously photographed many of the works illustrating this volume. Matthew Reynolds, Gloria Sutton, Genevieve Yue, Jason Hill, Rachelle Okawa, and Jannon Stein all played essential roles during their time as research assistants. Most important, we are grateful to Carlos Kase, whose patience, meticulousness, and keen intellect helped make this a better book, and to Michelle Bonnice, whose editorial input regarding the texts and images have much improved this publication. They asked valuable questions and endeavored to track down the most minute and esoteric details; Harry Smith would have approved!

Rani Singh would like to add to the thanks expressed above a note of personal appreciation to P. Adams Sitney, who as a scholar at the Research Institute during the 2004/2005 Scholar Year was an unflagging source of lucid memories of Harry Smith and clear-headed insight into the subject at hand—he offered an unpolished gem every day.

This volume is dedicated to Harry Smith, whose finite body of work affords an infinite amount of pleasure. His omnivorous and voracious intellectual curiosity sets an example we should all seek to follow, and his studious rigor presents a model every artist and scholar should seek to emulate. For those lucky enough to experience Smith's work, it will continue to unlock fresh insights, encourage the repatterning of the mundane, and impart nothing less than a unique way of seeing the world.

—Andrew Perchuk and Rani Singh

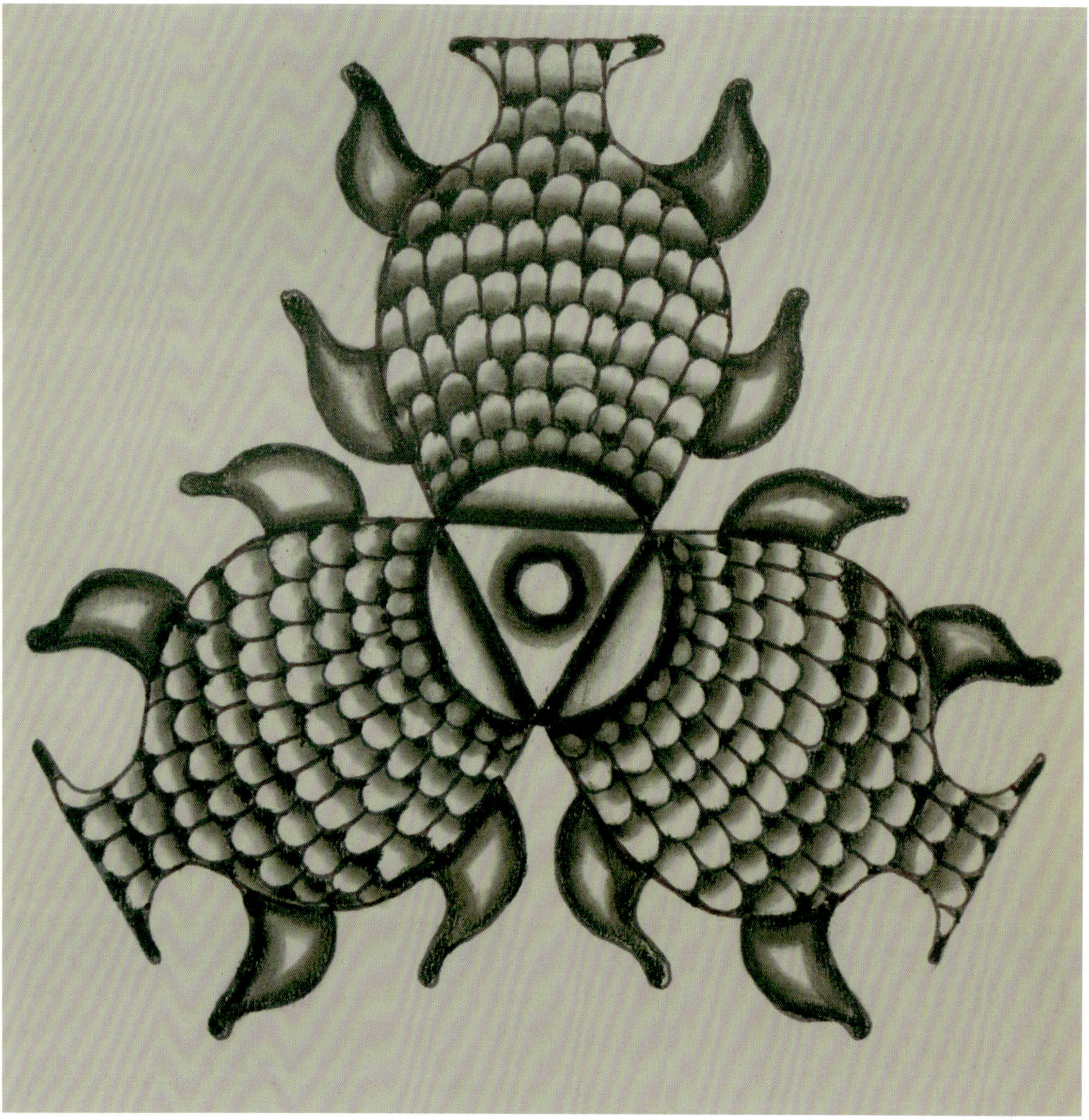

PART I
Harry Smith

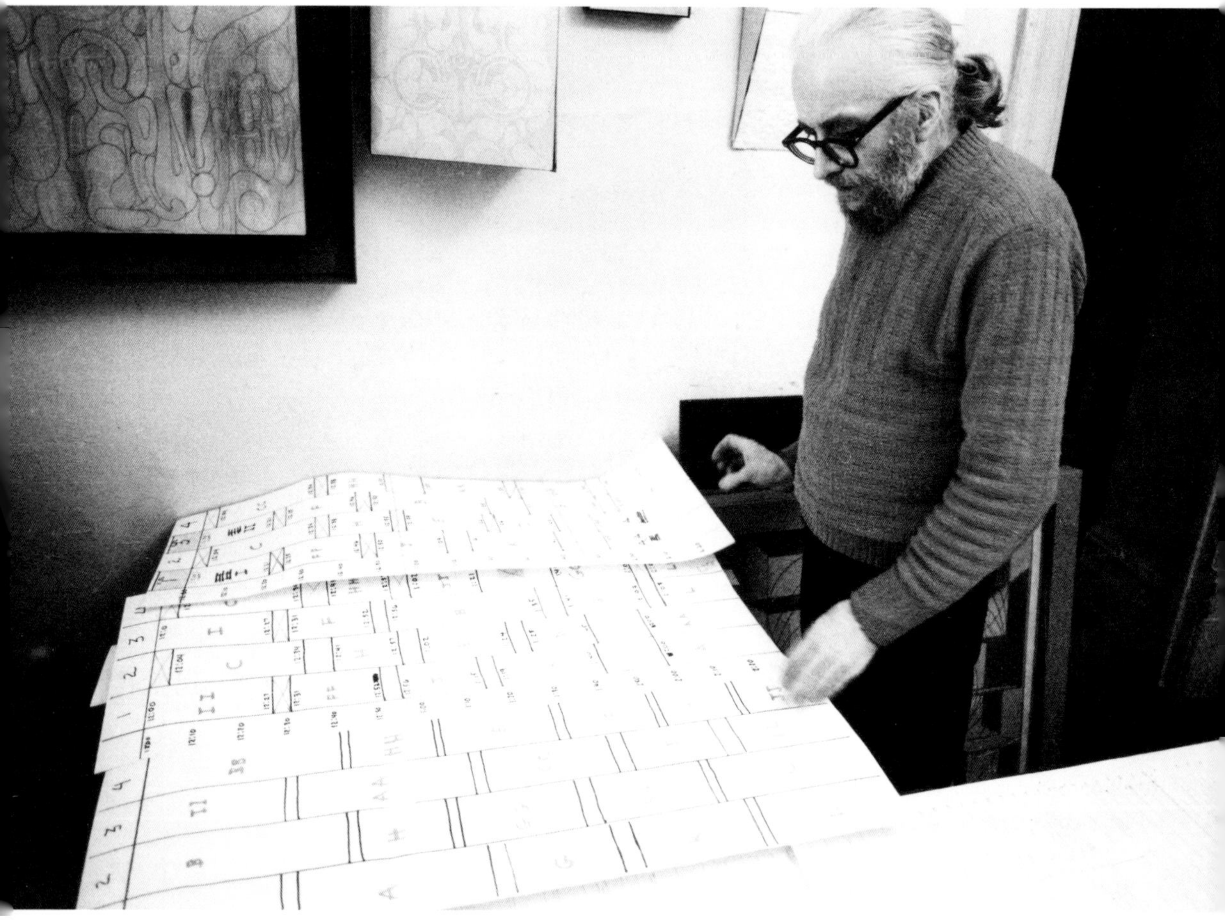

ANDREW PERCHUK

STRUGGLE AND STRUCTURE

Filmmaker, musicologist, anthropologist, ethnographer, collector of patterns and string figures—despite his multifaceted artistic endeavors and cultic status in the worlds of music and film, Harry Smith remains one of the least understood figures in postwar American culture. Since its creation in 1952, Smith's *Anthology of American Folk Music* (now distributed by Smithsonian Folkways) has educated and inspired musicians, fans, musicologists, and others interested in roots music. At the same time, Smith is known to filmmakers, film scholars, and devotees of experimental cinema as the creator of a unique body of abstract and nonnarrative films. The totality of his artistic output is, however, so little comprehended that it is possible to turn from a music publication on Smith to a film publication on him without realizing that they discuss the same person. This volume is a first attempt to bring together scholarly writings that stretch across Smith's oeuvre, surveying not only his contributions to American music and film but also his extensive visual arts endeavors and his vast collecting activities, all of which he considered of equal importance. As many of the authors in this book note, Smith is a difficult figure to pin down (no doubt partially because of his own self-mythologizing and perpetual evasions), but this volume aspires, by considering the fullness of Smith's activities, to locate him and his art more securely within the history of advanced art production in the postwar period.

Harry Smith undoubtedly made works of art that can rightfully be called avant-garde, but for all its apparent neutrality as a slimmer adjectival form for "advanced art practice," "avant-garde" could never have been a term that attached itself comfortably to Smith. The artistic sensibility that characterized the group of (mostly) men that dominated the era immediately after World War II when Smith came of age was far too triumphant, careerist, and heterosexual for Smith to have identified with or gained access to, even if he so desired. So, if "avant-garde" is a poor fit, should the natural place to locate Smith then be on the other side of T. J. Clark's still useful distinction: if not the avant-garde, then bohemia? Paradoxically, this might justify this volume's title, *Harry Smith: The Avant-Garde in the American Vernacular,* for Clark states that "the real history of the *avant-garde* is the history of those who bypassed, ignored and rejected it; a history of secrecy and isolation."[1] He then goes on to locate a postwar bohemia specifically in the place where Smith achieved artistic maturity: "the Bohemian style only works in a capitalism with a myth of itself, a belief in its future. Hence the failure of its British variants; hence its reappearance in California."[2]

This postwar bohemia stands in particular relation to its nineteenth-century Parisian ancestor, the proper subject of Clark's study; "its reappearance in California" can only be understood in specific terms central also to our understanding of Smith's work. Clark unmasks the Parisian avant-garde as a profoundly ideological

Page viii
Harry Smith
Buddha's Footprint, ca. 1983, ink and pencil on paper, 19 × 19 cm (7½ × 7½ in.)
Collection Allen Ginsberg Estate

Page 1
Harry Smith
Book-page border design, 1988
Harry Smith Archives

Fig. 1.
Scott A. Feero (American, b. 1955)
Harry Smith with charts for *Film #18: Mahagonny,* Hotel Breslin, New York City, 1980

construct, and one that, for all its protestations of subscribing to a more advanced mode of thought than the rest of the Parisian artistic world, actually aligned itself with bourgeois politics. In the French Revolution of 1848, it was not the avant-garde that stood with progressive forces, but bohemia. As Clark defines that contrast: "they fought, for a start, on different sides of the barricades in June: the Bohemians with the insurrection, and the *avant-garde,* of course, with the forces of order."[3] As part of its ideology, the avant-garde recast bohemia in terms of the still-current fantasy of the frivolous *la vie bohème.* Clark, however, asks us to recognize bohemia for what it actually was: a real social class, and one aligned not with the students of the Latin Quarter but with the *classes dangereuses*—the "vagabonds, discharged soldiers, discharged jailbirds, escaped galley slaves, swindlers, mountebanks, . . . , *literati,* organ-grinders, rag-pickers, knife grinders, tinkers, beggars" described by Karl Marx as opposed to bourgeois order.[4] The revolutionary work of the bohemians was to caricature bourgeois society by holding up the ideals that the bourgeoisie claimed as their own, the ideals of the French Revolution of 1789, and demonstrating how far from reality they were.

An antibourgeois stance emerged in California in the late 1940s and 1950s, but no actual revolution was in the offing. The distinction between avant-garde and bohemia was therefore reposited in less world-historical terms, specifically in relation to American consumer capitalism: in the words of the poet Robert Duncan, "Your art has to be posed with no guarantee and actually look like a very remote unreal activity to be in. Something that nobody values, and you couldn't explain why you're doing it—in order for it to be Bohemia. . . . Modern painting constantly tries to occupy an area that would be doubtful enough to be Bohemian, but it has become so much of a commodity that it's very hard to keep the Bohemian sense."[5] While Duncan graciously admits that modern painters could potentially be bohemian, he is deeply suspicious of precisely those artists who became the standard-bearers for the American postwar avant-garde. The subsequent financial success of many first-generation New York School painters and the later alliance of Clement Greenberg, at least, to the quintessential "forces of order" would only have confirmed these suspicions. Instead, Duncan identifies bohemia with the artists in his own San Francisco circle and in a closely related group of artists clustered around Wallace and Shirley Berman in Los Angeles. The locus of these artists' caricature of bourgeois ideals is personal politics, specifically family and domesticity, two of the major pillars of postwar Eisenhower conformity. Duncan rejects the bourgeois vision of the family as a self-sufficient organism sealed off from the outside world and comprising the nuclear family in favor of a much more permeable entity whose sociability defies traditional categories; he recasts domesticity from the maintenance of a space containing commodities purchased as a reflection of one's lifestyle to the celebration of things made—the most important being art, music, and poetry. In Duncan's formulation,

> In a Bohemian household you have immediacy to all the arts so that you are going to have some aspect of music, poetry, painting, and also the decoration of things at the same level. The minute they're picked up, it is part of the thing

> you do. Much of what you have around is either painted, composed, etc., either by you or your friends.... The Bohemian way is also a constant flow of people in and out, lots of entertainment. You're not surprised that so-and-so is married, or not married, to so-and-so. That's part of what we see—this network of people, this constant interchange.[6]

Harry Smith knew Duncan and for a brief period participated in at least one aspect of Bay Area bohemianism, the film series Art in Cinema. Smith played a part in the establishment of this early American outlet for experimental cinema, attending screenings, showing his own films, and even traveling down to Los Angeles to recruit filmmakers such as Oskar Fischinger and Kenneth Anger.[7] However, despite his acquaintance and perhaps friendship (more about this later) with numerous bohemian artists, Smith was never fully part of the sustaining networks that protected and encouraged these artists in the face of the often brutal suppression, both legal and mental, that characterized the early Cold War era. As Paul Arthur points out, "Smith did not actively collaborate with other filmmakers, disdained the widespread custom of group film programs, and took no role in the launching or administering of the avant-garde cinema's flourishing network of artist-run distribution and exhibition venues."[8]

If the two common descriptors of an advanced postwar artist—avant-garde or bohemian—both seem inadequate to describe Smith, what could that possibly mean for Smith and his work? It certainly does not mean that Smith did not make avant-garde art, or that he was somehow magically free of the constraints—whether Greenberg's "umbilical cord of gold" that defined the relationship of avant-garde to bourgeoisie[9] or the inner exile that characterized many bohemians' position within mainstream American society—under which all advanced artists were forced to work. But it may unbind Smith from some of the myths that continue to surround him, often obscuring both his own descriptions of what he was doing and his work. The first is Smith as a romanticized countercultural figure, a middle term between Woody Guthrie and Bob Dylan. While it is frequently stated that one of the seminal experiences that led Smith to become an artist took place at a Guthrie concert in the 1940s, Smith's own account of that experience is rarely mentioned: "It could have been at some longshoreman's hall.... I'm sure it was like Communists. But I didn't like his singing. It was too sophisticated and too involved with social problems, I felt. It wasn't the sort of stuff I was interested in."[10] The second is that, together with his friend Allen Ginsberg, Smith was part of a happy band of Beats. This similarly elides the fact that people who knew Smith well—Jordan Belson, Lionel Ziprin—have commented that Smith hated artists, that this antipathy meant that he did not refer to himself as an artist.[11] All this means that Smith could never have resided contentedly in some alternative bohemian milieu.

Although Smith, particularly through the *Anthology,* was undoubtedly one of the figures who inspired the counterculture of the 1960s, he was resolutely suspicious of politics in either its avant-garde or its bohemian inflection. When John Cohen interviewed Smith in 1969 and asked him to reflect on "what happened in politics last summer"—presumably the wave of student-led protests in 1968, that watershed moment of countercultural politics—Smith responded: "That brought the ideas home a little, although it was also disillusioning that so many apparently intelligent people could have any faith in politics. Yet there was some protest against the general notion of politics."[12] Smith's comments do not mean that he was for the status quo or against the transformation of society, much less that he was in agreement with Greenberg's neoconservative revisionism that what "started out more or less as 'Trotskyism,' turned into art for art's sake, and thereby cleared the way, heroically, for what was to come."[13] Instead, as Stephen Fredman suggests, he believed that politics per se was a shallow and ineffective means to change society and that a more profound change could come from altering the music to which people listened. Smith related to Cohen the effects he expected from releasing the *Anthology:* "I felt social changes would result from it. I'd been reading Plato's *Republic.* He's jabbering on about music, how you have to be careful about changing the music because it might upset or destroy the government. Everybody gets out of step."[14]

Smith's distrust of politics is related to his dislike for artists, as he was much more interested in deep structure than manifest form,[15] and therefore often referred to himself as an anthropologist—the only subject in which he had any significant formal training. As opposed to acting as an avant-garde or bohemian artist, Smith practiced a kind of aesthetic anthropology, but from a position not normally aligned with the authority of the anthropologist and instead more in tune with the social position of Clark's *classes dangereuses.* In other words, and as referenced by Greil Marcus, Arthur, and Fredman, Harry Smith was a bum. To some degree, this is not simply a description—Smith, especially later in life, toothless and unable to ingest solid food while barely subsisting in flophouses—but also a strategy. The bum was a figure much in the popular imagination during Smith's depression-era childhood, very distinct from the homeless of our own era. In fact, as the social realist painter Philip Evergood explained, there were both representationally and literally different types of bums. In distinguishing the benighted popular front bums of Reginald Marsh from the angry, ungrateful figures he himself painted, Evergood declared: "Marsh saw the sadness and the unfairness and Marsh was sorry for the bums, but he accepted this state of society and this picturesque scene, representing New York as inevitable. Hence, Marsh's bums are 'classical,' 'acceptable' bums, acceptable as lost souls and classical in their tragic hopelessness. *My* bums, which I painted at the same time as Marsh, were dangerous bums, discontented bums, because mine had not accepted their lot. Mine were not congenital bums, but transient bums."

Harry Smith lived and worked as just such an angry bum, setting up transient networks of support, as bums are forced to do, never knowing when someone around them will die or be dragged off to hospital or prison. He interacted with, and frequently used, those he needed to carry off a particular project, and he never seems to have been especially grateful or particularly sorry when he did things like pawn a borrowed camera. And if the avant-garde was parasitic on the bourgeoisie, tied by that umbilical cord of gold, Smith was parasitic off the avant-garde and bohemia alike, as Cohen decried: "You've bothered me, my friends, and others in the sense that you don't accept the fact that you have to earn money to be a fruitful part of society."[17] Part of their displeasure was no doubt that Smith's angry bum caricatured bohemian ideals—"art as life," "life as art"—just as bohemia caricatured the bourgeoisie.

Smith made his identification, and often very real cohabitation, with bums explicit as a strategy when he stated, "We're all trapped in a social system where you have to do something to provide food and shelter. I thought for a while that drinking got me out of food and shelter, but it's a way of living that is pushed underground. Thousands and thousands of derelicts."[18] The bum is, of course, a figure who is almost by definition considered dangerous to the bourgeois social order, a person whose very existence is criminalized—vagrant/vagrancy—rather than just his actions—arsonist, murderer. Smith's sustained penury, as well as his extended artistic engagements with African American jazz musicians and Native American artists, was a solidarity with those who do not choose the fringes but are forcibly, and physically (even more so in Smith's day), excluded from the spaces and opportunities of white, bourgeois American society. At the same time, it risks an unfortunate identification of Smith with otherness, a further instance in the disturbing history, stretching from Paul Verlaine to Norman Mailer, of casting the bohemian artist as the "white Negro."[19] Smith, however, was extremely dubious of this sort of identification, as instanced by his withering comments on the hippies' embrace of Native American customs as style: "I'm pretty sure there have always been things like people dressing up in Indian clothes. It's a romanticism of a sort to be followed by something else when this dies down. I would say it hasn't much association with the Indians, other than that everybody is now more sympathetic to the Indians. After all, their grandparents were murdering millions of them. I suppose that children dressed up like Saracens during the Crusades."[20] What saves Smith, other than the miserable facts of his own existence, is his anthropology, the fact that neither in his own social position nor in the work of artists of color is he looking for authenticity; instead he is searching for structure.

Through his twin vocations of artistic collagist and taxonomic collector (fig. 2), Smith locates nonverbal ways of ordering information and then of communicating these formations so as to make transhistorical patterns, the deep structures of society, emerge for the viewer or listener. As he explains,

> It has something to do with the desire to communicate in some way, the collection of objects. Now I like to have something around that has a lot of information in it, and since then, it seems to me that books are an especially bad way of recording information.... So I've been interested in other things that gave a heightened experience in relation to the environment.... So I'm interested in getting a series of objects of different sorts....
>
> ...The type of thinking that I applied to records, I still apply to other things, like Seminole patchwork or to Ukrainian Easter eggs. The whole purpose is to have some kind of series of things. Information as drawing and graphic designs can be located more quickly than it can be in books. The fact that I have all the Seminole designs permits anything that falls into the canon of that technological procedure to be found there. It's like flipping quickly through. It's a way of programming the mind, like a punch card of a sort.[21]

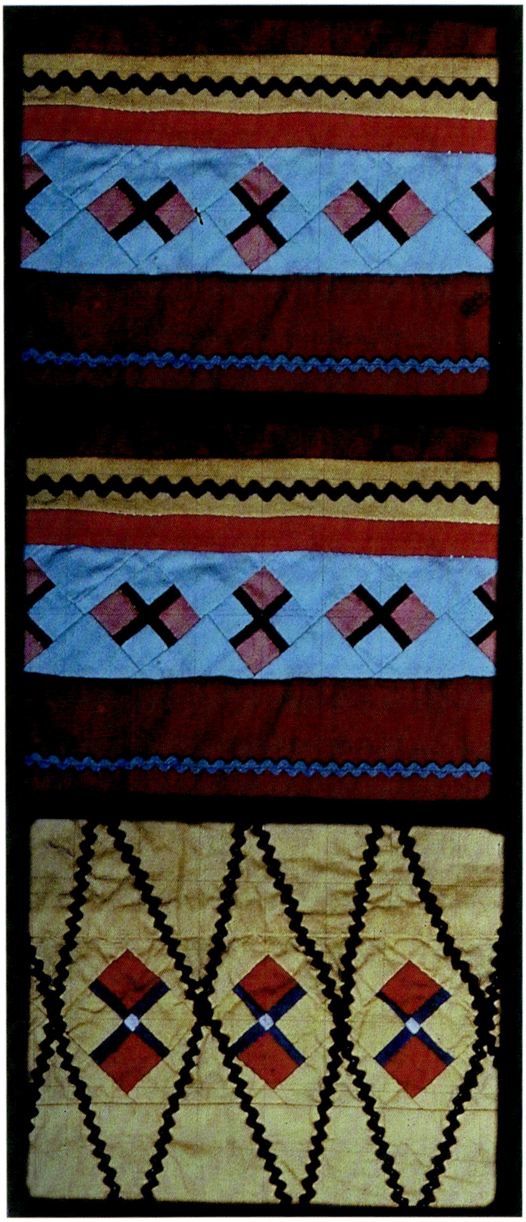

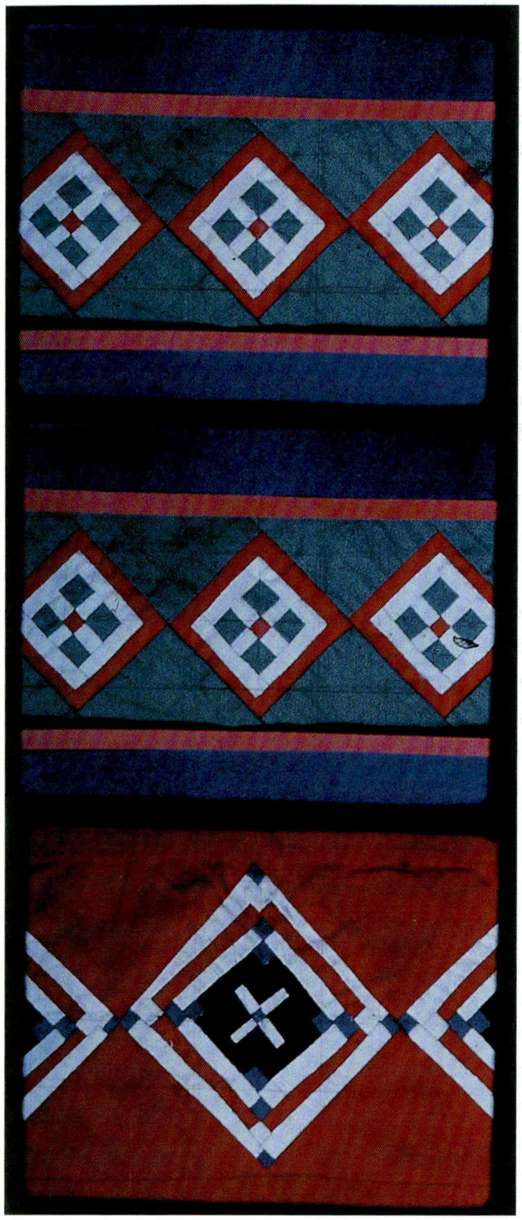

What makes Smith in some ways a modernist, as well as a mystic, is that he believes that the uncovering of these patterns unlocks powerful truths, whether esoteric or more prosaic, that are fundamental to understanding all human creation and have the power to change society. As an elderly Smith said of the impact of his *Anthology*, "I've seen America changed through music."[22]

The essays in this volume employ a range of approaches to engage with Smith's structures but can usefully be divided into attempts to trace the genealogies that shaped Smith as an artist, to map Smith's art onto other structural systems, to apply the comparative structures of analogy or allegory to Smith's work, and to define the procedural logic through which Smith constructs and uncovers his systems. Rani Singh and William Moritz have mined personal memory as well as the available archival resources to present, respectively, a fuller picture of Smith's overall career and an account of Smith's specific relationship to experimental film in California in the 1940s. Singh pulls out several of the remarkably diverse intellectual threads that the largely autodidact Smith wove together to construct his mature work. Beginning with a childhood steeped in theosophy and Freemasonry, an adolescence immersed in amateur and then more formal anthropology, and an adult devotion to Aleister Crowley's Ordo Templi Orientis, linguistics, and esoteric philosophy, Smith ultimately arrived at what Singh terms an ethnographic modernism. Moritz likewise portrays Smith as a mythologist but does so in order to deconstruct some of Smith's own self-mythologizing, detailing how the artist's encounters with experimental filmmakers such as Oskar Fischinger and John and James Whitney provided the necessary framework for Smith's early hand-painted abstract films.

In the extended back and forth that constitutes P. Adams Sitney's and Annette Michelson's contributions to this book, the authors engage in a debate as to the proper structural system to elucidate Smith's *Film #12: Heaven and Earth Magic:* mythopoesis or psychoanalysis. The sequence begins with an excerpt from "Absolute Animation," the chapter in Sitney's *Visionary Film* that constituted one of the first significant attempts to engage with Smith's work. Sitney details Smith's elaborate alchemical and kabbalistic operations, connecting them to the Romantic theme of the splintered self that must be reintegrated. For Sitney, Smith conflates heaven and the human brain, and the journeys of the woman and the magus alike are ultimately directed toward a restorative telos in which "Everything returns to its place of origin."[23] Michelson counters that the structure of the disintegrative and restorative operations that make up the majority of *Heaven and Earth Magic* are better understood through psychoanalysis than through myth. She turns to the two principal positions that ground the formation of infantile psychoses in the theory of Melanie Klein: the paranoid-schizoid position in which the infant relates to the world as a group not of whole objects but of "part objects" that split the ego into good and bad elements (paradigmatically, good breast and bad breast); and the depressive position that tries to repair the violence of the splitting of bad from good.

Fig. 2.
Harry Smith
Stills from *Film #15*
(Untitled animation of Seminole patchwork patterns), ca. 1965–66, ca. 10 min., 16 mm, color, silent

Ultimately, Michelson asserts that *Heaven and Earth Magic* is "the representation of an elaborate working through, in the form of a prodigally generous form of reparation offered by artistic practice, of the spectrum of infantile development through paranoid-schizoid and depressive positions."[24]

The conversation about *Heaven and Earth Magic* continues in Sitney's essay on Smith as a bibliophile. He adds to Singh's and Moritz's genealogies by delving further into the sources that Smith was reading at the time he made the film and proposing a series of close correspondences between Smith's film and the work of the pioneering French filmmaker Georges Méliès. A different vantage on the subject of *Heaven and Earth Magic* is provided by Smith himself. In the talk he gave at the Queens Museum of Art in 1978 (offered here in a new transcription), Smith demonstrates that he—along with Andy Warhol—was one of the intractable masters of the interactive talk, or interview form, in postwar art.

Both Paul Arthur and Stephen Hinton analyze Smith's *Film #18: Mahagonny* in terms of what they see as structures integral to, respectively, certain types of experimental film and modernist music. Arthur claims that prior to the emergence of New Narrative film in the 1980s, a vital if impossible goal of an avant-garde cinema that equated historical consciousness with the despised convention of linear narrative was to stand outside history, in a space of cinematic *presentness*. This goal aligns, of course, with Smith's antipathy to historical explanation and with his preference for the transhistorical methods of anthropology and structuralism. But Arthur is interested in particular in the relation between *Mahagonny* and aspects of a specific structuralist logic of experimental film of the 1970s that he terms the "first film/last film" syndrome. This meant that filmmakers strove to make either works so elemental that no prior work was conceivable or works that represented the last possible terms in their respective lines of development. Arthur sees *Mahagonny* as one of these last films not only for its conceptual rigor and formal exhaustiveness and for providing probably the last word on nondramatic adaptation of opera but also because its projection—*Mahagonny* was originally meant to be shown on the tops of four billiard tables enclosed in a boxing ring—stretched the cinematic apparatus to its limits.

Hinton, by contrast, adduces a relation between *Mahagonny* and Kurt Weill and Bertolt Brecht's *Aufstieg und Fall der Stadt Mahagonny* (1930; *Rise and Fall of the City of Mahagonny*), particularly in terms of the opera's complex structural manipulations of *Songspiel* and *Songstil* and its interruptions that clearly reference German opera history. At various points in the opera, the music seems neoclassical or neobaroque, suffused with academic counterpoint, only to be contaminated by contemporary dance music. In opposition to the uninterrupted flow of the Wagnerian *Gesamtkunstwerk*, *Mahagonny* is divided into closed musical numbers that place "greater dramaturgic importance on musical form." While Hinton sees Weill's lyrical, universal vision for the opera negotiating structuralist binaries—the old and the new, tradition and modernity, responsibility and freedom, order and anarchy—he ultimately argues that Smith's film "is composed according to an aesthetic thoroughly at odds with Weill's own"[25] even as the film radicalizes Weill's proposition of an autonomous role for music within the opera.

Robert Cantwell proposes that we are separated from the *Anthology of American Folk Music* by a double distancing, in that at the time that Smith compiled the *Anthology* the world of the recordings he assembled was already fading into memory, and in that today the world of the *Anthology* and the folk revival it launched has similarly receded. He proposes that we can overcome this distance either through an allegorical structure or through a structure that recaptures the immediacy of hearing the *Anthology* as if for the first time. His essay enacts this process through an extended allegorical reading of John Keats's "Ode to a Nightingale" that makes the *Anthology* strange both by displacing its themes to the England of the early nineteenth century and by the heightened unfamiliarity of Keats's and Cantwell's own language. This estrangement then provides the proper *Verfremdung* to listen to the *Anthology* with fresh ears.

Greil Marcus's essay is about the literal instantiation of a situation that recaptures the *Anthology*'s immediacy through the unlikely structure of the academic seminar. Marcus details that in the 1960s to be initiated into "the brotherhood of the *Anthology*" was to discover "an occult, Gothic America of terror and deliverance inside the official America of anxiety and success" but that over time the songs had desiccated into a canon exemplifying the authenticity of a harmless American folk. The academics with whom Marcus relistens to the *Anthology* are unfamiliar with the pieties surrounding the *Anthology,* or folk music more generally, and thus are able to argue directly "with Uncle Dave Macon, not with whatever tradition he might represent."[26]

Stephen Fredman and Thomas Crow primarily focus on the overarching organizing structure of Smith's art: collage. Fredman argues that Smith "composed not in a narrative sequence but by juxtaposition," the defining operation of collage. The argument proceeds by comparing Smith's output to the work of the poets Allen Ginsberg, Jack Spicer, and Robert Duncan, which Fredman places into a tripartite architectonics of collage. Ginsberg's method is summed up in his maxim "First thought, best thought," which ties collage to a deeply personal, stream of consciousness creativity. In stark contrast, Spicer sees the collage form as something wholly impersonal, with the poet's main job being to get out of the way so that the poem can be dictated from "outside," as if written by Martians (Spicer's term).[27] Duncan occupies a middle term: his grand collage consists in locating "hidden correspondences among disparate sources, claiming no originality for his art other than in the finding and arranging of the materials." For Fredman, Smith's collage art rejects the personal and is, like Duncan's and Spicer's, legitimately visionary. Noting that, for Smith, "Reality is made up of just the placement of objects" and that the universe operates on the principle of spontaneous juxtaposition, he defines Smith's artistic mission as studying "in great detail the conjunctions that actually occur in reality and to submit the meaning he finds there to laborious compositional techniques."[28]

If Fredman elucidates how Smith's collage method orders reality, Crow demonstrates how it is profoundly American. Crow likewise lays out a tripartite structure, in his case to describe the poles of American art at mid-twentieth century. At one extreme is the aggressively avant-garde practice of Robert Rauschenberg, whose violent juxtapositions of vernacular and Abstract Expressionist elements were off-putting to prominent tastemakers. At the opposite pole is the utilitarian and ornamental restraint of American folk art, with its emphasis on the homespun achievements of the anonymous American everyman, which occupied a surprisingly prominent place in the imagination of American modernists such as the Museum of Modern Art's Alfred J. Barr. The middle ground was established by Jasper Johns, whose paintings attained almost instantaneous acceptance by combining the avant-garde sophistication of Rauschenberg with the modesty and symmetry of folk forms. Crow argues that if contemporary critics had been less aesthetically balkanized (and balkanizing), they would have realized that a crucial precursor to this infusion of vernacular imagery into advanced art was Smith's handbook for the *Anthology of American Folk Music,* which manages to bridge the otherwise irreconcilable gulf between the folk revival and Pop art.

It is our hope that in bringing together scholarship reaching across the varied media in which Smith worked, this volume will advance our understanding of his achievements. Yet numerous areas for research and discussion remain nearly untouched. In particular, comprehension of the scope of Smith's collecting and anthologizing endeavors awaits a thoroughly cataloged and accessible archive of the considerable material that Smith left behind. What is certain is that within a reconsidered contemporary art history in which stuff that was not deemed worthy of the term *art* is now recognized as some of the most important art of the postwar period, the work of Harry Smith will occupy an increasingly central place.

Notes

1. T. J. Clark, *Image of the People: Gustave Courbet and the 1848 Revolution* (London: Thames & Hudson, 1973), 14. Over the years scores of critics have attacked Clark's distinction between the avant-garde and bohemia, but to my mind no one has seriously challenged the productiveness of the distinctions that Clark draws.
2. Clark, *Image of the People* (note 1), 34.
3. Clark, *Image of the People* (note 1), 14.
4. Karl Marx, "The Eighteenth Brumaire of Louis Bonaparte," in Karl Marx and Frederick Engels, *Selected Works* (Moscow: Progress, 1969), 1:442.
5. Quoted in Richard Cándida Smith, *Utopia and Dissent: Art, Poetry, and Politics in California* (Berkeley: Univ. of California Press, 1995), 170.
6. Smith, *Utopia and Dissent* (note 5), 169.
7. See, for example, Scott MacDonald, *Art in Cinema: Documents toward a History of the Film Society* (Philadelphia: Temple Univ. Press, 2006), 2, 5–6, 10, 159, 163, 174, 242.
8. Arthur, this volume, 132.
9. See Clement Greenberg, "Avant-Garde and Kitsch" (1939), in idem, *The Collected Essays and Criticism,* vol. 1, *Perceptions and Judgments, 1939–1944,* ed. John O'Brian (Chicago: Univ. of Chicago Press, 1986), 10–11.
10. Harry Smith, "John Cohen—Chelsea Hotel, NYC [*Sing Out!* Volume 19, No. 1, 1969]," interview by John Cohen, in idem, *Think of the Self Speaking: Harry Smith—Selected Interviews,* ed. Rani Singh (Seattle: Elbow/Cityful, 1999), 71.
11. See, for example, Jordan Belson, "Jordan Belson—3 October 1995," interview by Paola Igliori, in Paola Igliori, ed., *American Magus Harry Smith: A Modern*

Alchemist (New York: Inanout, 1996), 27; and Lionel Ziprin, "Lionel Ziprin—May and June 1993," interview by Paola Igliori, compiled with previous interview by Clayton Patterson with K. K., in Paola Igliori, ed., *American Magus Harry Smith: A Modern Alchemist* (New York: Inanout, 1996), 41.

12. Smith, "John Cohen" (note 10), 93.
13. Clement Greenberg, "The Late Thirties in New York," in idem, *Art and Culture: Critical Essays* (Boston: Beacon, 1961), 230.
14. Smith, "John Cohen" (note 10), 83.
15. Smith was one of the first artists to make significant use of both Chomskyan linguistics and Claude Lévi-Strauss's brand of structural anthropology. The term *deep structure* is from Noam Chomsky's transformational-generative grammar, which distinguishes between two levels of structure in sentences: "surface structures," which are the actual words and sounds used in a sentence, and "deep structures," which carry a sentence's underlying meaning and are fairly uniform across human languages.
16. Philip Evergood, "There Is a Difference in Bums," unpublished draft of an undated essay, American Contemporary Artists Gallery Paper, roll D-304, frame 315, Archives of American Art, Washington, D.C.; as quoted in Ellen Wiley Todd, *The "New Woman" Revised: Painting and Gender Politics on Fourteenth Street* (Berkeley: Univ. of California Press, 1993), 134.
17. Smith, "John Cohen" (note 10), 80.
18. Smith, "John Cohen" (note 10), 80.
19. For Verlaine and the "white Negro," see Elizabeth Wilson, *Bohemians: The Glamorous Outcasts* (London: Tauris Parke Paperbacks, 2003), 139. In 1894, a few years after Arthur Rimbaud's death, Verlaine described him as "The white Negro, the splendidly civilized, carelessly civilizing savage"; cited in James Campbell, *This Is the Beat Generation: New York–San Francisco–Paris* (London: Secker & Warburg, 1999), xi. Mailer picks up on the term in the 1950s: "So there was a new breed of adventurers, urban adventurers who drifted out at night looking for action with a black man's code to fit their facts. The hipster had absorbed the existentialist synapses of the Negro, and for practical purposes could be considered a white Negro"; see Norman Mailer, "The White Negro: Superficial Reflections on the Hipster" (1957), in idem, *Advertisements for Myself* (New York: G. P. Putnam's Sons, 1959), 341.
20. Smith, "John Cohen" (note 10), 99.
21. Smith, "John Cohen" (note 10), 79, 81–82.
22. Harry Smith, Chairman's Merit Award acceptance speech, Grammy Awards, Radio City Music Hall, New York City, 10 February 1991.
23. Sitney, "*Film #12*," this volume, 81.
24. Michelson, this volume, 90.
25. Hinton, this volume, 164, 167.
26. Marcus, this volume, 175, 181.
27. See, for instance, Jack Spicer, "Vancouver Lecture 1: Dictation and 'A Textbook of Poetry,'" in idem, *The House That Jack Built: The Collected Lectures of Jack Spicer,* ed. Peter Gizzi (Hanover, N.H.: University Press of New England, 1998), 8–9 and passim.
28. Fredman, this volume, 225, 231, 235, 226, 231.

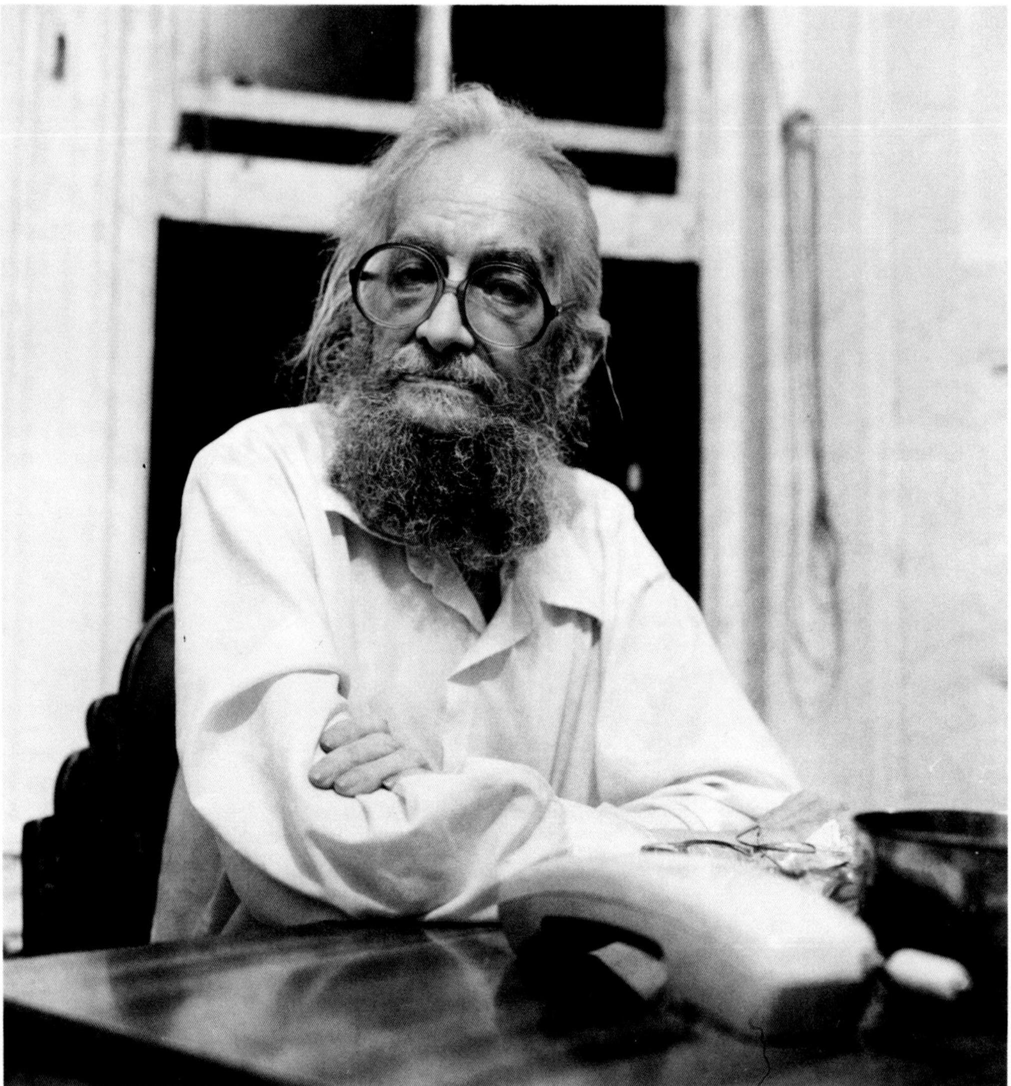

Harry Smith at kitchen table 437 E 12 St. Apt. 22, he lived in tiny guest room off to the side of the kitchen, suffered compression fracture of knee, bumped by car on First Avenue corner – so stayed on nine months before moving up to Cooperstown for half a year – still drank 2 bottles of beer in his room, taped ambient sounds of New York Lower Manhattan with a Sony Pro Walkman microphone wrapped in towel on outside window ledge, kitchen and front room. Night, June 16, 1988 another stay for several weeks before we both moved to Boulder-Naropa for the summer – there he settled down.

Allen Ginsberg

RANI SINGH

HARRY SMITH, AN ETHNOGRAPHIC MODERNIST IN AMERICA

Myth and mystery entangle with fact in all aspects of Harry Smith's multifaceted legacy. He engaged many different disciplines, and his creative endeavors were so seemingly dissimilar as to be perceived as the products of separate artistic intelligences. Indeed, some thought he was several discrete people or that "Harry Smith" was a pseudonym. Yet there was a grand scheme behind his practice. Smith delved into disparate forms in search of the essence of what he considered universal patterns. In his cosmological worldview, everything was connected across cultural lines, including all artistic ventures, from string figures to folk music to the high modernism that dominated the avant-garde discourse of the twentieth century. His grand project was to synthesize universal patterns into a unified theory of culture—much like the alchemists' ambition for their Great Work, whose goals were the magical conversion of common materials into precious objects and the purification of the alchemist into a being with a deep mystical understanding of the universe and the divine. He had a voracious appetite for information and looked at the world as might a cultural anthropologist such as Claude Lévi-Strauss, whom he greatly admired. His work accordingly explores the language and interconnectedness of symbols from dead, forgotten worlds as well as living, vibrant cultures. It is the product of sifting through wildly varied sources to create a singular if protopsychedelic vision.

The way Smith lived his life is an essential part of the stories, and the work, he left behind. Smith once wrote that his films "should be observed together in order, or not at all."[1] This essay is an attempt to provide an overview and a synthesis of Smith's body of work, which must be regarded as encompassing his willfully varied presentations of his own life story. His creative multidisciplinarity, coupled with his penchant for self-mythologizing and self-destruction, make writing his biography a unique challenge, especially as half-truths seem to play longer, and more colorfully, than nonfiction. Nevertheless, whether the stories that circulate about Harry Smith are ultimately based on fact or fiction, and whether they were propagated by Smith himself or by the people he encountered, each story merits attention, as each yields insight into the methods and motivations of a modernist pioneer. Without denying the very real importance of mythmaking within Smith's world, this essay tries to set at least some of the record straight.

Northwestern Washington: Genesis of an Ethnographic Modernist

Born on 29 May 1923 in Portland, Oregon, Harry Everett Smith spent his early years in Washington, moving between the small rural towns of Anacortes and Bellingham,

Fig. 1.
Allen Ginsberg (American, 1926–97)
Harry Smith at Allen Ginsberg's kitchen table, New York City, 16 June 1988

in the heart of Pacific Northwest Coast Indian territory. The Smith family had a long history of involvement with metaphysics. Smith's parents were theosophists who exposed him to a variety of pantheistic ideas, which led to an early and ongoing fascination with unorthodox spirituality, comparative religion, and philosophy.

> When I was a child, there were a great number of books on occultism and alchemy always in the basement.
>
> Like I say, my father gave me a blacksmith shop when I was maybe twelve. He told me I should convert lead into gold. He had me build all these things, like models of the first Bell telephone, the original electric light bulb, and perform all sorts of historical experiments. I once discovered in the attic of our house all those illuminated documents with hands with eyes in them, all kinds of Masonic deals that belonged to my grandfather. My father said I shouldn't have seen them, and he burned them up immediately. That was the background for my interest in metaphysics and so forth....
>
> Very early, my parents got me interested in projecting things.[2]

Smith's esoteric upbringing planted the seeds of what would become a lifelong interest in an ethnological approach to world cultures and rituals. After the Civil War, General John Corson Smith (1832–1910), Smith's paternal great-grandfather, would eventually be elected state treasurer of Illinois and then lieutenant governor. He was active in the Knights Templar Freemasons, a Christian fraternal organization founded in the eleventh century, in which he reached the level of grand commander. His son, Robert A. Smith (1857–after 1904), followed in his father's footsteps and became a master mason in 1889. He moved from Illinois to Fairhaven, Washington, at the turn of the century, where he soon became assistant manager of the local Pacific American Fisheries cannery.[3] The boom-bust salmon industry had a profound effect on the economy of the area, employing two generations of the Smith family. Harry's father, Robert James Smith (1880 or 1881–1959), worked in that industry as a marine engineer and boat captain and then, after its decline, as a night watchman for Pacific American Fisheries.

Although Smith claimed that his mother was the Romanov Grand Duchess Anastasia of Russia,[4] she was actually Mary Louise Hammond (1889–1949), born in Sioux City, Iowa, and a teacher on the Lummi Indian Reservation, near Bellingham, from 1925 to 1932.[5] Emotionally, Smith was very close to his mother. Inspired by her work on the Lummi reservation, he took an interest in local Indian cultures. "When I was a child, somebody came to school one day and said they'd been to an Indian dance, and they saw somebody swinging a skull on the end of a string, so I thought, 'Hmm, I have to see this.'"[6] He began spending time on the Lummi, Swinomish, and other Coast Salish reservations and was soon recording songs and rituals, collecting sacred religious objects, and compiling a dictionary of several Puget Sound dialects. Throughout his adolescence and into his college years, Smith attended various Native American rituals, including potlatch ceremonies and winter dances. He frequently documented these activities by making sound recordings on discs of acetate- or shellac-coated paper using a 78 rpm disc

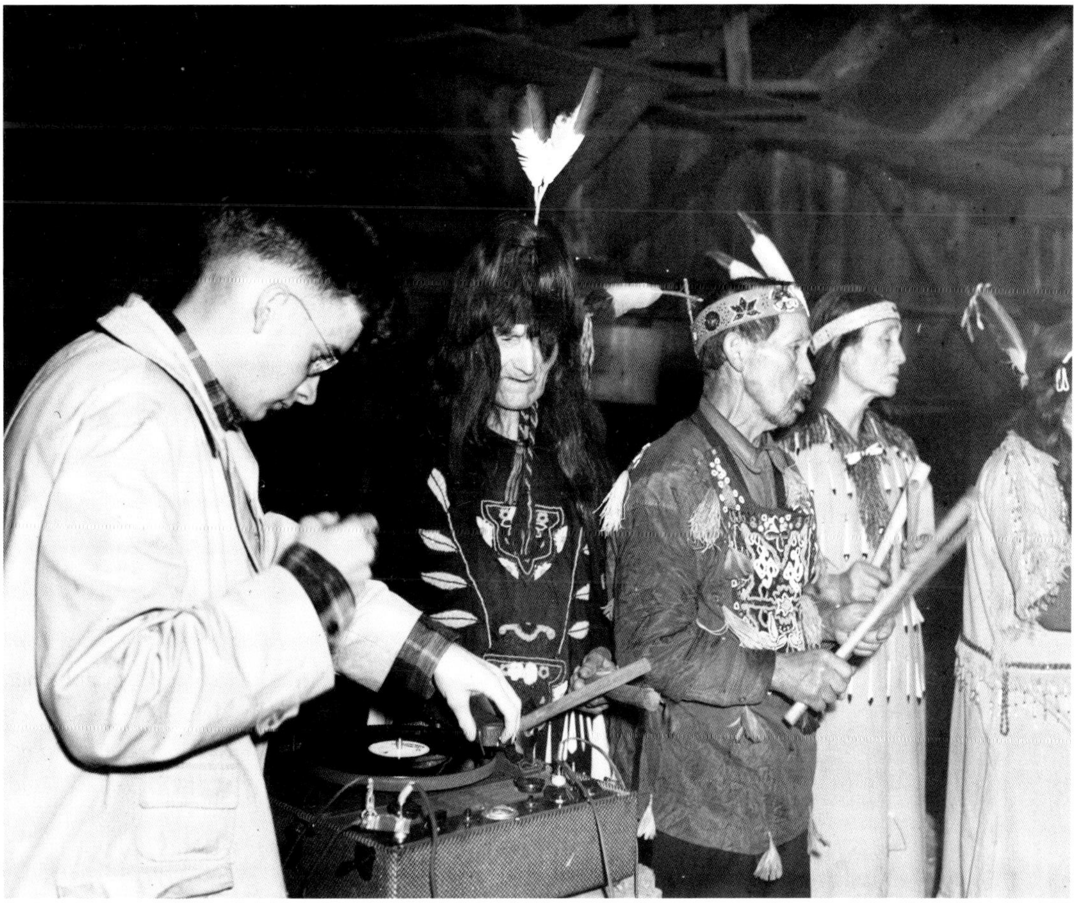

Fig. 2.
K. S. Brown
Harry Smith recording a Lummi ceremony, with Julius Charles (next to Smith) and August Martin, Lummi Smokehouse, Lummi Indian Reservation, Washington, ca. 1942–43

recorder (fig. 2), which required transporting heavy recording equipment (including a car battery that supplied the power) for long distances, often by hitchhiking or by bicycle.

> I sometimes spent three or four months with them during summer vacation, or sometimes in the winter, while I was going to high school or junior high school.... In an effort to write down dances, I developed certain techniques of transcription. Then I got interested in the designs in relation to music. That's where it started from. Of course! It was an attempt to write down the unknown Indian life.... I took portable equipment all over that place long before anyone else did and recorded whole long ceremonies sometimes lasting several days. Diagramming the pictures was so interesting that I then started to be interested in music in relation to existence.[7]

Smith had a sophisticated understanding of ethnographic research methods that far surpassed his years, a situation that was the result of a combination of a progressive education, his parents' untraditional lifestyle,[8] and Smith's obsessive reading of ethnographic materials. He utilized techniques of an experienced ethnographer, keeping detailed notes, developing phonetic dictionaries of Native American languages, and taking hundreds of photographs (fig. 3), which he numbered and precociously stamped "Not for Reproduction, Harry E. Smith." A scant selection of this material survives.[9] By the time he was a freshman in high school, he had developed relationships with several of the Lummi elders, especially Julius Charles and Chief August Martin. At that point, the younger generation of the Lummi community had begun to lose interest in tribal traditions and ceremonies, but Charles and Martin recognized Smith's sincere interest in their culture. As a term of endearment they gave him the name *We<u>k</u>a* (pronounced *way-ka*), which means "boy" in Lummi.[10]

Smith's fascination with Native American linguistic and material culture had already begun to flourish when he met fellow high school student Bill Holm at the Swinomish Smokehouse in 1940 on Treaty Day, a significant holiday marking an agreement made with local settlers in 1855.[11] Smith and Holm had accompanied a group of ethnography students from the University of Washington led by anthropology professors Melville Jacobs and Erna Gunther, who were following in the footsteps of Franz Boas, the father of modern anthropology, with whom both had studied. Smith later claimed to have corresponded with Boas while in high school, and Holm has confirmed this.[12] Boas had challenged the prevailing "evolutionary" mode of anthropology by arguing that all cultures have progressed equally but in unique ways. He worked extensively with the Kwakwaka'wakw (then known as the Kwakiutl) of the northeast Vancouver Island area, and his approach influenced Gunther and Jacobs, who would compile comprehensive collections of Northwest Coast Indian ethnographic material during the postwar years. Holm went on to become a noted expert on the material culture of the Northwest Coast Indians, writing the foundational and still essential text *Northwest Coast Indian Art: An Analysis of Form* (1965). He continues to act as curator emeritus at the Burke Museum of Natural History and Culture at the University of Washington—the museum to which Smith donated various ethnographic objects in the 1940s.

The youngest members of the group, Smith and Holm became instant friends, and together they recorded tribal ceremonies (fig. 4). Holm described these sacred dances as total sensory experiences. On the occasions they witnessed, the smokehouse would be packed with people, some in traditional Indian garb, and the ceremony would begin with the low, repetitive boom of drums, which became increasingly forceful as the deep, rhythmic sound took over the space. As smoke filled the room, the participants would begin to dance as they were gradually possessed and overtaken by spirits. As the dancers moved into the spirit world, the chief signaled that the spiritual climax of the ritual was near and Smith would lay the needle down on a blank disc to record the ecstatic moment.[13] Among his figurative works from these years, few of which survive, are paintings inspired by such events in which Smith combined a palette of warm, earthy tones with detailed renderings of costumes and ritual objects (fig. 5).

Smith acquired Native American objects of all sorts, including a canoe bailer, a smoking pipe, a massive six-foot bear monument, house posts, and funerary figures in the shapes of birds or frogs. How he transported and stored them in his bedroom remains a mystery. An article in the *Bellingham High Beacon,* the local

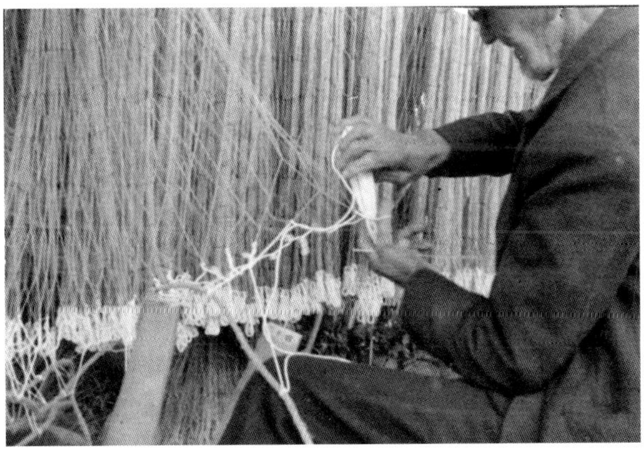

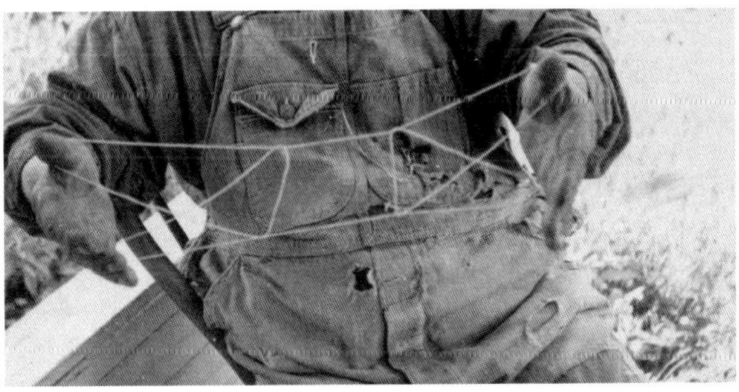

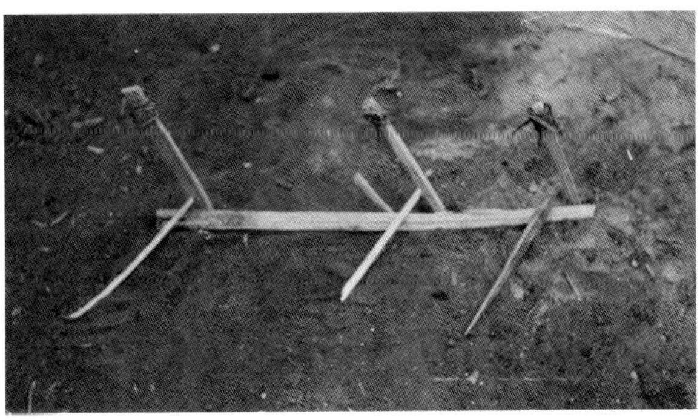

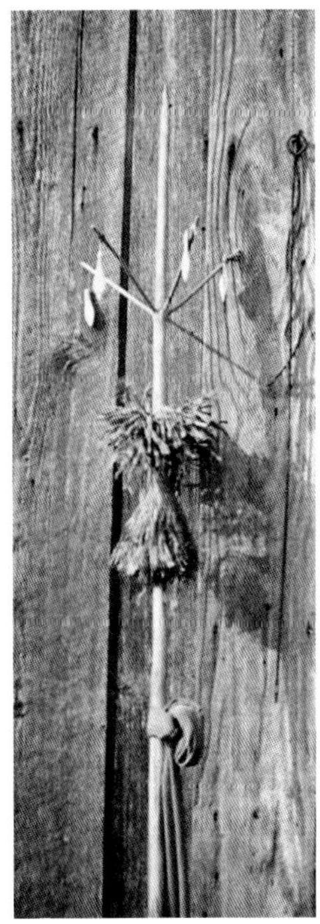

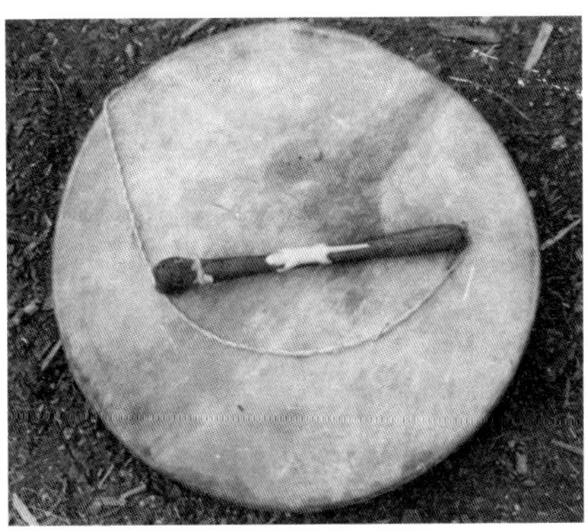

Fig. 3.
Harry Smith
Julius Charles working on gill net, Lummi, 1942
String figure made by Joe Billy, Swinomish, 1942
Sign left to show that the family is away on a canoe trip, set up by Julius Charles, Lummi, 1942
Drum owned by Charles Edwards, Swinomish, 1942
Top of staff carried by Joe Washington as a new dancer, Swinomish, 1942
(As notated by Smith)

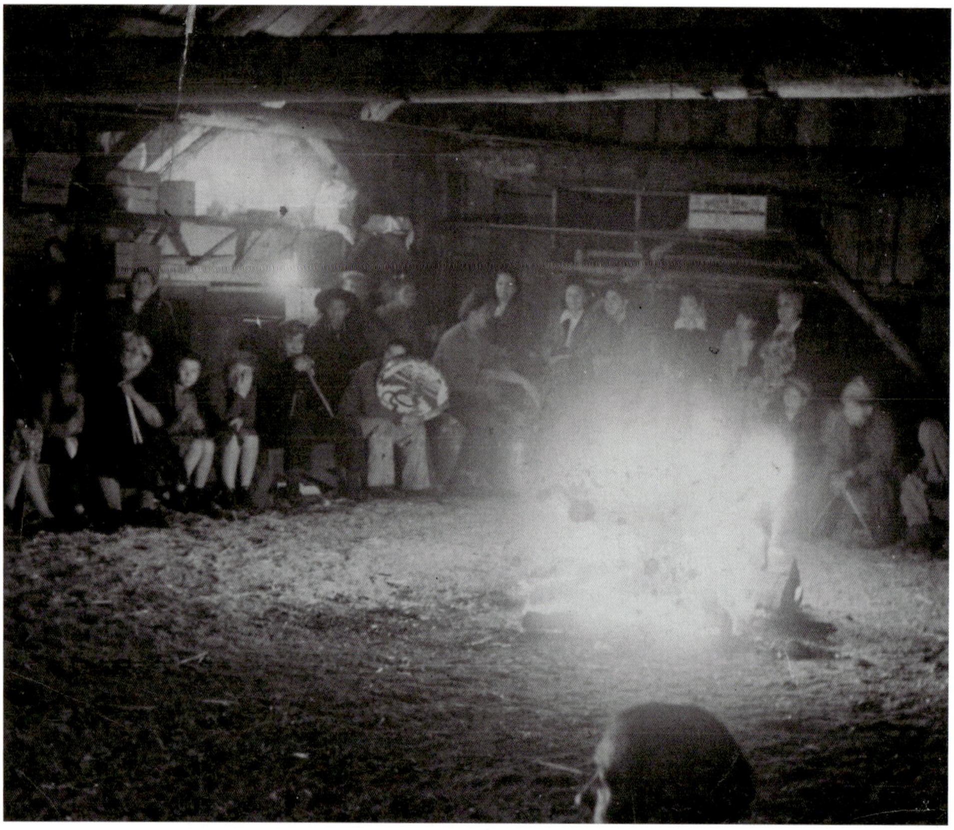

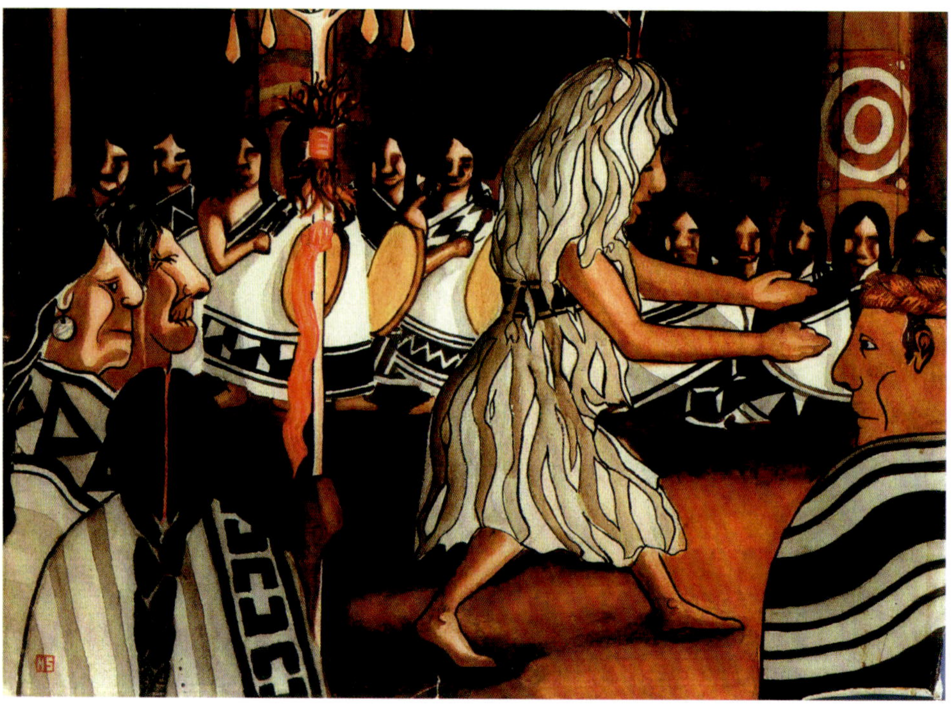

high school newspaper, singled Smith out as an "interesting" high school senior with "an unusual hobby. He studies anthropology, the science of mankind, in the Indian division. Harry's hobby covers the habits, languages, dress, and customs of the Indians of Northwestern Washington. Among his collections of Indian curios, some of which are on display at the University of Washington Museum in Seattle, are photographic records of the different Indian rites and ceremonies taken on the Lummi Reservation."[14] Several of these cultural items remained in the university's collection until 2003, when they were repatriated to the descendants of their original owners in compliance with the Native American Graves Protection and Repatriation Act (NAGPRA).

Smith also applied his anthropological training to another lifelong obsession, record collecting. As a teenager, he scoured secondhand stores for used 78 rpm records; the first one that he bought was "a Tommy McClellan record that had somehow got into this town by mistake. It sounded strange and I looked for others." He was looking not for the "best records" but for unique and unusual examples of obscure American music. "I started looking in other towns and found Yank Rachell records in Mt. Vernon, Washington." In support of the war effort, people donated their records to be melted down for shellac, and Smith recalled that "during the record drive—I then arranged for other people to look for old records.... People collected records because you could sell them for scrap."[15]

Smith received average grades and had few childhood friends. Holm remembered Smith as "a loner with a head of blond, curly hair and stooped posture that was the result of a bout with rickets." Gordan Tweit, a high school friend, described Smith quite distinctly as "keeping to himself, an intense fellow, a very studious type, with a slight hunchback. He always carried a 4 × 5 camera around."[16] Smith was active in the chess club and the senior class production of the comedy *You Can't Take It with You* and was also on the yearbook staff. His stated ambition in the high school yearbook was to be a "Composer of symphonic music" (fig. 6).

Following graduation in 1943, Smith received a medical exemption from military service. Between 1943 and 1944, he spent five semesters at the University of Washington, where he took classes in the evolution of man, American indigenous linguistics, geology, and principles of race and language. He was a satisfactory student and received mostly Bs and Cs. During his college years, he worked for six months at a local Boeing Airplane Company plant as an engine degreaser operator—a job he was given because he was small enough to easily maneuver inside the fuselage of the aircraft.

Fig. 4.
Bill Holm (American, b. 1925)
Event at Lummi Smokehouse, with August Martin in the foreground, Lummi Indian Reservation, Washington, ca. 1942

Fig. 5.
Harry Smith
Untitled (Precontact Samish spirit dance), ca. 1940, watercolor, 24 × 30.5 cm (9½ × 12 in.)
Anacortes, Washington, Samish Indian Nation

Fig. 6.
Harry Smith, Bellingham High School Yearbook, Bellingham, Washington, 1943

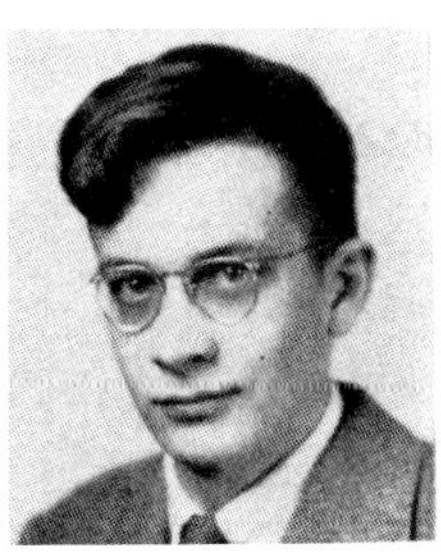

JEANNE WORLEY—Beacon, Ad Staff; Service Club; What-A-Sho; "Naughty Marietta." Ambition —Costume designer.

GEORGE SMITH—Traffic Squad; Ticket Squad.

HARRY SMITH—Entered from Anacortes; Chess Club; Senior Play; Shuksan, Photographic Staff. Ambition —Composer of symphonic music.

San Francisco Bay Area: Artistic Beginnings

The day after World War II ended, Smith was invited to visit the Bay Area, where he attended a Woody Guthrie concert and smoked marijuana for the first time.[17] The Bay Area had a thriving bohemian scene supportive of experimentation in drugs, sex, music, and alternative spirituality; Smith felt a connection to the milieu and soon relocated to Berkeley. By 1946, he was living in a small ground-floor room with its own entrance (see p. 177) attached to the house of Bertrand H. Bronson, an English professor at the University of California, Berkeley, and a noted Child ballads expert. Although Smith did not continue his formal studies, he thus had the luxury of an ongoing dialogue with an authority in the field of folk music (and vice versa: Jordan Belson noted that Bronson would regularly consult with Smith about musical matters[18]). He was also put in contact with like-minded record collectors, often adding to his own growing music library by "borrowing" from others; when accused of stealing, he replied that the records would be of better use in his collection "because his was a research collection." With fellow aficionado Luis Kemnitzer, he took weekend bus trips to the nearby towns of Richmond and Vallejo to hunt for records.[19]

In this setting, Smith flourished, pursuing a myriad of new artistic directions. In addition to collecting cultural artifacts, he maintained an experimental art practice of his own that generated paintings, drawings (fig. 7), and works on film. The density of Smith's creative production was something his friends experienced firsthand when they visited his cramped living quarters at 5½ Panoramic Way. His cluttered live-work space was the incubator for current projects, collections, and experimental techniques. Unfinished paintings hung on the walls, strips of film

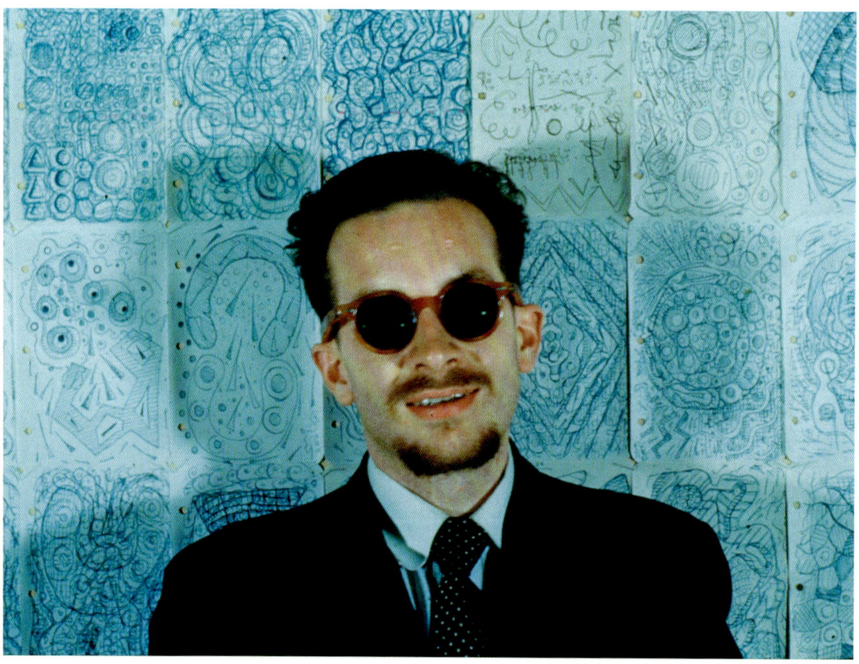

Fig. 7.
Hy Hirsh (American, 1911–61)
Harry Smith with his "brain drawings," San Francisco, ca. 1950

were strung across the room, tubes and jars of paint were scattered about, piles of books and records covered the floor, and a small cot sat inconspicuously in the corner. Throughout his life, Smith struggled to maintain a delicate balance between order and chaos in his living conditions.

While living in Berkeley, Smith regularly attended Art in Cinema, a series of avant-garde film programs screened at the San Francisco Museum of Art. Organized by Frank and Jack Stauffacher and Richard Foster in 1946, over the next eight years Art in Cinema played a crucial role in exposing West Coast audiences to avant-garde films from Europe and the United States. It was at these screenings that Smith first saw the work of pioneering abstract filmmakers such as Oskar Fischinger, Hans Richter, and Norman McLaren. Art in Cinema exposed Smith to the avant-garde film world in other important ways as well. Smith volunteered to contact filmmakers and film libraries in order to locate and book the films shown in the series. In July 1947, Frank Stauffacher (who regularly gave him small sums of money) asked Smith to travel to Los Angeles on Art in Cinema's behalf to make contact with Southern California filmmakers. There he met James and John Whitney, Kenneth Anger, and, most important, Fischinger, who became a seminal influence. Fischinger was one of the few artists Smith ever credited as an inspiration for his work. "You can tell how much I admire Fischinger: the only film of mine that I ever gave a real title to was *Homage to Oskar Fischinger*," he told William Moritz in 1977. "I learned concentration from him."[20]

Art in Cinema was the first public venue in which Smith's films were shown, but dating the beginning of Smith's film production is difficult, as there are conflicting accounts. Smith himself was the chief obfuscator, making contradictory claims on a number of occasions. In a letter written to Hilla Rebay in 1950, Smith claimed that his first film was "made in 1946 and called on the Reel 'A Strange Dream.'"[21] But in 1965, Smith stated in a well-known interview with P. Adams Sitney that he made his first film in 1939, a claim he repeated in his often quoted entry regarding his "cinematic excreta" in the *Film-Makers' Cooperative Catalogue*.[22] Moritz has suggested that Smith's statement about his making films in 1939 is a defensive myth, intended as an assertion of originality.[23] He argues that Smith did not start making films until he was exposed to the work of contemporaries such as Norman McLaren and Len Lye through the Art in Cinema screenings. Jordan Belson reinforces this idea in an interview with Scott MacDonald in July 2000: "He claims to have started making films that way when he was 13 or 14 years old, but *I* never saw anything like that.... My sense was that we went there [Art in Cinema] together and discovered new ways of making films."[24] There is no doubt that the array of work that Belson and Smith saw at these screenings had a profound effect on their own output.

On 24 October 1947, Art in Cinema premiered a work by Smith at the San Francisco Museum of Art. The program notes for the evening included this description:

> FILM NUMBER FIVE (FAST TRACK) (American, 1947) by Harry Smith. (The color films originally scheduled for this program [*Absolute Films No. 2, No. 3,* and *No. 4*] have not yet been returned from the processing plant where

> 16mm reductions are being made from the 35mm originals. These films will be shown on a later program.) Although the images of NUMBER FIVE are closely synchronized with sound, they are to be viewed as a purely visual sequence with themes and rhythms for the eye, completely independent of the musical score which augments what is on the screen, without determining its direction or commenting upon it. (Time 10 min. Loaned by Harry Smith)[25]

This is the first documented public screening of a film by Smith. Another film titled, for the occasion, *Primitive Visual Rhythm* (1947–48) was screened by Art in Cinema on 24 September 1948, and two more films, titled *Film No. 1* and *Film No. 4* (both 1949) were shown on 11 February 1949.[26] Made using an extremely labor-intensive process, Smith's early films were meticulously hand-painted frame by frame on 35 mm film stock using a unique method of his own invention, derived from batik techniques, involving the use of stencils, cutouts, tape, and various layers of petroleum jelly, paint, and color dyes.[27]

The next time Art in Cinema screened a set of Smith's films would be on 12 May 1950. The four films on the program that evening—titled *A Strange Dream, Message from the Sun, Circular Tensions,* and *Interwoven*—were accompanied live by a jazz sextet under the direction of Atlee Chapman (figs. 8, 9),[28] reflecting a new passion in Smith's life. Jazz and bohemian culture had by then brought Smith across the bay from Berkeley to San Francisco, where bebop was in its heyday during the late 1940s. The worlds of advanced jazz and avant-garde film might seem to have little in common, but Smith found jazz's complex structures and improvisation uniquely suited to his cinematic investigations. He became a regular in the Fillmore district, a hub of Bay Area jazz culture, and he moved to a rented room over the club named Jackson's Nook in 1948.[29] Live gigs in small clubs often stretched into early morning sessions, where Smith had ample access to the musicians and drugs that were integral to the scene. The films shown at Art in Cinema in 1950 were part of a series of films conceived as a visual response to music by Charlie Parker, Dexter Gordon, Chet Baker, and Dizzy Gillespie. "I had a really great illumination the first time I saw Dizzy Gillespie play," Smith said. "I had gone there very high, and I literally saw all kinds of colored flashes. It was at that point that I realized music could be put to my films."[30]

At about the same time, he embarked on a series of jazz paintings, murals for the walls of Jimbo's Bop City, and performance pieces at museums and small nightclubs that conjoined screenings of his films and live music. At Jimbo's Bop City, an infamous waffle house and after-hours jazz club, Smith showed his films while Gillespie, Parker, Thelonious Monk, and other musicians responded musically to his imagery. This was probably one of the first times jazz virtuosos improvised to film imagery, and Smith regarded these evenings as an "investigation of intuitive creation."[31] These encounters represent some of the most extraordinary interactions between advanced artists of the postwar era. The exploratory collaboration of the world's most progressive jazz artists with a young visionary filmmaker in a smoky after-hours club represents a pinnacle of Beat-era pollination across different art forms.

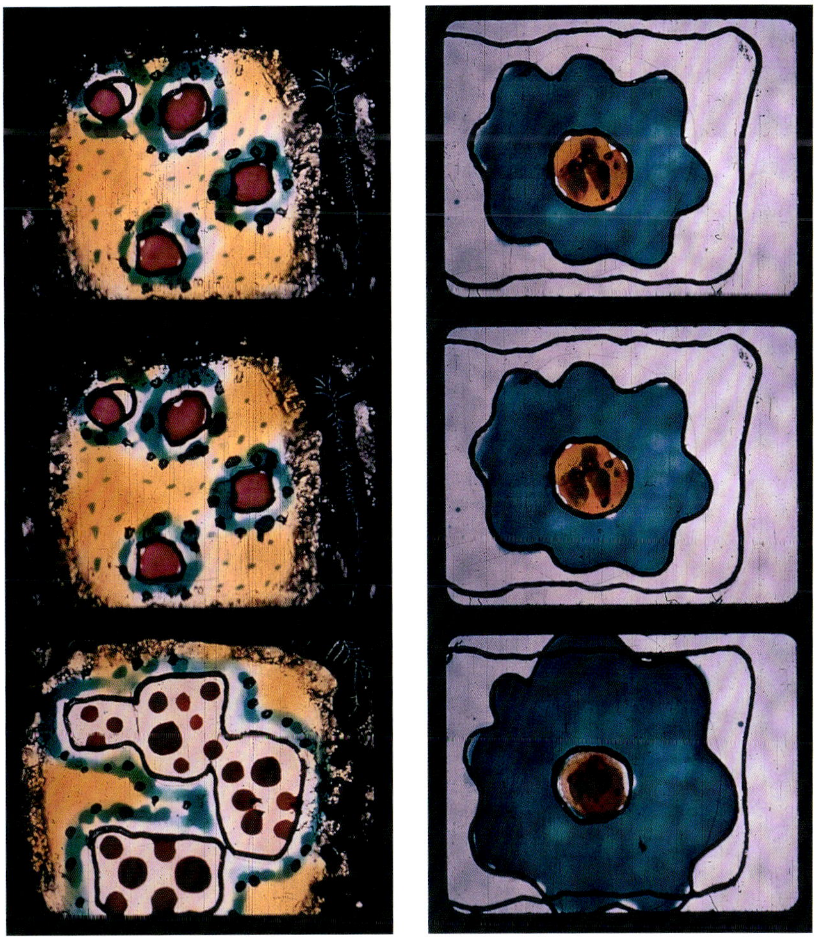

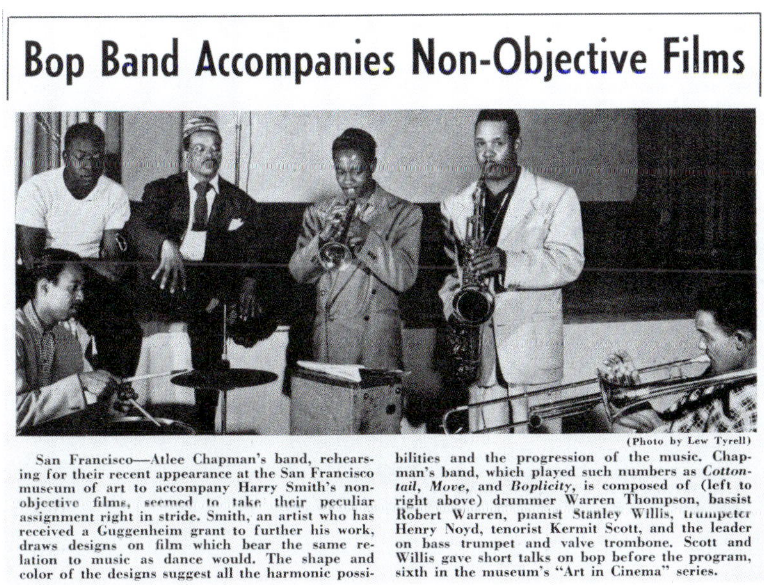

Bop Band Accompanies Non-Objective Films

(Photo by Lew Tyrell)

San Francisco—Atlee Chapman's band, rehearsing for their recent appearance at the San Francisco museum of art to accompany Harry Smith's non-objective films, seemed to take their peculiar assignment right in stride. Smith, an artist who has received a Guggenheim grant to further his work, draws designs on film which bear the same relation to music as dance would. The shape and color of the designs suggest all the harmonic possibilities and the progression of the music. Chapman's band, which played such numbers as *Cottontail*, *Move*, and *Boplicity*, is composed of (left to right above) drummer Warren Thompson, bassist Robert Warren, pianist Stanley Willis, trumpeter Henry Noyd, tenorist Kermit Scott, and the leader on bass trumpet and valve trombone. Scott and Willis gave short talks on bop before the program, sixth in the museum's "Art in Cinema" series.

Fig. 8.
Harry Smith
Stills from *Film #1: A Strange Dream*, ca. 1946–48, 2 min. 20 sec., hand-painted 35 mm film stock photographed in 16 mm, color, sound

Fig. 9.
"Bop Band Accompanies Non-Objective Films," *DownBeat*, 30 June 1950, 3

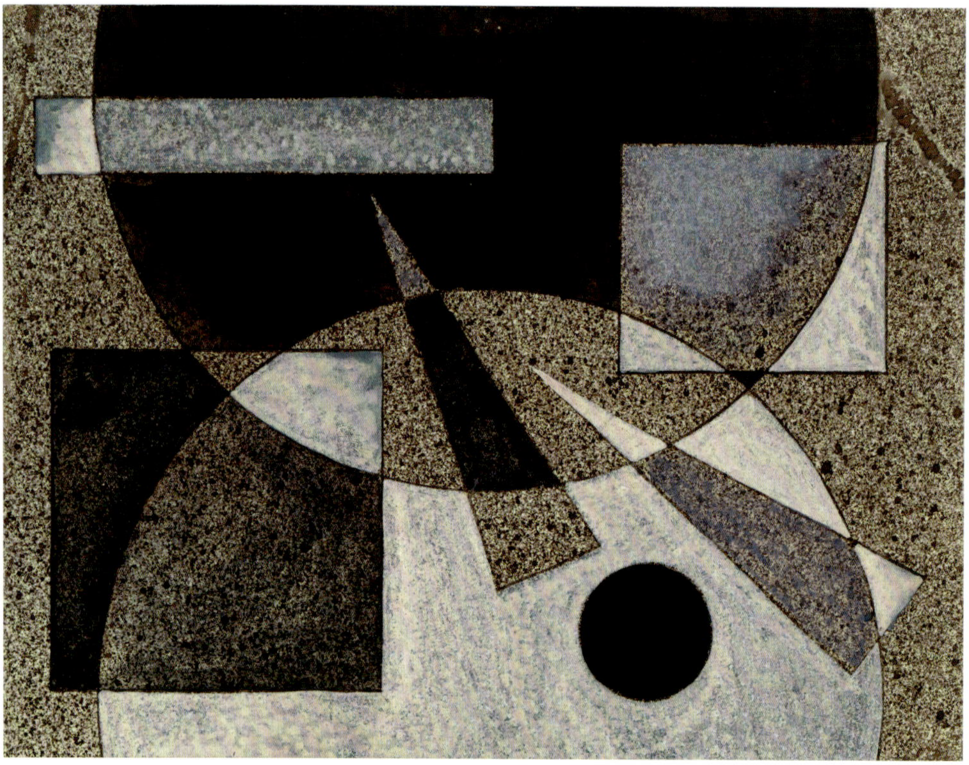

Fig. 10.
Harry Smith
First Note, Fourth Chorus, Boplicity, ca. 1950, india ink and gouache on paper, 17.8 × 22.9 cm (7 × 9 in.)
Annotation of "Boplicity," Miles Davis Orchestra, ca. 1950
Harry Smith Archives

Smith painted several murals inside Jimbo's Bop City (see p. 195), probably in payment for his overextended bar tab. While working on the murals (which took over a year), he played records to suit his moods. Dexter Gordon often spent hours listening with Smith as he painted, and Smith became increasingly interested in exploring the combination of abstract art and jazz, an interest that found outlet in a series of paintings synchronized to specific jazz pieces. In these works, each paint stroke corresponded to a musical note in a recording (fig. 10; see also p. 198). He later described the process in terms of both working method and the investment of time it required:

> It is a painting of a tune by Dizzy Gillespie called "Manteca." Each stroke in that painting represents a certain note on the recording. If I had the record, I could project the painting as a slide and point to a certain thing. This is the main theme in there, which is a-doot-doot-doot, doot-doot-doottadootdoot—those curved lines up there. See, ta-doot-doot-doot-doot-dootaloot-dootaloot, and so forth. Each note is on there. The most complex one of these is this one, one of Charlie Parker's records, I don't remember the name of it. That's a really complex painting. That took five years. Just like I gave up making films after that last hand-drawn one took a number of years, I gave up painting after that took a number of years to make. It was just too exhausting. There's a dot for each note and the phrases that the notes consist of are colored in a certain way or made in a certain path.[32]

Little serious attention has been given to Smith's paintings; most of his surviving work resides in private hands, making access difficult. Throughout his life, Smith's creative output took on a variety of forms with visual expression at its core, and his paintings constitute an essential part of his oeuvre. Smith himself stated, "I was mainly a painter. The films are minor accessories to my paintings. It just happened that I had the films with me when everything else was destroyed. My paintings were infinitely better than my films."[33]

Although Smith's early films were initially made without sound, the films that followed were experiments in visualizing music. Smith's practice of blending sound, image, and the senses was enhanced by drug use, and this became an essential part of his creative process. Synesthesia involves the overlapping of the senses, as in seeing colors on hearing particular sounds, tastes that invoke visual impressions, images that trigger auditory sensations. For Smith, the fusion of visual imagery with music was a form of synesthesia, an act that held cosmic implications. His interest in the mystical correspondence of the senses may be traced to his explorations of nonobjectivity, a movement that emphasized the combination of pure abstraction

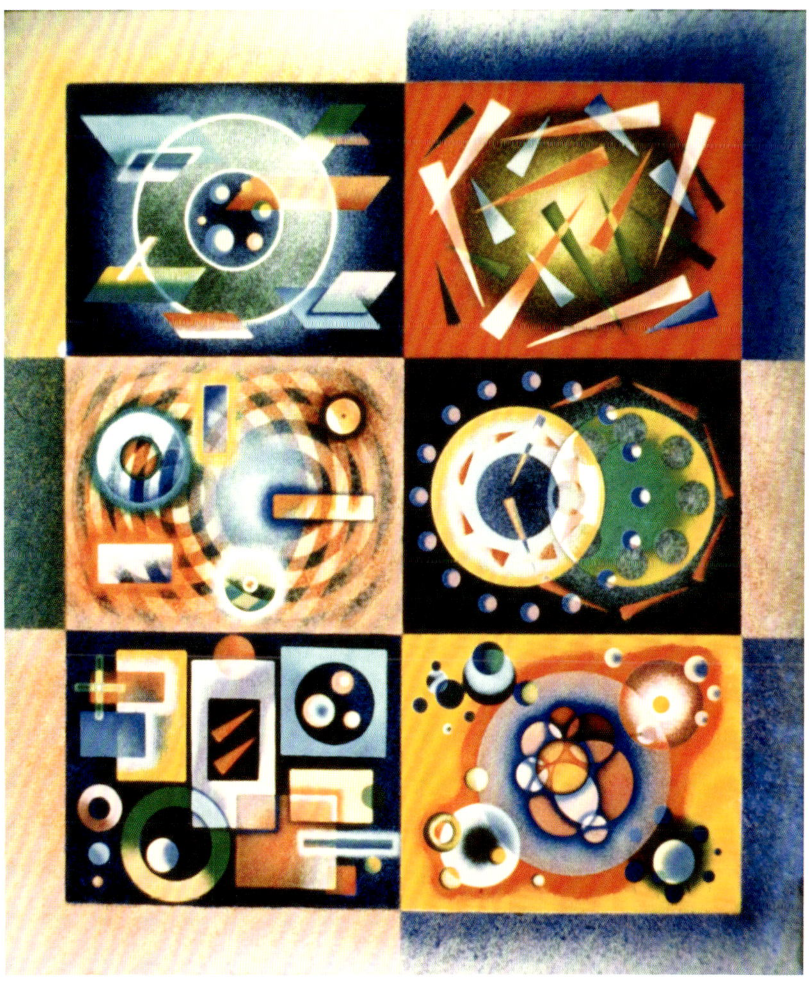

Fig. 11.
Harry Smith
Study for Film #9: Prelude and Fugue, ca. 1950
Whereabouts unknown

and cosmic spirituality in art. He began studying the work and theories of Vassily Kandinsky, Rudolf Bauer, and Franz Marc, all artists who advanced a concept of inner expression through nonrepresentational painting. After 1948, his own painting style underwent a significant transformation, dissolving into the flat geometrical forms of pure abstraction. Smith was particularly enamored with Bauer's *Triptych, Symphony in Four Parts,* which inspired him to create a series of paintings in which he attempted to convey a feeling of virtual movement. Such works were often executed in concert with the films he completed during the late 1940s and early 1950s. Smith also created studies in a similar style titled *Prelude and Fugue* (fig. 11) for the incomplete *Film #9*.

More important, in terms of the trajectory of Smith's career, Belson initiated correspondence with Hilla Rebay, the first director of the Museum of Non-Objective Painting, which eventually became the Solomon R. Guggenheim Museum. At Belson's invitation, Rebay came to San Francisco to visit his studio. After her return to New York City, she and Smith began to correspond. In exchange for small sums of money, Smith sent her at various times his early animated films, experiments in three-dimensional cinema, slides, and painted film frames. Smith usually accompanied his packages with letters that today provide rare samples of his writing as well as focused reflections on his own thinking about spirituality and art. The letters written between April 1950 and May 1952, in particular, lend insight into Smith's then-developing desire to represent spiritual concerns artistically through abstract forms.[34]

New York City: Pursuit of the Grand Project

In 1951, with patronage from Rebay, Smith moved to New York City. He cited three reasons for this change: he wanted to see Rebay, hear jazz at Birdland, and meet Marcel Duchamp.[35] Smith would live and work primarily in New York City until 1988, pursuing interests in music, filmmaking, and visual arts. Over the next several decades, he would immerse himself in a cycle of intense creation and destruction, ultimately becoming a deeply influential figure for several generations of underground and bohemian artists.

American Musical Landscapes

Shortly after arriving in New York City, Smith was in need of money and looked up Moses Asch of Folkways Records, hoping to sell some of his record collection. Asch had launched Folkways in 1948 as a small label devoted to traditional and contemporary music from around the world. His goal was to document the entire world of sound, and to this day, Folkways keeps nearly all its releases in print. Asch was impressed with Smith's erudition as well as intrigued by his collection—but rather than buy the records outright, Asch challenged Smith to produce a compilation for release on Folkways.

The *Anthology of American Folk Music* was the result of Asch's challenge. Issued in 1952 in three volumes, each in the form of a two-LP hinged set (Folkways FP 251–FP 253), the *Anthology* comprised eighty-four music tracks from commercially recorded 78 rpm records that included the genres of Appalachian folk, fiddle tunes, gospel, hillbilly, blues, and Cajun, and was accompanied by a twenty-eight-page handbook written and designed by Smith (see pp. 212, 214). Eschewing standard musicological categories, Smith titled the volumes *Ballads, Social Music,* and *Songs.* Of dubious legality (neither Folkways nor Smith ever bothered with licensing or artist fees), the *Anthology,* with Smith as its pioneering disc jockey, marks one of the first times that a collection of music was curated and presented as a unified work of art. It was to become Smith's best-known work and an inspiration for generations of singers and songwriters: as Luc Sante commented, "it is a philosopher's stone or a Rosetta stone, a treasure map of an ancient and now-hidden America,"[36] and its reverberations are still felt today.

The *Anthology* was a modernist collage in sound and image. A dark and mysterious panorama of America, the *Anthology* offered firsthand accounts of trials and travails, assassinations, loves lost, and burdens found. Although Smith did not purport to furnish a definitive version of folk culture in late-nineteenth- and early-twentieth-century America, he attempted to use the wisdom of the country's marginalized populations to portray a distinctly American experience in all its oddity and complexity. Using vernacular music as raw material, the *Anthology* presented a previously unexplored cultural history of America.

The cover of each volume was a different color, each associated with an element: green for water (*Ballads*), red for fire (*Social Music*), and blue for air (*Songs*). Each featured an engraving by seventeenth-century publisher Johann Theodor de Bry of what is known as the celestial monochord (see pp. 186, 228); Smith found the image in alchemist Robert Fludd's *Utriusque Cosmi Maioris Scilicet et Minoris Metaphysica, Physica atque Technica Historia* (1617–21; The metaphysical, physical, and technical history of the two worlds, namely the greater and the lesser), a compendium on mysticism and a grand summation of centuries of Western esotericism. An image of the instrument of the cosmos being tuned by the hand of God, the celestial monochord was indicative of the larger aspirations of the *Anthology.* Smith's strange-looking booklet was embellished with clippings from Sears, Roebuck and farm catalogs, illustrations of 78 rpm record covers, pictures of musical instruments from turn-of-the-century sources, and muddy photographs of performers.

Smith numbered each cut using heavy black type and listed each recording by its original title, performer, instrumentation, and discographic information (recording date, label, and master number). This was followed by various notes and citations to sources, both published and recorded. Faux newspaper headlines created by Smith offered darkly humorous summaries of each song's lyrics. For example, Smith's entry for "Mississippi Boweavil Blues" (no. 26) read: "Bollweavil survives physical attack after cleverly answering farmers questions." A song about the *Titanic* (no. 22) states: "Manufactures proud dream destroyed at shipwreck. Segregated poor die first." For "Old Shoes and Leggins" (no. 8): "Mother hospitable, but girls find shoddy older's actions perverse." The booklet was not only humorous but also a testament to Smith's encyclopedic knowledge of relevant source material and song provenance. The inclusion of quotations from mystics Robert Fludd, Rudolph Steiner, Aleister Crowley, and R. R. Marrett reflected his spiritual bent; Smith pointedly acknowledged them as having "been useful to the editor in preparing the notes for this handbook."[37] Together, the records and the booklet functioned as a cryptic whole that begged to be examined further.

The *Anthology* was restricted to commercial recordings issued "between 1927, when electronic recording made possible accurate music reproduction, and 1932 when the depression halted folk music sales." As Smith explains in his foreword, "During this five year period American music still retained some of the regional qualities evident in the days before the phonograph, radio and talking picture had tended to integrate local types."[38] In this short window of time, singers and musicians in small towns were still relatively isolated from outside sources and could be recorded *before* they knew how they sounded on records, while performing vernacular music learned through oral tradition for local audiences. Technological advances brought rapid change to the recording industry; many performers altered their styles after they heard themselves in recorded form or in response to new recording and broadcast technologies such as microphones, studio sound mixing, and radio.

Smith explained to John Cohen:

> The *Anthology* was not an attempt to get all the best records . . . , but a lot of these were selected because they were odd—an important version of the song, or one which came from some particular place. . . . Instead, they were selected to be ones that would be popular among musicologists, or possibly with people who would want to sing them and maybe would improve the version. They were basically picked out from an epistemological, musicological selection of reasons. . . .
>
> I was looking for exotic records. . . .
>
> Exotic in relation to what was considered to be the world culture of high class music.[39]

Taken as a whole, the *Anthology* presented a narrative of "the old, weird America," as Greil Marcus described it in his book *Invisible Republic*.[40] It was an America of many voices, speaking of poverty, violence, oppression, spiritual ecstasy, and unrequited love. Smith's sequencing was a deliberate act that created an active dialogue among individual tracks. The complex interweaving of themes and ideas generated multiple narratives—one of the most striking of which addressed racial categorization within the music industry. During the 1920s, so-called race records had been marketed exclusively to black audiences, and Smith felt that record companies made caricatures of the performers in the way they presented them. Smith refrained from identifying musicians in racial terms in his liner notes, and he made his feelings on the subject clear with his observation that "The advertising on these envelopes gives a good idiea of the companies attitude toward their artists."[41] Crossing racial and ethnic boundaries, he deracialized the recordings and recast the songs as "characteristic of American music,"[42] deliberately leaving the listener without a basis for bias. Fans who were initially enchanted by the *Anthology* experienced it in racially ambiguous terms.

The *Anthology* was released at the height of McCarthyism, when popular folk-infused music extended from the light Top 40 sounds of the Weavers to the left leaning, politically aware protest songs of Woody Guthrie. Smith had a decidedly different take from the prevailing activist attitudes of folk music. Never overtly political, his approach subtly juxtaposed rural attitudes about mortality with the tragic effects of industrialization, and the result had a profound effect on the music of the 1960s—which was precisely what Smith had intended. "That's what I was trying to do, because I thought that is what this type of folk music would lead to. I felt social changes would result from it."[43]

Anthology fans of the 1950s became the folk revivalists of the 1960s. Bohemians and beatniks who responded to the records were part of a cult following who played the records obsessively, learned the songs, and even sought out some of the musicians, most of whom were living in obscurity and no longer performing. Folk enthusiasts such as Tony Seeger, Eric von Schmidt, John Cohen, and Ralph Rinzler tracked down Clarence Ashley, Mississippi John Hurt, Dock Boggs, and Furry Lewis, among others. Several of the *Anthology*'s musicians had renewed careers in the 1960s playing at folk festivals and concerts for supportive young audiences. Artists such as Bob Dylan, Joan Baez, Phil Ochs, and Jerry Garcia credited the *Anthology* with exposing them to songs that inspired both their own careers and the folk revival movement that was essential to their repertoires. "That's where the wealth of folk music was, on that particular record," Dylan said. "It's all poetry, every single one of those songs."[44]

Although the *Anthology* is Smith's best-known work, it occupied his creative life for a relatively short time. As soon as he finished it, he moved on. This was a consistent pattern in his life; he approached projects with tremendous energy and obsessiveness, but he often switched his focus upon their completion just as readily. After the *Anthology* was released, Smith began recording the Jewish liturgical songs of the famed Talmudic scholar Rabbi Naftali Zvi Margolies Abulafia—the kabbalist Lionel Ziprin's grandfather—in the basement of a Lower East Side yeshiva. Though Smith did not speak Yiddish, and Abulafia did not speak English, they succeeded in compiling fifteen LPs worth of recordings, two of which were released by Folkways Records in 1954 as *Prayers and Chants by Rabbi Naftuli Zvi Margolies.*[45]

Smith's peripatetic and edgy lifestyle also led to his ethnographic documentation of the music of the transformative peyote rituals of the Native American Kiowa Indians. Invited by Conrad Rooks in 1964 to assist with the peyote ritual segment of his film project *Chappaqua* (1966)—a surrealistic, hallucinatory depiction of a drug addict's withdrawal—Smith went to Oklahoma by train ahead of the film crew.[46] By the time they arrived, he was in jail in Anadarko, where networking with his fellow inmates allowed him to connect with the singers he would record, members of the Native American Church, a religious denomination formed in the late nineteenth century based on the consumption of peyote, a natural hallucinogen. His selection of fifty-three songs, *The Kiowa Peyote Meeting,* was released on three LPs by Folkways Records in 1973 (fig. 12). These field recordings were not made during an actual ceremony but rather in private recording sessions with Smith and the singers. While peyote meetings are usually accompanied by a peyote drum, these recordings

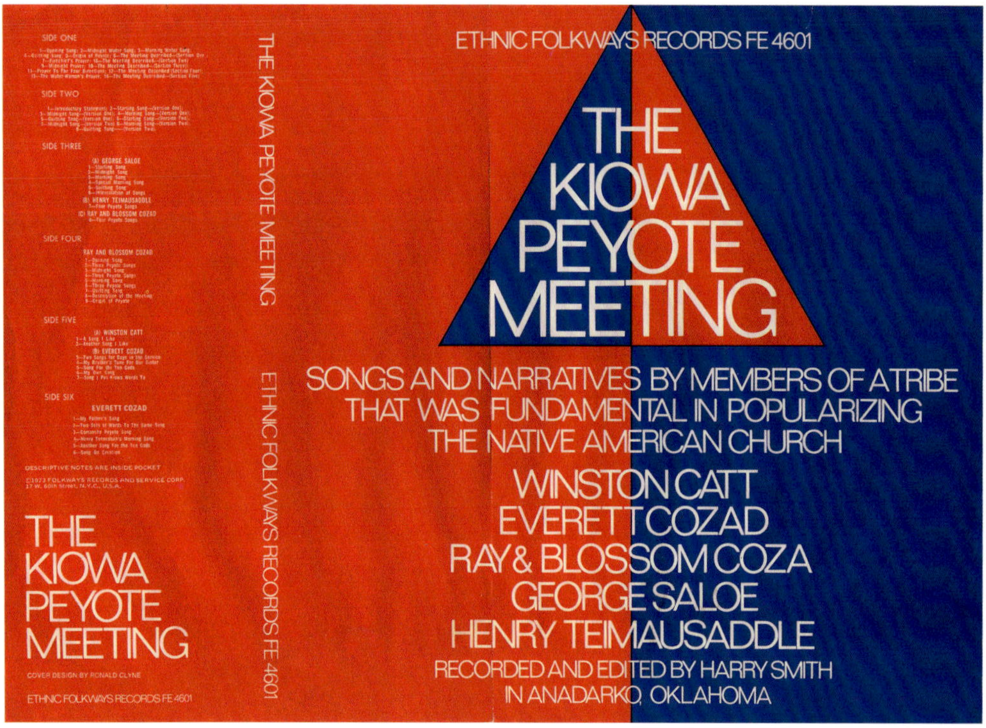

Fig. 12. Slick of album cover designed by Ronald Clyne for Harry Smith, ed., *The Kiowa Peyote Meeting,* Ethnic Folkways Records FE 4601 (New York: Folkways Records, 1973)

feature a rattle in its place, giving the listener a rare chance to hear the singing clearly. The singers preface each song with explanatory comments, which comprise a third of the recording. In his liner notes, Smith recommends that the listener take peyote before playing the records.[47]

The following year, Smith produced the debut album for the Fugs, an anarchist folk-rock/poetry band that had been performing at galleries, clubs, and theaters in New York City. Smith persuaded Moses Asch to give the group studio recording time by introducing them as the Fugs Jug Band. Tracks from two recording sessions in April and June 1965 were edited and sequenced by Fugs founder Ed Sanders and Smith and released as *The Village Fugs Sing Ballads of Contemporary Protest, Point of Views, and General Dissatisfaction* by Broadside Records (BR 304) through Folkways Records (FW 05304) in fall 1965. It marked, as Philip Smith notes, "a pioneering incursion by bohemian literati into the exploding rock scene."[48]

Smith also recorded the tracks that would appear as Allen Ginsberg's *First Blues: Rags, Ballads and Harmonium Songs,* released by Folkways Records (FW 37560) in 1981. Ginsberg had been chanting his poetry since his return from India in 1963 and began experimenting with improvising poetry in the 1970s at the suggestion of the Tibetan Buddhist monk Chögyam Trungpa Rinpoche, his meditation teacher and personal guru. By singing—an interest fueled by sessions with Dylan and Happy Traum—he hoped to unlock the seeds of creativity as well as tap into free and direct expression. The sessions were recorded in Smith's room at the Chelsea Hotel, mostly in 1971 and 1972; Ginsberg later remembered Smith instructing him to tap his foot loudly during the recording, to mimic the sound of the old blues artists. Smith's inability to complete the liner notes probably led to Ann Charters making the final selection of songs for the album; according to Ginsberg, Smith was quite unhappy with her choices.[49]

Over the years, Smith made recordings of the poets Gregory Corso and Peter Orlovsky, the protest singer Phil Ochs, American shape-note singers, and the ambient sounds of Manhattan and other environments he passed through, none of which has been released to date. His constant struggle to secure the basic elements of survival—food, shelter—coupled with his untraditional lifestyle, often verging on the derelict, and unconventional mind-set led to many projects remaining unfinished. However, his life's work was shaped by a central desire to synthesize the various subjects, languages, and mediums that caught his interest. Whether on canvas, celluloid, magnetic audiotape, or any of the various other media he used, Smith was obsessed with documenting the world around him.

Expanded Cinematic Visions

During the 1950s, Smith devoted most of his energy to filmmaking. He experimented constantly with different approaches and techniques, moving from hand painting to photographic representation and superimposition. In 1965, in his description for the *Film-Makers' Cooperative Catalogue,* Smith defined his film work in diverse and wide ranging terms:

> My cinematic excreta is of four varieties:—batiked abstractions made directly on film between 1939 and 1946; optically printed non-objective studies composed around 1950; semi-realistic animated collages made as part of my alchemical labors of 1957 to 1962; and chronologically superimposed photographs of actualities formed since the latter year. All these works have been organized in specific patterns derived from the interlocking beats of the respiration, the heart and the EEG Alpha component and should be observed together in order, or not at all, for they are valuable works, works that will live forever—they made me gray.[50]

Historically there was little communication between experimental filmmakers in California and those on the East Coast. When Smith arrived in New York City in 1951, he and his work were virtually unknown—and remained unknown for the rest of the decade, as Smith worked on films and his occult studies in self-imposed obscurity. His extremely commonplace name may have contributed to the confusion regarding his identity; no one seemed to realize that Harry Smith the filmmaker had also compiled the *Anthology of American Folk Music.*[51] The photographer Robert Frank was among the first to make the connection. In the late 1950s, John Cohen, a photographer himself as well as a member of the New Lost City Ramblers, loaned the records to Frank, who lived next door. According to Miles Frost, another neighbor, Frank played the LPs incessantly, especially the rendition of "He Got Better Things for You" by the Memphis Sanctified Singers.[52] The *Anthology* could well serve as an inspired sound track for Frank's seminal photography book of 1958, *The Americans.*

Like Frank, Allen Ginsberg moved in the same downtown bohemian circles as Smith. In 1960, Ginsberg spotted a man sitting at a bar "listening to Thelonious Monk, and sort of notating something." When Ginsberg asked what he was doing, Smith replied, "I'm trying to determine where Monk comes in on the beat—before or after, what are the recurrent syncopations, what is the pattern, the mathematical pattern of syncopations in his solos.... I'm keeping track of his time, because I'm using his music as background to films that I'm making."[53] Smith invited Ginsberg back to his apartment, offered him marijuana, and after it took effect, showed him some of his early hand-painted films as well as his work in progress, the animated collage masterpiece now known as *Film #12: Heaven and Earth Magic* (see pp. 70, 74–75, 91, 108, 233). Soon after, Smith sold a print of *Film #12* to Ginsberg, who took it to Jonas Mekas, a well-known critic for the *Village Voice,* a founder of Anthology Film Archives, and a champion of the avant-garde. When he projected the film, Mekas said to Ginsberg, "Who is this Harry Smith? He's an absolute genius."[54] Mekas had a significant effect on Smith's career as a filmmaker; he showed his work at various public screenings of underground films, and both Mekas and Ginsberg were major supporters of Smith during his lifetime and long after.

By 1957, Smith had finished his first eleven films (two of which are lost). The earliest films were meticulously hand-crafted and painted, then optically printed. Around 1964, a series of these short films (*Films #1–5, 7, 10*) were strung together and titled *Early Abstractions* by Mekas. As a group, they ranged from geometric patterns in black and white and color to complex collages revolving around a surrealistic barrage of disparate esoteric imagery culled from various texts. *Film #1* is loosely hand-painted and visually fluid. Over the series of seven films, the imagery grows increasingly geometric and more rigorously patterned and rhythmic. Throughout, the circle and square are basic components in the exploration of the possibilities of one- and two-dimensional space (fig. 13). The intensity and complexity of design builds as the films became more hard-edged, with Smith becoming more assured in his explorations of tension and depth.

Initially, Smith numbered his films rather than naming them, as an expression of his support for the nonobjective aesthetic. Though he continued to number his films sequentially throughout his life, Smith did assign titles to some of his early films for their West Coast screenings, in an effort to accommodate the expectations of a museum-going audience, abandoning the titles afterward. In a letter to Hilla Rebay, Smith commented, "Originally they were not titled and I still feel that giving specific titles is destructive because it tensions them to specific emotions, and for these particular films are as out of place as a chemest (sic) naming his experiments according to the colour they produce, rather than the purpose."[55] The titles currently attached to several of Smith's films—*Early Abstractions, Heaven and Earth Magic,* and *Late Superimpositions*—are Jonas Mekas's.

Over the years, Smith experimented with a variety of different sound tracks for his films, and the issue of how to reconcile Smith's multiple, fluid, and sometimes contradictory aesthetic visions for the presentation of his films has been the source of much debate. When Smith screened the films in the early 1950s, he showed them without sound or, occasionally, with a live jazz band. He later reedited the

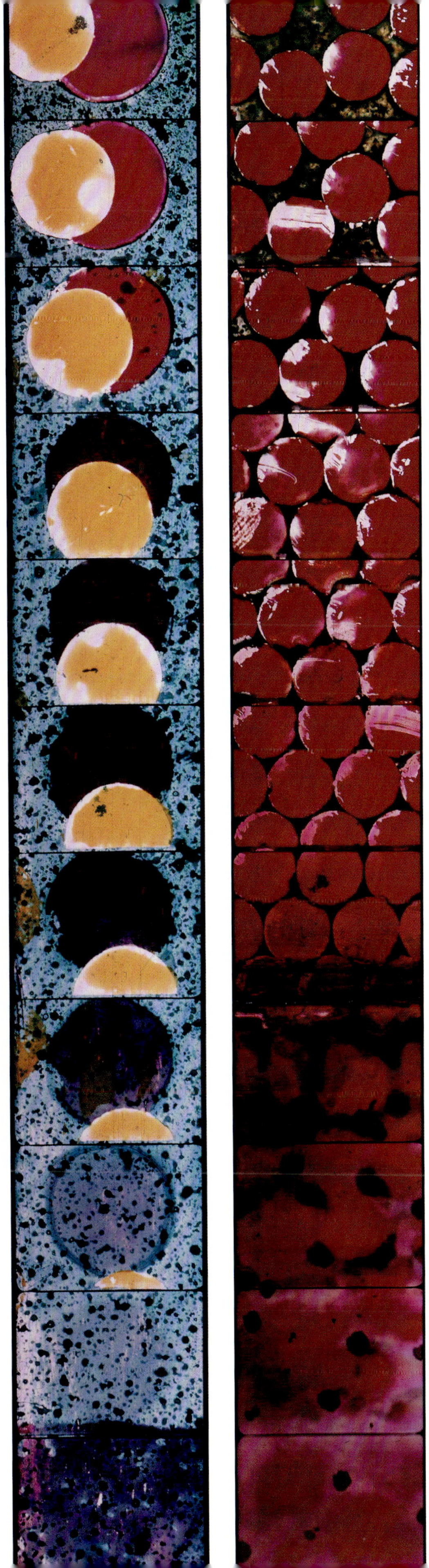

Fig. 13.
Harry Smith
Stills from *Film #2: Message from the Sun,* ca. 1946–48, 2 min. 15 sec., 16 mm, color, sound

films, synchronizing them to well-known 78 rpm recordings of the Dizzy Gillespie Orchestra playing "Guarachi Guaro" or "Manteca." In fall 1965, Smith began using the newly issued LP *The Village Fugs* as the makeshift sound track for the films, playing the record from the back of the room at screenings. Soon, however, the popularity of the Beatles influenced Smith's decision to use the monophonic mix of *Meet the Beatles* (1964, their first U.S. release on Capitol Records) as a sound track, via reel-to-reel tape, for his films. When a sound version of *Early Abstractions* was finally being made, Smith reportedly chose the Beatles' album in the hopes that his film would achieve a comparable popularity. This sound track continues to be the one associated with the film, and remains on the distribution prints to this day, despite Smith's intention to have the films seen with a variety of music and accompaniment.

Film #10, the final selection in *Early Abstractions,* was recut in 1957 to create *Film #11,* also known as *Mirror Animations* (fig. 14). The film is meticulously synchronized to Thelonious Monk's signature piece, "Misterioso." Smith said that he originally intended to base a painting on Monk's work, but "I realized that it would be impossible to make it in the form of a painting, because his music was so complex, and it would be better to make a film."[56] In 1979, Smith expanded the film again, printing it (and the corresponding sound track) forward, then backward, and finally forward once again to create *Film #17.* In these films, Smith arranged alchemical and hermetic imagery to Monk's piano pyrotechnics in a precise and rigorous way. Using cutouts of found materials, Smith assembled a mandala-like collage. Smith situates the action inside the center of the screen, using movement in the foreground, background, and off-screen space, creating a play of surface and depth.

From 1957 to 1962, Smith focused on creating *Film #12,* which Mekas later titled *Heaven and Earth Magic.* The extant version is a 16 mm film with a running time of about sixty-six minutes; Smith claimed to have completed a much longer 35 mm version, although no evidence of it has survived. Conceived as a black-and-white collage, the film draws imagery from such disparate sources as an exercise manual and ladies' wear catalogs. A surrealist study in transformation, the film unfolds through a montage of eclectic images and varied sounds. Smith utilized sortilege and appropriation to structure his cryptic narrative, at once terrifying and captivating. The film's intricate sound track is the only one composed by Smith himself. A howling dog, a screeching cat, wind, dripping water, breaking glass, a tolling bell, and train whistles coalesce to create multiple layers of noises, organically building into a series of dramatic crescendos. The correlation of sound to image is at times synchronous, at times uncannily disjunct.

Fig. 14.
Harry Smith
Stills from *Film #11: Mirror Animations,* ca. 1957, 3 min. 35 sec., 16 mm, color, sound

Film #12 foregrounded the subconscious in terms of subject matter and construction. While working on the film, Smith used sleep deprivation as a strategic creative tool. Positioning his camera and worktable next to his bed, he would work to the point of exhaustion, sleep, then wake up and transfer his dream imagery to film. Inspired by the surrealist process of automatic writing, Smith explained that he "tried as much as possible to make the whole thing automatic, the production automatic rather than any kind of logical process.... It wasn't just chance. Some kind of universal process was directing these so-called arbitrary processes."[57]

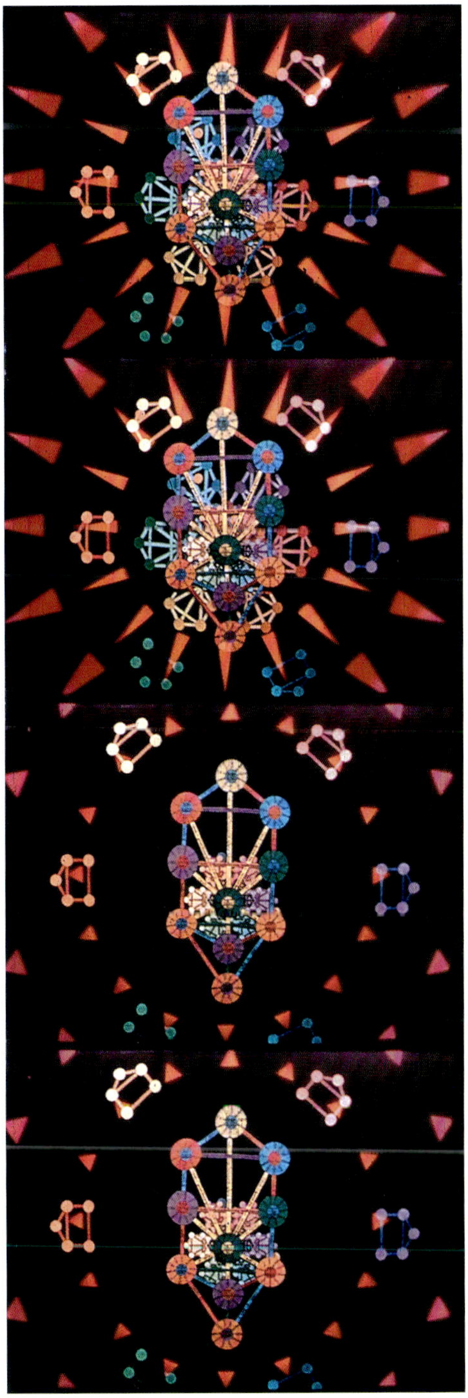

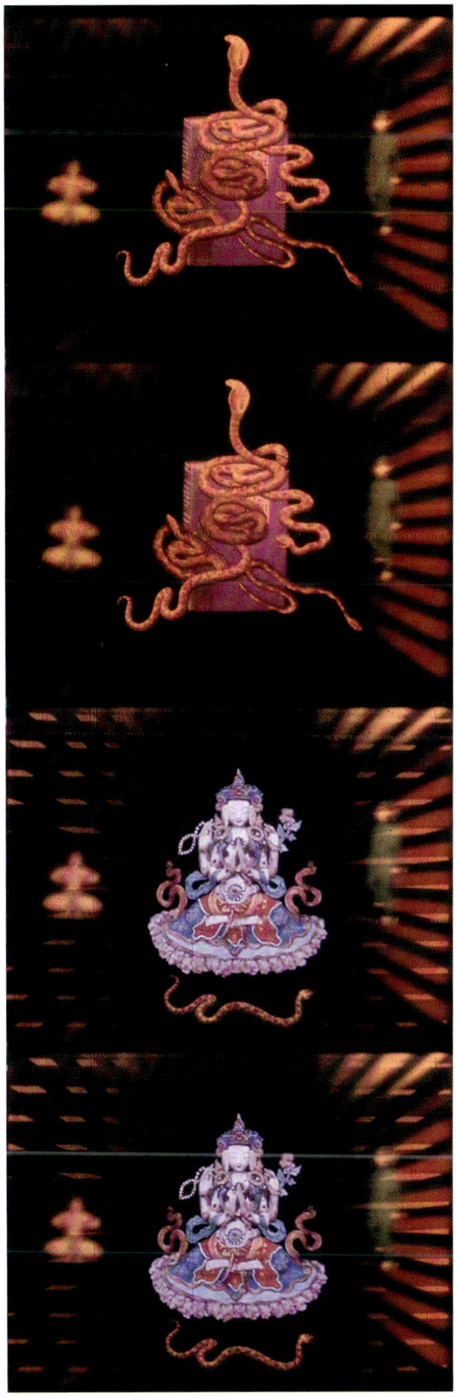

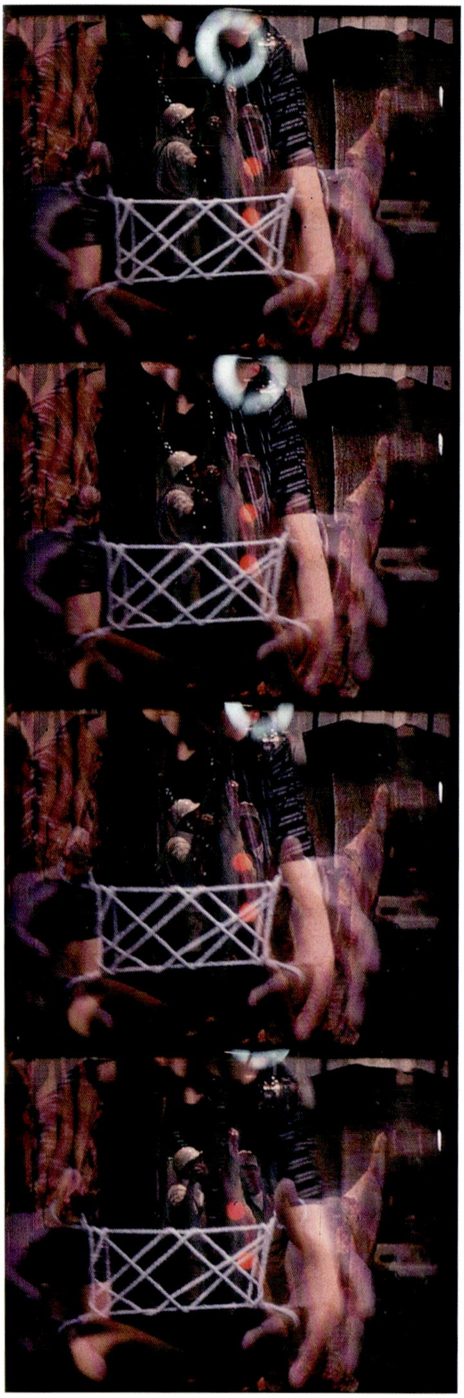

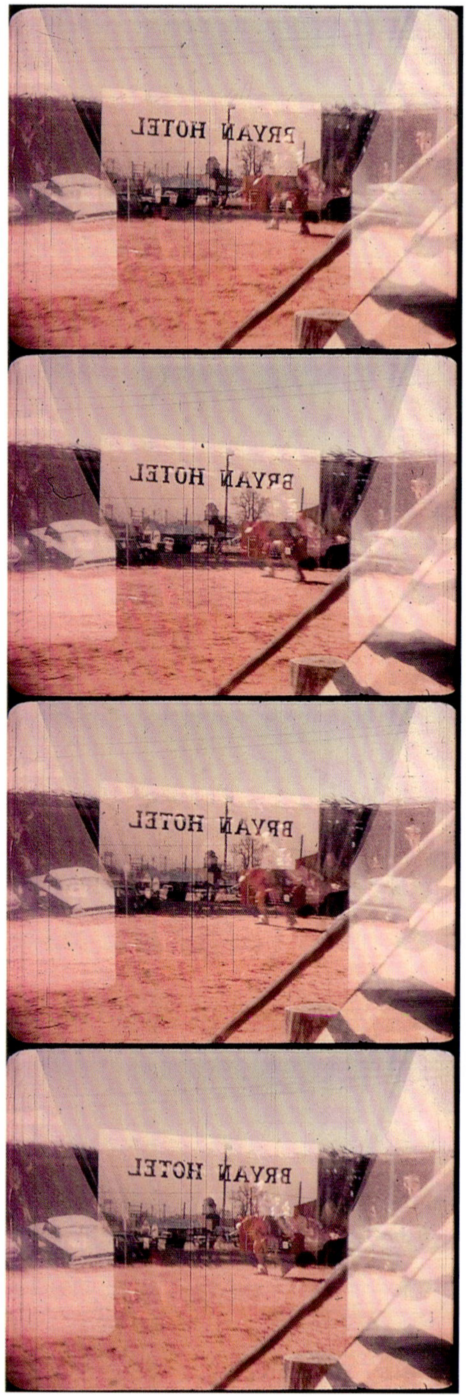
BRYAN HOTEL

Smith envisioned an "expanded" screening of the film that involved theater seats designed to resemble images from the film as well as colored gels and slide overlays that changed in response to the movement of viewers in their seats. He succeeded in organizing less elaborate presentations of the film in the late 1950s and early 1960s, one of which took place at Steinway Hall in New York City.[58] During these screenings, he manipulated the colored gels and slide overlays by hand, creating the impression of a magic lantern show with an animated shadow play at its center. It was characteristic of Smith to have constructed an antiquated, rather than naturalistic, form of color presentation, similar to the tinting and toning of silent films. With the slides and gels, *Film #12* regained its aboriginal character as a dramatic alchemical ritual.

In the early 1960s, Smith began work on his most autobiographical film, *Film #14* (fig. 15), a work that was part travelogue, part home movie. Dubbed *Late Superimpositions* by Mekas, it catalogs Smith's interests and activities during that period. Various sequences feature footage shot in Anadarko, staged Native American ceremonies, and scenes of Manhattan street life. The filmmaker himself can be seen in a few of these sequences. The sound track for this film features the opening sequence of Bertolt Brecht and Kurt Weill's *Aufstieg und Fall der Stadt Mahagonny* (1930; *Rise and Fall of the City of Mahagonny*) from a recording with vocals by Lotte Lenya issued by Columbia Records in 1957. This marked the beginning of Smith's obsession with the opera, which he eventually used as the framework and inspiration for his final film, *Mahagonny. Late Superimpositions* likewise marked a dramatic stylistic shift: for the first time, Smith left his animation table behind and moved into the real world, using live-action photography. Smith's strategy was to shoot hundred-foot reels of film, rewind them, then shoot over them again to create multiple layers of imagery in-camera that were partially determined by happenstance. Within each layer, the compositions were carefully controlled; Smith expertly juxtaposed foreground and background, creating tension between the different planes of action. Smith also included the head and tail leaders of the film reels in the piece, crediting Andy Warhol for the idea.

After unsuccessfully attempting to produce footage for Conrad Rooks's *Chappaqua,* Smith was left stranded and broke in Oklahoma. He pawned his borrowed camera, along with a Wollensak recorder paid for by Asch; this last-ditch solution to a financial bind was a lifelong pattern for Smith, who once informed Sitney, "I've never owned a camera. I've usually just borrowed one, then pawned it. That's always an embarrassing scene, trying to explain to the person where his or her camera is."[59] One of Smith's early films was made courtesy of a camera lent by Hy Hirsh. It was Stuart Reed who lost his camera to an Anadarko pawn shop, while *Film #11* and *Film #12* were shot with a camera belonging to Sheba Ziprin, Lionel's mother, which Smith pawned in Oklahoma City. Throughout his life Smith exploited the generosity of his friends and patrons, and his ability to charm money out of even the most frugal was equaled by his tendency to turn ornery when denied. Despite this pathological cycle, his betrayals and demonstrations of punishing behavior, his supporters sympathized with his artistic vision and continued to support his art.

Fig. 15.
Harry Smith
Stills from *Film #14: Late Superimpositions,* 1964,
31 min., 16 mm, color, sound

During the 1960s, Smith was preoccupied with the *Oz* project—his planned feature-length fiction film based on the series of books by L. Frank Baum. Smith believed that given adequate resources, he could achieve an international reputation with this project. As he explained, "It was to be a commercial film. Very elaborate equipment was built. The animation stand was about the size of a floor and exactly fourteen feet high. Oz was laid out on it, then seven levels built up. . . . I ditched the Munchkins, Quadlings, Gillikins, and Winkies in their original form. What I was really trying to do was to convert Oz into a Buddhistic image like a mandala."[60]

At the outset of the project, several of Smith's patrons—including George Huntington Hartford, Henry Ogden Phipps, Peggy Hitchcock (or "Peggy Richcock" as Smith would call her), Elizabeth Taylor, and Van Wolf—financed the rental of an elaborate and costly animation studio where he worked with Joanne Ziprin (the wife of his friend Lionel Ziprin) every day for over a year. At the end of that year, his investors asked to see what he had created only to discover a mere nine minutes of the film were complete. Smith called it "perhaps the most expensive animated film ever made."[61] When Phipps—Smith's main financier—was discovered dead of a drug overdose in April 1962,[62] funding for the project ended abruptly. Smith arrived at work to find the locks had been changed, and he later discovered that nearly all his work had been destroyed. The footage that survives provides a seductive taste of what could have been a stunning expansion of the characters and themes of *The Wizard of Oz*. Smith's *Film #16: Oz: The Tin Woodsman's Dream* consists of a short animated segment entitled "The Approach to Emerald City" (the surviving fragment) (fig. 16), supplemented by some kaleidoscope footage shot in the mid- to late 1960s.

Smith considered his final film, his cinematic interpretation of Bertolt Brecht and Kurt Weill's *Aufstieg und Fall der Stadt Mahagonny*, to be his magnum opus. The project took him more than ten years to complete, and friends recall him perpetually playing his Columbia recording of the opera in his room at the Chelsea Hotel.

Fig. 16.
Harry Smith
Still from "The Approach to Emerald City" (sequence from *Film #16: Oz: The Tin Woodsman's Dream*), ca. 1962, ca. 5 min., 35 mm, color, silent

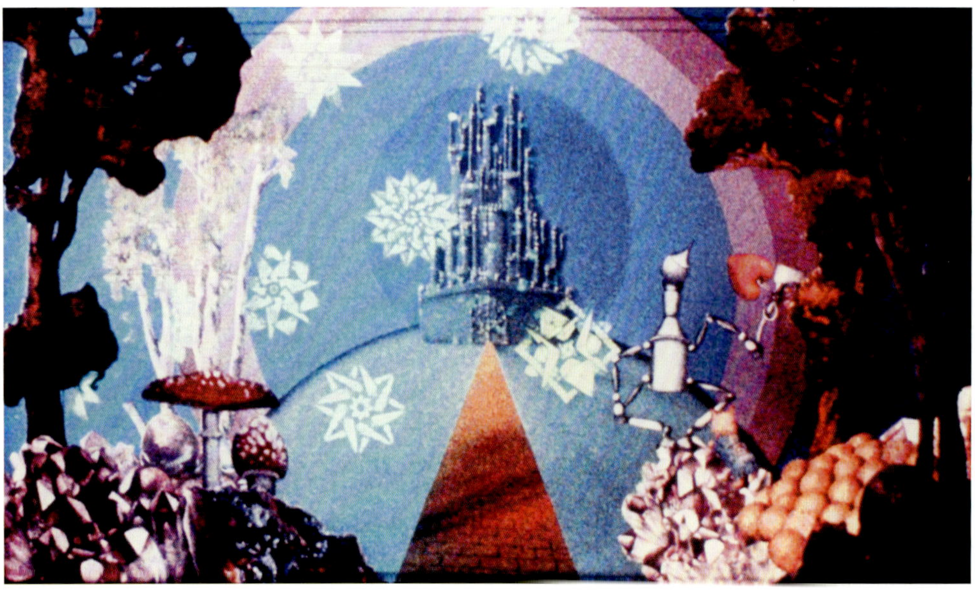

As was the case with various of his previous projects, Smith's *Film #18: Mahagonny* took quotidian elements that surrounded him—people, locations, objects—out of their original contexts, then recontextualized them in an effort to unveil underlying patterns that recur in every culture.

Smith's *Mahagonny* is an allegory of contemporary life that explores the needs, desires, and rituals of people moving through the streets of Manhattan (see pp. 128, 147, 148, 166). Like Weill's imaginary city Mahagonny, New York City is portrayed as a place where everything is permitted and poverty is the only sin. Much of the film takes place in the Chelsea Hotel, where Smith lived at the time, and he would film his friends—Allen Ginsberg, Jonas Mekas, and Patti Smith, among others—when they stopped by to visit. These sequences are intercut with shots of Robert Mapplethorpe's work installed in his studio, New York street scenes, and stop-motion sequences of shifting pills, bottles, and powdered pigments. These elements are woven together for projection onto a four-part split screen.

Smith shared Weill's interest in transforming popular culture into avant-garde art. Just as Smith had blurred the line between high and low culture in taking existing recordings of American folk music and reshaping them into the complex aural collage that was the *Anthology,* he hoped to transform Weill's opera—which was regarded as a successful synthesis of high and low—into a work of popular culture with universal appeal. Smith also shared Weill's desire to create a radical work of transformative art. Brecht and Weill's *Mahagonny* caused a riot when it premiered in Leipzig in 1930, and Smith hoped his film would have a comparable power—that it would redefine cinema.

In a grant application to the Committee on Poetry, Smith explained his vision for *Mahagonny:*

> the final film will be just as intelligible to the Zulu, the Eskimo, or the Australian Aborigine, as to people of any other cultural background or age.
>
> In its final form the film will be a series of scenes of varying lengths synchronized to the time of an entire song, and on occasion, synchronized to the length of a single line of the lyrics, but all designed to translate the opera into a universal script based on the similarities of life and aspiration in all humans. As far as I know, the attempt to make a film for all people whether they be Papuans or New Yorkers, has not been so far attempted. It is by far the most complex of the 20 or so films I have made in the last 30 years; and my hope is that it will not only be successful, but will introduce a new theoretical basis for films and through the use of world wide symbols, help to bring all people of the Earth closer together.[63]

Smith spent 1970 through 1972 shooting footage for *Mahagonny,* then devoted the next eight years to editing it according to a meticulously detailed program based on a numerological and symbolic system of his own conception. The completed work consists of four 16 mm images projected simultaneously to form a single four-part image that is two frames wide and two frames high. Synchronizing each of the four screens with the operatic score, Smith made elaborate scrolls

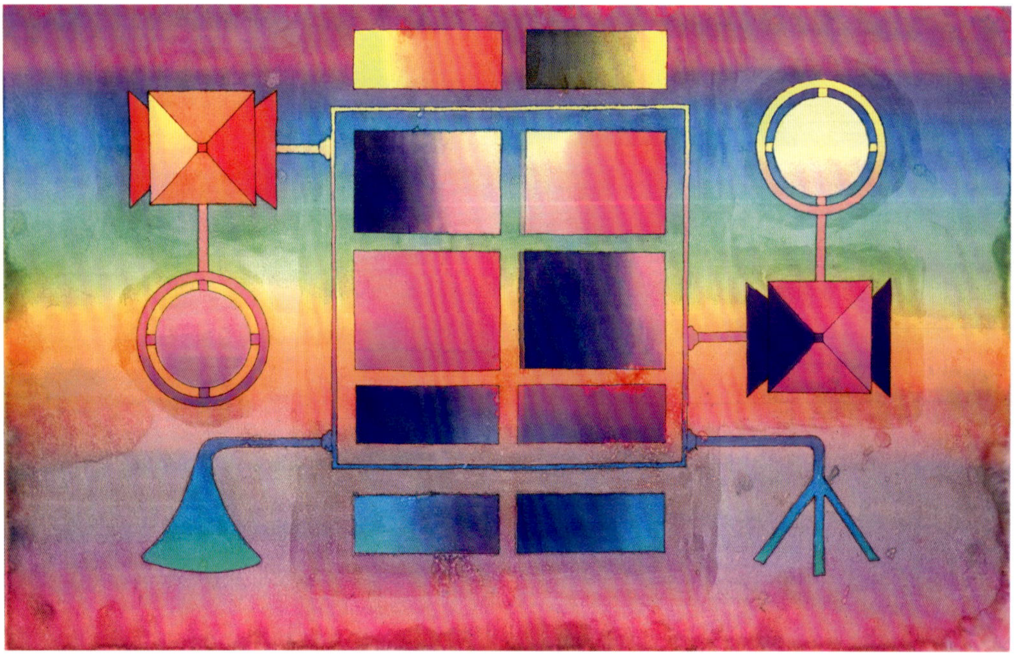

Fig. 17.
Harry Smith
Untitled (Scheme for projection of *Film #18: Mahagonny*), ca. 1978, watercolor on paper, 30.5 × 50.8 cm (12 × 20 in.)
Harry Smith Archives

Fig. 18.
Harry Smith
Untitled, ca. 1950
Whereabouts unknown

Fig. 19.
Harry Smith
Still from *Film #3: Interwoven*, ca. 1947–49, 3 min. 20 sec., 16 mm, color, sound

representing each edited reel, and a fifth scroll with a time code that included a list of scenes from the opera. The editing of *Mahagonny* was a byzantine process (see pp. 2, 143). Smith created index cards for each scene and organized them according to various mathematical permutations that corresponded, in Smith's mind, to particular parts and thematic moments in the opera. Twenty-four "units" (images or scenes) appear on each reel of the twelve reels of film. Smith categorized each of his film images as either portrait (P), animation (A), symbol (S), or nature (N), and the units on each reel appear in the order of the near palindrome PASAPASNAPASAPANSAPASAPN.[64] Smith determined the length of each scene based on the viewer's rates of respiration and heartbeat.

Smith would probably have worked on the film for the rest of his life, except the curator and art critic Henry Geldzahler, then the commissioner of cultural affairs for New York City, offered completion funds for *Mahagonny* on the condition that Smith stop editing, finish the film, and actually screen it. *Mahagonny* debuted at Anthology Film Archives in 1980, and Smith was present for each of the six screenings. As with *Heaven and Earth Magic,* he had to relinquish his desire for an extravagant mode of presentation—involving, in this case, projecting the film on the tops of four pool tables set up vertically within a boxing ring and accompanied by scrolling subtitles of the opera's text (fig. 17). He did, however, design slides, colored gels, framing masks, and other elements that he attempted to use for the initial screenings. He reportedly broke them in the street in a fit of anger after one of the shows.[65]

Like his filmmaking contemporaries Jack Smith and Ken Jacobs, Smith saw the projection of films as an opportunity for performance. More than a film, *Mahagonny* was structured to incorporate complex ritual elements, and each screening was meant to provoke different symbolic associations. Smith often caused

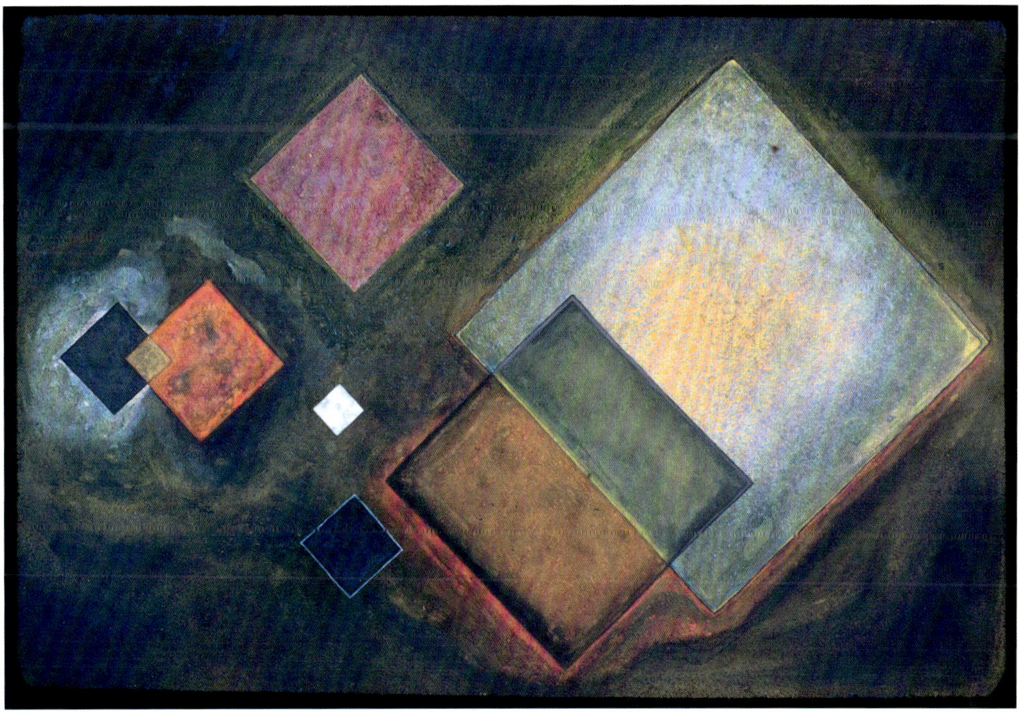

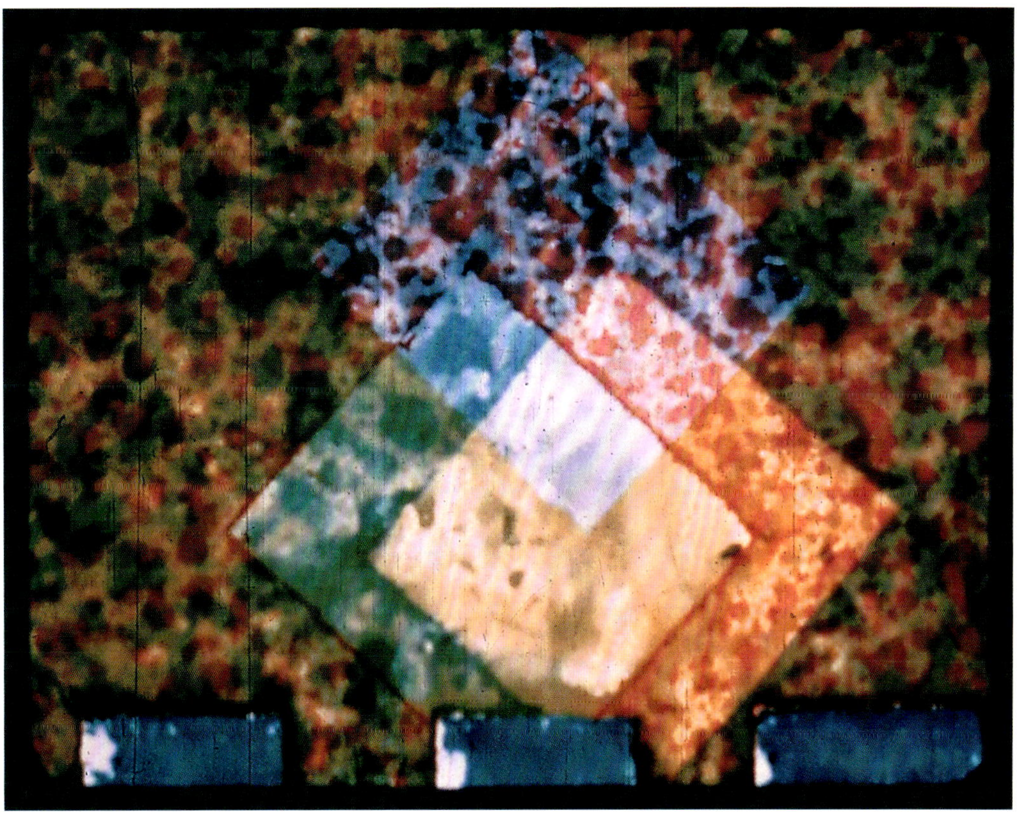

disruptions during screenings of his films, and the commotion he created became part of the performance. The mythology surrounding these screenings includes stories of Smith setting off fireworks during a showing, keeping his semen in the auditorium to absorb audience energy, and throwing a projector out of a third-story window onto Park Avenue South.[66]

Screenings with Smith in attendance were edgy, destabilizing events for the spectator,[67] and this erratic behavior extended to his personal life. His chronic drinking and drug abuse alienated many of his most ardent friends and supporters. He preferred the cheapest vodka available (usually Popov) and eventually invented a beverage to satiate both his alcohol addiction and his damaged health—a milk and beer fusion that was easy on his ulcerated stomach. Just as Smith welcomed technological evolution, he was open to new developments in recreational pharmacology; his use of drugs was both wide-ranging and opportunistic. When Smith discovered he could order peyote directly from the Sears, Roebuck catalog in the 1950s, he immediately purchased a supply. A chronic marijuana smoker and self-medicator, Smith also had a taste for amphetamines and barbiturates. Smith maintained lengthy and close relationships with his doctors, especially one he called Dr. G. (Dr. Joe Gross), who was a longtime patron and medical consultant.

Smith's paintings and films share an iconography, drawing from both symbolic systems and patterns of abstractions (figs. 18, 19). The glyph, a nonverbal symbol that imparts structural information about the object that it represents, is a foundational visual device for Smith, and central to understanding the connection between his work in different media. In his book *Visionary Film,* Sitney recounts an episode at Anthology Film Archives in 1971 in which Smith encountered a group of students sitting in an auditorium watching a film—not one of his, a work in the realist tradition. "You shouldn't be looking at this as a continuity," he admonished. "Film frames are hieroglyphs, even when they look like actuality. You should think of the individual film frame, always, as a glyph, and then you'll understand what cinema is about."[68] His iconographic images are intended to function as symbols that have universal meanings.

Cosmic Visual Patterns

Smith's paintings of the 1960s through the 1980s are significantly more complex than the figurative works of his teenage years, the jazz paintings of the late 1940s, and his nonobjective studies of the early 1950s. Freighted with allusions to magic, cosmology, and esoteric systems of metaphysics, they are densely layered, less hard-edged, and rely heavily on design and pattern (figs. 20, 21). In such works, Smith worked through ideas by cross-referencing and mapping comparative systems of knowledge on canvas or paper. In the five works in his *Enochian Tablet* series, for instance, he linked what he regarded as the principles underlying Highland tartans to the Enochian language (figs. 22, 23), which was said to have been communicated by angels to John Dee through his medium, Edward Kelley, in the sixteenth century.

Smith's most widely circulated graphic work is his four-color silk screen collotype print the *Tree of Life* (fig. 24). Smith credited his father with teaching him the geometry intrinsic to this image, which draws from the kabbalah, the mystical branch of

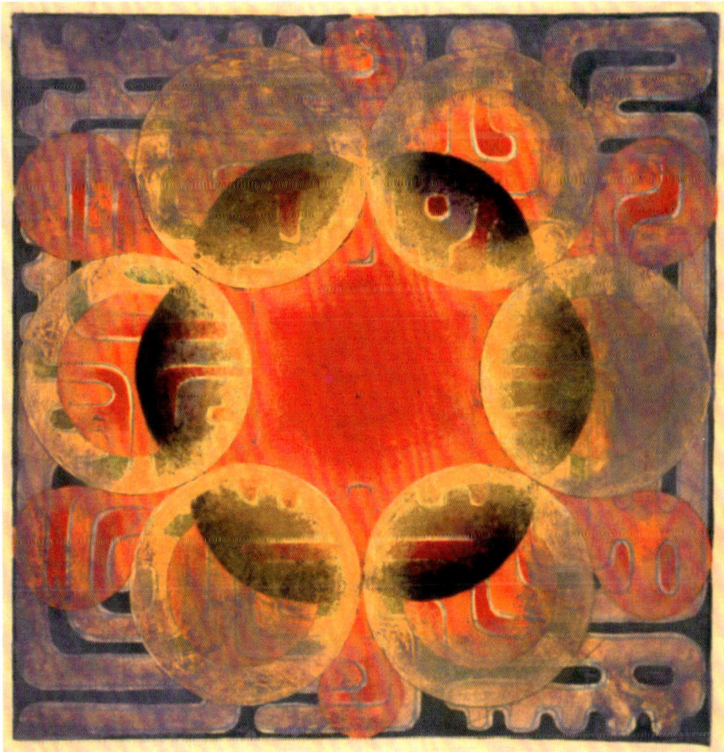

Fig. 20.
Harry Smith
Untitled (Zodiac sign),
ca. 1974, mixed media on
board, 36.8 × 37.5 cm
(14½ × 14¾ in.)
Harry Smith Collection

Jewish esoteric practice, in which the tree of life is the most significant symbol of the cosmos. The entirety of the spiritual and material world is represented in this visual map (fig. 25). A navigational tool, Smith's *Tree* is an extrapolation from this central icon of the kabbalah, which has as its structural origins an emphasis on the twenty-two letters of the Hebrew alphabet and the divine numbers from one to ten.

Smith created his version of the tree of life while working for Inkweed Arts, a greeting card company owned by his friend Lionel Ziprin. An underground figure and renowned Talmudic scholar, Ziprin had an affinity for eccentrics of every stripe—including the artists and filmmakers Bruce Conner and Jordan Belson—many of whom made a point of contacting him for work when they were in New York City. During the period when he and Ziprin were closest, Smith spent a good deal of time at the New York Public Library, where he created intricate tracings from assorted esoteric, religious, and alchemical texts in the public collection. Hours spent paging through these metaphysical texts inspired Smith to make his own drawing of the tree of life, which he and Ziprin printed in conjunction with their commercial work. Smith designed a silk screen that took advantage of the nearly five-inch-wide margins of paper generated, and generally discarded, in the making of greeting cards. Belson contributed to Smith's *Tree of Life* by cutting the intricate stencils required for the four-color printing process.[69] Smith's financially precarious existence caused him to become skilled at making use of whatever scavenged materials were available to him; his ingenious recycling of the paper remainders from a printing press is a good instance of his relentless resourcefulness.

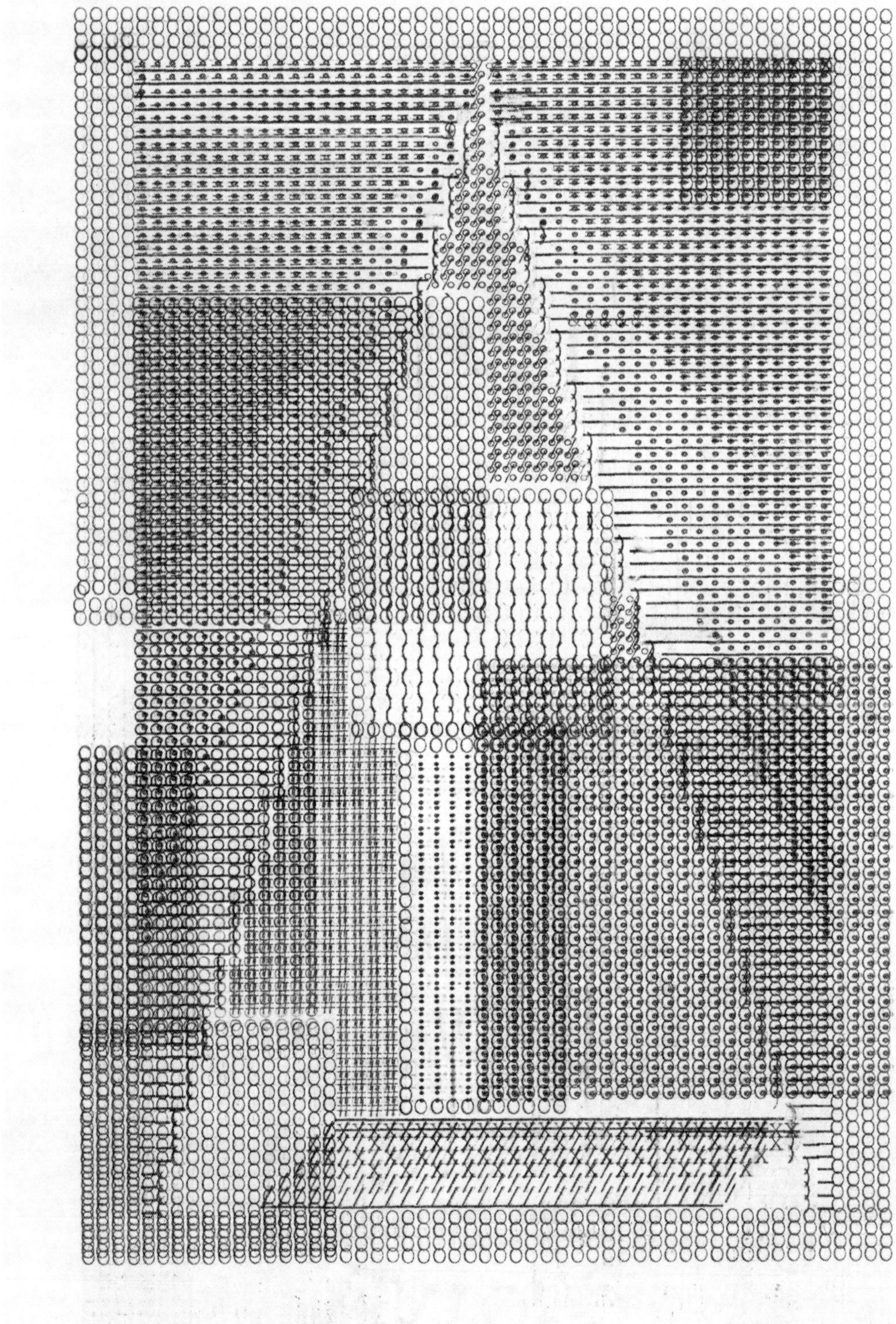

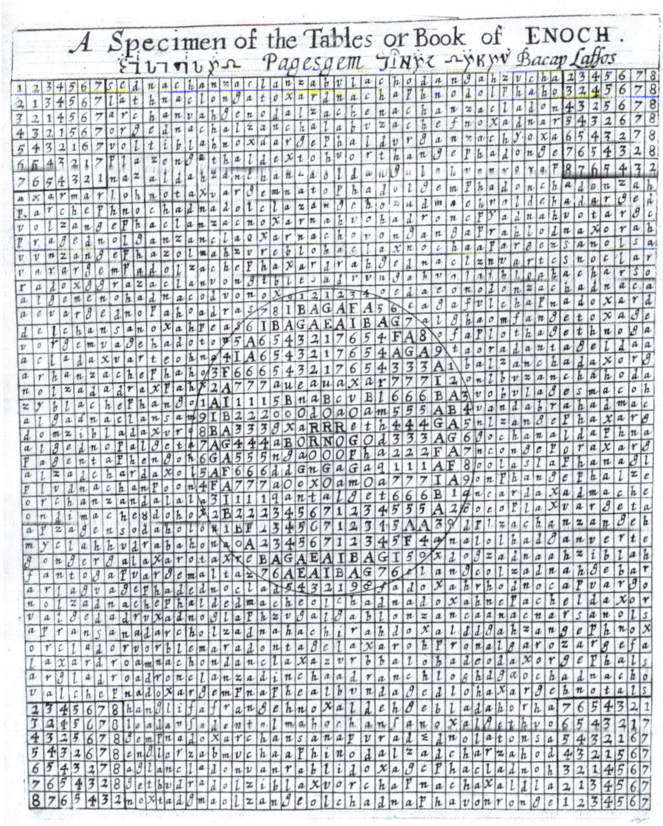

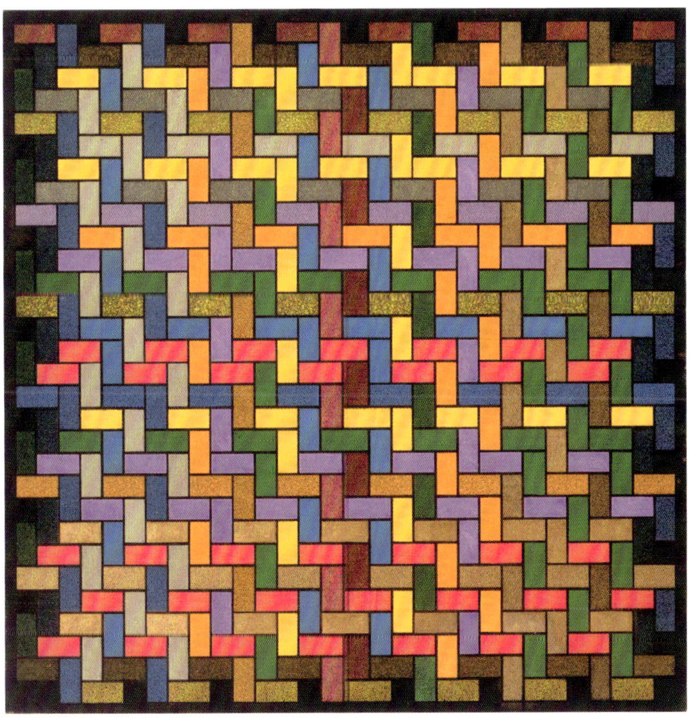

Fig. 21.
Harry Smith
Typewriter drawing, ca. 1980, typewriter on paper,
28 × 21.5 cm (11 × 8½ in.)
Harry Smith Archives

Fig. 22.
A Specimen of the Tables or Book of Enoch
From John Dee, *A True and Faithful Relation of What Passed for Many Yeers between Dr. John Dee... and Some Spirits...* (London: printed by D. Maxwell for T. Garthwait..., 1659), before p. 1

Fig. 23.
Harry Smith
Enochian Tablet, ca. 1979, watercolor, gouache, ink, acrylic, and enamel on board,
78.7 × 78.7 cm (31 × 31 in.)
Harry Smith Collection

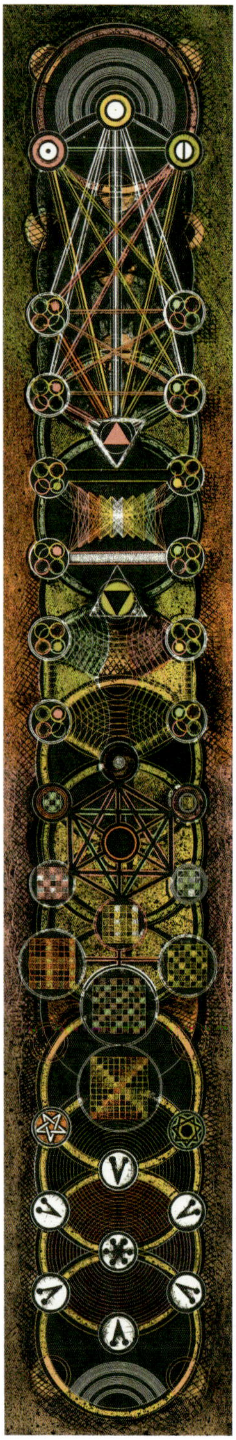

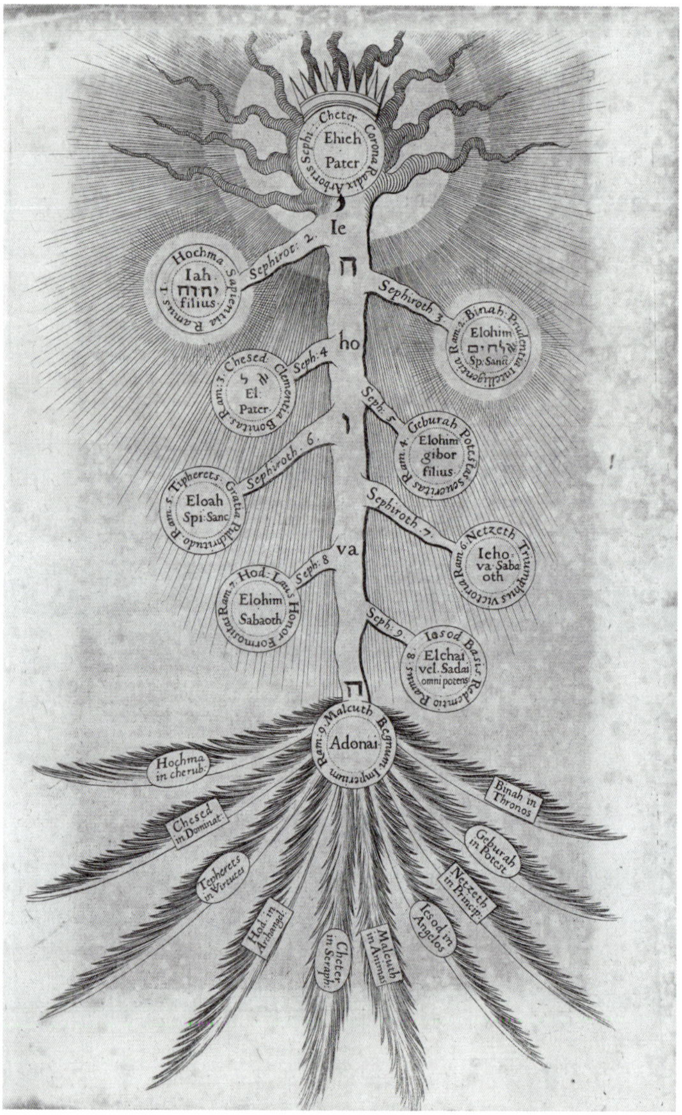

Smith's *Tree of Life* is likewise indicative of his lifelong interest in esotericism. According to William Breeze, the well-known occultist, the current leader of the Ordo Templi Orientis (OTO), and a longtime friend of Smith, in the late 1940s Smith began an earnest course of study in the A∴A∴ system, a magical order founded by Aleister Crowley. His first teacher was the highly influential Canadian kabbalist Charles Stansfeld Jones, famed as the occult teacher of the novelist Malcolm Lowry and the model for the Consul in Lowry's *Under the Volcano.* Smith continued his studies in New York in the 1950s with Jones's colleague Albert Handel. In 1986, Breeze consecrated Smith as a gnostic bishop in the Ecclesia Gnostica Catholica, the ecclesiastical branch of the OTO, the order founded in 1906 by Theodor Reuss, which Crowley joined in 1910 and led from 1922 until his death in 1947. The OTO performed a gnostic mass in Smith's honor at the memorial service

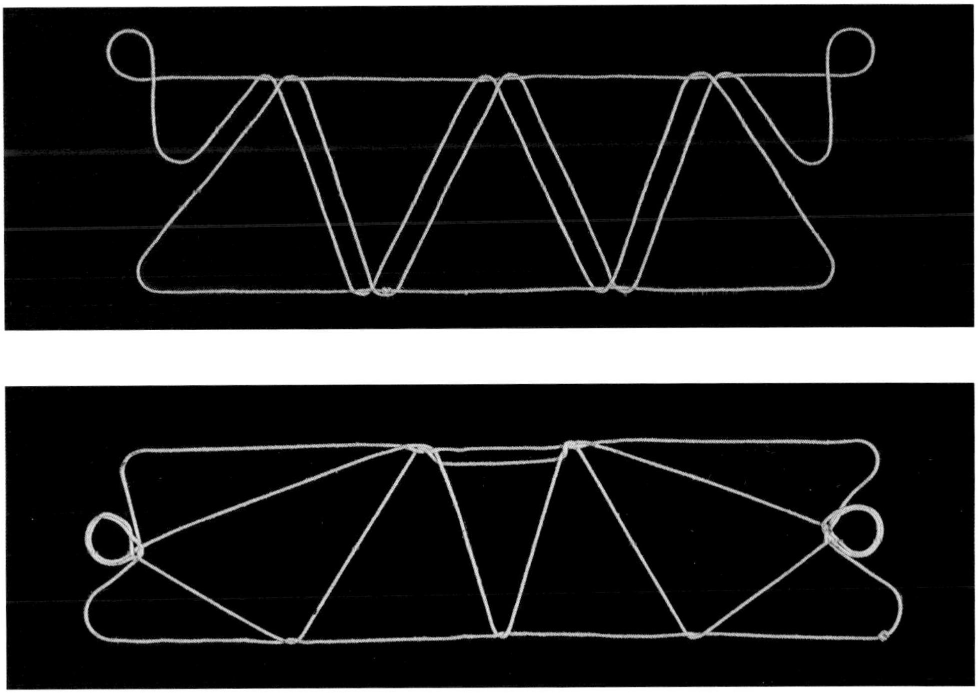

held for him at St. Mark's Church in-the-Bowery in New York City in 1991. In 2006, Breeze stated that "Aside from Kenneth Anger, it is hard to point to anyone in the twentieth century who better exemplifies the whole point of the 'universality' of Aleister Crowley's A.:.A.:. teaching curriculum than Harry."[70]

Throughout his life, Smith compulsively collected everything from books, pop-up books, audio recordings, Indian women's beaded costumes, tarot cards, and gourds to things shaped like other things (spoons shaped like ducks, banks shaped like apples, anything shaped like a hamburger). Quality, in the conventional sense, was not a criterion for Smith, who considered souvenir-grade folk items as equal in import to Fabergé eggs. One of his most astonishingly original accumulations was the collection of paper airplanes he amassed from the streets of New York City; whenever he came across a paper airplane there, he noted the time, date, and location where he picked it up, then filed it away. The collection was donated to the Smithsonian Institution's National Air and Space Museum, where it languished in storage because the curators did not know quite what to make of it. The collection was transferred to the Harry Smith Archives after Smith's death.

Another of Smith's ongoing collections consisted of instructions for string figures, which track the manipulation of an ordinary piece of string into an elaborate handwoven design (fig. 26). Smith regarded the construction of string figures as a universal form of expression; he claimed that all cultures use such figures as a storytelling device in one way or another. He first learned of them from "some cousins of mine [who] had a book on string figures, and in learning them I realized that this is happening north of Seattle, Washington."[71] Indeed, string figures were commonly performed by the elders of the Lummi and Swinomish on the Native

Fig. 24.
Harry Smith
Tree of Life, 1954, four-color screen print, 63.5 × 12.4 cm (25 × 4⅞ in.)
Harry Smith Archives

Fig. 25.
Johann Theodor de Bry (Franco-Flemish, 1561–1623)
Arboris Sephi[rothicae]
(Tree of the ten *Sefirot*)
From Robert Fludd, *Anatomiae Amphitheatrum Effigie Triplici, More et Conditione Varia, Designatum* (Frankfurt: sumptibus Iohannis Theodori de Bry, 1623), 157

Fig. 26.
Harry Smith
String figures, 1960s, string, glue, and poster board, each: 20.4 × 50.1 cm (8 × 20 in.)
Top: Harry Smith Archives
Bottom: John Cohen Collection

American reservations Smith visited during the late 1930s and early 1940s. Smith's interest in string figures continued throughout his life, and he eventually compiled a lengthy manuscript on the subject that remains unpublished. In an interview with Cohen for *Sing Out!,* Smith commented on what he saw in such figures: "Oh, it was some universal thing that seemed to be more widely distributed than anything else in places that didn't have so-called 'civilization.' It was the only thing that I could isolate off hand that was produced by all primitive societies and by no 'cultured' societies."[72]

Two of Smith's other collections of patterns—Seminole textiles (see p. 8) and Ukrainian Easter eggs—were often on display in his Chelsea Hotel room, a magical zone where disparate objects seemed to be in conversation among themselves. Smith regarded each object, and each collection, as offering insight into the culture that created it.

> It has something to do with the desire to communicate in some way, the collection of objects.... I presume that all these are methods to communicate according to the cultural background that they have. So I'm interested in getting series of objects of different sorts. It's a convenient way of finding information, for whatever use. It does seem apparent, since I started collecting records, that there are definite correlations between different artistic expressions in one particular social situation.[73]

Smith lost all his belongings while he was in Oklahoma in 1964 and 1965 when he failed to pay the rent on his apartment at 300½ East 75th Street—belongings that included major paintings and other works of art. Attempts to rescue them from the Fresh Kills Landfill on Staten Island were unsuccessful. But one of the great ongoing contradictions in Smith's life was his ever-expanding mass of personal property and his nomadic existence. He was often forced to move, sometimes at a moment's notice and under cover of night, from one hotel to another, but he usually returned to the Chelsea Hotel, on West 23rd Street between 7th and 8th avenues. Visitors to his room were greeted by a sign with "Do Not Disturb" neatly lettered on an index card. If granted entry, visitors never knew whom they might encounter, what chaos might ensue, or what mood Smith himself might be cultivating. A number of the Chelsea Hotel's most eccentric denizens, as well as celebrated artists, the local drug dealer, assorted sycophants, and runaway teenagers (whom Smith recorded reading desperate letters from their parents), regularly visited his room. Robert Frank once remarked that Smith's genius lay in the fact that he made little distinction between a Bowery bum and an erudite scholar and freely associated with both.[74]

Visitors were forbidden to touch anything in Smith's room, as he was fastidious about the handling and condition of his books and belongings. Often gray industrial metal shelving provided storage, a small bed occupied one corner, and folding card tables covered with open books served as a workspace. Objects were stacked in orderly piles beside beer cans and unemptied ashtrays, and a few of Smith's beloved parakeets were allowed to fly around the room. When one of his birds died, he preserved it for eternity in his freezer, alongside various unidentifiable petri dish experiments.

Smith lived at the Chelsea Hotel from 1968 until 1975, when he moved to the Hotel Breslin on 28th Street and Broadway. He stayed there for nearly a decade, until he could no longer avoid the manager seeking back rent—a sad turn of events that Robert Frank captured on video. Smith's eviction in December 1984 inaugurated an increasingly unstable period in his life, during which his ability to deal with day-to-day existence became severely compromised. Allen Ginsberg invited Smith for a temporary stay at his 12th Street apartment, which in the end lasted "Eight stormy, but amazing months."[75] Around this time, Ginsberg commissioned Smith to design the image used on the covers of Ginsberg's books *Collected Poems, 1947–1980* (1984) and *White Shroud* (1986). The image Smith created—three fish with a single head (see p. viii), inspired by a stone footprint left by the Buddha that Ginsberg had seen in India in 1963—now serves as the logo for the Harry Smith Archives. When Ginsberg was pushed beyond the limits of generosity, he arranged for Smith to move to Cooperstown, New York, to the home of the French poet Claude Pélieu and his wife, the artist Mary Beach (the couple made an appearance in Smith's *Mahagonny*).

The minute Smith got off the bus in Cooperstown, he made a beeline for the local antique shops, where he spent all the money Ginsberg had given him on obsolete farm tools, old keys, and items unique to the area and arranged to have his new purchases delivered to his unsuspecting hosts. Following this rather startling arrival, Smith, alcoholic and irascible, wore out his welcome in fairly short order. Within six months, he landed in a men's flophouse in the Bowery where, remarkably, he marshaled his creative energies and made audiotapes of different snoring sounds and the sounds of dying men. After a visit to the flophouse, the squalor of which he found appalling, Ginsberg again invited Smith to become his temporary houseguest and again began seeking a workable long-term living situation for Smith. After Smith returned from a trip with Ginsberg to the Center for the Study of Southern Culture in Oxford, Mississippi (where he made recordings of local musicians), Ginsberg arranged for him to teach at the Jack Kerouac School of Disembodied Poetics at the Naropa Institute in Boulder, Colorado.

Colorado: Coda, Part I

Smith spent his last years, from 1988 to 1991, as shaman in residence at the Naropa Institute, where he gave lectures on every aspect of his life's work and continued his research and collecting (fig. 27). It was in Colorado that I met Smith. I had been aware of Smith's films since my first year at the University of Colorado at Boulder, where I studied with the experimental filmmaker Stan Brakhage. Brakhage included Smith's work in his film history classes and prefaced each screening with the words, "You are about to see the work of one of the most extraordinarily inventive artists of all time." Brakhage spoke passionately about the fact that he never painted a frame of film without feeling that Smith was looking over his shoulder, and he regaled students with outrageous (and, it turns out, sometimes exaggerated) stories of Smith's magical experiments. I came away with the sense that this mysterious, larger-than-life character was so extraordinary that he could not possibly exist.

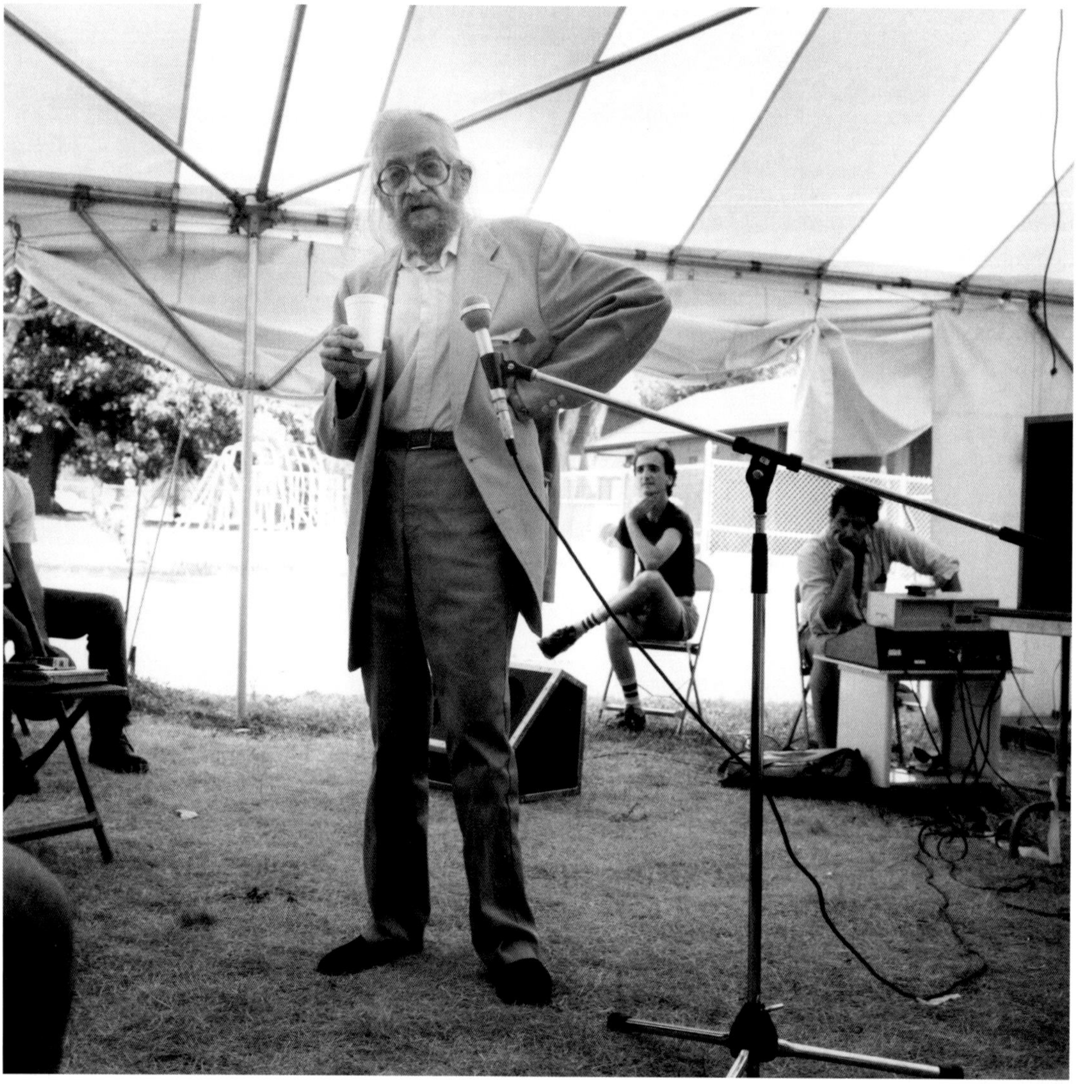

Fig. 27.
Allen Ginsberg (American, 1926–97)
Harry Smith, Naropa Institute, Boulder, Colorado, 16 July 1988

In 1986, I began working as assistant to Allen Ginsberg during the summer writing program at the Naropa Institute. Two years later, Ginsberg told me he was bringing Harry Smith to Boulder for the summer. "You know, the filmmaker and folk music collector." It took me some time to comprehend that the mythical figure that Brakhage spoke about was a living, breathing person. Smith made his first appearance in 1988 at Naropa's annual Fourth of July holiday picnic. He showed up wearing a trench coat in ninety-degree heat and strolled elegantly across the great lawn holding a Sony Walkman Professional cassette recorder (the second one he had "borrowed" from Ginsberg) in one gloved hand and a microphone in the other. He spent the entire day making audiotape recordings of the sounds at the party, which culminated in a fireworks display at evening's end.

At the end of the summer, Smith discovered, much to his surprise, that Ginsberg intended to leave him in Boulder, and he settled into a small cabin on the grounds of the institute (fig. 28). On the door, he placed his customary handwritten "Do Not Disturb, I Am Either Sleeping Or Working" index card. He had little furniture aside from a folding card table, a log to sit on, and a rock (which he called the vulva rock) strategically placed under the ceiling heater to warm a privileged guest. His bedroom floor was covered with neat stacks of books, and the built-in cabinets were crammed with more texts and various collections of objects. Smith and I had become friends by then, and when I expressed concern about his sleeping on the floor on a thick pile of blankets, he eventually permitted me to take him to a local futon store. Before Smith would enter the store, he insisted that we spend a while in the car so he could smoke enough marijuana to prepare himself for the upcoming purchase. Once inside, he zeroed in on a child-size futon on a platform that was about four inches off the ground. Although the store clerk wondered aloud about the appropriateness of the fit, Smith purchased the futon and happily took it home.

To converse with Smith was to experience total disorientation of the mind and senses. Marijuana nearly always played a prominent part in a visit with him. His nearly photographic memory along with an expansive range of references allowed him to make startling leaps from one subject to the next. A citation from an ethnographic journal published in 1933 might be followed by a reference to the latest issue of *Nature* or a recording of birdcalls. Incredibly, he always managed to lead the conversation back to the central topic from which he had digressed.

Smith taught at Naropa for three summers (1988 through 1990), presenting courses titled Surrealism, Alchemy, and Native American Cosmologies. His classes reflected longtime interests but also incorporated his newfound knowledge of the area garnered by prowling neighborhood bookstores and conferring with a variety

Fig. 28.
Peter Cole (American, b. 1957)
Harry Smith, Naropa Institute, Boulder, Colorado, 1988

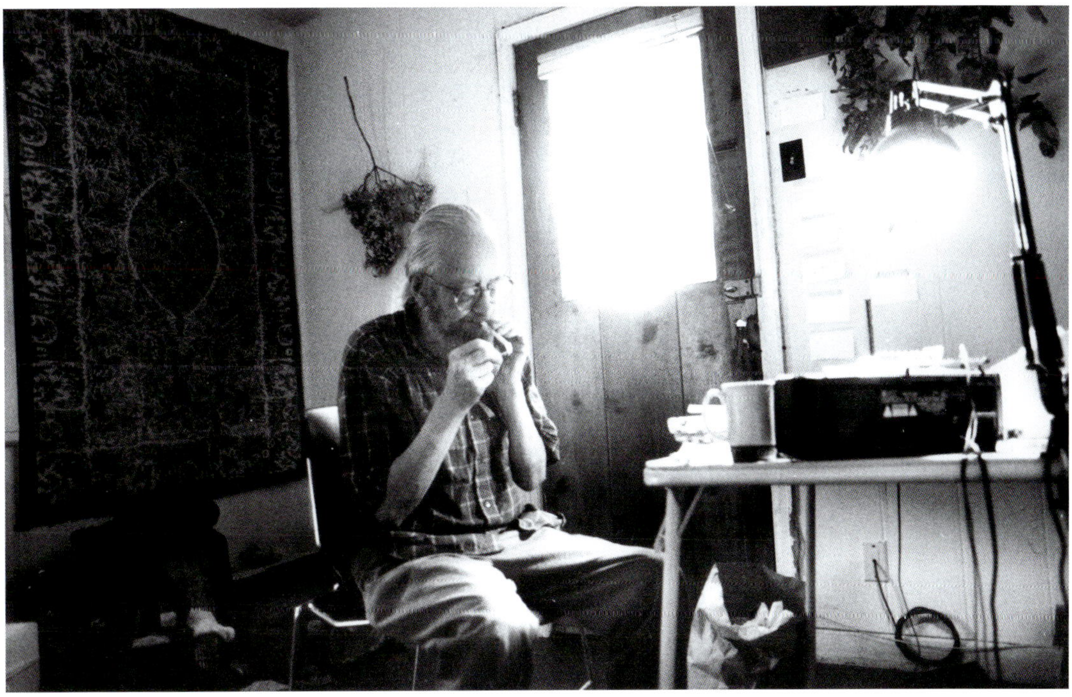

of local characters. As soon as he moved to Boulder, Smith began a "saturation job"—a term coined by the poet Charles Olson in the 1950s (and constantly evoked by Ed Sanders during the classes he taught at the Naropa Institute) to describe the practice of immersing oneself completely in a particular subject.[76] Returning to the American West at the age of sixty-five reignited Smith's early interests and inspired him to reconsider many of the subjects and materials that fascinated him as a young adult. He amassed a collection of materials on the Arapaho, Cheyenne, and Apache, and for his Native American Cosmologies class he compiled an extensive two-volume reading packet that included scholarly articles on ritual, religious symbolism, and creation myths; to show the interconnectedness of all things, he included in the packet a few of Rube Goldberg's comical cartoons.

Most of Smith's students had no knowledge of his pioneering work in American vernacular music. One day he offhandedly mentioned that he had produced a collection of records. Chuck Pirtle, a student, borrowed a copy of the *Anthology* from the Boulder Public Library and brought it to Smith, who claimed that he had not heard it in over thirty years. When Pirtle returned later that afternoon, he found him sitting at his table with his headphones on, listening to familiar voices from the past, tears in his eyes.

Smith's last years were relatively tranquil. He spent his time in Boulder buying books, reading, and making audio recordings, surrounded by a coterie who regularly arrived at his cabin with offerings. He had stopped drinking alcohol because of chronic throat and dental problems. He was on a diet of bee pollen, raw hamburger, ice cream, instant coffee, and Ensure liquid nutritional supplement that made him gain a healthy thirty pounds, giving him a renewed sense of well-being and vigor. He supplemented his diet with marijuana and whatever combination of Sinequan and Valium he found in his jacket pocket.

During these years, he subscribed to a telephone message service from US West. For three dollars a month, the telephone company would allow customers to record up to 175 three-minute messages that could be stored and retrieved at will. Intrigued by the possibilities of this technology, Smith would ask people to call and leave messages containing dreams, songs, stories, or sounds from any unique location. He would then arrange and transcribe the information, noting caller, date, time, and place. These tapes demonstrate his continued ability to transform everyday experience and recast it as a work of art.

His last formal project was a series of audio recordings entitled *Materials for the Study of Religion and Culture in the Lower East Side or Movies for Blind People* that he began in New York City and continued in Boulder. This collection consists of cassette tape recordings featuring the sounds of Haitian street fairs, Hispanic celebrations, church bells, children's jump rope rhymes, folk and rock music performed on the streets and in music clubs, and Bowery bums coughing and praying, as well as readings by the poets Gregory Corso and Allen Ginsberg, the noises of Tompkins Square Park, and many other found soundscapes. In Boulder, he recorded cows at sunset, crickets at dawn, the Boulder County Fair, rodeos, dances, and lectures held at Naropa Institute. Listening to these recordings, it becomes clear that Smith approached the project as a found sound symphony.

In 1991, Smith was honored with the National Academy of Recording Arts and Sciences's Chairman's Merit Award for lifetime achievement for "his deep commitment to presenting folk music as a vehicle for social change."[77] He returned to New York City in February to receive the award at Radio City Music Hall. In his acceptance speech he stated, "I'm glad to say my dreams came true, that I saw America changed through music. And all that stuff that the rest of you are talking about."[78] He stayed on in New York at the Chelsea Hotel for nine months, never coming back to Boulder despite continually making promises to me of his imminent return. As his health declined, he refused to see a doctor. He suffered from paranoid fantasies and believed he was being poisoned. He died at the Chelsea Hotel on 27 November 1991.

Coda, Part II

Historicizing a person requires a journey along an odd and imprecise trajectory. This volume is part of that process. We have begun the task of examining Smith's output from a number of diverse perspectives, each person drawn into the work by a different strand. Many people who came into contact with him have profound stories to tell, while others who encounter his work feel compelled to respond to it. Smith was a self-mythologist who delighted in throwing red herrings across the paths of would-be historians. The tales he propagated are just as important as the truth, and often more bizarre. Entering Harry Smith's world is like venturing into a cabinet of curiosities, a *Wunderkammer,* a museum unto itself, where the viewer is beguiled by the mysterious and intriguing.

Assessment of Smith's contributions to twentieth-century culture is in the formative stages. His influence goes far beyond the individual works he produced, having seeped into the general culture shared by successive generations of artists and performers. Musicians continue to reinterpret songs from the *Anthology,* while painters, graphic designers, and filmmakers have been inspired by Smith's pioneering techniques in cut-up and collage.

One of the characteristics of the twentieth century was a breaking down of boundaries between different artistic media and between high and low forms of art, as the rise of abstraction saw the demarcation between cinematic, musical, and visual arts increasingly blurred. Smith was at the epicenter of this convergence. Prescient in his use of different media, he anticipated both the challenges and the opportunities provided by multimedia artistic production in the information age of the twenty-first century. He was a walking Internet search engine before such a thing existed, with an amazing capacity for recall and the ability to make connections between seemingly random bits of esoterica.

Smith should be situated with the likes of Joseph Cornell and Marcel Duchamp in the lineage of modernist pioneers. Cornell and Duchamp were interested in appropriating everyday objects for artistic purposes while simultaneously exposing hierarchies of taste and class. Smith's approach was similar to theirs, though the objects he chose were quite different. However, unlike Cornell and Duchamp, who wanted to see the artistic value in mass-produced objects, Smith was interested in using cultural detritus to reach a mass audience. He took what had been cast off by society and imbued it with his esoteric knowledge, reframing and recontextualizing it, in the hopes of giving discarded materials newfound recognition and popularity.

For alchemists in the hermetic tradition, turning the ordinary into the extraordinary is an ongoing goal, as alchemy is the attempt to transform common elements into precious metals while also achieving personal transcendence. The quest is both spiritual and physical. Alchemists in the sixteenth and seventeenth centuries devoted themselves to a lifetime of preparation, study, and practice. Smith, who was often referred to as "the Paracelsus of the Chelsea Hotel,"[79] lived a life wholly focused on an ascetic existence and the suffering that it entailed. One of the possibilities that Smith's work offers us is a portal into other worlds, where forms of knowledge that have been neglected are revivified. It was by searching for the interconnections that bridge the infinite and the finite that Smith found a place to situate himself within the universe. By connecting ancient spiritual traditions and American folk cultures, Smith's work in music, film, and the visual arts gives us access to a cultural constellation that is perfect and strange, extraordinary in its breadth and focus, and surprisingly compelling in its coherence.

Notes

1. "Smith, Harry," *Film-Makers' Cooperative Catalogue,* no. 3 (1965): 57.
2. Harry Smith, "P. Adams Sitney—NYC [*Film Culture,* no. 37, 1965]," interview by P. Adams Sitney, in idem, *Think of the Self Speaking: Harry Smith—Selected Interviews,* ed. Rani Singh (Seattle: Elbow/Cityful, 1999), 47–48.
3. For Robert A. Smith's involvement with Freemasonry, see *Souvenir of the Semi-Centennial of Garden City Lodge No. 141, A. F. & A. Masons, Chicago, Illinois* (Chicago: [Rogers & Smith], 1903), 30–35, portrait facing p. 44; for his involvement with the Fairhaven cannery, see August C. Radke, *Pacific American Fisheries, Inc.: History of a Washington State Salmon Packing Company, 1890–1966,* ed. Barbara S. Radke (Jefferson, N.C.: McFarland, 2002), 28, 29, 42, 65. John Corson Smith is discussed in *History of the Grand Commandery of Knights Templar of the State of Illinois from October 27, A.D. 1857 to October 25, A.D. 1881* (Chicago: Grand Commandery, 1885), 317–19, portrait facing p. 329; and *History of the Grand Commandery of Knights Templar of the State of Illinois,* vol. 2, pt. 1, *From October 27, A.D. 1857 to June 1, 1907*... (Chicago: Grand Commandery, 1908), 187–96, 432–33, portrait facing p. 187. See also John Corson Smith, *History of Freemasonry in Illinois, 1804–1829* (Chicago: Rogers & Smith, 1903), which is posted in its entirety at http://www.archive.org/details/historyoffreemasoosmit (accessed 8 June 2009).

   For more on Smith's family history, see Darrin Daniel, *Harry Smith: Fragments of a Northwest Life* (Seattle: Elbow, 2000), 11–13.

   It is worth noting, given Smith's ongoing engagement with Native American cultures, that General John Corson Smith was sent a pictographic autobiography of Sitting Bull in about 1882, which Robert A. Smith eventually donated to the Bureau of American Ethnology of the Smithsonian Institution. See National Anthropological Archives, Smithsonian Institution, Museum Support Center, NAA MS 1929-b; and M. W. Stirling, *Three Pictographic Autobiographies of Sitting Bull* (Washington, D.C.: Smithsonian Institution, 1938), 25–48.

4. Smith, "P. Adams Sitney" (note 2), 44.
5. Daniel, *Harry Smith* (note 3), 12–14.
6. Smith, "P. Adams Sitney" (note 2), 56.
7. Smith, "P. Adams Sitney" (note 2), 56.
8. Smith's parents lived in two different houses on the street. They later lived as a couple in a semicommunal arrangement with Miss Henrietta "Bubble" Blaisdell, according to the musician and Anacortes historian Bret Lunsford.
9. See Daniel, *Harry Smith* (note 3), 10, 17–18.
10. Bill Holm, personal communication, 9 July 2001; and Bill Holm, email messages to Rani Singh, 11 and 15 February 2008.
11. Treaty Day is held every year during the weekend nearest to 22 January, to commemorate the signing of the Point Elliott Treaty, near Mukilteo, on that day in 1855. The treaty transferred most of the territory around Puget Sound eastward to the summit of the Cascade Range, and from the 49th parallel down to Point Pully (Three Tree Point), south of Seattle, from local Indian tribes to the United States government.
12. Bill Holm, personal communication, 9 July 2001; and Bill Holm, email messages to Rani Singh, 11 and 15 February 2008.
13. Bill Holm, personal communication, 9 July 2001; and Bill Holm, email messages to Rani Singh, 11 and 15 February 2008.
14. George Casey, "Indian Life and Radio Building Are Interests of Two B. H. S. Boys," *Bellingham High Beacon*, 5 December 1942.
15. Harry Smith, "John Cohen—Chelsea Hotel, NYC [*Sing Out!* Volume 19, No. 1, 1969]," interview by John Cohen, in idem, *Think of the Self Speaking: Harry Smith—Selected Interviews*, ed. Rani Singh (Seattle: Elbow/Cityful, 1999), 68, 70.
16. Gordon Tweit, personal communication, 6 July 2001. See also Tony Stasiek, "Ahead of His Time: Bellingham Youth's Folk Recordings Reverberate through the Years," *Bellingham Herald*, 2 December 2001, http://www.newslibrary.com/sites/behb (accessed 1 October 2008).
17. Harry Smith, "Gary Kenton—Breslin Hotel, NYC [March 1983/84]," interview by Gary Kenton, in idem, *Think of the Self Speaking: Harry Smith—Selected Interviews*, ed. Rani Singh (Seattle: Elbow/Cityful, 1999), 16.
18. Jordan Belson, personal communication, 2003; see also Luis Kemnitzer, "West Coast Record Collector," in *A Booklet of Essays, Appreciations, and Annotations Pertaining to the "Anthology of American Folk Music" edited by Harry Smith* (Washington, D.C.: Smithsonian Folkways Recordings, 1997), 30.
19. Kemnitzer, "West Coast Record Collector" (note 18), 29–31; and Luis Kemnitzer, personal communication, 29 July 2000.
20. Harry Smith, "Oskar Fischinger" (from an interview by William Moritz, 1977), in Gerald O'Grady and Bruce Posner, eds., *Articulated Light: The Emergence of Abstract Film in America* ([Cambridge]: Harvard Film Archive/Anthology Film Archives, 1995), 9.
21. Harry Smith to Hilla Rebay, 17 June 1950, 2, Hilla Rebay Archive, Solomon R. Guggenheim Museum Archives, New York. The letter is reprinted in this volume, 261–64.

22. Smith, "P. Adams Sitney" (note 2), 44; and "Smith, Harry" (note 1), 57.
23. Moritz, this volume, 64.
24. Scott MacDonald, ed., *Art in Cinema: Documents toward a History of the Film Society* (Philadelphia: Temple Univ. Press, 2006), 174 ("Conversation with Jordan Belson, 7/22/00").
25. For the program notes for 24 October 1947, see this volume, 255.
26. For the program notes for 24 September 1948, see this volume, 256; for the program note regarding the two films shown on 11 February 1949, see Moritz, this volume, 68 n. 9.
27. The 35 mm originals for these films no longer exist. Smith describes some of the processes in Smith, "P. Adams Sitney" (note 2), 52–57; see also P. Adams Sitney's commentary in his *Visionary Film: The American Avant-Garde, 1943–2000,* 3rd ed. (New York: Oxford Univ. Press, 2002), 238–49.
28. Program notes, Art in Cinema, Series 6, 12 May 1950, San Francisco Museum of Art, Pacific Film Archive Library and Film Study Center, University of California Berkeley Art Museum and Pacific Film Archive, Berkeley. Preceding Smith's films were *Begone Dull Care* (1949) by Norman McLaren and *Love and Bullets* (1914) by Roscoe "Fatty" Arbuckle; Fritz Lang's *Destiny* (*Der Müde Tod,* 1921) closed the program. The note on Smith's film describes them as follows:

    > In contrast to Lye and McLaren, who start their patterns after the sound track, Smith's carefully measured rhythmic designs are composed visually first and the music added or evoked after. His approach to this difficult technique is probably more complex than either Lye's or McLaren's in that each frame itself is considered as a separate composition, altering gradually from frame to frame, whereas the patterns of the other two extend along the film strip in a manner much resembling the sound track.

29. Kemnitzer, "West Coast Record Collector" (note 18), 31.
30. Smith, "P. Adams Sitney" (note 2), 56. On Jimbo's Bop City and Jackson's Nook, see also Roy Porter and David Keller, *There and Back: The Roy Porter Story* (Baton Rouge: Louisiana State Univ. Press, 1991), 4–6; for an overview of the Fillmore jazz scene, see Elizabeth Pepin and Lewis Watts, *Harlem of the West: The San Francisco Fillmore Jazz Era* (San Francisco: Chronicle, 2005).
31. Smith to Rebay (note 21), 2; see this volume, 262.
32. Smith, "P. Adams Sitney" (note 2), 55.
33. Smith, "P. Adams Sitney" (note 2), 52.
34. Three letters between Smith and Rebay are reprinted in this volume, 258–64.
35. Lionel Ziprin, "Lionel Ziprin—May and June 1993," by Paola Igliori, compiled with previous interview by Clayton Patterson with K. K., in Paola Igliori, ed., *American Magus Harry Smith: A Modern Alchemist* (New York: Inanout, 1996), 39.
36. Luc Sante, May 1977; as quoted in *A Booklet of Essays, Appreciations, and Annotations Pertaining to the "Anthology of American Folk Music" edited by Harry Smith* (Washington, D.C.: Smithsonian Folkways Recordings, 1997), 30.
37. Harry Smith, handbook to the *Anthology of American Folk Music,* FP 251–FP 253 (New York: Folkways Records, 1952), [18]. Smith's typography is retained unchanged in all quotations from the booklet.

38. Smith, handbook (note 37), [2].
39. Smith, "John Cohen" (note 15), 68–70.
40. Greil Marcus, *Invisible Republic: Bob Dylan's Basement Tapes* (New York: Henry Holt, 1997), chap. 4.
41. Smith, handbook (note 37), [25].
42. Smith, handbook (note 37), [2].
43. Smith, "John Cohen" (note 15), 83.
44. Bob Dylan, "'I've Got New Eyes… Everything Looks Far Away,'" interview by Serge Kaganski, *Mojo,* February 1998, 64.
45. [Harry Smith, ed.,] *Prayers and Chants by Rabbi Naftuli Zvi Margolies,* Special Record Q1 (New York: Folkways Records, 1954). See John Freeman Gill, "Giving Voice to Sacred Prayers," *New York Times,* 5 February 2006, sec. 14, p. 6; David Katz, "'Angels Are Just One More Species,'" *Jewish Quarterly,* no. 204 (2006/7): 61–64; and William Grimes, "Lionel Ziprin, 84, Mystic of Lower East Side, Dies," *New York Times,* 21 March 2009, A15.
46. In an email message sent to Rani Singh on 1 January 2004, Conrad Rooks described his arrangement with Smith:

> I cannot remember when he was supposed to be in Anadarko but he received around $5000 to cover all his expenses—recording equipment, film, etc. He didn't show up in Anadarko at the agreed time, and when he did just as we were leaving to go back to a peyote ceremony in Lame Deer, Montana, he showed up totally pissed with a drunken Indian. No one was amused. He was sent to find a peyote ceremony, and we were all on a tight schedule as a lot of money was gone already, he wanted more money. He was told to f— off.

For a description of the film and its making, see Jack Sargeant, "Hallucinations and Homecomings: Notes on Conrad Rooks' *Chappaqua,*" in idem, *Naked Lens: An Illustrated History of Beat Cinema,* new ed. (Washington, D.C.: Creation, 2001), 147–56.

47. Harry Smith, liner notes for *The Kiowa Peyote Meeting,* FE 4601 (New York: Folkways Records, 1973), 2: "I particularly hope that examples of the Kiowa approach to things will give an insight into how one people has dealt with the problem of rhythm in relation to thought, and that persons interested in the Ritual, but unable to attend a Meeting, will partake of the herb while listening to the records." An excerpt from the liner notes is reprinted as Harry Smith, "The Kiowa Peyote Meeting," in Paola Igliori, ed., *American Magus Harry Smith: A Modern Alchemist* (New York: Inanout, 1996), 162–67.
48. Philip Smith, "Harry Smith," in Eric Olsen, Paul Verna, and Carlo Wolff, *The Encyclopedia of Record Producers* (New York: Billboard, 1999), 740.
49. Allen Ginsberg, "Introduction," interview by Hal Willner, in Harry Smith, *Think of the Self Speaking: Harry Smith—Selected Interviews,* ed. Rani Singh (Seattle: Elbow/Cityful, 1999), 6–7.
50. "Smith, Harry" (note 1), 57.
51. Rumors often circulated on New York's downtown scene that Harry Smith was a pseudonym for several different artists. It seemed unlikely that one person would be capable of all of his divergent accomplishments, and Jonas Mekas even went so

far as to open a column in the *Village Voice* with the question, "Does Harry Smith even exist?" There were men in the 1970s who dubbed themselves "Harry Heads," dressing in trench coats and making recordings of street noises as Smith himself had done. See Jonas Mekas, "Movie Journal," *Village Voice,* 18 March 1965, 23; for the complete text of this particular column, see this volume, 267–68.

52. John Cohen, email message to Rani Singh, 21 October 2008.
53. Ginsberg, "Introduction" (note 49), 2.
54. Ginsberg, "Introduction" (note 49), 4. Mekas's account of his early encounters with Smith and his work does not match Ginsberg's version; see Jonas Mekas, "Jonas Mekas—10 July 1993," interview by Paola Igliori, in Paola Igliori, ed., *American Magus Harry Smith: A Modern Alchemist* (New York: Inanout, 1996), 80–81.
55. Smith to Rebay (note 21), 2; see this volume, 262.
56. Smith, "P. Adams Sitney" (note 2), 57.
57. Smith, "P. Adams Sitney" (note 2), 58.
58. Sitney, *Visionary Film* (note 27), 250.
59. Smith, "P. Adams Sitney" (note 2), 57.
60. Smith, "P. Adams Sitney" (note 2), 60.
61. Sitney, *Visionary Film* (note 27), 236.
62. "Henry Phipps, 31, Found Dead Here," *New York Times,* 12 April 1962, 22.
63. Harry Smith to the Committee on Poetry, New York City, typescript grant application, ca. 1973, ii–iii, Harry Smith Archives. Reprinted in this volume, 272–73.
64. According to a newly discovered score by Smith held by the Harry Smith Archives; see also Harry Smith, "P. Adams Sitney—NYC [*Mahagonny,* 1977]," interview by P. Adams Sitney, in idem, *Think of the Self Speaking: Harry Smith—Selected Interviews,* ed. Rani Singh (Seattle: Elbow/Cityful, 1999), 106–7.
65. Mekas, "Jonas Mekas" (note 54), 80–81.
66. Stan Brakhage told such stories to his students at the University of Colorado at Boulder in the 1980s; see also Mekas, "Jonas Mekas" (note 54), 80.
67. For a taste of one of Smith's performances before a screening, see Smith, this volume, 115–24.
68. Sitney, *Visionary Film* (note 27), 257.
69. For Smith's work with Ziprin, see Ziprin, "Lionel Ziprin" (note 35), 42–45.
70. Breeze made this statement during the film conference "Magic and the Avant-Garde in Cinema," Princeton University, 11 March 2006.
71. Harry Smith, Native American Cosmographies lecture, 8 July 1990, Allen Ginsberg Library, Naropa University, Boulder, Colorado; as quoted in Daniel, *Harry Smith* (note 3), 15.
72. Smith, "John Cohen" (note 15), 90.
73. Smith, "John Cohen" (note 15), 79.
74. Robert Frank, personal communication, 1991.
75. Ginsberg, "Introduction" (note 49), 9.
76. See Charles Olson, *A Bibliography on America for Ed Dorn* (1954), in idem, *Collected Prose,* ed. Donald Allen and Benjamin Friedlander (Berkeley: Univ. of California Press), 306–7: "Best thing to do is *to dig one thing or place or man* until you yourself know more abt that than is possible to any other man. It doesn't matter whether it's

Barbed Wire or Pemmican or Paterson or Iowa. But *exhaust* it. Saturate it. Beat it. And then U KNOW everything else very fast: one saturation job (it might take 14 years). And you're in, forever."

77. Bill Ivey, presentation of Chairman's Merit Award of the National Academy of Recording Arts and Sciences to Harry Smith, Grammy Awards, Radio City Music Hall, New York City, 20 February 1991.
78. See clip posted as "Harry Smith ackowledged" at http://www.youtube.com (accessed 8 June 2009).
79. See Marcus, *Invisible Republic* (note 40), 97.

WILLIAM MORITZ

HARRY SMITH, MYTHOLOGIST

I am very happy that in 2001 Harry Smith is being celebrated by a prestigious symposium at a major museum—a symposium that should place him, most correctly, among the "major artists" of our era.[1] But at the same time I feel a little chilled and shocked, remembering the first time I met Harry, at the Chelsea Hotel in 1961, when he was clearly a pariah, reviled and mocked by seemingly everyone. The Chelsea management had turned off the elevator closest to his room because, it said, he had used it too much. He was penniless and hadn't anything to eat. When I gave him a little money to buy some food, he hurried off to buy a book he had wanted for some time. I felt like his brother or son: I too would have bought a record or a book before paying the rent or eating. Fortunately, though, I never fell into the desperate poverty and alienation that Harry suffered. California winters are kinder than the frostbite of New York.

Harry Smith was a mythologist in two senses. He had an encyclopedic knowledge of the mythologies of many cultures from antiquity to the present day, including their cult practices, their sacred texts, their symbolisms, their music, and their magic. He gorged his living quarters with grimoires and anthropological studies which he practically knew by heart. But he was also the mythologer of his own personal legend. Was he, as a boy, initiated into sacred rites of the Native American tribes of the Pacific Northwest? Who knows, and why should we care, since he was so knowledgeable about them?

He had a small, fragile body, but he was capable of feats of considerable strength and agility. When I was driving to Canada with Elfriede Fischinger for a retrospective of her husband's films, we stopped in New York City, and I took her to visit Harry,[2] whom she had not seen since 1947. His room at the Chelsea Hotel was crowded from floor to ceiling with boxes and stacks of books, artworks, periodicals, records, figurines, and many other things, so that one could hardly get around much. I had visited him twice before, so I knew what to expect, but Elfriede was flabbergasted, and then thrilled, by the dozens of curious and priceless things that kept emerging from the seeming chaos (which Harry, however, seemed to know down to the last scrap, and from which he could retrieve any particular item with relative ease). He spoke glowingly of how inspirational Oskar Fischinger had been to him and said it must be nice for her to have his legacy so well preserved. Elfriede told him frankly how many things—films, paintings, and papers—had not been properly preserved yet. "Well, something should be done about that!" Harry proclaimed and disappeared for a moment into his "archive." He emerged shortly with a few magic paraphernalia and a live chicken and proceeded to perform a ritual, chanting, dancing around, and finally sacrificing the chicken to use its blood to mark symbols on various objects, including Elfriede's hand. "Now," he said in conclusion, "you should not be having so much financial worry, and most of your precious things will be taken care of in the next few years." Indeed, within a few years the Deutsches Filmmuseum in Frankfurt am Main paid a substantial amount of money to acquire a representative cross section of Oskar's works (films, paintings, animation drawings, photographs, documents, and so on) for archival preservation in Germany, and Elfriede used her fee to preserve more of Oskar's works in Los Angeles. She also received several grants from the National Endowment for the Arts and other foundations that contributed to the restoration and preservation of more of Oskar's things. Harry's magic seemed to have worked.

I knew Harry would enjoy seeing Elfriede because some years before, when I was preparing a text about Fischinger for *Film Culture,*[3] Harry had given me a lovely testimonial about Oskar:

> You can tell how much I admire Fischinger: the only film of mine that I ever gave a real title to was *Homage to Oskar Fischinger* [*Film #5,* in the current scheme of things]. I learned concentration from him—visiting his home and seeing how he could sit serenely in that small house, crawling with what seemed like a dozen children, and still paint those stunning pictures. That great film *Motion Painting* makes the process seem deceptively simple—and it was simple for him: the images really did just flow from his brush, never a ruler or compass, all free-hand—but you can't see all the obstacles he had to overcome in order to even work at all. Something so wonderful happened in that film, and in those paintings, something so much better than all the Pollocks and other stuff that the museums fight to get hold of. Did anyone ever fight to save Fischinger's things?

In many interviews and statements Harry created a mythological version of his own life and works. He claimed to have made his first film in 1939, but that was not just a lie: it was rather a strategy to prove that he had not followed or copied filmmakers such as Norman McLaren and Len Lye who had been making works painted directly on the film surface since the 1930s. Harry should not have worried about that, since his own films have a style and intricacy quite different from Lye's and McLaren's. However, government sponsorship made their films widely available, well publicized and well known. Harry was on his own, often with only one or two prints of any given film.

In fact, Harry had seen films by McLaren and Lye (*Colour Box* [1935] in 1948) and Fischinger and John and James Whitney before he made his first painted films. Harry was studying painting in San Francisco (and was a friend of Jordan Belson, another painting student) in 1946, when Frank Stauffacher, along with his brother Jack Stauffacher and Richard Foster, began preparing the Art in Cinema series, which would screen at the San Francisco Museum of Art for the next eight years. The screenings included most of the classic avant-garde experimental films (many of them available then through the Museum of Modern Art in New York City) as well as new experimental works from around the world. Belson and Smith volunteered to help out with the project (in exchange, of course, for free tickets to all the screenings), and Harry would boast that he had seen every one of the Art in Cinema screenings, even the repeat showings. As luck would have it, in 1947 Harry was sent to Los Angeles to convince Oskar Fischinger and the Whitney brothers that they should come to San Francisco to screen a program of their films.[4] Harry was amazed by the brilliance of Fischinger's new film, *Motion Painting No. 1* (1947),[5] as well as the dozens of canvases that had preceded it. He had mixed feelings about the Whitney brothers' *Five Film Exercises* (1943–44):[6] *No. 1* and *No. 5* seemed more mechanical to him, while the other three impressed him by their musical values. *No. 4* particularly, Harry said, contained all the anguish and terror of World War II and managed to survive. Both Fischinger and the Whitneys did go to San Francisco for Art in Cinema screenings.

Harry wanted to extend his painting into this exciting new medium of film, but he lacked the equipment and the technical skills as well as the significant amount of money that processing and making copies in a laboratory could cost. The angel who enabled him was a photographer named Hy Hirsh, who had been a cinematographer at Columbia Studios in the 1930s but now worked freelance with still photography (an official photographer of artworks at the de Young Museum in San Francisco, he also did many fashion and commercial shoots, which sometimes took him to exotic locales such as Jamaica, Amsterdam, Paris, and Morocco). Hirsh also made his own experimental films, often abstract ones. Hirsh was what the French call a *bricoleur:* someone who can make everything himself. He built his own optical printer so that he could create "special effects" for his films. And he generously taught filmmaking skills and loaned his own equipment to a whole generation of Bay Area filmmakers, including James Broughton, Sidney Peterson, Jordan Belson, and Harry Smith.

While Belson first experimented with painting hundreds of sequential images on long scrolls, Harry opted for creating geometric and abstract shapes that occurred in everyday city situations, which he shot in black and white but then could "colorize" with filters handheld during projection. The first of these films, titled *Film Number Five (Fast Track),* was screened at Art in Cinema on 24 October 1947. It was listed as ten minutes, with sound, in the program notes.[7] The second of these (probably the current *Film #4*) appeared on 31 October 1949, listed as *Film No. 6,* in black and white, with no mention of sound.[8]

Then Harry began painting directly on the film strip, thus avoiding the cost of extra negatives and prints, except, of course, Hirsh had to help with the optical printing to ensure that the delicate painted film strip was not scraped or scratched during the printing process. On 12 May 1950, Art in Cinema premiered four painted films by Harry Smith.[9] They were titled *A Strange Dream, Message from the Sun, Interwoven,* and *Circular Tensions,* and the program notes remark that each of their hundreds of painted film frames is a work of art (see pp. 25, 35, 43).[10] The films were accompanied by a live jazz band consisting of Atlee Chapman on trombone and bass trumpet, Henry Noyd on trumpet, Kermit Scott on tenor saxophone, Robert Warren on bass, Warren Thompson on drums, and Stanly Willis on piano. It is easy

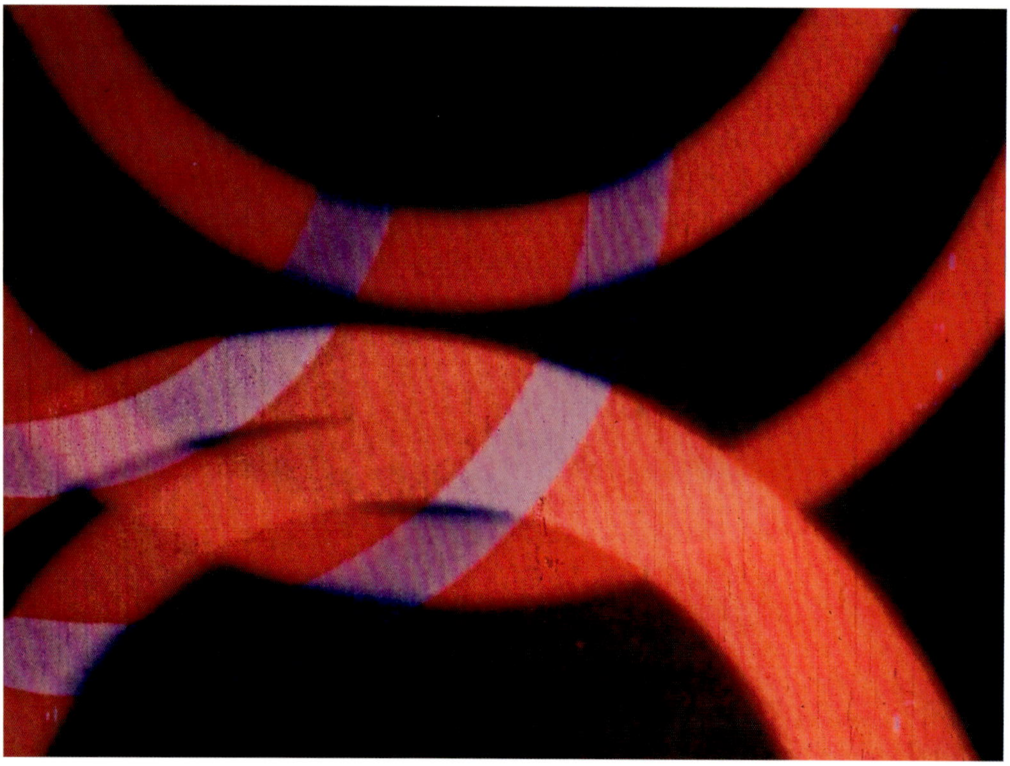

Fig. 1. Harry Smith Still from *Film #5: Circular Tensions (Homage to Oskar Fischinger),* ca. 1950, 2 min. 30 sec., 16 mm, color, silent

to recognize these four films as those currently known as *Film #1, Film #2, Film #3,* and *Film #5* (fig. 1). Harry told me that he was jazz-crazy at that time, particularly for Dizzy Gillespie and Thelonious Monk, and insisted that he had synchronized the first three to jazz performances by Gillespie: "Guarachi Guaro," "Algo Bueno," and "Manteca." He said that Hirsh had recorded live performances of Gillespie's orchestra doing these three pieces and that he had carefully synchronized the images to the tape recording. But he was not able to afford the cost of transferring the music to an optical sound track and then making the more expensive sound release prints. Hence the live jazz accompaniment at the Art in Cinema premiere. Harry also screened the films with live jazz performances at Jimbo's Bop City nightclub in San Francisco. In the 1970s, I found a pirate LP called *Dizzy Gillespie Live in Sweden.* I played it for Harry, and he insisted it was the same as the recording that Hirsh had given him in the late 1940s.

In May 1950, Harry received a grant from the Solomon R. Guggenheim Foundation, and after several months of working on new films to fulfill the terms of his stipend, he traveled to New York City, where he would spend most of the rest of his life. The baroness Hilla Rebay, then the curator of Guggenheim's Museum of Non-Objective Painting, supervised the artists with creative grants.[11] Harry presented her with three films that he had prepared: *Homage to Oskar Fischinger* (who had recommended him for the grant), which used materials from the *Fast Track* film colorized by Hirsh to recall Fischinger's *Kreise* (1933; *Circles*); a 3-D film that required the viewer to wear special glasses fitted with one red lens and one green lens in order to experience strange "supernatural" depth and antidepth phenomena among moving geometrical shapes;[12] and the brilliant film *Color Study,* which was shot live from the screen during a performance at the Guggenheim museum, in which Harry used several slide projectors and film projectors simultaneously to create complex layered imagery. These three films are now known as *Film #5: Circular Tensions, Film #6,* and *Film #7.*

That constitutes the accurate details of Harry Smith's early California films. The various things he may have said or written about them later, giving them different dates, different titles and numbers, and so on, were, as I said before, not meant to be fraudulent. Harry wanted his films to be a Great Work in the mystical alchemical sense. With or without the special numerology, they certainly are a Great Work.

Notes

1. William Moritz submitted this essay in September 2002 for publication in this volume. It is a revision of the talk "Early Abstraction, California Films" that he gave at "Harry Smith: The Avant Garde in the American Vernacular," a symposium organized by the Getty Research Institute and held 20–21 April 2001 at the Getty Center, Los Angeles. The current version incorporates a number of minor editorial changes not seen by William Moritz himself before his death on 12 March 2004. All notes are editorial additions.
2. They probably visited Smith in 1976.
3. William Moritz, "The Films of Oskar Fischinger," *Film Culture,* no. 58–60 (1974): 37–187. Smith's comment was not published in that essay, but it does appear in William Moritz, *Optical Poetry: The Life and Work of Oskar Fischinger* (Bloomington: Indiana Univ. Press, 2004), 168 (where it is dated to 1977).
4. This anecdote is incorrect. Smith went to Los Angeles to meet Fischinger, whom he admired. A screening of Fischinger's films had already occurred at the first Art in Cinema series in October 1946, and Fischinger was already discussing others of his films with Richard Foster in 1947. See Scott MacDonald, ed., *Art in Cinema: Documents toward a History of the Film Society* (Philadelphia: Temple Univ. Press, 2006), 159.

   A substantial number of documents regarding Art in Cinema are held by the Pacific Film Archive Library and Film Study Center at the University of California, Berkeley Art Museum and Pacific Film Archive. See also MacDonald, *Art in Cinema* (this note); Harry Smith, "Harry Smith Interview," interview by P. Adams Sitney, *Film Culture,* no. 37 (1965): 4–13; "Smith, Harry," *Film-Makers' Cooperative Catalogue,* no. 3 (1965): 57–58; and Scott MacDonald, "Jordan Belson (and Collaborator Stephen Beck)," in idem, *A Critical Cinema 3: Interviews with Independent Filmmakers* (Berkeley: Univ. of California Press, 1998), 67–71.
5. First screened by Art in Cinema on 17 September 1948.
6. First screened by Art in Cinema on 1 November 1946.
7. For the program notes for the evening, see this volume, 255.
8. We have not been able to verify the screening of this film by Art in Cinema, as there is no mention of a program on 31 October 1949 in the extant documentation—which is, we note, incomplete.

9. For the program announcement for this evening, see this volume, 257. Before this, three of Smith's works were screened by Art in Cinema. *Primitive Visual Rhythm* (1947–48) was shown on 24 September 1948, on a program that also included Fischinger's *Motion Painting No. 1;* for the program notes for this evening, see this volume, 256. On 11 February 1949, Art in Cinema presented an evening of "Contemporary Experimental Films" that included two hand-painted films by Smith. The program note for his films reads:

   Films No. 1 and 4 by Harry Smith, 1949. The designs in these two films were applied directly to transparent 35mm. film base without use of photographic means. In *No. 1,* the organic forms were drawn with a crow-quill pen and color added with a small brush. In *No. 4* small pieces of masking tape were cut to the shape of the design and applied to the film which was then painted the background color. In *No. 4,* the colors have been limited mainly to reds and blue-greens and the forms to quadr[i]laterals except for a short sequence of more restful circles at the very end. Types of movement employed have also been limited to the smallest possible number so that whatever interest and sequence the film possesses can depend on the rhythmic recurrence of a few specific non-objective tensions rather than curiosity on the part of the spectator as to what the forms are going to do next.

10. The program note for Smith's films reads (leaving out here the titles of his films and the listing of the musicians):

    Four films by Harry Smith. In contrast to Lye and McLaren, who start their patterns after the sound track, Smith's carefully measured rhythmic designs are composed visually first and the music added or evoked after. His approach to this difficult technique is probably more complex than either Lye's or McLaren's in that each frame itself is considered as a sep[a]rate composition, altering gradually from frame to frame, whereas the patterns of the other two extend along the film strip in a manner much resembling the sound track. Smith is now at work on the first full-color, three-dimensional, non-objective film, under the sponsorship of the Solomon R. Guggenheim Foundation.

11. For transcriptions of three letters between Smith and Rebay, see this volume, 258–64. Smith apparently also sent Rebay, along with the letter dated 17 June 1950, the four films shown by Art in Cinema on 12 May 1950.
12. Several of Smith's three-dimensional films were screened by Art in Cinema on 27 April 1951, sharing the program with four films by Maya Deren. The program notes for the screening state: "Notes on tonight's films will take the form of addresses by both Miss Deren and Mr. Smith"; the description on the program announcement for the seventh series read: "The premiere public showing of the first three-dimensional non-objective films to be made. There will be four short subjects. They will be projected both with synchronized sound track of Balinese, Hopi and Yorouba music, and also accompanied by modern instrumentalists and a vocalist improvising directly from the visual stimuli. (By permission of The Solomon R. Guggenheim Foundat[i]on.)" The only three-dimensional film by Smith currently extant is *Film #6,* ca. 1950, 90 sec., 16 mm red/green anaglyphic 3-D, silent.

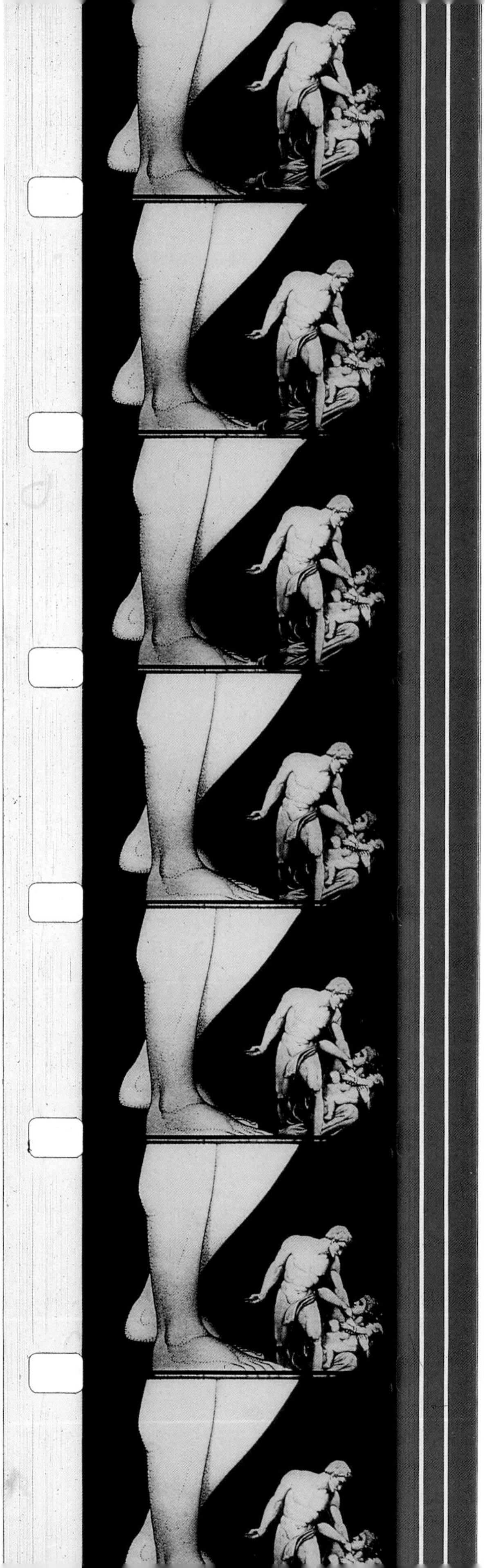

PART II
Heaven and Earth Magic

P. ADAMS SITNEY

FILM #12: HEAVEN AND EARTH MAGIC

This film, sometimes called *The Magic Feature* or *Heaven and Earth Magic,* is Harry Smith's most ambitious and most difficult work. Although it is particularly difficult to assign dates to the animated films he made in New York, *Film #12* seems to have occupied him through most of the 1950s, especially toward the end of that decade.

The original conception of this film exemplifies the myth of the absolute film[1] in its expansive form. The hour-long version that can be seen today is but a fragment of the original plan, but even so, it is among the very highest achievements of the American avant-garde cinema and one of the central texts of its mythopoeic phase.

In the interview published in *Film Culture* [in 1965], the filmmaker describes the plan for the whole film [(fig. 1; see also pp. 70, 91, 108, 233)]:

> I must say that I'm amazed, after having seen the black and white film (*#12*) last night, at the labor that went into it. It is incredible that I had enough energy to do it. Most of my mind was pushed aside into some sort of theoretical sorting of the pieces, mainly on the basis that I have described: first I collected the pieces out of old catalogues and books and whatever; then made up file cards of all possible combinations of them; then I spent maybe a few months trying to sort the cards into logical order. A script was made for that. All the script and the pieces were made for a film at least four times as long. There were wonderful masks and things cut out. Like when the dog pushes the scene away at the end of the film, instead of the title "end" what is really there is a transparent screen that has a candle burning behind it on which a cat fight begins—shadow forms of cats begin fighting. Then all sorts of complicated effects; I had held these off. The radiations were to begin at this point. Then Noah's Ark appears. There were beautiful scratch-board drawings, probably the finest drawings I ever made—really pretty. Maybe two hundred were made for that one scene. Then there's a graveyard scene when the dead are all raised again. What actually happens at the end of the film is everybody's put in a teacup, because all kinds of horrible monsters came out of the graveyard, like animals that folded into one another. Then everyone gets thrown in a teacup which is made out of a head, and stirred up. This is the Trip to Heaven and the Return, then the Noah's Ark, then The Raising of the Dead, and finally the Stirring of Everyone in a Teacup. It was to be in four parts. The script was made up for the whole works on the basis of sorting pieces. It was exhaustingly long in its original form. When I say that it was cut, mainly what was cut out was, say, instead of the little man bowing and then standing up, he would stay bowed down much longer in the original. The cutting that was done was really a correction of timing. It's better in its original form.[2]

Page 70
Harry Smith
Still from *Film #12: Heaven and Earth Magic,* ca. 1957–62, 66 min., 16 mm, black and white, sound

Page 71
Harry Smith
Book-page border design, 1988
Harry Smith Archives

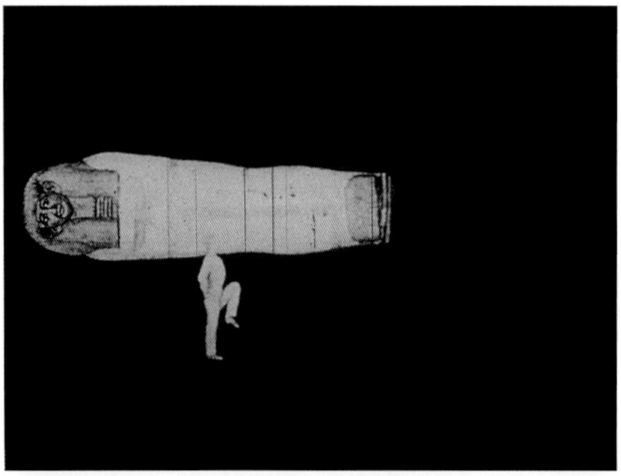

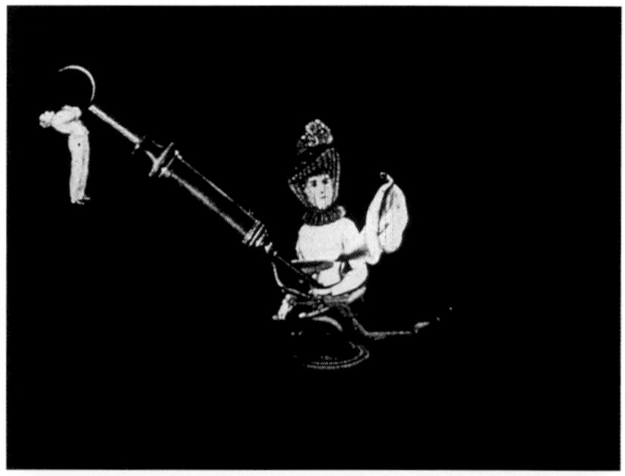

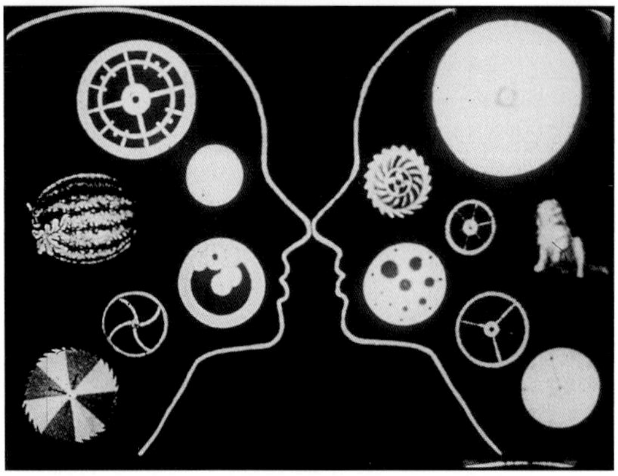

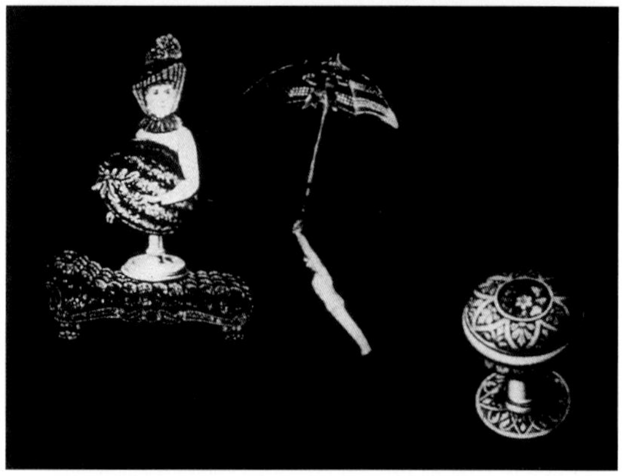

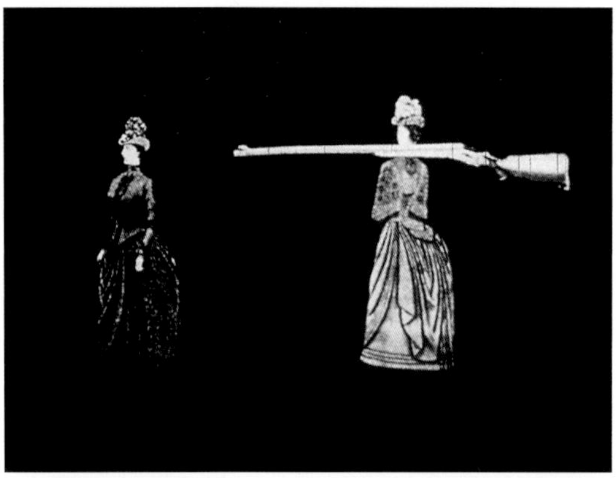

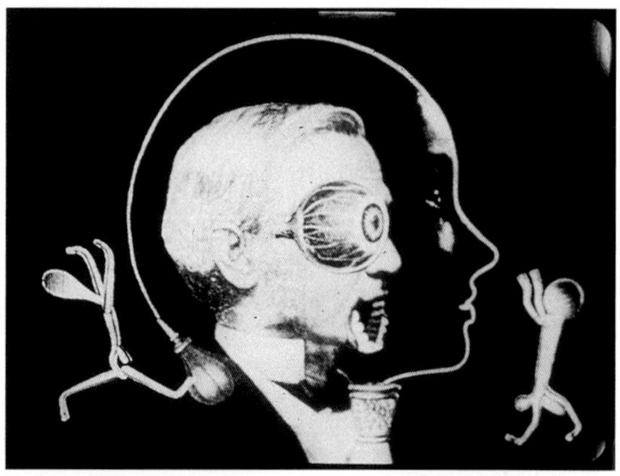

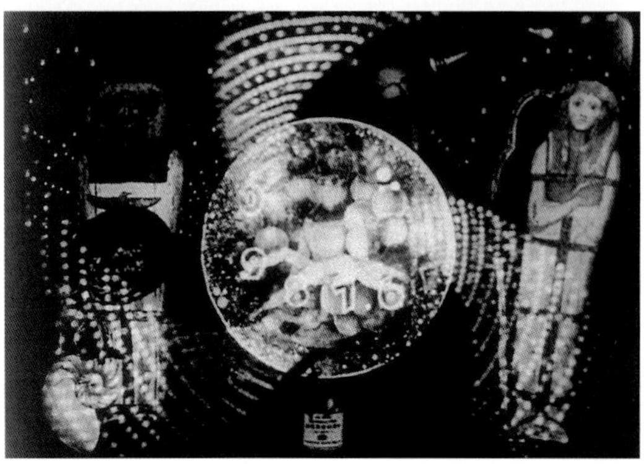

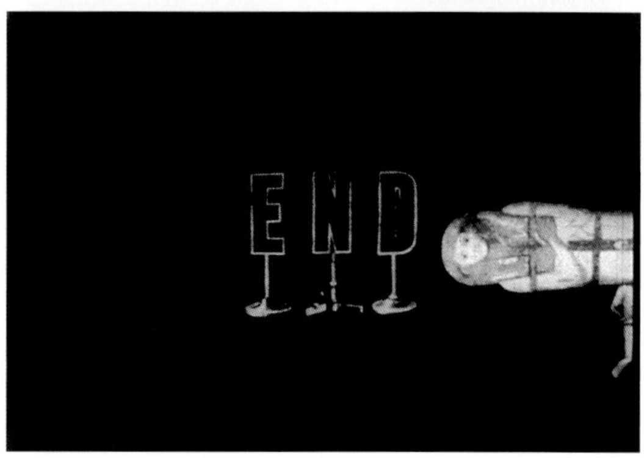
END

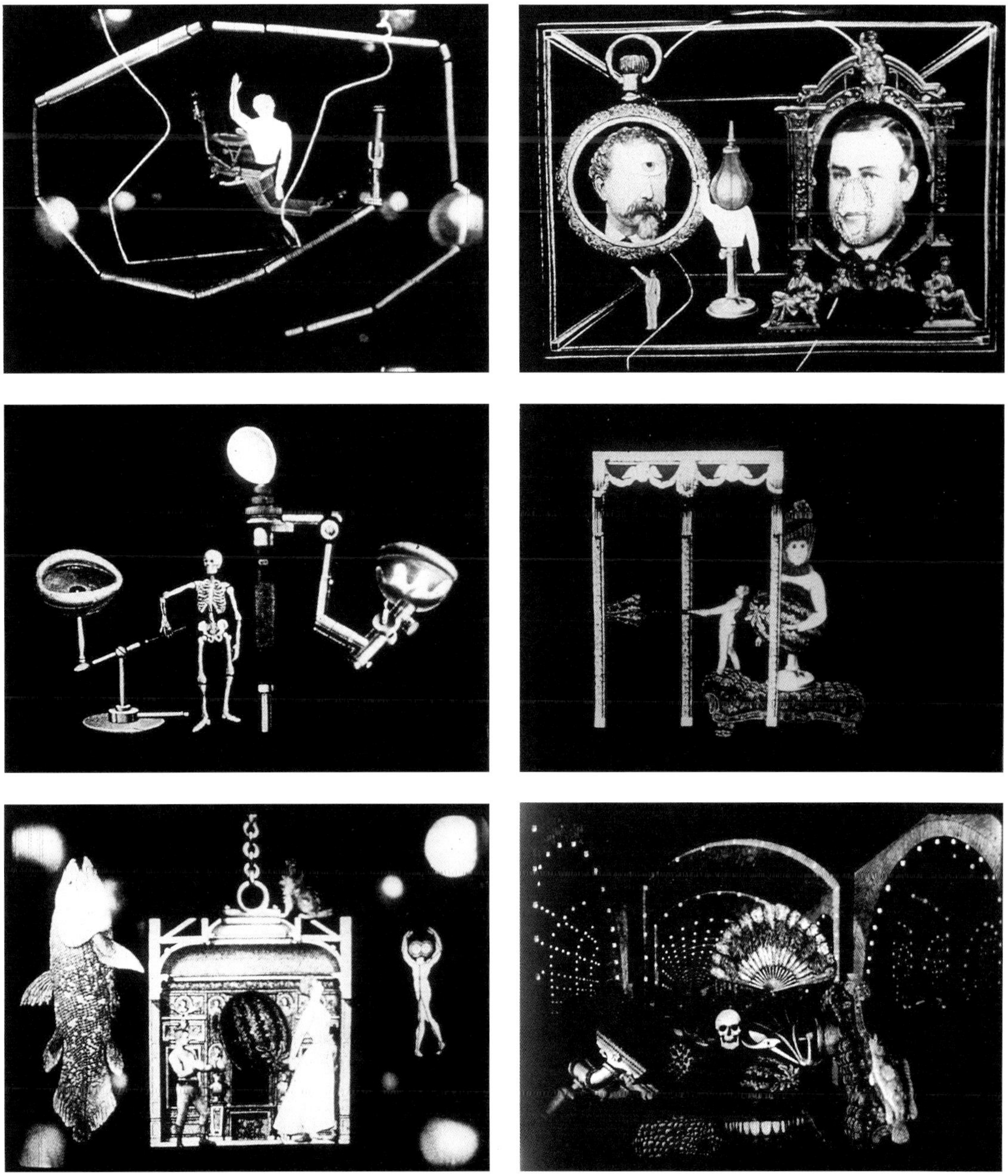

Fig. 1.
Harry Smith
Stills from *Film #12: Heaven and Earth Magic*, ca. 1957–62, 66 min., 16 mm, black and white, sound

Although the film was shot in black-and-white, he built a projector with color filters that could change the tint of the images. Furthermore, the whole film was to be projected through a series of masking slides which would transform the shape of the screen. The slides take the form of important images within the film, such as a watermelon or an egg. Thus, the entire movement would be enclosed within the projection of the slide. A different filter could determine the color of the surrounding slides. The whole apparatus functioned only once. In the late 1950s or early 1960s he presented the film for potential backers at Steinway Hall in New York.[3] He would have liked to have installed seats in the form[s] of the slide images—a watermelon seat, an egg seat, etc.—with an electrically controlled mechanism that would have changed the colors and the slides in accordance with the movements of the spectators in their seats.[4] Lacking the extravagant means necessary to achieve this, he manipulated the changes by hand.

Despite the multiplicity of their references and obscure allusions, *Film #10* and *Film #11* offer easier access to the viewer than *Film #12*. Here Smith avoids historical iconography, with the possible exception of the universally understood skeleton. The form of the film evokes hermetic maneuvers, which are all the more distanced because of their abstraction and lack of specificity. The tone of the film seems to call for a close reading which the form frustrates. Furthermore, the investigation of his sources, which he alludes to obliquely in his note on the film [for the *Film-Makers' Cooperative Catalogue* of 1965], opens up seemingly fruitful approaches to the film without ever providing satisfying insights.

The note veers from an elliptical description of the film's images to allusions about its sources. When he writes, "Next follows an elaborate exposition of the heavenly land in terms of Israel, Montreal and the second part depicts the return to earth from being eaten by Max Müller on the day Edward the Seventh dedicated the Great Sewer of London,"[5] he is deliberately obscuring the film with hints about it. By Israel he means the Cabala, particularly the three books translated by [S. L.] MacGregor Mathers as *The Kabbalah Unveiled* [(1887)]: "The Book of Concealed Mystery," "The Greater Holy Assembly," and "The Lesser Holy Assembly." Here the Cabalists interpret the tree of life in terms of the body of God, with intricate and detailed descriptions of features, members, configurations of the beard, and so on.

The reference to Montreal, he later explained, indicates the parallel influence of Dr. Wilder Penfield of the Montreal Neurological Institute, whose extensive open brain operations on epileptics are described in *Epilepsy and the Functional Anatomy of the Human Brain* (Little, Brown, Boston, 1954). Several aspects of Penfield's book intrigued Smith: the hallucinations of the patients under brain surgery; the topology and geography of the cerebral cortex [(fig. 2)]; and the distribution and juxtaposition of nervous centers. His occasional remark that *Film #12* takes place in the fissure of Silvius, one of the major folds in the brain, is another allusion to Penfield.

A photograph of [F.] Max Müller, the nineteenth-century philologist and [series] editor of *The Sacred Books of the East* [(1879–1910)], actually appears in the film. What Smith does not say is that this is the only face, out of several, which has a specific reference. Naturally, Smith's identification of this figure, which has a privileged place in the film, leads us to wonder, fruitlessly, who[se] the other Victorian visages might be.

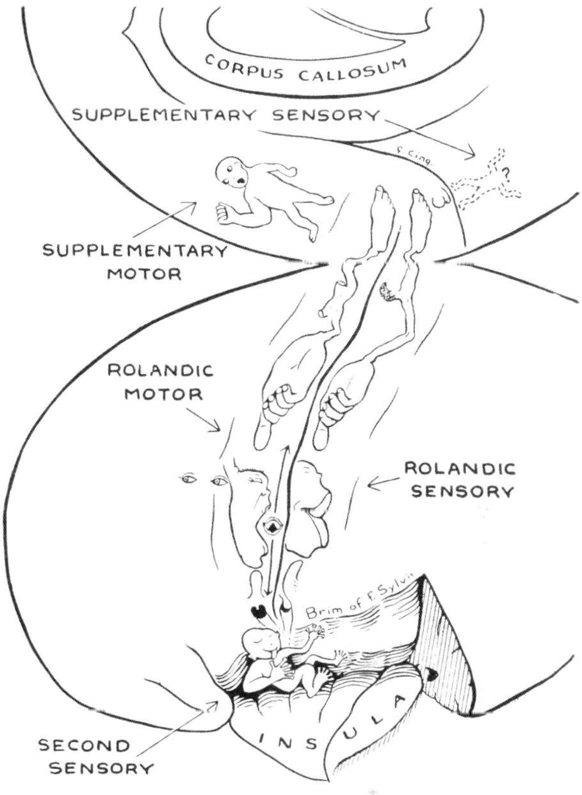

Fig. 2.
Somatic figurines drawn on the left hemisphere
From Wilder Penfield and Herbert Jasper, *Epilepsy and the Functional Anatomy of the Human Brain* (Boston: Little, Brown, 1954), fig. III-36

Finally, the allusion to the day the London sewers were inaugurated turns out to refer to the cover story of an illustrated magazine [(fig. 3)] that provided many of the elements of [*Film #12*'s] collage. The very choice of late-nineteenth-century engravings as the materials for his collage brings to mind the influence of Max Ernst's books *La femme 100 têtes* [(1929)] and *Une semaine de bonté* [(1934)]. As we shall see, there are other, structural links with Ernst in this film.

The broadest outline of the "action" of *Film #12* [(see fig. 1)] agrees with the filmmaker's ironic note. As in *Film #10,* there are two main characters, a man and a woman; but here the man assumes the role of the priestess from *Film #11,* not that of the postman. Although Smith has described him as having the same function as the prop-mover in traditional Japanese theater, [the man's] continual manipulations in the alchemical context of *Film #12,* coupled with his almost absolute resistance to change when everything else, including the heroine, is under constant metamorphosis, elevates him to the status of a magus. According to the argument of the film, he injects her with a magical potion while she sits in a diabolical dentist's chair. She rises to heaven and becomes fragmented. The "elaborate exposition of the heavenly land" occurs while the magus attempts a series of operations to put her back together. He does not succeed until after they are eaten by the giant head of a man (Max Müller) [(see p. 108)] and they are descending to earth in an elevator. Their arrival coincides with an obscure celebration, seen in scatological imagery

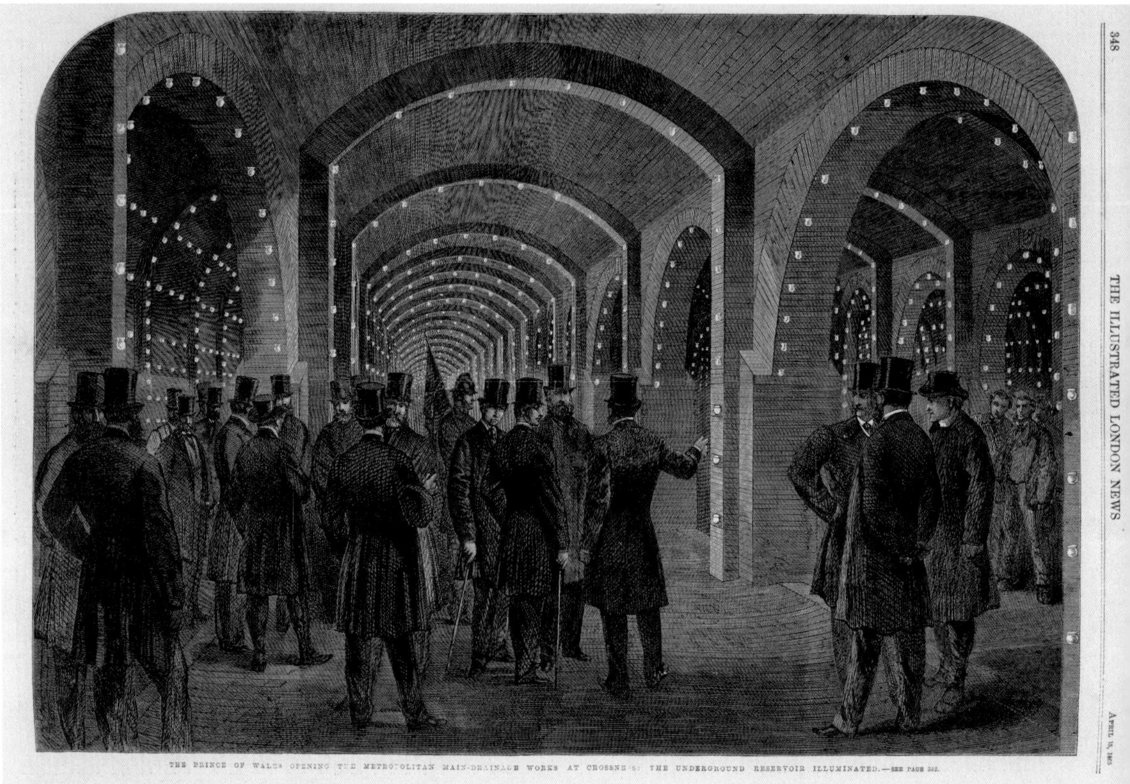

Fig. 3. *The Prince of Wales Opening the Metropolitan Main-Drainage Works at Crossness: The Underground Reservoir Illuminated* From *Illustrated London News,* 15 April 1865, 348

(the Great Sewer), in which a clima[c]tic recapitulation of the journey blends into an ending which is the exact reversal of the opening shots.

The reader of Dr. Penfield might identify the injection of the heroine and the subsequent explosion of her cranium with the effects of open brain surgery on the conscious patient. Since the operation is painless, after a local anesthetic has been applied to the surface of the skull, Penfield had his patients talk while he probed their brains with his surgical needle. Individual patients' visions, memories, sensory illusions, and motor reactions when particular areas of their brains were touched were recorded by Penfield in numerous case histories.

A significant case of the fusion of a religious cosmology with mental disorder would be Daniel Paul Schreber's *Memoirs of My Nervous Illness* [(1955)].[6] Harry Smith first brought this book to my attention in a context unrelated to *Film #12,* but later he referred to the first tableau after the ascent as "Schreber's heaven." In the book, a well-educated, influential German jurist vividly describes two periods of extreme paranoia in 1884 and 1893. The text is neither clinical nor apocalyptic. Although Schreber sees himself as mentally disturbed, he presents his fantasies as metaphysical revelations and himself as the privileged martyr to these insights. In essence, his thesis is that God attracts human nerves to the "forecourts of heaven." Among his numerous paranoid hallucinations were the ideas that he had contact on the nerve plane with other people, which they refused to admit in the flesh; that his stomach had been replaced with an inferior one; and that the boundaries of male and female were confused

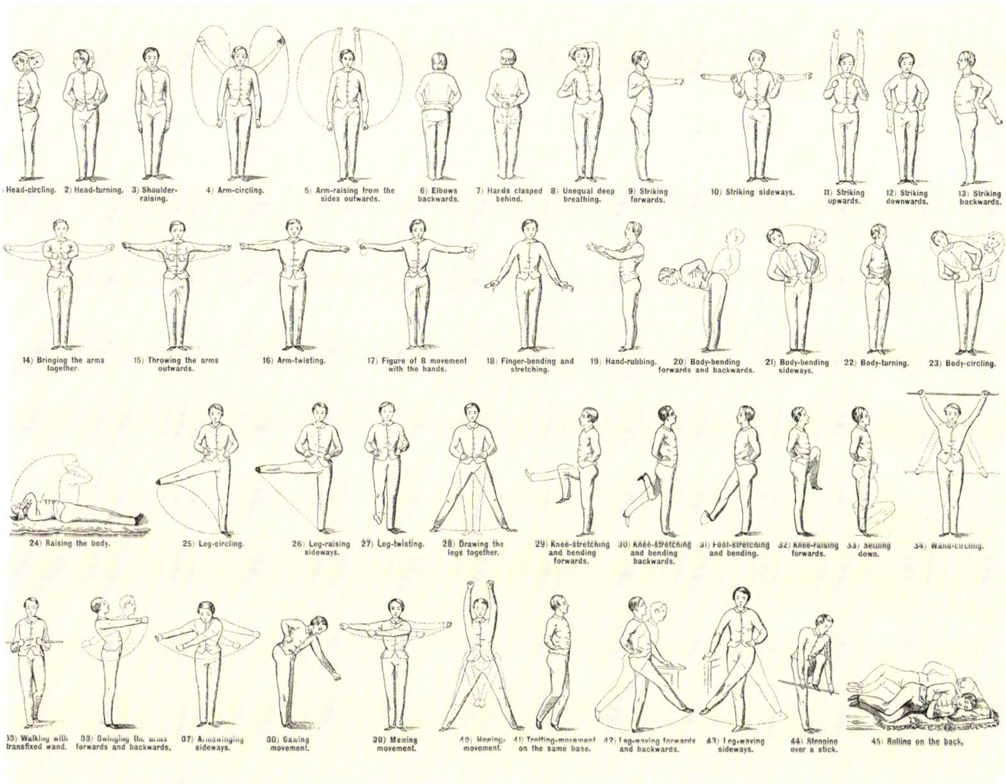

within him. [Sigmund] Freud wrote a psychoanalytical study of the book, finding in it a psychosis based on homosexual fears. Harry Smith seems to be interested in it, as in all psychological phenomena, because of the quality of its imagination.

Fig. 4.
Exercise placard: *Table of Diagrams for the Prescriptions of the Fifth Part*
From Daniel Gottlob Moritz Schreber, *Medical Indoor Gymnastics; or, A System of Hygienic Exercises for Home Use*..., ed. Rudolf Graefe, trans. Herbert A. Day (London: Williams & Norgate, 1899), foldout endsheet

Schreber's father, Daniel Gottlob Moritz Schreber, was a physician and author of a very popular exercise book, *Medical Indoor Exercises*.[7] From this book Smith took the character of the magus. By cataloging the illustrations for the exercises [(fig. 4)], he collected a sequence of gestures which he animated into all the movements of the film's main character.

What makes *Film #12* much more complicated than its argument and what obscures its outlines is the multiplicity of details filling the images and the refusal on the part of the filmmaker to indicate levels of importance among these details. For example, before the dentist's chair can be used, it must be adjusted. A bird might lay an egg, out of which comes the hammer with which the magus can transform the dentist's chair. Other figures carry out bottles, mortars and pestles, and enema bulbs to prepare a liquid with which to oil the chair, and an almost identical set of operations is repeated for the preparation of the potion to be injected into the heroine. Since the viewer never knows the desired end of an operation or a series of operations, he must divide his attention evenly among these endless and varied procedures.

In addition to this, countless creatures and things are crossing the screen while these actions are going on—a dog, a cat, a skeleton horse, a walking house, a cow, a sheep, two spoonlike creatures, a homunculus, birds. At times they contribute to the operation at hand, but just as often their participation is deliberately obscure.

The technique of distancing the dramatic focus of a story behind a continual foreground of evenly accented detail is a literary tactic dating from the novels of Raymond Roussel, before the First World War, and periodically revived, most recently in the plays of Richard Foreman. In *Film #12* Harry Smith has offered its hypostatic equivalent in cinema. His continual alternation of associative and disassociative sound effects underlines this distancing; for as often as he will synchronize the sound of a dog barking when the dog crosses the screen or of screams when the woman is being dismembered, he will connect mooings with a horse, suddenly inject applause, or preface or follow an event with the sound appropriate to it.

Perhaps even more disorienting than the pressure of detail or the dialectic of sound is the random combination of certain recurrent images. Like [Stan] Brakhage in *Prelude: Dog Star Man* [(1961)], Harry Smith found a way of incorporating chance operations in his film without sacrificing its structure. In *Film Culture* he says:

> All the permutations possible were built up: say there's a hammer in it, and there's a vase, and there's a woman, and there's a dog. Various things could then be done—hammer hits dog; woman hits dog; dog jumps into vase; so forth. It was possible to build up an enormous number of cross references....
>
> I tried as much as possible to make the whole thing automatic, the production automatic rather than any kind of logical process. Though at this point Allen Ginsberg denies having said it, about the time I started making those films he told me that William Burroughs made a change in the Surrealistic process—because, you know, all that stuff comes from the Surrealists—that business of folding a piece of paper: one person draws the head and then folds it over and somebody else draws the body. What do they call it? The Exquisite Corpse. Somebody later, perhaps Burroughs, realized that something was directing it, that it wasn't arbitrary, and that there was some kind of what you might call God. It wasn't just chance.[8]
>
> I never did finish that sentence about the relation of Surrealism to my things: I assumed that something was controlling the course of action and that it was not simply arbitrary, so that by sortilege (as you know, there is a system of divination called "sortilege") everything would come out all right.[9]

Smith's use of chance coincides with his idea of the mantic function of the artist. He has said, "My movies are made by God; I was just the medium for them."[10] The chance variations on the basic imagistic vocabulary of the film provide yet another metaphor between his film and the Great Work of the alchemists. For the Renaissance alchemist, the preparation of his tools and of himself equaled in importance the act of transformation itself. Since every element in an alchemical change had to be perfect, each instrument and chemical had its own intricate preparation. Alchemical texts tend to read like endless recipes of purification, fire-making, etc. The commitment to preliminaries is so strong that in its spiritual interpretation, alchemy becomes the slow perfection of the alchemist; the accent shifts from goals to processes. The viewer of *Film #12* finds himself confronted with repetitive scenes of preparation—an egg hatches a hammer, which changes a machine, which will produce a liquid, etc.—toward a *telos* that brings us back to the beginning. The characters of the film end up precisely as they were at the beginning. Everything returns to its place of origin.

Film #12 shares with the mythopoeic cinema of Brakhage, [Kenneth] Anger, and [Gregory] Markopoulos the theme of the divided being or splintered consciousness which must be reintegrated. As I have shown in the previous chapters, this theme is an inheritance from Romanticism.[11] In Smith's version of the myth, heaven and the human brain are conflated. When the physically divided woman first arrives in heaven, she is seen within the frame of a female head. Her release from the anxieties of selfhood comes at the end of the film when the elevator brings her back to earth, down through the titanic body of Max Müller, who is last seen circumscribed by the same female head. Her disappearance from the action of the middle of the film cannot be construed as an escape from her anxiety, which I have called selfhood; these are her moments of maximal fragmentation, when all of the magus's efforts are directed at bringing her back, or at least preparing the tools to do so.

Although there is no movement into or out of screen depth, various strategies are employed to suggest, at times, a recess of space there. The radiating balls, which help to create the illusion of ascent and descent to and from heaven, are the first of these. A room or theater is suggested immediately afterward in the first of the heavenly landscapes. Finally, the image of the Great Sewer, the last backdrop of the film, gives the impression of a group of receding arcades.

Among the more interesting spatial strategies in *Film #12* are the sudden manifestations of the law of gravity. Through most of the film, figures simply move along virtual horizontal lines imagined within the black background. They do not need the support of a floor or structure to keep from falling out of the frame. But occasionally, as when the arch forms in the lower part of the screen, such support suddenly becomes necessary. The most dramatic use of this change of pace occurs during the episode in which a line of couches descends vertically down the screen. They create a void within the screen. The magus cannot pass without leaping onto one of the passing couches for support. His alternative, of course, is to float over the void by using the umbrella.

A related configuration of space within the black background would be the series of arches through which the magus walks or rides on the couch-boat. Normally, passage across the screen is smooth, along a single plane. When he begins to pass through arches by crossing in front of the right-hand pillar and behind the left-hand pillar of the arch, a sense of depth emerges without the illusion of diminishing into the vanishing point of the screen.

The circularity of the film's form, the use of nineteenth-century engravings, and above all the theme of the mutable woman recall Max Ernst's collage novel, *La femme 100 têtes* (1929), whose title in French puns as the woman with one hundred (*cent*) heads or the woman without (*sans*) heads. That novel, in collage pictures, begins and ends with the same image. Within it are sections and subsections built on varying degrees of thematic and narrative sequence. Whenever a series of plates has a specific narrative and therefore temporal logic, Ernst introduces another image or images into the collage which does not follow the same unity of time or scale.

The collages abound in complex machinery and scenes of violence and dismemberment. Studying the images in sequence, the reader experiences promises of narration which continually evaporate or transform into chains of metaphor. The ultimate unity of the book is that of the dream. Harry Smith has said that he let his dreams determine the filming of *Film #12*. According to his account, he slept fitfully in the studio where he was filming for the entire year in which the film was being shot. He would sleep for a while, then animate his dreams.[12] The exact relation between his dreams and the structure of the film is ambiguous, unless we can suppose that he dreamed the life of the figures he had already cut out and assembled for his film. What is more likely is that he established an intuitive relationship between the structure of his dreams and the substructure of the film.

In 1971 at Anthology Film Archives, Smith spontaneously delivered a lecture to a group of students he happened upon in that theater. As they were looking at a film, not by him, in the realist tradition—a film of photographed actuality—he said, "You shouldn't be looking at this as a continuity. Film frames are hieroglyphs, even when they look like actuality. You should think of the individual film frame, always, as a glyph, and then you'll understand what cinema is about."

Notes

Reprinted from P. Adams Sitney, "Absolute Animation," in idem, *Visionary Film: The American Avant-Garde, 1943–2000*, 3rd ed. (New York: Oxford Univ. Press, 2002), 249–57.

This excerpt has been selected by the volume editors and does not reflect the intent of the author. P. Adams Sitney believes that his text is best read in its entirety and not taken out of context. The editors agree, yet they feel that this excerpt provides crucial background for understanding not only the other three pieces in this part of the volume but also the complexity of *Heaven and Earth Magic*, the framework in which that film was conceived, and Harry Smith's oeuvre as a whole. We have silently substituted "*Film #12*" for "*No. 12*" and so on for the designations of Smith's films throughout Sitney's text; all other substantive editorial changes to the running text are enclosed in brackets. The expanded notes are editorial additions; the illustrations that accompany this excerpt were also selected by the editors.

1. The term *absolute film* was coined in the 1920s by analogy with *absolute music*. In contrast to documentary and narrative cinema, absolute films present a visual spectacle of fluid, dynamic imagery rhythmically paced by editing, dissolving, superimposition, segmented screens, contrasts of positive and negative, color ambiance, and other purely cinematic devices.
2. Harry Smith, "Harry Smith Interview," interview by P. Adams Sitney, *Film Culture*, no. 37 (1965): 10–11. This interview has been reprinted, with minor modifications, in P. Adams Sitney, ed., *"Film Culture" Reader* (New York: Praeger, 1970), 260–76.
3. According to Jonas Mekas (personal communication to Rani Singh, 2008), the screening at Steinway Hall was canceled.

4. See Smith, "Harry Smith Interview" (note 2), 11–12.
5. "Smith, Harry," *Film-Makers' Cooperative Catalogue,* no. 3 (1965): 58. This issue of the catalog was appended to *Film Culture,* no. 37 (1965).
6. Originally published as Daniel Paul Schreber, *Denkwürdigkeiten eines Nervenkranken: Nebst Nachträgen und einem Anhang über die Frage "Unter welchen Voraussetzungen darf eine für geisteskrank erachtete Person gegen ihren erklärten Willen in einer Heilanstalt festgehalten werden?"* (Leipzig: Oswald Mutze, 1903). Sigmund Freud analyzed Schreber's book; see Sigmund Freud, "Psychoanalytic Notes upon an Autobiographical Account of a Case of Paranoia (Dementia Paranoides) (1911)," in idem, *Three Case Histories,* ed. Philip Rieff (New York: Collier, 1966), 103–86. Annette Michelson has presented a psychoanalytic reading of *Film #12* in "The Mummy's Return: A Kleinian Film Scenario," in Irving Lavin, ed., *Meaning in the Visual Arts: Views from the Outside: A Centennial Commemoration of Erwin Panofsky (1892–1968)* (Princeton: Institute for Advanced Study, 1995), 335–50; her essay is reprinted in this volume, 85–101. See also Noël Carroll, "Mind, Medium, and Metaphor in Harry Smith's *Heaven and Earth Magic,*" in idem, *Interpreting the Moving Image* (Cambridge: Cambridge Univ. Press, 1998), 178–90.
7. The title of the two English editions, of 1856 and 1899, is actually *Medical Indoor Gymnastics,* not *Medical Indoor Exercises.* Originally published as Daniel Gottlob Moritz Schreber, *Ärztliche Zimmer-Gymnastik oder Darstellung und Beschreibung der unmittelbaren, keiner Geräthschaft und Unterstützung bedürfenden, daher stets und überall ausführbaren heilgymnastischen Bewegungen für jedes Alter und Geschlecht und für die verschiedenen speciellen Gebrauchszwecke* (Leipzig: Fleischer, 1855); as of 1914, the book had been published in German in at least thirty-three printings and several editions.
8. Smith, "Harry Smith Interview" (note 2), 10.
9. Smith, "Harry Smith Interview" (note 2), 12.
10. See, for example, Harry Smith, book page doodle, ca. 1970; illustrated in Paola Igliori, ed., *American Magus Harry Smith: A Modern Alchemist* (New York: Inanout, 1996), 2.
11. See, for example, P. Adams Sitney, *The American Avant-Garde, 1943–2000,* 3rd ed. (New York: Oxford Univ. Press, 2002), 150–51, 166–68, 205–6.
12. See, for example, Harry Smith, "A. J. Melita—Chelsea Hotel, New York City, 1976," interview by A. J. Melita, in idem, *Think of the Self Speaking: Harry Smith—Selected Interviews,* ed. Rani Singh (Seattle: Elbow/Cityful, 1999), 139, 140.

ANNETTE MICHELSON

THE MUMMY'S RETURN: A Kleinian Film Scenario

I

> My movies are made by God; I was just the medium for them.
>
> — Harry Smith[1]

In offering elements for a textual analysis of Harry Smith's epic collage film, *The Magic Feature,*[2] I pay tribute to the men responsible for its preservation and dissemination. To them, as well, we owe the first important critical assessment of a work whose visual splendor is grounded in that artisanal mode of production that has sustained the American cinema of independent persuasion. Jonas Mekas and P. Adams Sitney, in their passionate dedication to that cinema in general and to the work of Harry Smith in particular (a dedication resistant to public indifference and to the very caprices of the author himself) have retrieved this work for the corpus of the New American Cinema.

It is, moreover, Sitney's assiduous investigation of the sources of Smith's iconography that continues to provide the basis for any reading of this film-text. And we are further indebted to Sitney for something of comparable value: his ability to draw from Smith, in conversation, the phantasmatic construction of a life history. I stress the importance of this latter element insofar as these extravagant musings demand, in my view, acknowledgment as constitutive, together with Smith's film practice, of a field that must be studied as such. Text and film-text, then, are to be considered, for the purpose of an iconological project, as reciprocally illuminating within a unified field.

My reading, its method, leads me, however, to differ with Sitney in many important respects. For Sitney, whose pioneering account of the cinema of the American avant-garde, *Visionary Film,* first published in 1974, remains a major text within its field of study, *The Magic Feature* is the narrative of a spiritual quest, sharing with the mythopoeic cinema of Stan Brakhage, Kenneth Anger, and Gregory Markopoulos "the theme of the divided being or splintered consciousness which must be reintegrated."[3]

Now this first intuition may appear sound, but only on condition that we examine the ground and nature of that division and splintering. They cannot, I believe, be understood as yet other elements of Romanticism's legacy, within which a drama of spiritual salvation and transcendence is enacted; they must be explicated in terms that are more concrete and more fully explanatory.

Noël Carroll, the other prime exegete of this film-text, has offered a reading wholly antithetical to that of Sitney and equally subject to question. He sees it as an articulation of the epistemology of British empiricism, literalizing John Locke's image of the mind as "a cabinet or closet, full of simple impressions of perception" and David Hume's notion of the mind as "a heap or collection of different perceptions united together by certain relations."[4] If, however, one is to understand this film as a whole, in the full range of its imagery, its pace and rhythm, its parametric construction, its serial repetition, and permutational structure, if one is to account for its constantly postponed resolution of action, one requires an approach that is, again, more fully explanatory. One wants, as well, to consider its material aspect as collage animation. And one must confront the manner in which this form, this work, offers the incessant fragmentation and restoration of the body, of a woman's body, in particular. Moreover, the performance of these assaults and of all other operations is of a magical character, the work of a man of singularly small stature and hyperagility. A homunculus is, in fact, the central, dominant, omnipotent protagonist of the action articulated through apparitions, transformations, and vanishing acts effected by the constant invention, supply, and deployment of magical instruments and weapons. As Smith himself remarked,

> first I collected the pieces out of old catalogues and books and whatever; then made up file cards of all possible combinations of them; then I spent maybe a few months trying to sort the cards into logical order.[5]

> All the permutations possible were built up: say there's a hammer in it, and there's a vase, and there's a woman, and there's a dog. Various things could then be done—hammer hits dog; woman hits dog; dog jumps into vase; so forth. It was possible to build up an enormous number of cross references.[6]

If I am led to differ from Sitney's reading of *The Magic Feature,* that is because it accepts Smith's discourse, epitomized in my epigraph, as scripture, so to speak. If it be such, one is bound to further persevere in one's hermeneutic efforts. Both readings heretofore offered confuse, as it were, the order of those principles of exegetical tradition which, deriving from Origen, read scripture through the Platonic topos of body/soul/spirit, passing from the literal to the allegorical, and thence to the analogical register of faith. It is the median term of allegory—that of the soul which we now term the psyche—that I shall claim as the ground of a coherent reading.

Smith, talking to a group of students in 1971, advised them to look at films as discrete systems of signs, bearing in mind their character as such as against the reality effect of the motion picture. One recognizes the stress upon the acknowledgment of persistence of vision characteristic of a generation of American modernists and salient in the work and theoretical production of Hollis Frampton, Paul Sharits, Michael Snow, and Ernie Gehr, among others. Smith, however, presses on: "You shouldn't be looking at this as a continuity. Film frames," he declares, "are hieroglyphs, even when they look like actuality. You should think of the individual film frame, always, as a glyph, and then you'll understand what cinema is about."[7]

From the time of their insertion into European discourse, Egyptian hieroglyphs were known, as in John Florio's sixteenth-century definition, as "mysticall or enigmaticall letters,"[8] a view that persisted into the nineteenth century, when they were characterized as sacred writing. And certainly Smith, in his role as divine instrument, as bearer of a gnosis, enjoins upon us the attentive reverence owed to the hieroglyphic inscription of that gnosis. However, we now possess the key to Egyptian hieroglyphic writing, the Rosetta Stone. And *The Magic Feature,* presumably dictated by God, presents itself as a mixture of pictures, visual puns, conventional signs, that is to say, as a rebus for our deciphering. Following Thomas Carlyle's advice, as offered in *Sartor Resartus,* I shall consequently not proceed to receive "as literally authentic what was but hieroglyphically so."[9] It is by now most surely evident that I shall take my cue from the prime interpreter of the rebus, that my approach, through the median term of the psyche, is to be psychoanalytic.

Now, recent film theory has been most extensively concerned, in its highly developed psychoanalytic register, not with the analysis of the film-text itself but rather with the positioning of the spectator within cinematic construction. Its work has been grounded largely in Sigmund Freud's paper, published in 1927, in which the position of the fetishist is described as one of disavowal. "To put it plainly," Freud writes, "the fetish is a substitute for the woman's (mother's) phallus which the little boy once believed in and does not wish to forego—we know why," for if mother has lost hers, he, too, is subject to that threat of castration.[10] The child "retains this belief"—in the woman originally endowed with a phallus—"but he also gives it up; during the conflict between the deadweight of the unwelcome perception and the force of the opposite wish, a compromise is constructed such as is only possible in the realm of unconscious modes of thought—by the primary processes." He knows, but all the same...[11]

Such then, as claimed by a dominant trend in contemporary film theory, will be the position of the film viewer in relation to the reality effect of cinematic representation.

In the exercise of decipherment to follow, I shall want to shift the psychoanalytic method of inquiry, back to the film-text. In so doing, I shall take as my structural model a quotation not from Freud's essay on fetishism but rather from an earlier paper of 1919, entitled "Psycho-analysis and Religious Origins," that I have found helpful and suggestive when confronted with the hermeneutic task posed by singularly complex and enigmatic works:

> A little reflection was bound to show that it would be impossible to restrict to the provinces of dreams and nervous disorders a view such as this of the life of the human mind. If that view has hit upon a truth, it must apply equally to normal mental events, and even the highest achievements of the human spirit must bear a demonstrable relation to the factors found in pathology—to repression, to the efforts at mastering the unconscious and to the possibilities of satisfying the primitive instincts. There was thus an irresistible temptation and, indeed, a scientific duty, to apply the research methods of psycho-analysis, in regions far remote from its native soil, to the various mental sciences. And indeed psycho-analytic work upon patients pointed persistently in the direction of this new task, for it was obvious that the forms assumed by the different neuroses echoed the most highly admired productions of our culture. Thus

> hysterics are undoubtedly imaginative artists, even if they express their phantasies *mimetically* in the main and without considering their intelligibility to other people; the ceremonials and prohibitions of obsessional neurotics drive us to suppose that they have created a private religion of their own; and the delusions of paranoics have an unpalatable external similarity and internal kinship to the systems of our philosophers. It is impossible to escape the conclusion that these patients are, in an *asocial* fashion, making the very attempts at solving their conflicts and appeasing their pressing needs which, when they are carried out in a fashion that has binding force for the majority, go by the names of poetry, religion and philosophy.[12]

In following the Freudian model, I shall draw as well upon the theory of object relations formulated and documented for us by Melanie Klein in the psychoanalysis of young children. Klein, stressing the importance of the psyche's developments with the very earliest period of life, radically revised our view of early infancy and its consequences for later development. Given the relative neglect of Kleinian theory within the recent literature of cinema studies, I shall allow myself to retrace its account of the human subject's formation in those aspects that I judge to be pertinent for my project.[13]

The relational aspect of a primordial dyad is fundamental to her analysis of successive positions as the ground of the formation of infantile psychoses. Like D. W. Winnecott, Klein tended to believe that not babies but babies-with-mothers formed the proper object of analysis. Moreover, Klein, in strong opposition to the dominant psychoanalytic thinking, extended the trajectory of the human subject into the earliest stages of existence, laying stress upon anxieties, defenses, and relations as constituting, from earliest infancy on, the crucial factors in the development of two successive infantile positions. The first of these, known as the paranoid-schizoid position, is operative within the first three to five months of the infant's life. The infant at this earliest stage of development relates to external reality not as a group of "whole objects" (mother, father) but rather as "part objects"—first and foremost, the mother's breast. When present to satisfy the infant's hunger, this part object functions as a "good breast," nourishing and satisfying. When absent during hunger, it acts as a "bad breast," frustrating and denying. It is consequently experienced as dual and persecutory: bent on the annihilation of the infant.

The dynamics of this relatively simple schema are nonetheless complex: the mechanism of "projective identification" is that which allows the object to become a representative of the developing ego—the identification of an object with the hated parts of the self, endowed with qualities of independence. At the same time, the infant introjects the object and its associated qualities, creating within its own psyche an internalized good breast or bad breast. The internal objects, as idealized constructs, become the prototypes of all helpful and gratifying objects, or—as in the case of the bad breast—the prototype of all external, persecutory objects. Such a process of introjection and holding of internal objects corresponds, in Kleinian thought, to the beginning of the formation of the superego. Interestingly enough, however, the splitting of the object necessarily involves concurrent splitting of the ego, as the infant attempts to separate its good and bad objects.

The bad breast comes to possess the oral-sadistic impulses deriving from the infant's own feeling of envy. Destructive phantasies of biting, devouring, and annihilating the breast and the mother's body are prevalent when the infant is in a state of such paranoid anxiety. Later psychosexual stages will bring phantasies constructed about the infant's urethral and anal-sadistic impulses. Throughout, however, consistent defense mechanisms continue to operate—splitting projection/introjection, a hallucinatory phantasy of control over the object (phantasies of omnipotence), and complete denial of the object, expressed by phantasies of annihilation.

I began this schematic exposition of Kleinian theory by remarking that its insistence upon extending the subject's psychoanalytic history back into the very earliest months of infancy met with great resistance, and I now want to stress the extreme hostility it elicited, which continues to this day. This we must understand as generated by the extreme violence of the infantile psyche's psychotic states as described in the theory of object relations. Both precocity and violence were, as we know, derived from and confirmed by Klein's extensive work over several decades in the as yet undeveloped field of the psychoanalysis of children, now shaped, nonetheless, by her pioneering efforts. In that process, she delivered to us a scenario of infantile development whose complex violence does indeed require a considerable adjustment of perspective, even from those already disabused, by Freudian theory, of the idealization of childhood so deeply embedded in our culture.[11]

I now return to the account of infantile development and its analysis of the second, crucial stage: that of the depressive position. Those physiological changes that extend the child's perceptual faculties now render it capable of establishing connections among the part objects of breast, hands, voice, gaze, so as to perceive the mother as a unified whole. The separating of good from bad which produces splitting is reduced, and the infant accedes to the depressive position through a growing awareness that the mother, embodying good and bad, is source of both love and hate, of satisfaction and frustration. It is then that the child comes to believe that it can, through projection of aggressive and destructive phantasies onto the mother, destroy and consequently lose the mother. The depressive anxieties thus generated produce a sense of loss of the good external object, a sense that the infant has, in its destructive phantasies, caused that loss. Good and bad breasts are now seen as the same object. It is this realization, and its consequent anxiety, that generates, in turn, an impulse toward reparation. The infant defends itself against those feelings of loss partly through manic defenses. For, Klein tells us, in describing the mourning that occurs during the depressive state, the ego is driven by depressive anxiety to build up omnipotent and violent phantasies, partly for the purpose of controlling and mastering the bad and dangerous objects, partly in order to save and restore the loved ones. Omnipotence, denial, and idealization, closely bound up with ambivalence, enable the early ego to assert itself to a certain degree against its internal persecutor and against a perilous dependence upon its loved objects, and thus to make further advances in its relation with its loved objects.

Together with these defenses and in place of these, Klein tells us, the child cultivates what she holds as the primordially significant aspect of the depressive position—reparative tendencies, in which the subject actively seeks to repair the damage (the loss inflicted on the good object), thereby successfully working through the depressive position. Reparation is, however, a complex process, for it involves impulses of control and phantasies of omnipotence, and therefore is closely aligned with sadistic impulses leading to reintroduction of manic defenses. It is only through *repetition* of reparative tendencies, through reinforcement and successful introjection of strong internal good objects, that the child comes to trust its own constructive bent, and its capacity for love. And this, finally, is of especial importance, for to Klein and to her followers the reparative impulse is the ground of creative action. Confidence in one's reparative powers appears to be important, fundamentally so, for development in general, but, more particularly, it is the generative source of artistic production.

II

> Allegory dwells in a palace of transparency.
>
> — Antoine-Marin Le Mierre[15]

It is by now surely evident, after this long expository excursus, that what is proposed is a reading of *The Magic Feature* as the representation of an elaborate working through, in the form of a prodigally generous form of reparation offered by artistic practice, of the spectrum of infantile development through paranoid-schizoid and depressive positions. And our first step toward that reading will entail an account of the initial image of the film, which I note, with more than casual interest and amusement, neither of the exegetes cited above troubled to include in his own reading: that of the homunculus who sets in motion this epic of repeated slaughter and resurrection by introducing (literally carrying onto the screen or scene) (see pp. 74–75) the other member of the primordial dyad, whose name we read, as in a rebus: "Mummy." She is dead, embalmed, encased Egyptian-style, imprisoned in her coffin (fig. 1). It is from that initial point on that one is impelled to read *The Magic Feature* as an elaborate articulation by an artist of what has come to be known as the Kleinian scenario of infantile development. It is, of course, the scenario of a horror feature, and the longest running one known to us. For it presents the narrative of the ever-recommencing struggle of the little man, endowed in phantasy with magic powers (of aggression, insemination, destruction, and restoration), constantly engaged in the repetition compulsion of murderous assault upon and fragmentation of Mummy's body and the restoration of its integrity in an act of reparation. To cite Smith:

> Then there's a graveyard scene when the dead are all raised again. What actually happens at the end of the film is everybody's put in a teacup, because all kinds of horrible monsters came out of the graveyard, like animals that folded into one another. Then everyone gets thrown in a teacup which is made out

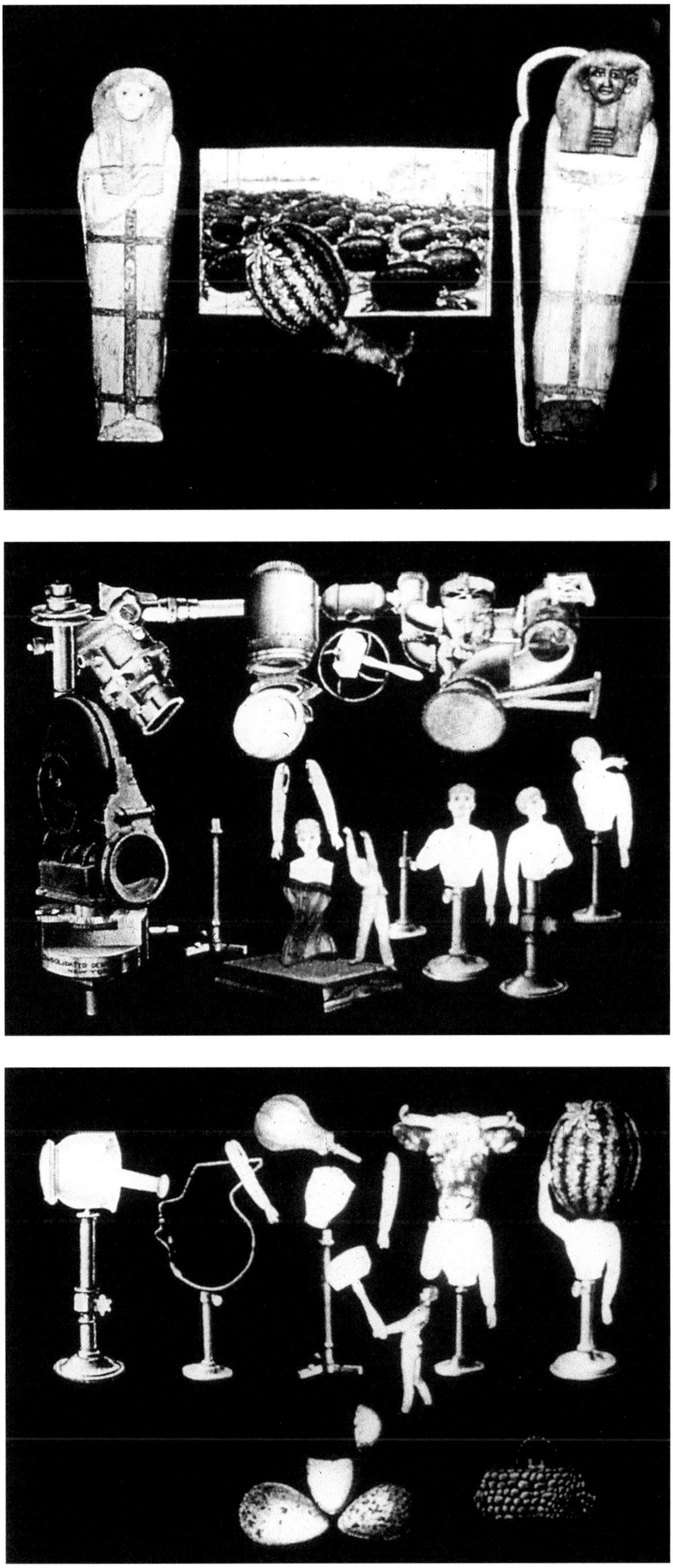

Fig. 1.
Harry Smith
Stills from *Film #12: Heaven and Earth Magic,* ca. 1957–62, 66 min., 16 mm, black and white, sound

of a head and stirred up. This is the Trip to Heaven and the Return, then the Noah's Ark, then The Raising of the Dead.[16]

Sitney offers the following account of the little man, his actions and his role.

> Although Smith has described him as having the same function as the prop-mover in traditional Japanese theater, his continual manipulations in the alchemical context…, coupled with his almost absolute resistance to change when everything else, including the heroine, is under constant metamorphosis, elevates him to the status of a magus. According to the argument of the film, he injects her with a magical potion while she sits in a diabolical dentist's chair. She rises to heaven and becomes fragmented. The "elaborate exposition of the heavenly land" occurs while the magus attempts a series of operations to put her back together. He does not succeed until after they are eaten by the giant head of a man (Max Muller) and they are descending to earth in an elevator. Their arrival coincides with an obscure celebration, seen in scatological imagery (the Great Sewer), in which a climactic recapitulation of the journey blends into an ending which is the exact reversal of the opening shots.[17]

The reference to the "alchemical context" is clarified by reference to the phantasmatic autobiography elicited by Sitney in the interview of Smith previously cited. Additionally and most importantly, that text foregrounds an etiology of infantile aggression and phantasies of omnipotence.

> Like I say, my father gave me a blacksmith shop when I was maybe twelve; he told me I should convert lead into gold. He had me build all these things like models of the first Bell telephone, the original electric light bulb, and perform all kinds of historical experiments. I once discovered in the attic of our house all those illuminated documents with hands with eyes in them, all kinds of Masonic deals that belonged to my grand-father. My father said I shouldn't have seen them and he burned them up immediately. That was the background for my interest in metaphysics.[18]
>
> I mostly lived with my mother. I performed what might now be considered sexual acts with her until I was eighteen or nineteen maybe. No actual insertion or anything, but I would always get up in the morning and get in bed with her because she had a long story she would tell me about someone named Eaky-Peaky. She was a really good story teller. My posture is derived from trying to be exactly her height; for she was shorter.[19]
>
> She would leave me in a theater. I saw some good films there which I wish it was possible to locate again. I saw one, for example, which was pretty good in which bad children put caps into the spaghetti at a fancy Italian dinner. (That was one of the first sound films that I ever saw.) When the people chewed their spaghetti there was a BAAAKH that was about all that was on

the soundtrack. The mouth would fly open and false teeth would go across the dinner table and so forth.[20]

I saw all those Fu Manchu movies; they were some of my favorites. There was also some serial that had a great big spider about the size of this room, which would be chasing Pearl White down through tunnels. That thing scared the shit out of me, but I probably had erections during it, it was so terrifying. I was very interested in spiders at about the age of five.[21]

Klein, in characterizing infantile sexuality between the ages of three and five, tells us that it is in this phase that we can locate the origin of the unconscious equation of breast, penis, feces, child. The infant's phantasies at the polymorphous stage of instinctual development, when excitations form all bodily zones, and libidinal and destructive aims rival one another, produce the theory of parental intercourse as a feeding or an excretory act, of conception through the mouth and birth through the anus: in them are superimposed oral, excretory, and procreative urges and phantasies. And, indeed, the film's little man alternates his destructive acts with a spectrum of actions of insemination of the maternal figure. Adolescence normally shows the reemergence of early infantile sexuality. When the adolescent in horror turns away from his impulses, it is not only because he discovers his incestuous object choice, the wish to sleep with his mother, but also because he becomes aware that he is attracted and excited by perverse and cruel phantasies.

Textual analysis of *The Magic Feature* requires, however, the unveiling, as it were, of the scenario's third leading actor, for the Baby/Mummy dyad is, of course, extended into a trio, completed by Daddy. Our scenario's Baby, is, naturally, a homunculus, or little man, formed in Daddy's very image and wielding that same powerful instrument as Daddy, the secret of his power over both Mummy and Baby, and over all things in general. Represented by syringe or by hammer (see fig. 1), it is the instrument of destruction, vivification, transformation; it is magical, the source of the homunculus's omnipotence.

But the homunculus of *The Magic Feature,* this protagonist of the Kleinian scenario, is not just any anonymous little man; he is a very particular one. Mummy's chic and dainty avatars have been culled from the nineteenth-century fashion plates of *Godey's Lady's Book,* cut, dismembered, placed on pedestals, encased, entombed, revived, framed, and elevated (see fig. 1). But the homunculus is taken from the illustrations for the volume *Kallipädie* (1858)—the subtitle of which translates, in part, as *Education to Beauty through Natural and Symmetrical Promotion of Normal Body Growth, Functional Health, and Mental Refinement*—by Dr. Daniel Gottlob Moritz Schreber.[22] This celebrated German pedagogue of an earlier century has now receded into the past, eclipsed by the celebrity of his son, Daniel Paul Schreber (1842–1911), the presiding judge of a division of the court of appeal in Dresden, whose *Denkwürdigkeiten eines Nervenkranken,* or *Memoirs of a Mental Patient,* first published in Leipzig in 1903, narrated in great detail his stays in various mental institutions as well as the excruciating periods of disturbance that preceded them.[23] These crises were described with a candor that led the Schreber family to buy up and destroy the book after publication. The few copies that remained attracted, as we know, considerable and enduring interest in psychiatric circles. One of these copies came into Freud's possession in Vienna, in 1910; the eventual result was Freud's penetrating analysis of the case, published in 1911, the only major case study he undertook and published without direct contact with the patient, on the basis of this admittedly abundant documentary evidence.[24] Generally considered a seminal text, and the forerunner of numerous related studies in the area of paranoia, Freud's analysis has, since the 1970s, been subject to a widespread renewal of interest and to intensive revision of approach to the case. I shall in what follows draw upon the pioneering work of William G. Niederland, whose investigation extends to analysis of Schreber's family history and research into the father's biography.[25]

Schreber's long phantasmatic narrative presents all the density of and obsession with detail and all the "invented logic" that characterize the discourse of the paranoiac. Schreber invents special terminology, which he calls *Grundsprache* (ground language or root language) and which he attributes to God or to divine rays emanating from God. These were the means of communication between himself and the divine source of his mission.

His delusional system, as revealed in the *Memoirs,* has been summarized *briefly* by Niederland as follows:

> He felt he had a mission to redeem the world and to restore it to its lost state of bliss.
>
> This mission must be preceded by the destruction of the world and by his personal transformation into a woman.
>
> Transformed into a female, he—Schreber, now a woman—would become God's mate, and out of such union a better and healthier race of men would emerge.[26]

Schreber, whose sleep depended "totally on the celestial constellations," claimed: "*A force of attraction* emanating...from [my] single human body over such enormous distances...may appear quite absurd. Nonetheless, the action of the force of attraction is a fact that for me is absolutely unquestionable."[27]

He, Schreber, was awakened by rays to a new heavenly life, "a *state of bliss*...for God...only pure human nerves were usable, because they were destined to become attached to God himself and finally to turn into parts of God as 'forecourts of heaven,'"[28] as he termed them.

A male state of bliss occupied (Schreber speaking) an even "higher level than the female state of bliss; the latter seems to have consisted of an uninterrupted sensation" that "it was the ultimate goal of all souls, merged with other souls, to coalesce into higher entities and to feel themselves as parts of God ('forecourts of heaven')."[29]

Schreber's discourse on the omniscience and omnipresence of God stresses, as well, the importance of the connection, preestablished, in his view, more than a century before, between the names of Flechsig, his doctor, and Schreber—a connection that was not, as we shall see, limited to himself as a merely individual member of one of those families.[30]

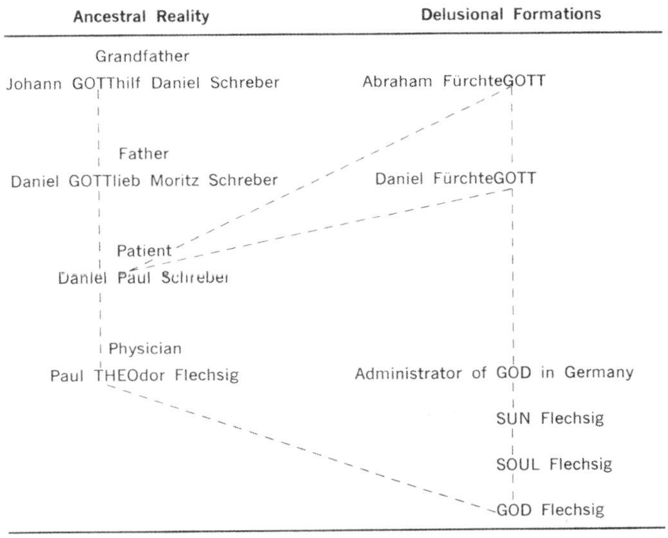

Fig. 2.
Daniel Paul Schreber's delusional use of the presence of God in personal names for the deification of his ancestors and his physician
From William G. Niederland, *The Schreber Case: Psychoanalytic Profile of a Paranoid Personality* (New York: Quadrangle/New York Times, 1974), 47

The undergoing, at the hands of the doctor, of a "soul murder" is woven into the narrative of Schreber's feminization, a process involving unutterable pain and issuing in ecstatic surrender. Schreber eventually developed the delusion that he actually was a woman, declaring that he had the breasts of a woman and experienced the "soul voluptuousness" of a female being. He was, in fact, "the last real person left," whereas others, including Dr. Paul Emil Flechsig, attendants, and other patients were merely "miracled-up," cursorily sketched, many-headed little men.[31] We know that Freud was particularly interested in the psychopathological process that led or ascended from Flechsig, Schreber's persecutory physician, to the figure of God. A partial family tree shows the various steps in the production of the delusional system that culminates in the Flechsig-father-God identification (fig. 2). The diagram shows the patient's delusional use of the presence of *Gott* (God) in his father's and grandfather's names and of *Theo* (the Greek root meaning God) in his physician's name.[32] It presents, we are told, the linguistic basis for the deification of the ancestors and, via psychotic transference, of Flechsig. It also illustrates Schreber's statement: "I have parts of their souls in my body." Freud analyzed the patient's psychotic thought process as an "attempt at restitution." One of the characteristic manifestations of this attempt consists of an effort to regain lost libidinal objects by reinforcing the cathexis of the verbal representations standing for the lost objects. The outstanding libidinal object in Schreber's case was the father. The verbal representation of his father—his given name, Daniel Gottlob—is recathected, and in all the variations of the delusional names "God" (*Gott* or *Theo*) occurs. *Fürchtegott* (fear God) is of especial interest, revealing the patient's ambivalence, his fear of God as well as the threat he addresses to God. And the patient, as we see, shared the name of Daniel with his father and the name of Paul with his physician.[33]

Considering the photographic portrait of Flechsig installed behind his desk, with the contextual confirmation of his professional capacity and status, the huge

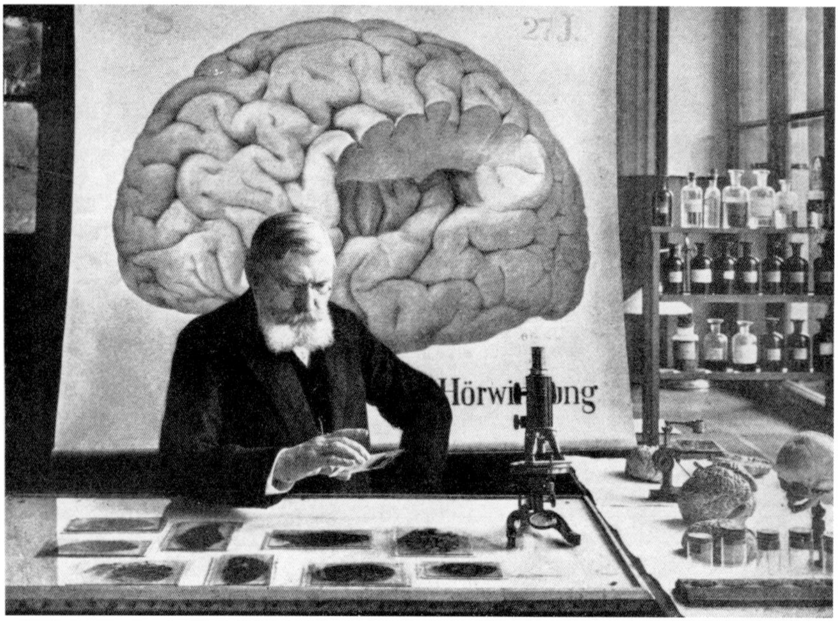

Fig. 3.
Dr. Paul Emil Flechsig at his desk
From Daniel Paul Schreber, *Memoirs of My Nervous Illness*, trans. and ed. Ida Macalpine and Richard A. Hunter (London: Wm. Dawson, 1955), pl. 1

map of his domain of sovereignty, the brain (fig. 3), one wonders, indeed, how his patient could not take him for that omniscient, omnipotent object of veneration and of fear?[34] Benefiting from Niederland's research offering a more precise identification of the father-figure in the case, we learn that Dr. Daniel Gottlob Moritz Schreber (1808–61) was a celebrated social, medical, and educational reformer, who taught in the medical school of the Universität Leipzig. He wrote and published close to twenty books on health and pediatric care. He was described in his obituary as "physician, teacher, nutritionist, anthropologist, therapeutic gymnast and athlete, and above all as man of action, of tremendous enthusiasm and endurance."[35] Among the twenty books mentioned was the *Kallipädie,* the popular guidebook for parents and educators, which after his death was reissued, in expanded form, as *Das Buch der Erziehung an Leib und Seele* (Book for the education of body and soul). And it was an especial and important point of pride with Dr. Schreber that his methods, theoretically derived, were, nevertheless, "regularly, actively, and personally applied by him in the rearing of his own children."[36] His educational system, as set forth to his readership of parents and educators, was based on the application of firm discipline, control, pressure, in the expectation that an early discipline will establish, in the malleable years of childhood, a moral discipline and a physical, muscular control that will ensure bodily health and mental soundness. He invented for this system a set of exercises and physical controls that were to be applied to children and were certainly applied to his own children, including young Daniel Paul. He seems to have been particularly concerned about the development of upright, straight posture.[37] In this he was not alone, certainly, in Germany, but he was singular in his construction of varied and elaborate apparatuses for the training in question, as illustrated by his recommendations for application of the following elements of his orthopedic apparatus (figs. 4–7):

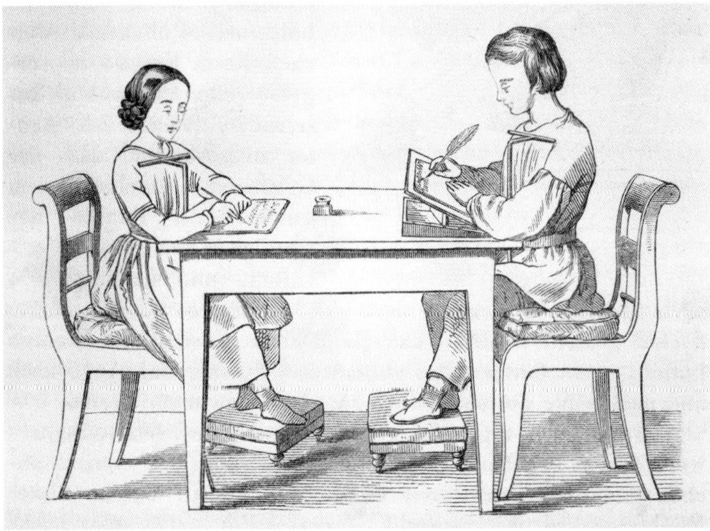

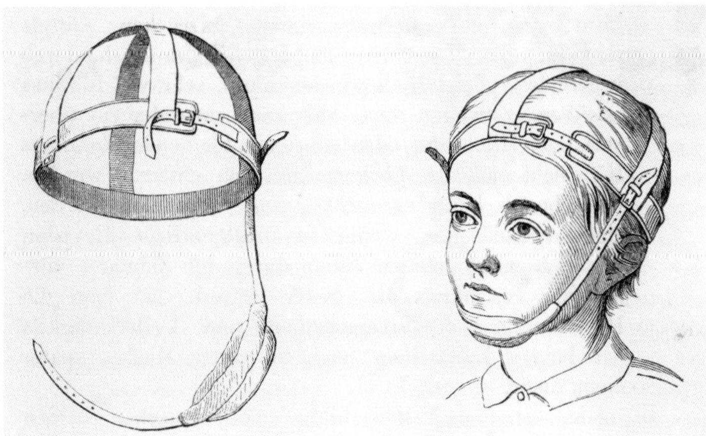

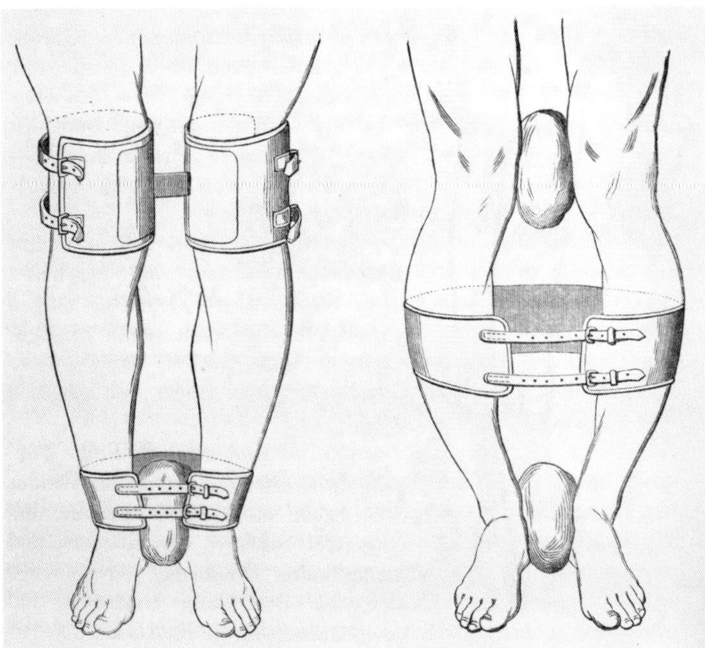

Fig. 4.
Use of *Geradhalter*
From Daniel Gottlob Moritz Schreber, *Kallipädie; oder, Erziehung zur Schönheit...* (Leipzig: Friedrich Fleischer, 1858), figs. 66, 67

Fig. 5.
Kopfhalter, and its use
From Daniel Gottlob Moritz Schreber, *Kallipädie; oder, Erziehung zur Schönheit...* (Leipzig: Friedrich Fleischer, 1858), figs. 71, 72

Fig. 6.
Orthopedic braces to correct knock-kneed or bowed legs
From Daniel Gottlob Moritz Schreber, *Kallipädie; oder, Erziehung zur Schönheit...* (Leipzig: Friedrich Fleischer, 1858), figs. 5, 6

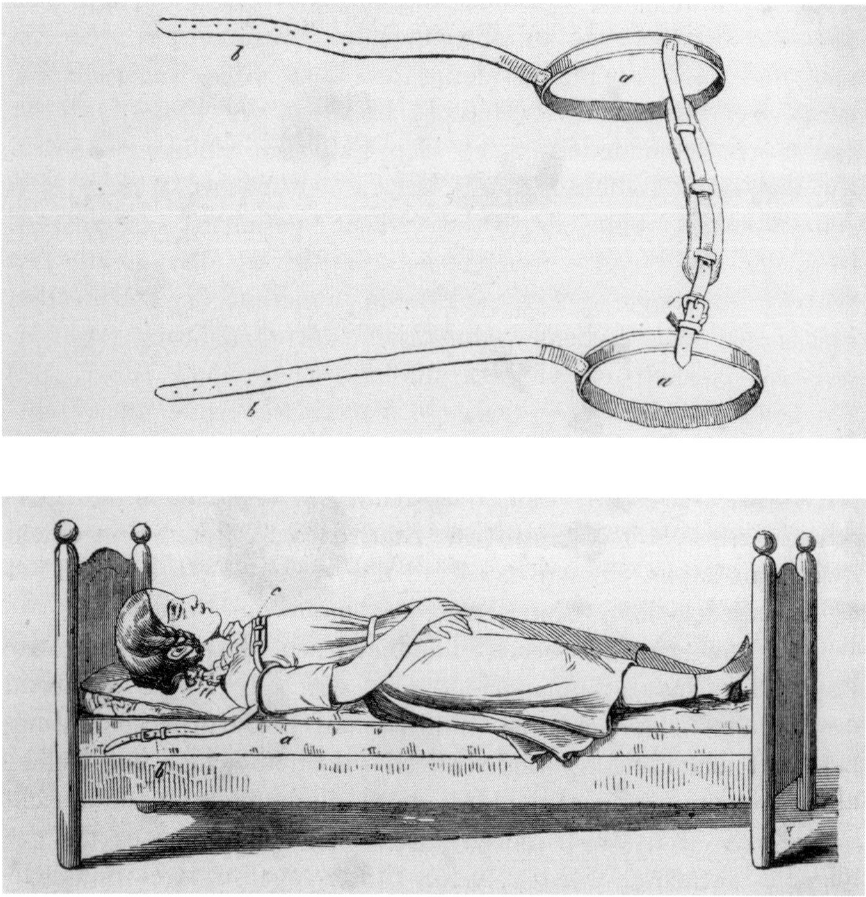

Fig. 7. Apparatus for maintaining perfect posture while asleep, and its use
From Daniel Gottlob Moritz Schreber, *Kallipädie; oder, Erziehung zur Schönheit...* (Leipzig: Friedrich Fleischer, 1858), figs. 25, 26

Geradhalter (upright brace) designed to ensure a rigidly erect sitting posture.
Kopfhalter (head belt) designed to correct the alignment of the jaws.
Braces designed to straighten the legs.
Apparatus designed to maintain perfect posture in sleep.

The pedagogue's *pangymnastikon* offered an entire gymnastic system condensed into one apparatus—consisting of two large rings suspended from the ceiling—the construction and application of which are described in his book of the same name.[38] This device, ensuring that all gymnastic exercises were brought within the compass of a single piece of equipment, was viewed as the simplest means for achieving the fullest development of muscular strength and endurance.[39]

It is from this book's set of illustrations (fig. 8), no doubt, that Schreber derived his own images of cursorily sketched little men with multiple heads.[40] And indeed, Schreber's entire delusional system can be seen as the projection of the system of constraints imposed upon the body of the psyche of the child of this extraordinary, totally controlling, Godlike father. As Schreber put it, "a miracle *directs the movements of my eyes.* I have not mentioned this miracle before, but it has been regularly enacted for years. Rays [father], after all, want constantly to see what pleases

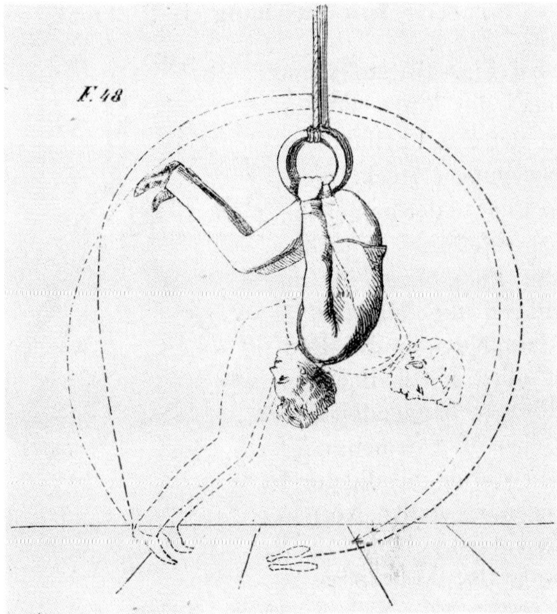

Fig. 8.
Exercise on the *pangymnastikon: Umschlag mit Auffussen* (Turn over with kick) From Daniel Gottlob Moritz Schreber, *Das Pangymnastikon; oder, Das ganze Turnsystem an einem einzigen Geräthe ohne Raumerforderniss*. . . (Leipzig: Friedrich Fleischer, 1875), fig. 48

them. . . . My eye muscles are therefore influenced to move in that direction toward which my glance *must* fall on things just created or else on a female being."[41]

Although an iconological study of *The Magic Feature* hardly requires that we situate the operation of the family triad more exactly within its text, we will want, however, to recall that Smith received, at the age of puberty, the command from his own father, of a task impossible to fulfill. "You must perform that magic feat which no one in the history of the world has yet performed: the conversion of lead into gold." (And Smith, in a spontaneous articulation of the accepted relation between gold and stool, speaks of his works as "excreta.")[42] Smith has offered us, in the visual splendor of his magic feature, the reparative offering in which the grief and anger of infantile psychosis are rehearsed and resolved. Out of the existing body of nineteenth-century illustration he cut, tore, then restored by collage and montage the turbulent saga of a passage from schizoid paranoia to depression. Smith's claims that his films were made by a force speaking through him has only to be translated from the rhetoric of transcendence to that of immanence. It was the force of the little man, the homunculus, acting through him that converted that grief, that anger, those leaden directives of fashion and of pedagogic control into the reparative gold of *The Magic Feature.*

Notes

Reprinted, with minor changes, from Irving Lavin, ed., *Meaning in the Visual Arts: Views from the Outside: A Centennial Commemoration of Erwin Panofsky (1892–1968)* (Princeton: Institute for Advanced Study, 1995), 335–50.

1. See, for instance, Harry Smith, book page doodle, ca. 1970; reproduced in Paola Igliori, ed., *American Magus Harry Smith: A Modern Alchemist* (New York: Inanout, 1996), 2.

2. The alternate title for this work is *Film #12: Heaven and Earth Magic.*
3. For a comprehensive survey and interpretation of Smith's oeuvre, see P. Adams Sitney, *Visionary Film: The American Avant-Garde* (New York: Oxford Univ. Press, 1974), 270–300; *The Magic Feature* is described on pp. 287–99. An excerpt of Sitney's discussion appears in this volume, 73–83.
4. Noël Carroll, "Mind, Medium and Metaphor in Harry Smith's *Heaven and Earth Magic*," *Film Quarterly* 31, no. 2 (1977–78): 39.
5. Harry Smith, "Harry Smith Interview," interview by P. Adams Sitney, *Film Culture,* no. 37 (1965), 11; cited in Sitney, *Visionary Film* (note 3), 287.
6. Smith, "Harry Smith Interview" (note 5), 10; cited in Sitney, *Visionary Film* (note 3), 294.
7. Harry Smith in 1971; as cited in Sitney, *Visionary Film* (note 3), 299.
8. John Florio, *A Worlde of Wordes; or, Most Copious, and Exact Dictionarie in Italien and English* (London: printed by Arnold Hatfield for Edw. Blount, 1598), 146, s.v. "geroglifico."
9. Thomas Carlyle, *Sartor Resartus: The Life and Opinions of Herr Teufelsdröckh,* rev. ed. (Boston: James Munroe, 1840), 205.
10. Sigmund Freud, "Fetishism (1927)," trans. Joan Riviere, in idem, *Collected Papers,* vol. 5, *Miscellaneous Papers, 1888–1938,* ed. James Strachey (New York: Basic, 1959), 199.
11. Freud, "Fetishism" (note 10), 200.
12. See Sigmund Freud, "Psycho-analysis and Religious Origins (1919)," trans. James Strachey, in idem, *Collected Papers,* vol. 5, *Miscellaneous Papers, 1888–1938,* ed. James Strachey (New York: Basic, 1959), 94. For a demonstration of its explanatory power in the construction of the semiotics of the oeuvre of Marcel Duchamp, see Annette Michelson, "*Anemic Cinema:* Reflections on an Emblematic Work," *Artforum* 12, no. 2 (1973): 64–69.
13. For the following exposition of Kleinian theory, I have drawn upon Melanie Klein, *Contributions to Psycho-analysis, 1921–1945* (New York: McGraw-Hill, 1964); and Melanie Klein, *Envy and Gratitude and Other Works, 1946–1963* (New York: Dell, 1977).
14. A recent example would be the extraordinary statement by Sally Mann, the remarkable photographer of children whose work has been the subject of much critical debate: "I think childhood sexuality is an oxymoron"; cited in Richard B. Woodward, "The Disturbing Photography of Sally Mann," *New York Times Magazine,* 27 September 1992, 52.
15. Antoine-Marin Le Mierre, *La peinture: Poëme en trois chants* (Paris: chez le Jay, 1769), 60: "L'allégorie habite un palais diaphane."
16. For this description and that of the larger conception and realization of *The Magic Feature,* see Smith, "Harry Smith Interview" (note 5), 10 and passim.
17. Sitney, *Visionary Film* (note 3), 292.
18. Smith, "Harry Smith Interview" (note 5), 5.
19. Smith, "Harry Smith Interview" (note 5), 6.
20. Smith, "Harry Smith Interview" (note 5), 6.
21. Smith, "Harry Smith Interview" (note 5), 7.

22. Daniel Gottlob Moritz Schreber, *Kallipädie; oder, Erziehung zur Schönheit durch naturgetreue und gleichmässige Förderung normaler Körperbildung, lebenstüchtiger Gesundheit und geistiger Veredelung und insbesondere durch möglichste Benutzung specieller Erziehungsmittel: Für Aeltern, Erzieher und Lehrer* (Leipzig: Friedrich Fleischer, 1858). Note that various authors (including Freud and Niederland) and other authorities mistakenly spell his second given name as "Gottlieb."
23. Daniel Paul Schreber, *Denkwürdigkeiten eines Nervenkranken: Nebst Nachträgen und einem Anhang über die Frage: "Unter welchen Voraussetzungen darf eine für geisteskrank erachtete Person gegen ihren erklärten Willen in einer Heilanstalt festgehalten werden?"* (Leipzig: O. Mutze, 1903).
24. See Sigmund Freud, "Psychoanalytic Notes upon an Autobiographical Account of a Case of Paranoia (Dementia Paranoides) (1911)," in idem, *Three Case Histories*, ed. Philip Rieff (New York: Collier, 1966), 103–86.
25. William G. Niederland, *The Schreber Case: Psycho-analytic Profile of a Paranoid Personality* (New York: Quadrangle/New York Times, 1974). For quotations from Schreber's text, I have drawn upon the translations in Niederland. For an English translation of the entire text, see Daniel Paul Schreber, *Memoirs of My Nervous Illness*, trans. Ida Macalpine and Richard A. Hunter (London: Wm. Dawson, 1955).
26. Niederland, *The Schreber Case* (note 25), 10.
27. Schreber, as translated in Niederland, *The Schreber Case* (note 25), 18, 11.
28. Schreber, as translated in Niederland, *The Schreber Case* (note 25), 11.
29. Schreber, as translated in Niederland, *The Schreber Case* (note 25), 11–12.
30. Niederland, *The Schreber Case* (note 25), 12.
31. Niederland, *The Schreber Case* (note 25), 16–17, 44–45.
32. "Paul Theodor" was a delusional construct too, apparently, as the doctor's given names were "Paul Emil." See Schreber, *Denkwürdigkeiten* (note 23), 23–25.
33. Niederland, *The Schreber Case* (note 25), 46–47.
34. See Niederland, *The Schreber Case* (note 25), 29, 105.
35. Niederland, *The Schreber Case* (note 25), 49–50.
36. Niederland, *The Schreber Case* (note 25), 50.
37. Niederland, *The Schreber Case* (note 25), 50–51.
38. Daniel Gottlob Moritz Schreber, *Das Pangymnastikon; oder, Das ganze Turnsystem an einem einzigen Geräthe ohne Raumerforderniss . . . für Schulanstalten, Haus-Turner und Turnvereine* (Leipzig: Friedrich Fleischer, 1862). Three editions of the English language translation of this work were published that same year by Ticknor and Fields in Boston in Dio Lewis, *The New Gymnastics for Men, Women, and Children, with a Translation of Prof. Kloss's Dumb-bell Instructor and Prof. Schreber's Pangymnastikon*, with over twenty editions to follow.
39. Niederland, *The Schreber Case* (note 25), 51.
40. Niederland, *The Schreber Case* (note 25), 94–95.
41. Niederland, *The Schreber Case* (note 25), 79 (brackets in Niederland's text; italics in Niederland's text and Schreber's original).
42. Cited in Smith, "Harry Smith Interview" (note 5), 5. The reference to "my cinematic excreta" opens the detailed description of his films that Smith prepared for the *Film-Makers' Cooperative Catalogue*, no. 3 (1965): 57.

P. ADAMS SITNEY

HARRY SMITH, BIBLIOPHILE, AND THE ORIGINS OF CINEMA

The scholarship and interpretation devoted to Harry Smith's *Film #12* (the so-called *Heaven and Earth Magic* or *The Magic Feature*) has developed significantly since I published the first edition of *Visionary Film* in 1974. Before that, there was very little on the film: Jonas Mekas had mentioned it in his *Village Voice* column; I had published an interview with Smith in *Film Culture* in which he described, often cryptically, how the film was made; and he himself had crafted an even more cryptic note for the *Film-Makers' Cooperative Catalogue*.[1]

Rereading my discussion of the film, I think my central contribution had been the explication of Smith's cryptic note:

> No. 12: A much expanded version of No. 8. The first part depicts the heroine's toothache consequent to the loss of a very valuable watermelon, her dentistry and transportation to heaven. Next follows an elaborate exposition of the heavenly land in terms of Israel, Montreal and the second part depicts the return to earth from being eaten by Max Muller on the day Edward the Seventh dedicated the Great Sewer of London. (Approx. 50 min.).[2]

Characteristically, Smith leads us back, from the very start, to an earlier point of origin, the now lost *Film #8,* which he described in the *Catalogue* thus: "No. 8: Black and white collage made up of clippings from 19th Century ladies' wear catalogues and elocution books. The cat, the dog, the statue and the Hygrometer appear here for the first time. (Approx. 5 min.)."[3]

Reading Smith's note in light of the interview in *Film Culture* and other clues he had provided for me over several years, I proposed a scenario—a plot summary—for the film and listed a few of its sources: Max Ernst's two collage novels, Daniel Paul Schreber's *Memoirs of My Nervous Illness,* Daniel Gottlob Moritz Schreber's *Medical Indoor Gymnastics.* I glossed "Israel" with S. L. MacGregor Mathers's *The Kabbalah Unveiled,* and "Montreal" with Wilder Penfield and Herbert H. Jasper's *Epilepsy and the Functional Anatomy of the Human Brain.*[4]

However, I had not noticed the publication dates of most of these crucial sources. Little, Brown brought out Penfield and Jasper's book in 1954; Ida Macalpine and Richard A. Hunter translated, edited, and provided an introduction to Schreber's memoirs in 1955. These two books, along with Carl Størmer's *The Polar Aurora* (1955) and Linn F. Cooper and Milton H. Erickson's *Time Distortion in Hypnosis* (1954), probably came into Smith's hands just before he started *Heaven and Earth Magic.* Smith mentions the first two in conjunction with the film and the other two more generally in the conversations recorded by A. J. Melita in 1976.[5] A frenzy of book buying and eclectic reading seems to have preceded the initiation of Smith's long projects. At the very least we can now conjecture that *Heaven and Earth Magic* was begun in 1955 or shortly after. There was even a 1951 reprint of Mathers's crucial translation of the Kabbalistic text, which the filmmaker could have found in Samuel Weiser's bookshop—one of his regular haunts in New York City[6]—although it is just possible that he might have had the edition published in 1926 or even one of the much rarer editions of this book, which originally appeared in 1887.

Although there is very little on *Heaven and Earth Magic* in *American Magus Harry Smith: A Modern Alchemist* (1996), edited by Paola Igliori, a careful reading of its interviews provides several interesting bibliographical leads. Lionel Ziprin indicates that Smith read aloud to his mother on her deathbed a chapter on sadism written by Karen Horney.[7] I presume that was "Sadistic Trends," the twelfth and final chapter (before the conclusion) of Horney's *Our Inner Conflicts: A Constructive Theory of Neurosis* (1945); the date is plausible: Mary Louise Smith died in 1949. There Horney emphasizes the sadist's compulsion to control and play on the emotions of another person, to exploit, disparage, and humiliate them, often while in the grip of "spells of an almost insane rage."[8] The idea of a deathbed reading of such a text seemed to characterize Harry Smith in Ziprin's mind, and so struck the interviewer that she repeated it to Smith's friend and protégé, Dr. Joseph Gross.[9] Was Smith trying to tell his mother something about her nature? Perhaps, but we cannot exclude the possibility that Smith was reading this passage in an effort to explain himself to her. No one familiar with Smith's behavior could fail to recognize him in Horney's sketch of the compulsive sadist.

In any case, this is one of many indications that Smith was reading psychoanalytic literature, particularly in the late 1940s and into the 1950s. Macalpine and Hunter, the editors of *Memoirs of My Nervous Illness,* were psychiatrists revising Sigmund Freud's pioneering work on Schreber.[10] Furthermore, I recall Smith's discussion of the psychoanalyst Géza Róheim's work on dreams, particularly on the associations of bed-wetting and myths of the flood.[11] (We might recall here that *Heaven and Earth Magic* is just a fragment of a film that was to include Noah's Ark and the Raising of the Dead.)[12] Yet again, the publication date of Róheim's *The Gates of the Dream* is 1952. The accumulation of texts from the first half of the 1950s is too significant to be coincidental. It is clear that a period of intense study preceded the making of the film. Smith repeatedly referred to the books he read in this period when discussing *Heaven and Earth Magic.*

Smith's familiarity with psychoanalytic literature is particularly interesting in light of Annette Michelson's discussions of *Heaven and Earth Magic.* In her fullest version, "The Mummy's Return: A Kleinian Film Scenario," Michelson offers a psychoanalytic reading of the film informed by Melanie Klein's work on infant development:

> what is proposed is a reading of *The Magic Feature* as the representation of an elaborate working through, in the form of a prodigally generous form of reparation offered by artistic practice, of the spectrum of infantile development through paranoid-schizoid and depressive positions. And our first step toward

> that reading will entail an account of the initial image of the film, which I note, with more than casual interest and amusement, neither of the exegetes cited above [myself and Noël Carroll, who read the film as a model of the Humean mind] troubled to include in his own reading: that of the homunculus who sets in motion this epic of repeated slaughter and resurrection by introducing (literally carrying onto the screen or scene) the other member of the primordial dyad, whose name we read, as in a rebus: "Mummy."[13]

That critical insight is so brilliant it whets our appetite for further revelations, say of the meaning of the watermelon, the dog, the strawberry, the elevator, to flesh out the Kleinian scenario she so provocatively initiates.

Nothing in *American Magus* takes us as far as Michelson's interpretation. Nevertheless, I think we can take an indirect path to yet other sources for *Heaven and Earth Magic* through that book. For my part, I want to pounce on a memory Jordan Belson offered Igliori: "He always had some interesting books around. I know he had a book on Méliès, for example."[14] I would bet that this was Maurice Bessy and Lo Duca's *Georges Méliès, mage* (1945). It was the sort of expensive, lavish, hard-to-get book Smith could hardly ever resist; there were two thousand numbered copies printed.[15] The publication date suggests that it would have been available in the early 1950s. There was no comparable volume on Méliès at that time, to the best of my knowledge. I will try to chart a few of the ways in which *Heaven and Earth Magic* could be viewed as an homage to Méliès.

Méliès hand-colored many of his films, producing a more vivid intensity of hue than later photographic processes could match, as the color illustrations of seven tinted stills in Bessy and Lo Duca's book bear out.[16] Similarly, Smith colored *Heaven and Earth Magic* with a series of masks, filters, and gels (see p. 138), hand-operated as he projected the film through a contraption of his own design (which he flung in a rage from the third-story window of the Film-Makers' Cooperative on Park Avenue South in the mid-1960s; mercifully no one was injured).[17] The mechanism resembled some of the devices Méliès invented to create his filmic effects, as illustrated by Bessy and Lo Duca,[18] including underwater illusions (fig. 1), flying figures, moving skies, and inflating heads.

These interesting but superficial similarities pale beside the remarkable echoes of images and structures found in Méliès's corpus and Smith's *Heaven and Earth Magic* (see pp. 74–75). The play between flatness and depth—exemplified in the opening moments of Smith's film by the photograph of a garden patch from which a dog steals a watermelon (see p. 91)—is a continual inspiration to Méliès, as *Le livre magique* (1900) illustrates.[19] In that film, the magician turns live figures into flat cards, and vice versa. Since *Heaven and Earth Magic* is a collage of flat cutout figures and objects, however, there is no true play between flatness and depth in it.

Smith would have found an evocation of Egyptology in two images from *La prophétesse de Thèbes* (1907) and in two illustrations identified as "Magie égyptienne" and "Scène égyptienne" in Bessy and Lo Duca's book.[20] The imaginary projection of women, as in *Le portrait spirite* (1903) and *Les illusions fantaisistes* (1909), are a part of the phantasmagoria of both Méliès and Smith. Likewise both invoke

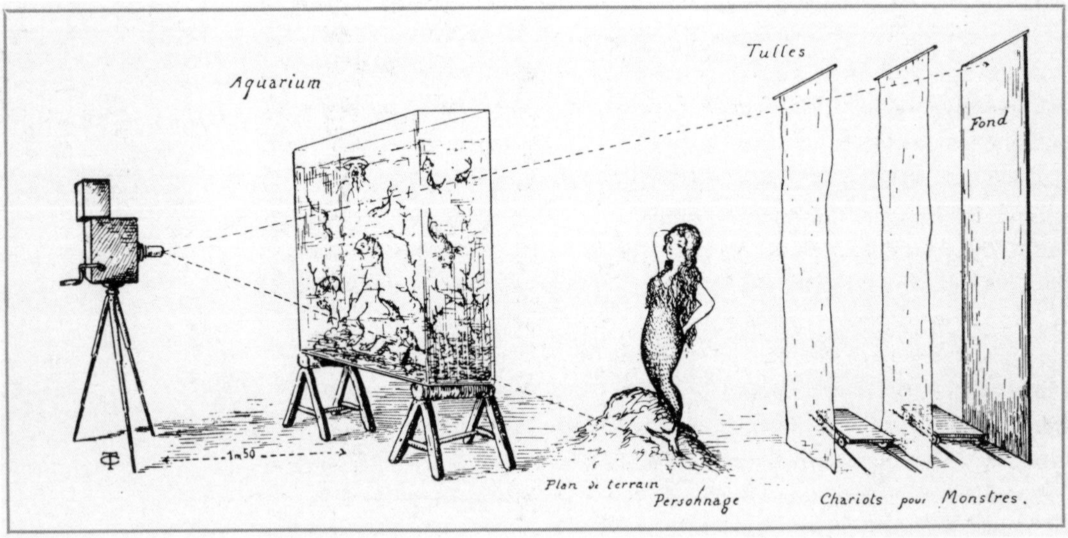

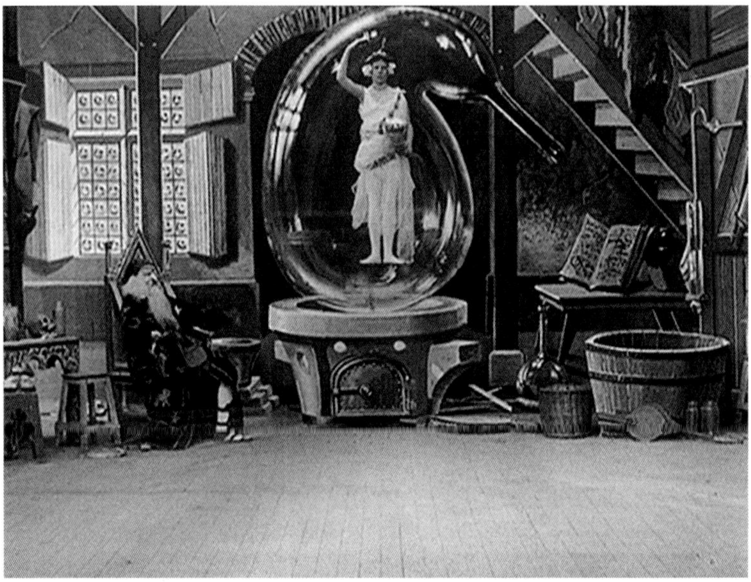

Fig. 1.
Le secret des abîmes sous-marins (The secret of the undersea abysses)
From Maurice Bessy and Lo Duca, *Georges Méliès, mage, et "Mes mémoires" par Méliès* (Paris: Prisma, 1945), 58

Fig. 2.
Georges Méliès (French, 1861–1938)
Still from *L'alchimiste Parafaragamus ou la cornue infernale,* 1906, 3 min. 25 sec., 35 mm, black and white, silent

extraordinary shifts of scale—among the obvious instances in Méliès's oeuvre are *La danseuse microscopique* (1902) and *Le voyage de Gulliver à Lilliput et chez les géants* (1902). Even Méliès's transformation of bodies into skeletons—see, for example, his *La crémation* (1899) as well as *Les illusions fantaisistes*—becomes a favored trope for Smith. The paraphernalia of an alchemical workshop appeared in *L'alchimiste Parafaragamus ou la cornue infernale* (1906) (fig. 2).[21]

The dismemberment and reconstitution of the human body is even more central to both. I presume Méliès's famous trick film, *Le mélomane* (1903), would have especially appealed to Smith, an artist who spent so much of his life exploring the visualization of music. Méliès's film has just one set: a stage with five parallel lines of telegraph wire. The artist marches on at the head of a line of six chorus girls and a drummer. He is carrying a huge G-clef, which he heaves into the wires to make a musical staff of them. Six times he removes his head to toss it onto the staff, then he heaves up wands to make the quarter and eighth notes of the tune. Finally, the six women holding cards with the names of the musical tones on them line up under the staff, and the artist conducts the music. I believe that the original sound of the film would have included a live orchestra's rendering of the notes, the opening measures of "God Save the King."[22] The film, likely inspired by the caricaturist Grandville's drawing replacing the notes of the "Marche militaire et orientale" with stick figures, evoked the *sparagmos,*[23] or dismembering, of the composer.

The elaborate variations on the dissection and transformations of Smith's woman lead to her ascent into the heavenly zone, where at several points she is multiplied like the heads of *Le mélomane.* The descent from that zone begins when the man throws his equipment, the woman (fig. 3), and eventually himself into the munching jaws of the head of the great German scholar of comparative religion, F. Max Müller. In Méliès's *Voyage à travers l'impossible* (1904) and in his *À la conquête du pôle* (1912), a large entity—respectively, the sun and a polar ice giant (fig. 4)—consumes without killing a group of explorers. A drawing of the huge machinery constructed for this illusion in *À la conquête* appears in *Georges Méliès, mage.* In addition, Smith would have seen the film in 1947, when it was screened at the San Francisco Museum of Art as part of the Art in Cinema series, in a program titled "Ingenuity and Wit" that featured Méliès's *L'impressionniste fin de siècle* (1899), *Le voyage dans la lune* (1902), *Le palais des Mille et une nuits* (1905), and *L'hydrothérapie fantastique* (1909) as well.[24] Deliverance by consumption, a version of Jonah and the whale, also occurs in Méliès's *Le royaume des fées* (1903).

In *Heaven and Earth Magic,* the scene then shifts to reveal an elevator—which emerges from within Müller—in which the magus and the woman, still undergoing transformations, descend from the heavenly zone, eventually splashing down into the sea—indicated much more by the sound of splashing water and rocking motions as if the elevator were being swayed by undersea currents than by imagery—and finally re-ascend to the surface, following the pattern of Méliès's most celebrated film, *Le voyage dans la lune,* in which we see the rocket pushed off the edge of the moon, splashing into the sea, then floating up to the surface.[25]

I have saved for my final comparison Méliès's *L'hydrothérapie fantastique.* Bessy and Lo Duca offer six stills on a two-page spread.[26] The film illustrates the

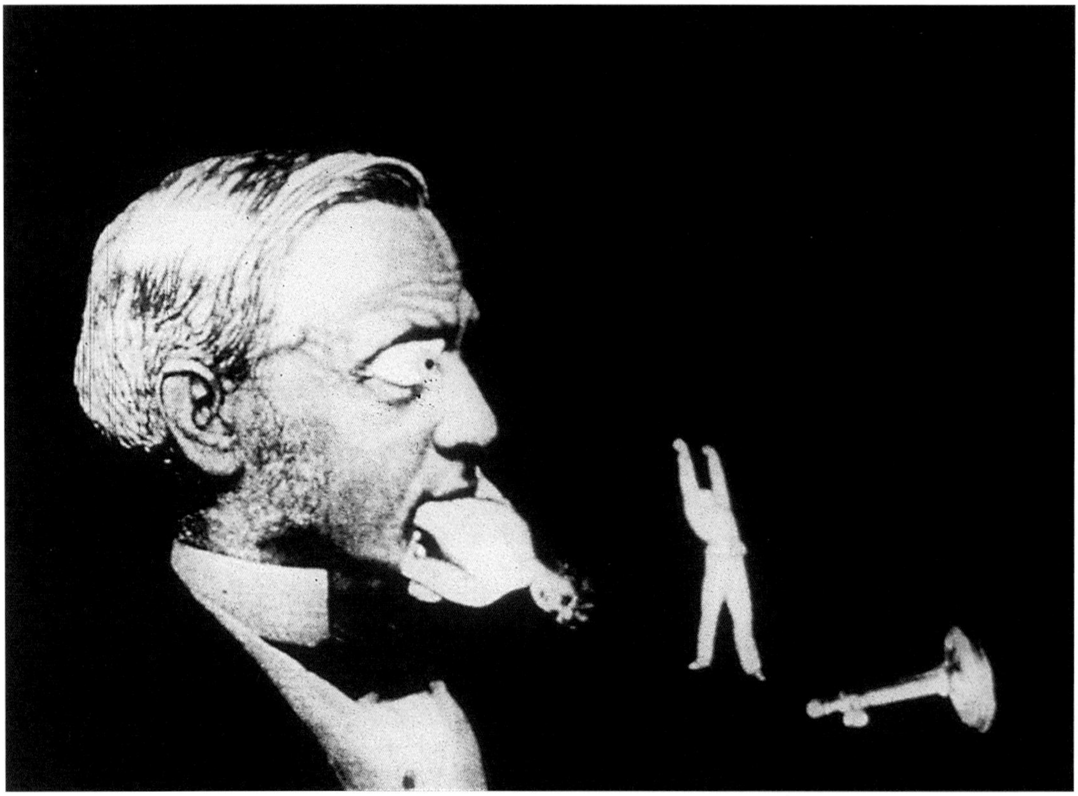

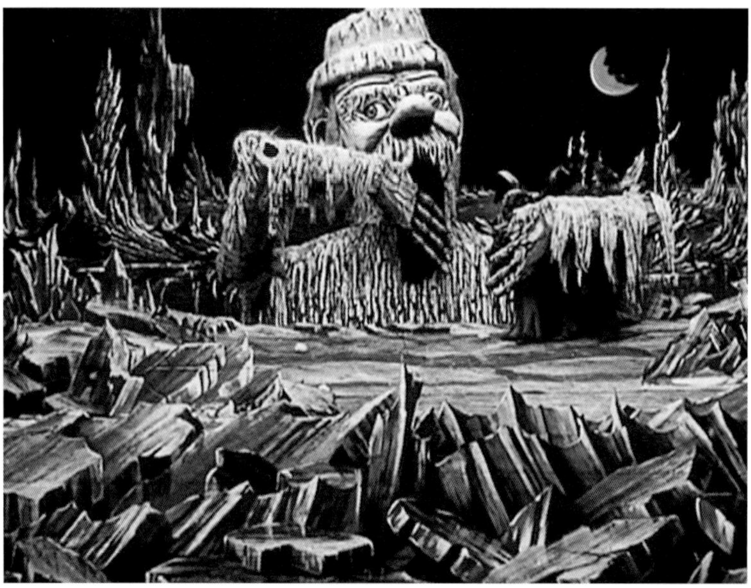

Fig. 3.
Harry Smith
Still from *Film #12: Heaven and Earth Magic,* ca. 1957–62, 66 min., 16 mm, black and white, sound

Fig. 4.
Georges Méliès (French, 1861–1938)
Still from *À la conquête du pôle,* 1912, 30 min. 22 sec., 35 mm, tinted, silent

transformation of an exhausted, debilitated, obese man into an energetic, self-sufficient, thin man. His subjection to a series of grotesque machines leads to an accidental explosion in which all his body parts fly apart, only to be reassembled by the frantic team of doctors. The overarching movement of the film reflects the way in which the female figure of *Heaven and Earth Magic* endures injections, dismemberment, reconstruction in elaborate mechanical contraptions, and a final restitution.

When the doctor initially examines the patient in *L'hydrothérapie fantastique,* he draws a liquid from him first with a huge syringe and then with an even huger one. Nevertheless, even the second syringe is not as outsize as the needle that the manipulating male figure in *Heaven and Earth Magic* uses: that is at least twice his height. Méliès next shows his patient attached to the first of several elaborate machines: containing a flywheel and a hydraulic pump, it draws liquid from his body through a large hose and drips the liquid into a pail. Dripping is a central, recurring image in *Heaven and Earth Magic.*

As in most of Méliès's films, a considerable part of the action consists in the wheeling into view or the removal of machinery, and the physical preparations of the magicians or, in this instance, doctors. In this respect, *Heaven and Earth Magic* goes Méliès one better: the process of preparation and removal is virtually indistinguishable from the main action of the film; it is one alchemical operation in serial variations.

Having drained liquid from the patient, Méliès's doctors lay him in a tub into which they put a fanlike machine with eight brushes that whirl in a cloud of steam, pummeling the man. Then, after removing his body and massaging it with hand rollers, they put him under a framework of five mechanical pistons that pound him into spasms. Then they place him in a chair and construct a box around him, leaving only his head showing. A gauge and a thermometer are attached. But the doctors become distracted in their consultations, and the overheated machine explodes, scattering the patient's limbs. Frantically, they reassemble him, wiggling piece by wiggling piece, on another specially constructed frame, from which he emerges delighted with his cure.

Smith called his later film *Mahagonny* an interpretation of Marcel Duchamp's *Large Glass*—that is, of *The Bride Stripped Bare by Her Bachelors, Even* (1915–23) (see p. 144).[27] He probably was unaware of Michel Carrouges's *Les machines célibataires* when that book was published in 1954; but he certainly learned of it when Harald Szeemann revived the notion of bachelor machines in the exhibition *Le macchine celibi/The Bachelor Machines,* for which Rizzoli published the catalog in 1975.[28] Smith would have seen the catalog because Szeemann included *Heaven and Earth Magic* in the show. I believe that catalog may have been the impetus for the ironic description of *Mahagonny.* But Smith's *Heaven and Earth Magic* already abounded in bachelor machines, as Szeemann realized as soon as he saw it. Méliès's films, too, had been a festival of bachelor machines. In that vein, we can call *Heaven and Earth Magic* an interpretation of the work of Georges Méliès.

How do we reconcile the sadistic Kleinian scenario with the homage to Méliès? Stan Brakhage has unwittingly provided us with a critical insight that may answer that question. As I read Michelson's essay, I was reminded of a daring, speculative meditation by Brakhage from almost twenty years earlier. I take the liberty of inserting Harry Smith's name in brackets in Brakhage's text:

> Young [Harry] then—already defeated by some-such creatures as we can begin to imagine on the barren planet of his foetal mind... completely overwhelmed, torn to pieces before what-we-would-call his 'birth'—begins as a child to invent a spirit-of-himself which will revenge him... a hero who will FREE the wickedly enchanted—or otherwise destroyed—pieces of his actual being [...] young [Harry], perhaps later then, begins to imagine a heroine who will restore him, a woman who will sew together or otherwise re-member his actual being.
>
> [Harry] himself decides to become just such a magician; but first he must make the hero of his invention a magician. As he is *imagining* the woman (rather than inventing her) she will always be victim of this magic—subject to the transformations of it: thus young [Harry] hopes to have power over her equal to her necessary ability to re-member and, as Mother then, to restore him. He must also manage some ultimate magic for his actual being which can defeat the magic he gives the hero-of-his-invention; and he begins, therefore, to create a demon-self (of himself-imagined-restored) who can tear his hero to pieces as he foetally once was.[29]

The informed reader will protest that there is no such discussion of Harry Smith in all Brakhage's voluminous writings—for Brakhage was not projecting this version of the Kleinian scenario onto Smith (and his *Heaven and Earth Magic*) in 1977 but onto Méliès (and all his films), and where I wrote "Harry," Brakhage wrote "George." Brakhage's phantasmal reconstruction of Méliès's psychic formation, which he derived from an exclusively intuitive reading of the films, bears a striking resemblance to the Kleinian narrative Michelson read into *Heaven and Earth Magic*.

There is no evidence that Smith was familiar with the writings of Melanie Klein. However, between 1948 and 1953 the Hogarth Press in London published many of her most important works in their prestigious International Psycho-Analytical Library. So, it is possible that he was acquainted with her work, although the relevance of Michelson's analysis in no way depends upon Smith's knowledge of "the Kleinian scenario." I conclude with the suggestion that Smith perceived and identified with, or was excited and inspired by, the latent psychodrama of Méliès's imagery in constructing *Heaven and Earth Magic*, his masterpiece of the mid-1950s. Brakhage's recuperation of Méliès, the prestidigitator, as an Oedipal magician neatly demonstrates the possibility of extracting a version of "the Kleinian scenario" from his films by a filmmaker unfamiliar with Klein's theses. Brakhage's insight coincides in this one instance with Smith's hermetic archaeology of popular culture.

Notes

1. P. Adams Sitney, *Visionary Film: The American Avant-Garde* (New York: Oxford Univ. Press, 1974), 270–300. Jonas Mekas, "Movie Journal," *Village Voice*, 12 August 1965, 16; see also 25 June 1964, 11; 7 January 1965, 12; 18 March 1965, 23; 23 June 1966, 29; 3 June 1971, 61. Harry Smith, "Harry Smith Interview," interview by P. Adams Sitney, *Film Culture*, no. 37 (1965): 4–13. "Smith, Harry," *Film-Makers' Cooperative Catalogue*, no. 3 (1965): 57–58.
2. "Smith, Harry" (note 1), 58.
3. "Smith, Harry" (note 1), 57.
4. Sitney, *Visionary Film* (note 1), 287–99. Max Ernst, *La femme 100 têtes* (Paris: Éditions du Carrefour, 1929); and Max Ernst, *Une semaine de bonté; ou, Les sept éléments capitaux* ([Paris]: J. Bucher, [1934]). Daniel Paul Schreber, *Memoirs of My Nervous Illness*, trans. and ed. Ida Macalpine and Richard A. Hunter (London: Wm. Dawson, 1955). Daniel Gottlob Moritz Schreber, *Medical Indoor Gymnastics*, ed. Rudolf Graefe, trans. Herbert A. Day (London: Williams & Norgate, 1899). Christian Freiherr Knorr von Rosenroth, *The Kabbalah Unveiled*, trans. and ed. S. L. MacGregor Mathers (London: G. Redway, 1887; reprint, London: Routledge & K. Paul, 1951). Wilder Penfield and Herbert H. Jasper, *Epilepsy and the Functional Anatomy of the Human Brain* (Boston: Little, Brown, 1954).
5. Harry Smith, "A. J. Melita—Chelsea Hotel, New York City, 1976," interview by A. J. Melita, in idem, *Think of the Self Speaking: Harry Smith—Selected Interviews*, ed. Rani Singh (Seattle: Elbow/Cityful, 1999), 152–53.
6. See, for example, Jim Wasserman, "Jim Wasserman—25 October 1995," interview by Paola Igliori, in Paola Igliori, ed., *American Magus Harry Smith: A Modern Alchemist* (New York: Inanout, 1996), 169–70.
7. Lionel Ziprin, "Lionel Ziprin—May and June 1993," interview by Paola Igliori, compiled with previous interview by Clayton Patterson with K. K., in Paola Igliori, ed., *American Magus Harry Smith: A Modern Alchemist* (New York: Inanout, 1996), 45–46.
8. Karen Horney, *Our Inner Conflicts: A Constructive Theory of Neurosis* (New York: W. W. Norton, 1945), 199.
9. Joe Gross, "Dr. Joe Gross—25 October 1995, 16 November 1995," interview by Paola Igliori, in Paola Igliori, ed., *American Magus Harry Smith: A Modern Alchemist* (New York: Inanout, 1996), 152.
10. Sigmund Freud, "Psycho-analytic Notes on an Autobiographical Account of a Case of Paranoia (Dementia Paranoides) (1911)," trans. Alix Strachey and James Strachey, in idem, *The Standard Edition of the Complete Psychological Works of Sigmund Freud*, vol. 12, *The Case of Schreber, Papers on Technique and Other Works* (1911–1913), gen. ed. James Strachey (London: Hogarth), 9–82.
11. Géza Róheim, *The Gates of the Dream* (New York: International Universities Press, 1952), 439–65.
12. Smith, "Harry Smith Interview" (note 1), 11.
13. Michelson, this volume, 90. Michelson's essay first appeared in Irving Lavin, ed., *Meaning in the Visual Arts: Views from the Outside: A Centennial Commemoration of Erwin Panofsky (1892–1968)* (Princeton: Institute for Advanced Study, 1995), 335–50.

14. Jordan Belson, "Jordan Belson—3 October 1995," interview by Paola Igliori, in Paola Igliori, ed., *American Magus Harry Smith: A Modern Alchemist* (New York: Inanout, 1996), 21.
15. In 1961, in honor of the centenary of Méliès's birth, a revised edition of Bessy and Lo Duca's book was issued, likewise in a limited edition of two thousand copies.
16. Maurice Bessy and [Giuseppe Maria] Lo Duca, *Georges Méliès, mage* (Paris: Prisma, 1945), 6, plates inserted after pp. 18, 40, 50, 72, 118, 152.
17. Jonas Mekas, "Jonas Mekas—10 July 1993," interview by Paola Igliori, in Paola Igliori, ed., *American Magus Harry Smith: A Modern Alchemist* (New York: Inanout, 1996), 80.
18. Bessy and Lo Duca, *Georges Méliès* (note 16), 55–63.
19. Bessy and Lo Duca, *Georges Méliès* (note 16), 124–25.
20. Bessy and Lo Duca, *Georges Méliès* (note 16), 140–41.
21. See Bessy and Lo Duca, *Georges Méliès* (note 16), 37, 76 (projected women); 64 (differences of scale); 202, 37 (skeletons); 197 (alchemist's laboratory). Michelle Bonnice pointed out several of these examples to me.
22. Bessy and Lo Duca, *Georges Méliès* (note 16), 126–28.
23. See Sitney, *Visionary Film* (note 1), 81n: "I have used the term *sparagmos* to underline the ritual origins of the numerous scenes of dismemberment in the American avant-garde cinema. I have also used it for both explicit thematic manifestations of the rite and for those cinematic tropes which more obliquely allude to it."
24. The program handed out on the evening of the Art in Cinema screening for 25 April 1947 shows five films by Méliès closing the event: *The Conjuror, A Trip to the Moon, The Palace of the Arabian Nights, The Doctor's Secret,* and *The Conquest of the Pole.* These films (except *The Conjuror*) were originally scheduled to be shown on 11 April 1947, as part of an Art in Cinema program titled "Trickery and Surrealism"; see Scott MacDonald, ed., *Art in Cinema: Documents toward a History of the Film Society* (Philadelphia: Temple Univ. Press, 2006), 64. I am indebted to Michelle Bonnice for having researched the Art in Cinema programs.
25. Bessy and Lo Duca, *Georges Méliès* (note 16), 87–88.
26. Bessy and Lo Duca, *Georges Méliès* (note 16), 142–43.
27. Harry Smith, "On *Mahagonny,*" in P. Adams Sitney, ed., *The Avant-Garde Film: A Reader of Theory and Criticism* (New York: New York Univ. Press, 1978), 105.
28. Michel Carrouges proposed the myth of bachelor machines in his *Les machines célibataires* (Paris: Arcanes, 1954). He was struck by the similarities between Duchamp's *The Large Glass* and Franz Kafka's short story "In der Strafkolonie" (written in 1914, published in 1919; "In the Penal Colony"). He saw in the invention of bizarre machines "the fourfold tragedy of our times: the Gordian knot of interconnections between machinery, terror, eroticism, and religion or anti-religion" (pp. 24–25, my translation). In the catalog for Szeemann's exhibition *Le macchine celibi/The Bachelor Machines,* Jean Clair defined the bachelor machine as "A fantastic machine. In contrast to the machines in futuristic literature and science fiction, which are ultimately rational, useful, even possible (for example, the *Nautilus* of Jules Verne), bachelor machines are ostensibly impossible, irrational, useless, pipe dreams.... The dominant characteristic of bachelor machines is their *sexuality*"; see

Hans Ulrich Reck and Harald Szeemann, eds., *Junggesellenmaschinen,* expanded ed., exh. cat. (Vienna: Springer, 1999), 12 (my translation). The exhibition catalog was first published as Marc Le Bot et al., *Le macchine celibi/The Bachelor Machines,* ed. Jean Clair and Harald Szeemann, exh. cat. (New York: Rizzoli, 1975); the exhibition was installed in Bern, Venice, and Paris. See also Smith, "A. J. Melita" (note 5), 161.

29. Stan Brakhage, *Film Biographies* (Berkeley, Calif.: Turtle Island, 1977), 17, 18.

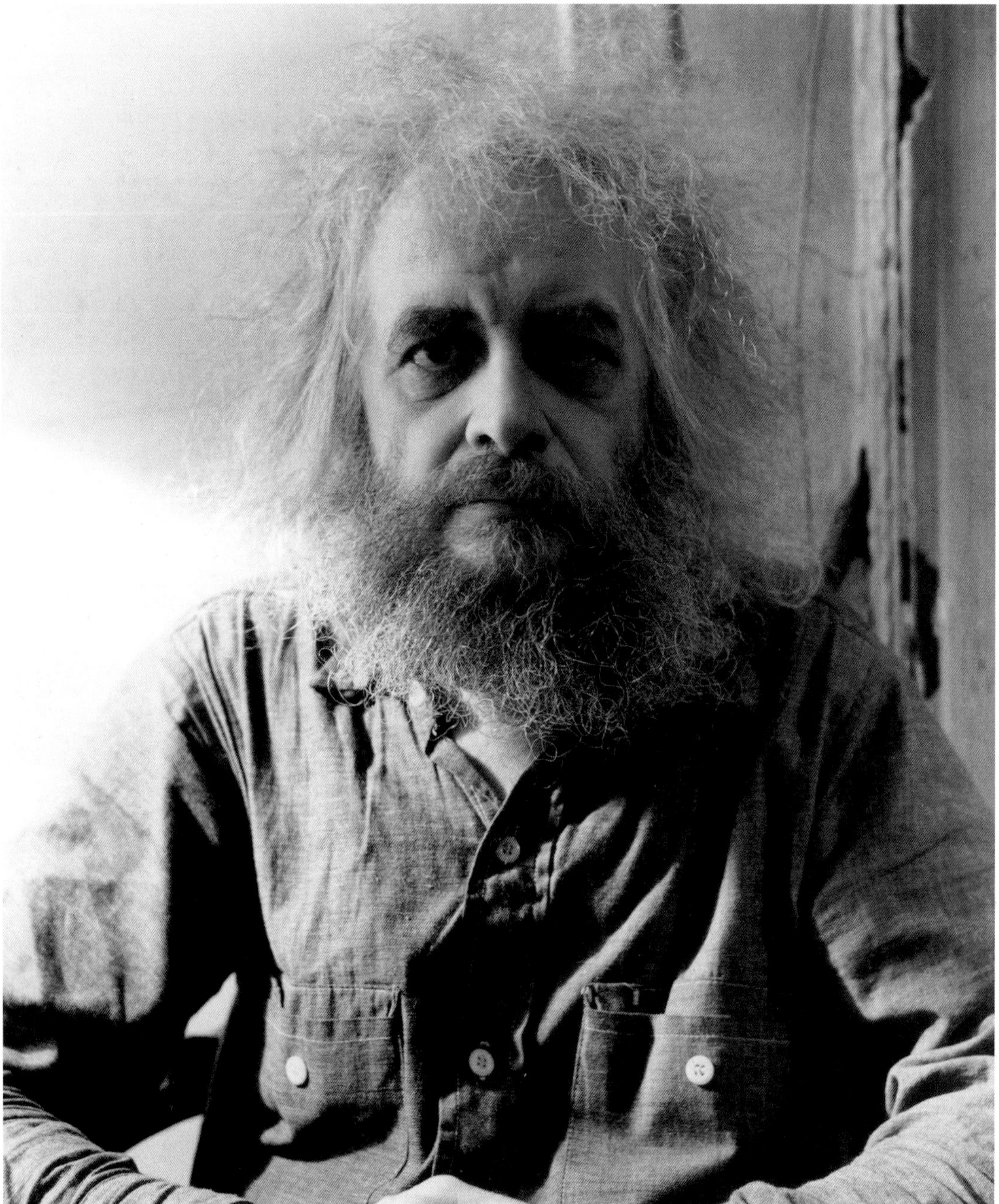

HARRY SMITH

QUEENS MUSEUM OF ART TALK, 11 NOVEMBER 1978

Editors' Note

This is a new transcription of Harry Smith's talk from a tape recording held by the Harry Smith Archives. A somewhat different version (by an unidentified transcriber) appeared in 1979 in *Cinema News,* a bimonthly film journal, edited by Henry Hills (East Coast) and Abigail Child (West Coast), published in San Francisco from 1977 to 1981.[1]

Since Harry Smith makes a point about his failure to complete sentences, we have marked where he trails off or pauses in his delivery. We have also corrected a few apparent errors, eliminated some incoherent phrases, added explanatory notes, and so forth. All editorial changes to the text of the talk are enclosed in brackets. Questions and answers from members of the audience, among them a photographer and some of Smith's friends, are in bold italic.

Smith seems to suggest that he periodically substitutes new texts as the "sources" for *Heaven and Earth Magic.* Here he does not mention *The Kabbalah Unveiled,* which, along with Daniel Paul Schreber's and Wilder Penfield and Herbert H. Jasper's books, was included in the triad of sources he listed for P. Adams Sitney in 1969 (see this volume, 76–78, 103). Smith first substitutes *The Polar Aurora* by Carl Størmer for *The Kabbalah Unveiled* and then indicates that this new triad has been superseded by works by Noam Chomsky, Claude Lévi-Strauss, and Ludwig Wittgenstein—although Smith's references seemingly confuse or conflate texts.

— Rani Singh and P. Adams Sitney

This is part of an animation series, of course, and the type of animation that I do is usually very slong, I mean slow, and often involves making a number of films at once. Lately I've been painting in the style of certain films we may look at later that I used from about 1939 to 1942, which were painted directly on the film, but when one film took five years, I quit that technique. This one [*Film #12: Heaven and Earth Magic*] was started twice. I have never looked at the film completely. It's based on a certain type of sortilege of parts. A large number of books were gone through, basically of the 1860s to about 1900.

I don't know the ethnic composition or education of any of you.

[*To photographer:*] I don't want any pictures taken of me. Recordings are all right though. Are you a good photographer?

Yes, I am. I would love to do your portrait.

Yeah! [*Laugh.*] Well... I'm having the lights turned off in a minute.

[*After some incoherent phrases indicating a gap in the tape or a distraction, Smith continues, giving as an example of sortilege the reconstruction of pottery from shards.*] So that, naturally, when any selection of objects is taken, as the exhibit of pottery in

Fig. 1.
Friedl Kubelka (Austrian, b. 1946)
Harry Smith, Chelsea Hotel, New York City, 1975

the gallery now, which was assembled from a number of sources and fits very well in with some of the shapes, as far as the earlier Grecian things at the Metropolitan [Museum of Art]. Although the designs are more closely allied to gourd designs of sort of northeastern Nigeria—which the museum there has brought up, now, you know, a corpus of two thousand of them or something... At base, the sorting process that occurs could be gone into at great length.

Today I was reading a book on a series of people from Aristotle to [William] Harvey that worked on the circulation of the blood—at first, of course, being thought to be these things like "natural spirit" or "animal spirit" or something like that.[2] I suppose it would be called *ruah* [breath, spirit] in the Bible... being one of the et cetera,...

So that any object can be taken and sorted, in this case all of the objects—*Has somebody here got a clock? I'm liable to talk forever*—were put in—*Can I watch the clock for a second, thank you; yeah, I have about twelve minutes more*... In any one case, I started to bring my catalogs for the Queens Museum so that I could illustrate to you how a limited number of words can encompass the whole meaning. This is because the exact references to the interpretation of the film having changed.[3] It took about twelve years to make the film, and it was finished in [*interruption from the back of the room*]. The film was originally composed on the use of three books. A book by Carl Størmer called *The Polar Aurora,*[4] who discovered radio reflections in about 1902 and spent the next fifty years... It's quite a touching book—how he describes it has taken him fifty years to write the book, which is for some... It's published by Oxford University [Press] in a particular series on geomagnetics. And Penfield and Jasper's *Epilepsy and the Functional Anatomy of the Human Brain.*[5] Now, people are going to say, "Uh, a book on epilepsy? You must be crazy." No: knowledge. Because they made a great number of discoveries while performing operations while the patient was describing what they were either feeling or seeing. And the third one, which I'm going to read parts of today, was Daniel Paul Schreber's *Memoirs of My Nervous Illness,* which is a particularly irritating one because people keep getting [Sigmund] Freud's interpretation of the book mixed with Schreber, like a recent article in *Film Quarterly* (I believe two issues ago) by Noël Carroll does that—mistranslates words that another sixty years of research has been made clearer in the light of advances in philosophy.[6]

In the meantime if anyone has read any of my recent stuff[7]... And I've also abandoned them now... Finally, they turned into Chomsky's effort to find the deep structure, Claude Lévi-Strauss's *Structural Anthropology,* and what is the third book? I'll think of it in a minute. Now in each case there have been... Wittgenstein, who has also been completely demolished in his attempt to solve the liar's paradox on the basis that a... I guess you're all familiar with the liar's paradox, which is the statement, "Everything I say is a lie." Now, this question has been discussed since biblical times right up to a recent symposi[um] at Harvard [University], there being no solution. If everything I say is a lie, I'm telling the truth. So everything I say isn't a lie. On the other hand, it can be interpreted as such. Bertrand Russell and so forth at one point thought they'd solved it on the basis that a statement cannot refer to itself and—however, that's somehow disproved by Wittgenstein, but somebody else has given him the ax. But I'm going to interpret it more or less on that level. Basically, I consider that Chomsky's notion that symbols are generated at the point where philosophy is turned into language still seems to be valid, which is statement 1.1 written in the Italian prison camp in 1918.[8] I like the way that Lévi-Strauss starts out in *The Raw and the Cooked,* sort of like: he's listening to [Igor] Stravinsky's, you know, *The Marriage* [*Les noces*] and says, "Well, I'm the world's greatest anthropologist, where shall I go? Well, it doesn't really matter, being as I'm the world's greatest anthropologist, I can go anywhere," and he's an entertaining writer, see, equating cooking with the problem of the consciousness in relation to what is there.

That's why I said, "What are you doing here?" I came here because each one of you was paid two dollars by the City of New York to get me here. You could have seen *Thank God It's Friday* and heard Donna Summer sing, which now has Spanish subtitles. It's a really good film. I saw it at a disco convention, and they set the thing quickly up in the grand ballroom somewhere in the Hilton Hotel, so quickly—it's wide-screen stereophonic sound and everything—they got the film all mixed up when they projected it, but the film is so amorphous that nobody noticed.[9]

So, originally this film [*Heaven and Earth Magic*] was shown—this is probably what's called a fifth-generation print or something, having thrown the film a number of times away but somebody always grabs it—it was originally shown in a series of round pictures and was in color through a series of filters, each little image, like the little man that is taken out of Schreber's father's book *Medical Indoor Gymnastics.*[10]

What time is it? I have five minutes. I've got to get this record by Johnny Cash, "25 Minutes to Go"—no, it's by Shel Silverstein.[11] You'll notice that I don't finish any sentences. [*Laughter.*] The laughter comes from the fact that that's what Chomsky is talking about, that you realize that there *is* an end to the sentence. Why finish the sentence? Everybody knows... is able in their own mind. Remember that this is 1978, I think. I haven't looked at what it says about my film but—did I get two copies of it here? [*To illustrate a principle of Chomsky's theory of syntax or Wittgenstein's "language games," Smith reads the words down the right-hand side of the handout from the Queens Museum accompanying his lecture.*] So that the last lines—I haven't examined it at all—the last words say, "Will illness the to in from of film? Whatever! Maybe for as criticism 1978." The first two words—you can do this in a variety of ways.

I hate to say that I believe in God, see, or something. I'm a preacher these days. In fact, as I was coming over here some teenagers almost ran over me. Sometimes I get rather profane, and I said, "You goddamn sons of bitches, have you no respect for the clergy!?" [*Laughter.*] Well, yeah, I need a light on me because I don't want you... To get Schreber's statement... remember he was the equivalent of the head of the Prussian Supreme Court.[12] He begins to get systematic illusions, a lot of which he proves—such as, the bill at a certain asylum where he was for a while for piano keys he had busted while playing the piano was twelve thousand marks; at that point, he rented a log and another piano and hit the piano with the log and was unable to break the strings. A number of phenomenon described by Størmer such as the way that a bundle of energy enters the earth's magnetic field from the sun... He one day saw, when he was in a little cold room during a storm and a thing fell off on his head, a beam, and he saw all these lights.

This man is making a nice recording of this because I talk too fast and it always looks better when it's typed up. Now, I haven't looked at the book by Macalpine and Hunter, and... Of course, like any other scientific book, [*Memoirs of My Nervous Illness*] gives the number of the page of the original. Senate president Schreber eventually got out an elaborate series... You must remember that the specialized words he coins... Can we turn the projector on now? I thought I'd try reading part of the book in relation to the sound effects. This is page 139—[*"Heaven and Earth Magic" starts.*]

> After a few days the miraculous phenomena of which I have spoken were over; the sun assumed the shape she has had since then retained without interruption.
>
> [*The reference number for footnote 65 appears in the published text after "interruption," and Smith proceeds to read that footnote.*] By the way, even today the sun looks different to me than before my illness. Her rays before me turn toward me. I speak with a loud voice. I can look into the sun unperturbed. I am dazzled only very little, whereas in days of health, I, like other people [*Breaks off with the interjection:*] et cetera.
>
> [*Twenty second pause.*]
>
> [*Begins reading footnote 66.*] In the description of the appearance of the posterior gods of realm in the pure form I have followed exactly the idea I had formed at the time (in July and August 1894) from the impressions I received, and which I retained throughout the years. Thinking it over again today, it seems that I made a mistake in believing that the phenomena during the night were those only of the lower God (Ariman) and the phenomena in the daytime *only* those of the higher God (Ormuzd). This error is explained by the fact that I did not then recognize the signs of distinction which I *now* make between the rays of Ariman and the voices of Ariman, and the rays of Ormuzd and the voices of Ormuzd which for years of further uninterrupted contact: the first name I heard was "Ariman" which led me to believe that the whole influx of rays during the night described starlets in the lower God Ariman. But in the course of the years that have since passed there has *never* been a time without both the lower God and the upper God appearing alternately in the short intervals.

[*Audio from film continues for ninety seconds while Smith pauses in his reading.*] This is the published version which he published privately, was published in 1903.

> I can clearly recognize the genuine feeling expressed in these words in contrast to the phrases "drummed-into" their nerves (compare chapter 15 of the *Memoirs,* footnote 92) both by their effect—real voices do not cause me pain or any other damage but help to increase the soul-voluptuousness—and by their *sound,* and particularly by the *tempo* in which they are spoken. The genuine words follow with the rapidity peculiar to all nerves and become more distinct from the drummed-into phrases.[13]

Everybody's leaving in my general area. [*Laughter.*] You really should look at the movie. Well, naturally the oilcan turns into a hypodermic needle, the lady is given an injection of something, this is an alchemical symbol, that's a bottle of mercury, and time marches on.

Why mercury?

Because the three books are equivalent to sulfur, salt, and mercury, or what Newton calls the centrifugal force, the centripetal force, and the gravitational force. It has to do with the binomial encoding of information in the... I don't want a lot of people to leave. You can ask your questions later. Now they're leaving back there.

[*To photographer:*] Why don't you take pictures of the movie?

Is that her head?

Yeah, it's a drawing I made of a head. It doesn't represent ANYTHING!!! I have never looked at the film. Don't you understand that I... There's no reason to look at it—which is the second reason for asking you, "What were you doing here?" [*For the remainder of the talk, Smith is periodically drowned out by the film's sound track, that is, by the sounds of cows, trains, sirens, typewriters, Tibetan chimes, a variety of birds, coyotes, dogs, machines, electronics, cicadas, baby cries and gurgles, wind, chickens, conversations, and so forth.*]

[*Two minute twenty second pause.*]

All those things have transformed into their opposites at that flash that occurs.

[*Forty second pause.*]

Naturally, you know, the images that occur... They were clearer. This is a copy of a copy of a copy of a copy...

I have been working for the last eight years on the filming of Kurt Weill [and] Bertolt Brecht's opera [*Aufstieg und Fall der Stadt*] *Mahagonny,* which is infinitely more complicated than this. The photography was finished six years ago. It's shown on four screens that are the tops of billiard tables, inside a boxing ring, with very elaborate charts that have been built up for that.

Is it animation?

It's, of course, ten hours long. That means if it's shown on four screens, it only lasts two hours and twenty-eight minutes; and about half is pure animation and about half is shots of real persons: everybody from the Duchess of Windsor to Patti Smith and a lot of other people...

This film [*Heaven and Earth Magic*] had been in the Venice Biennial. Then it hitched up with something called the Museum of Obsessions. The main showing was at the Musée des arts decoratifs [in Paris].[14]

[*Mahagonny* has] never been shown. It's on computer cards and punch tape and very long diagrams, which correlate the frame numbers with the sound track, which is 16 mm film, only coated with iron oxide and stuff. It has like four different light shows around it. It is shown on stages of theaters. It requires five movie projectors.

This [*Heaven and Earth Magic*] of course requires three movie projectors and four slide projectors, plus projection behind and in front of the screen, plus Tibetan block prints hanging from the ceiling with spotlights on them. This was in Steinway Hall [in New York]...

So you originally had other things happening with it?

Oh yes! That's what I was trying to say before! It was in color and was a round picture, the edges were black, special matting stuff was put there. If I sound cranky—but if they ever type this up, I'll sound beneficent... [*Smith trying to sound beneficent:*] This was a circular image, controllable in density, hue, and chroma...

Here we are on Coney Island: the reconstruction of the multum in parvo. When this thing was first shown, I limited the audience only to six people... That avoids the... and a red rug running up to the screen. The person who got most of the other people interested in it was Van Wolf, who got [George] Huntington Hartford and Elizabeth Taylor and Henry Ogden Phipps III et cetera.[15] We then made an *Oz* film that cost about a million and a half dollars which is 35 mm wide-screen. The film is about eight hours long, you know.

Is that "The Tin Woodsman's Dream"? Is that around?

Well, that's a little part of it, yes... Well, I waited quite a while until the public was prepared to look at that, a lot more than the *Tin Woodsman's Dream* problem. I'm dealing with Casablanca Records and Filmworks right now. Of course, because this record on Mecca was... *The Wizard of Oz* is ideal to resynchronize the thing... Too much of it is dreamy, amorphous scenes. See, typical Coney Island, you know.

Did you record this? Or did you get sound effects records? How did you get the sound?

Sound effect records. They're the same ones that are on the Mecca line. It's the biggest sound effect company: Valentino [Production Music and Sound Effects Library].

Did you write to them saying I want a cat meowing or Coney Island?

No! No! You go to their office on 57th Street or 47th Street... I don't know... in the music section and ask them for their catalog, which is about a hundred and two pages. They carry five or six lines of sound effects cat sets. There's a very good British set... Then I had the discs transferred to acetate discs, two sets, that I played by hand—there were occasionally mistakes. Nobody thought it would work, see. Valentino Sound Effects. If you don't have that Mecca record of *The Wizard of Oz*, it's twenty-seven minutes long. I think it's commercially available. There's also a seventeen-minute one and a seven minute forty-five second one...

[*First reel of "Heaven and Earth Magic" ends.*]

Are we going to see the rest of the film?

I guess so. It's more or less a continuation of the same. Actually, Andy Warhol thought of that first—showing one on top of the other.[16] It was because the screen or the wall was that shape. Several of the better performances of this film have been, for example, one at Harvard had sort of pillars on each side: they're rounded you know, and the black-and-white films were projected on them, whereas color films that I had made much earlier, from about [1946 to 1957], they were drawn on film. I didn't have the money for a camera. I'm very poor. If anybody here has any money... [*Laughter.*] I tried to fix myself up, see. I had no time to... I have new string that I changed into shoelaces but I didn't have it today; instead, like that man here, he's the only person I knew that came here, and how I knew he came here is because he had been to the same place that I had, the Strand [bookstore].

Now, this book [Schreber's *Memoirs of My Nervous Illness*], on the other hand, being impossible to get—I bought it in 1950—this is when I started making this. As I explained, it used to be in color and was limited to six people only, the color projection apparatus at the time being extremely primitive. The dimmers of any sort wouldn't carry 1500 watts.

What about your backgrounds? They're all black.

Well, that was because... being as the original was projected in a round image—for example, a bubble or a watermelon, any of the objects that are here, a variety of shapes of rooms, designs derived from American Indian art, Siberian maybe, or Tibetan. I wouldn't think of using those things now, Tibet has been so overworked, and it's sort of a relief to see something from Cyprus. They do good sculpture there. [*Aside:*] *You should try to get that. Send it to* [*the*] *Cyclades at once.* So, in order to color the entire image you see that each one of these little things operates as an aperture, the same as in the light; then this had a train of color filters that went in front of it; three movie projectors, although it could be easily reduced to two; and then a screen somewhat larger than this but square was hung in front of white drapes that were especially lit; and a room which was in Steinway Hall had been painted entirely black except that one wall was entirely mirrors—it just happened to be that way, something like it was a dance school, Marilyn Miller or somebody like that, no, Nola Studios...

[*Break in the tape to turn over audiocassette.*]

...was then overlain by drawings of the seven main objects; and, of course, the image was much clearer. After I made it, I went to Oklahoma to record American Indian music. I made about three thousand recordings. I made a survey of an entire small town: Anadarko, Oklahoma. It's basically American Indian, but there are also a great number of black people which aren't in the audiences, but they keep throwing me into the offices where I can smoke. In the meantime, the landlord foreclosed the mortgage you see;[17] it's proof of everything working out all right, that a person accumulates too much stuff; it's very fortunate that very often [your possessions are] thrown out, because it gives you the inclination to work further. I'm constantly being given offers to go to the YMCA and make bookends shaped like sailfish. Nobody ever gives me a ticket to go to the Fontainebleau [Hotel in Miami Beach] or anything, so I make this stuff.

[*To sculptor:*] You're probably a pretty good sculptor, because you ask why is the background all black. That is like saying why is the box of plasticine or the lump of marble or granite that whatever you sculpt out of, although I suspect you use plastic and old brooms and mummy wrappings and things in bottles.

See, there's a limited number of people, except I've never seen any of them before, except that man [*points into the audience*] who studies Pythagorean mathematics and makes monochords. We did some interesting experiments recently with Sue Dallas from the city of the same name, by attaching diffraction gratings to one of the monochords, and then, how was that done? [*To the monochord maker:*] A mirror was...

A light was on the monochord and the filament went in.

What was your longest monochord? Forty feet?

Thirty.

That produces the natural harmonies that the... never mind.

I want to see the children's drawings... But I understand they take them all home. [*Laughter.*] They're ashamed that the teacher might have, you know, something like kinetic family drawings or something that really reveals that the kids have some kind of Freudian bit...

Do you do the Greek stuff too?... A lot of the pottery was broken. Since they originally put out the original bunch of the *Corpus Vasorum* [*Antiquorum*],[18] they reput the pieces all together in various improved shapes. Well, it's like art imitating nature. There are all these studies by [E.W.] Handley. The proportions of the Greek vases being the same two hundred and sixteen units the... whoever it is... Vitruvius says that[19]... It's a difficult word to translate: it either means "comic" or "tragic"; I've never been able to get over that.

What's the Greek word?

I don't know! It's Greek to me. The Loeb Classical Library translates the thing as "comic" and the art historian from Yale [University] whose thing is published by Cornell [University Press] translates it as "tragic"—or vice versa, I forget.[20] They can't agree on the word. The Greeks had a word for it but it covers a number of subjects. They translate the one word differently. You see, it depends on whether you consider Aristophanes to be comic or tragic. A play like *The Birds* represents the deepest aspects of Orphic [religion], Orpheus being the first of the philosophers. We being basically Aristotelian still, it seems impossible, but the same ideas of force and matter being... but as Gilbert and Sullivan say, "The meaning doesn't matter if it's only idle chatter of a transcendental kind."[21] I can cover this whole thing by quoting Gilbert and Sullivan also, or Bob Dylan, if you want that. The times they are changing,[22] and you should get the reel change.

[*To projectionist:*] I'd rather look at the color ones [*Early Abstractions*].

Certain effects that look good here were not intended. In other words, it was drawn on 35 mm film and the ink cracked. I was using Higgins Ink at the time, you see, I didn't have any more sense. Now it looks real crazy, because in the meanwhile... Jackson Pollock or somebody, I don't know who... [Jean] Dubuffet! Anyway, Wittgenstein says that ethics are equal to aesthetics, which really covers that, although from the Chomskyan sense, I have used the example of symbols being generated when philosophy is transformed into language. Like we're trying to talk to each other, but we're thinking in a manner that does not involve verbalization. Now the same thing has happened in art. The first film that you see here was made in 1939, forty years ago; you see, I spend most of my time writing and painting. The current film that I'm working on, which is *Mahagonny* by Kurt Weill and Bertolt Brecht—all these other things like *Happy End* and *The Threepenny Opera* having been written to produce money for *Mahagonny,* but it has never been produced; it's always a failure; it's *ideal* for me![23] Now that has been worked on actively for about eight years now, although the music analysis had taken place before that, of course. I had to memorize the entire score, have a number of translations made, and then do about forty hours of photography that took a number of years.

Do you play any musical instruments?

I don't know; I never tried. [*Laughter.*] Yes, I'm very good at the piano. In a mediocre way. If you explain that it's the latest thing recorded by Hugo Zemp and released by the 'Are'are that you got in northern New Guinea... the Solomon Islands.[24] It sounds good; it *is* good. It's like that French atonal thing. But at this point I'm interested in Central African polyphonic music, whale recordings from the Australian block, and a variety of things. I make lot of recordings.

What did you do with the American Indian music that you collected?

Well, six sides of that have come out which is called *Kiowa Peyote Ritual*[25] and another six sides are about to come out which is *A History of Kiowa Love Songs.*[26] That's twelve albums. It has very thick notes. It had very good reviews in both the *Journal of American Folklore* and *Ethnomusicology,* a magazine.[27] The *Journal of American Folklore* said it's a great album except that I didn't supply any peyote buttons with it. The guy from University of Oklahoma who reviews it for *Ethnomusicology* says that his peyotist friends said that it was the very best record to learn songs from. The main thing was that the recordings were all made on a much cheaper recording machine than *that* [*points to the machine recording his talk*] but were remastered carefully, which is part of a general plan I had so everybody will drag Grandpa Blah's home recordings out of the attic. In 1978 it's possible to change the consciousness in such a way that even blurry pictures [and] poorly recorded things sound all right if you're happy.

[*Projectionist:*] **Should we put on the film?**

This film [*Early Abstractions*] goes through a number of vicissitudes; it was originally made as a silent film, then I began playing [J. S.] Bach with it, being young and impressionable. I didn't see it for ten years. I couldn't raise enough money to get a print made. I finally had to build an optical printer in order to get satisfactory reductions. Then come the Beatles, so I slapped them on—out goes Bach—and then they become *unpopular.* There's a ghastly review in the *Village Voice:* What do you mean by showing this with this?[28] [It should have] archaic Dixieland jazz or something? Now the Beatles are popular again. I don't like them, I mean I haven't even listened to Wings, people keep trying to play it. The only time I've been out here, I came with my girlfriend to the Beatles concert in Shea Stadium in some particular year.[29] I couldn't stand it, the crowd was too big. However, Rosebud [Rosemarie Feliu-Pettet] stayed. She said, "We got in. You couldn't hear the music of course, but we got in." I said, "How did you get in?" She said, "We picked up the police barricades and knocked down the fence."

OK. These are films that are made approximately between [1946 and 1957]. The first one took a week that she's going to show; the last one took five years. You understand these are all drawn on the film.

Is this what you call batik film?

Oh, you read that thing too.[30] Yeah. The two best analyses of my films are a radio interview and... I might say I'm staring at City Hall, out of Boss Tweed's office, which has now been converted into the WNY[C] studio. I tell one lie on the record; you try to figure out which one it is. It's recently been printed.[31] That's the one on *Mahagonny,* that you're talking about. It describes how *Mahagonny* has been made. And the one that you're speaking about. In between there's an *Oz* film that I made. It cost about a million and a half dollars. Now, these are the batiked animations. The first one took a week; the third one took five years.

What time is it? Turn off the lights and show it. Make the music loud. At this point I really like Pink Floyd better though. And Led Zeppelin is going to be on in about four weeks...

It's out of focus!

[*Parts of the remainder of the talk drowned out by the sound track of "Early Abstractions," the album "Meet the Beatles!"* (Capitol Records, 1964).]

...basically the heart beating at seventy-two times a minute and the respiration occurring at about thirteen times per minute, so that those produce counterpoints that probably at least 80 percent of the music produced in the world (and I include Outer Mongolia and Tierra del Fuego) will synchronize automatically with this. Actually, the film was made twenty years before there were any Beatles.

This [*Film #3: Interwoven*] was originally with a Dizzy Gillespie thing ["Guarachi Guaro"]. It shows the three converting into the four, I mean vice versa. This is the one that took five years. I'll never try that again! This is little pieces of masking tape stuck to the film. Those were the four colors representing earth, air, fire, and water. Which don't refer to those substances but refer to... I don't know. What? Something to do with spring, red-fired oxidizing pottery from about 3,500 years B.C.,...

What type of ink did you use? Did you use india inks?

These are dyes that were got in Hollywood; the Whitney brothers [John and James] got them for me. They were matched exactly in the final prints. But, of course, the originals have all been lost. The colors were really good in the originals. It *still* is good. They were real saturated.

Of course there isn't any real perfect synchronization, but it comes out pretty good.

Notes

1. Harry Smith, "Queens Museum, November 11, 1978," *Cinemanews*, no. 78-6/79-1 (1979): 3–5, 27; accompanying this transcription were three illustrations reproduced from William G. Niederland, *The Schreber Case: Psycho-analytic Profile of a Paranoid Personality* (New York: Quadrangle/New York Times, 1974), 54 (fig. 6), 81 (fig. 10), 95 (fig. 11)—all taken, in turn, from works by Daniel Gottlob Moritz Schreber; see Michelson, this volume, figs. 5, 6, 8, respectively.
2. Tibor Doby, *Discoverers of Blood Circulation, from Aristotle to the Times of Da Vinci and Harvey* (London: Abelard-Schuman, 1963).
3. In 1969, Smith spoke of Christian Freiherr Knorr von Rosenroth's *The Kabbalah Unveiled*, trans. and ed. S. L. MacGregor Mathers (London: G. Redway, 1887; reprint, London: Routledge & K. Paul, 1951); Daniel Paul Schreber's *Memoirs of My Nervous Illness*, trans. and ed. Ida Macalpine and Richard A. Hunter (London: Wm. Dawson, 1955); and the writings of Wilder Penfield as the prime sources for *Heaven and Earth Magic*. See P. Adams Sitney, *Visionary Film: The American Avant-Garde, 1943–2000*, 3rd ed. (New York: Oxford Univ. Press, 2002), 250–55.

   At the beginning of P. Adams Sitney's radio interview with Harry Smith, broadcast on 3 June 1977 on WNYC-FM, and published as Harry Smith, "On *Mahagonny*," interview by P. Adams Sitney, in P. Adams Sitney, ed., *The Avant-Garde Film: A Reader of Theory and Criticism* (New York: New York Univ. Press, 1978), 103–9, Smith listed as works that he assumed "the radio audience is familiar with" Claude Lévi-Strauss's *The Raw and the Cooked,* trans. John Weightman and Doreen Weightman (New York: Harper & Row, 1969); Noam Chomsky's *Aspects of the Theory of Syntax* (Cambridge: MIT Press, 1965); and an unnamed book by Ludwig Wittgenstein as his sources. In that opening statement, Smith misidentifies *Aspects of the Theory of Syntax* as Chomsky's doctoral dissertation for the University of Pennsylvania, *Transformational Analysis* (Ann Arbor, Mich.: University Microfilms, 1955), eventually published as *The Logical Structure of Linguistic Theory* (New York: Plenum, 1975); his dissertation and the later book were based on a much longer manuscript, "The Logical Structure of Linguistic Theory" (Massachusetts Institute of Technology, June 1955, typescript, 919 pages), that has been microfilmed by Harvard College Library and is now available from http://alpha-leonis.lids.mit.edu/chomsky (accessed 22 August 2008).

4. Carl Størmer, *The Polar Aurora* (Oxford: Clarendon, 1955).
5. Wilder Penfield and Herbert H. Jasper, *Epilepsy and the Functional Anatomy of the Human Brain* (Boston: Little, Brown, 1954).
6. See Sigmund Freud, "Psycho-analytic Notes on an Autobiographical Account of a Case of Paranoia (Dementia Paranoides) (1911)," trans. Alix Strachey and James Strachey, in idem, *The Standard Edition of the Complete Psychological Works of Sigmund Freud,* vol. 12, *The Case of Schreber, Papers on Technique and Other Works (1911–1913),* gen. ed. James Strachey (London: Hogarth), 9–82; and Noël Carroll, "Mind, Medium, and Metaphor in Harry Smith's *Heaven and Earth Magic,*" *Film Quarterly* 31, no. 2 (1977–78): 37–44.
7. Here Smith refers to the bibliography with which he opened his radio interview with Sitney on 3 June 1977; see Smith, "On *Mahagonny*" (note 3), 103.
8. In Ludwig Wittgenstein's *Tractatus Logico-Philosophicus,* proposition 1.1 is "Die Welt ist die Gesamtheit der Tatsachen, nicht der Dinge"; see Ludwig Wittgenstein, *Tractatus Logico-Philosophicus,* trans. D. F. Pears and B. F. McGuinness (London: Routledge, 1961), 5: "The world is the totality of facts, not of things." Wittgenstein finished the *Tractatus* (1921) in August 1918, while serving in the Austrian artillery, and the manuscript was sent to Bertrand Russell while its author was in an Italian prison camp at Monte Cassino.
9. The movie *Thank God It's Friday* was produced by Casablanca Filmworks and released in the United States on 19 May 1978 in New York City. By 1978, "the Hilton Hotel chain was converting its unfashionable bars into trendy new discos," according to Dave Thompson, *Funk* (San Francisco: Backbeat, 2001), 290; see also Albert Goldman, "The Delirium of Disco," *Life Magazine,* November 1978, 42–52.
10. Daniel Gottlob Moritz Schreber, *Medical Indoor Gymnastics; or, A System of Hygienic Exercises for Home Use . . . ,* ed. Rudolf Graefe, trans. Herbert A. Day (London: Williams & Norgate, 1899).
11. The song "25 Minutes to Go," written by Shel Silverstein, appeared on the album *Johnny Cash Sings the Ballads of the True West* (Columbia Records, 1965).
12. He was the Senatspräsident (presiding judge) of the Oberlandesgericht Dresden

(High Court of Appeals) in Dresden for the kingdom of Saxony, which was then part of the German Empire, as was the kingdom of Prussia (which included the province of Saxony).

13. Daniel Paul Schreber's *Denkwürdigkeiten eines Nervenkranken*... (Leipzig: Oswald Mutze, 1903) was translated by Ida Macalpine and Richard A. Hunter as *Memoirs of My Nervous Illness* (note 3). Smith's reading starts on page 126 of the *Memoirs,* which corresponds to page 139 in the *Denkwürdigkeiten,* according to the numbers in the margins of the *Memoirs.* Then he reads most of footnote 65 on page 126 of the *Memoirs,* half of footnote 66, and a passage from page 235 (*Denkwürdigkeiten,* page 328), which is from a postscript titled "Concerning the Nature of God." The text as rendered by Smith differs very slightly from the wording in the *Memoirs;* these differences in wording are probably mistakes or ad lib variations by Smith.
14. *Heaven and Earth Magic* was shown at the Venice Biennale in 1975, as part of Harald Szeemann's exhibition *Junggesellenmaschinen/Les Machines célibataires* (Bachelor machines), which between 1975 and 1977 traveled from Bern to Venice, Brussels, Düsseldorf, Paris, Malmö, Amsterdam, and Vienna. The catalog for this exhibition bears on its opening page the notations "3 Museum der Obsessionen 3" and "3 Musée des obsessions 3."

    After Documenta V (Kassel, 1972), Szeemann proposed an imaginary museum, the so-called Museum of Obsessions, for which he "settled on three fundamental themes, metaphors that had to be given visual form: the Bachelor, la Mamma, and the Sun"; see Hans-Ulrich Obrist, "Mind over Matter," *Artforum,* November 1996, 112, 119.
15. Van Wolf served as promotion director for Mike Todd's film *Around the World in 80 Days* (United Artists, 1956); see "Van Wolf, 45, Producer and Ex-Theater Executive," *New York Times,* 23 March 1972, 46. Elizabeth Taylor was married to Todd from February 1957 until his death in March 1958.
16. Smith may be referring to Andy Warhol's ★★★★ (*Four Stars*), shown 15–16 December 1967 at the New Cinema Playhouse in New York City; see Amy Taubin, "★★★★," in Colin MacCabe with Mark Francis and Peter Wollen, eds., *Who Is Andy Warhol?* (London: British Film Institute, 1997), 23–24, 27.
17. During Smith's extended trip to Oklahoma (1964–65), he neglected to pay the rent on his apartment in New York City. The landlords, rumored to be a pair of Hungarian midgets, reportedly threw out all Smith's belongings. The garbage was believed to have been sent to a landfill on Staten Island or in New Jersey. Efforts were made to locate the materials, but they were never found. See Lionel Ziprin, "Lionel Ziprin—May and June 1993," interview by Paola Igliori, compiled with previous interview by Clayton Patterson with K. K., in Paola Igliori, ed., *American Magus Harry Smith: A Modern Alchemist* (New York: Inanout, 1996), 51–52.
18. Begun in 1923, the Union académique internationale's *Corpus Vasorum Antiquorum* is an ongoing international project that, as of 2008, has published in some three hundred fascicules of text and plates an estimated 100,000 examples of ceramic vessels surviving from classical antiquity (circa 6000 B.C.–400 A.D.).
19. For the 216 "units," see Vitruvius, *De architectura* 5.*praef.*3–5.
20. Smith is referencing the translation of the Latin phrase "graeci... poetae comici"

(Vitruvius, *De architectura* 5.*praef*.4) correctly as "Greek dramatic poets" by George L. Hersey in his *Pythagorean Palaces: Magic and Architecture in the Italian Renaissance* (Ithaca: Cornell Univ. Press, 1976), 123, and erroneously as "Greek comic poets" in Vitruvius, *The Ten Books on Architecture,* trans. Morris Hicky Morgan (1914; reprint, New York: Dover, 1960), 130. Hersey was a professor in the Department of the History of Art at Yale University from 1963 to 1998.

21. This is a line from the song in Reginald Bunthorne's recitative and solo "Am I Alone and Unobserved?" in act 1 of W. S. Gilbert and Arthur Sullivan's comic opera *Patience or Bunthorne's Bride* (1881).
22. Smith is referencing the title (and title track) of Bob Dylan's third album, *The Times They Are A-Changin'* (Columbia Records, 1964).
23. Brecht and Weill's *Die Dreigroschenoper* (1928; *The Threepenny Opera*) was an immediate success, although their *Happy End* (1929) closed after a few performances. *Aufstieg und Fall der Stadt Mahagonny* (1930; *Rise and Fall of the City of Mahagonny*) had received several notable productions in Europe since its premiere in Leipzig in March 1930, so Smith's claim of it never being performed successfully is puzzling—unless he is pointing out that the opera had received, as of 1978, only one short-lived production in the United States or, perhaps, that the *Mahagonny Songspiel* had never been produced successfully since its premiere in 1927 or, more remotely, that Smith's own *Mahagonny* had not yet been screened.
24. Daniel de Coppet and Hugo Zemp, *'Are'are: Un peuple mélanésien et sa musique; avec des textes 'are'are et un disque* (Paris: Editions du Seuil, 1978), preceded by some nine LPs of recordings issued between 1971 and 1973 of music by Solomon Island societies; see Jane Mink Rossen, review of *Polyphonies des Îles Salomon,* recordings by Hugo Zemp, *Ethnomusicology* 23 (1979): 473–75.
25. *The Kiowa Peyote Meeting* (recorded 1964–65), a three-LP set with a twelve-page booklet by Smith, was released in 1973 by Folkways Records as Ethnic Folkways Library album no. FE 4601.
26. *A History of Kiowa Love Songs* was to be released on Folkways Records but was never completed.
27. David Evans, "North American Indian Music," *Journal of American Folklore* 90 (1977): 369; and James H. Howard, review of *The Kiowa Peyote Meeting,* recording and commentary by Harry Smith, *Ethnomusicology* 19 (1975): 330–31.
28. Jonas Mekas, "Movie Journal," *Village Voice,* 29 June 1967, 25. Mekas was not so much taking Smith to task for using music by the Beatles as his sound track as he was critiquing American and European audiences and critics for wishing all avant-garde films to similarly "swing" or otherwise amuse.
29. The Beatles played Shea Stadium twice, on 15 August 1965 and 23 August 1966.
30. "Smith, Harry," *Film-Makers' Cooperative Catalogue,* no. 3 (1965): 57.
31. On 3 June 1977, Sitney interviewed Smith on his monthly *Arts Forum* radio program for WNYC-FM; for an edited and annotated transcription of that broadcast, see Smith, "On *Mahagonny*" (note 3). The offices of WNYC are still located in the Municipal Building at 1 Centre Street, across from New York City's City Hall.

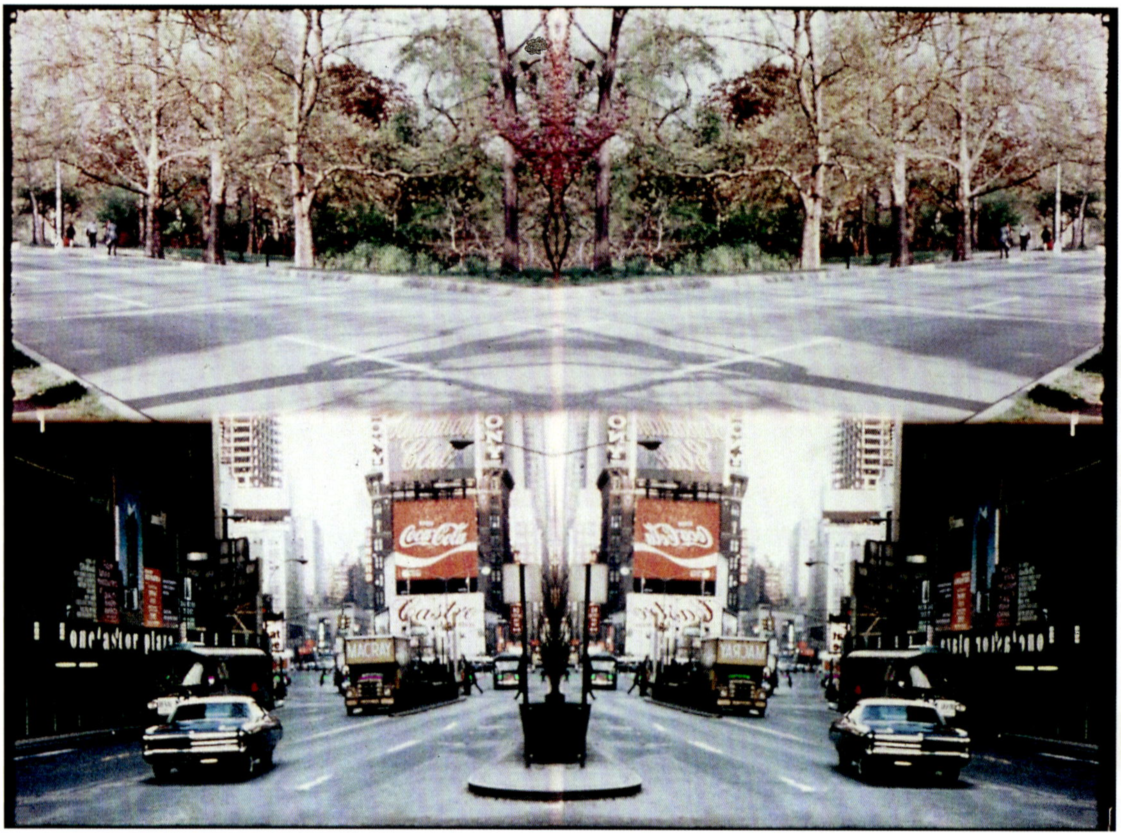
Coca-Cola
MACRAY

PART III
Mahagonny

PAUL ARTHUR

THE ONUS OF REPRESENTATION: Harry Smith, *Mahagonny*, and Avant-Garde Film in the 1970s

According to the published transcript, the talk given by Harry Smith prior to a screening of his *Film #12: Heaven and Earth Magic* at the Queens Museum of Art in 1978 was a typically tumultuous affair: sprinkled with lengthy digressions, hostile exchanges involving members of the audience, and the random interjection of recorded sound effects.[1] At one point, Smith broke off reading from the English translation of Daniel Paul Schreber's infamous *Denkwürdigkeiten eines Nervenkranken* (Memoirs of a mental patient), a 1903 account of the German jurist's deranged thoughts while incarcerated in various hospitals, to continue his comments on the significance of images being projected in the auditorium:

> Everybody's leaving in my general area. [*Laughter.*] You really should look at the movie. Well, naturally the oilcan turns into a hypodermic needle, the lady is given an injection of something, this is an alchemical symbol, that's a bottle of mercury, and time marches on.
>
> ***Why mercury?***
>
> Because the three books are equivalent to sulfur, salt, and mercury, or what Newton calls the centrifugal force, the centripetal force, and the gravitational force. It has to do with the binomial encoding of information in the… I don't want a lot of people to leave. You can ask your questions later…
>
> ***Is that her head?***
>
> Yeah, it's a drawing I made of a head. It doesn't represent ANYTHING!!! I have never looked at the film. Don't you understand that I… There's no reason to look at it—which is the second reason for asking you, "What were you doing here?"

The transcriber then notes: "*talk… periodically drowned out… by the sounds of cows, trains, sirens, typewriters, Tibetan chimes, a variety of birds, coyotes, dogs, machines, electronics, cicadas, baby cries and gurgles, wind, chickens, conversations, and so forth.*"[2] The slides and sound fragments accompanying the filmmaker's introduction were likely extracted from the work about to be screened; his attempts at annotating key iconographic allusions and scholarly influences harbor, at the least, a mixture of genuine edification and aggressive obscurantism that is consistent with Smith's overarching career, not just in cinema but in a spectrum of interlocking cultural pursuits.

Lacking any further testimony—of which there is, in fact, an abundance—it would seem foolhardy to designate the artistic sensibility displayed here as an

Page 128
Harry Smith
Still from *Film #18: Mahagonny*, 1970–80 (restored 2002), 141 min., 35 mm, color, sound

Page 129
Harry Smith
Book-page border design, 1988
Harry Smith Archives

exemplar, or avatar, of avant-garde cinema's reigning visual practices and its institutional prerogatives during a period of unprecedented growth. Nonetheless, despite an extravagant reputation as a contrarian, Smith was no recluse. He had a host of film-world friends and acquaintances, attended screenings by colleagues in the movement, and, judging from interviews, possessed a tolerably eccentric grasp of film history. He freely acknowledged the technical guidance provided by pioneers such as John Whitney and claimed a disparate aesthetic heritage encompassing surrealism, Native American artifacts, and Thelonious Monk. Yet as someone who disseminated conflicting versions of his childhood background and refused to supply films with fixed dates of completion—although the term *completion* is problematic here—it is hardly surprising that Smith did not actively collaborate with other filmmakers, disdained the widespread custom of group film programs, and took no role in the launching or administering of the avant-garde cinema's flourishing network of artist-run distribution and exhibition venues. Iconoclastic even by the relaxed standards of postwar American bohemians, Smith's early films confound established avant-garde categories of style while his storied social aversions can be addressed as the flipside of his passionate commitment to vernacular, demotic idioms in music, textiles, and other modes of cultural production.

A lifelong student of hermetic philosophical disciplines, he joined no discernible causes or public campaigns. He gained initial notoriety as a filmmaker during the rebellious 1960s, yet his career evinces a stubborn resistance to the demands of collective participation—hence to the burdens of *representing anything*, much less generational ideals associated with a boisterously profane film movement quickly grown too large, too "organized," for his tastes. Still, all evidence to the contrary notwithstanding, there are in his final film certain symptomatic convergences that cast *Film #18: Mahagonny* as a signal achievement in the avant-garde cinema of the 1970s. That *Mahagonny* has failed to receive the kind of critical attention garnered by, say, Ernie Gehr's *Serene Velocity* or Hollis Frampton's *Zorns Lemma* (both 1970) is attributable perhaps to a paucity of public exposure (due largely to the film's technical demands), to the difficulty of the operatic score by Bertolt Brecht and Kurt Weill, and to the film's ostensible immunity from the period's heated theoretical controversies. Although its arc of production spans the decade—it was shot between 1970 and 1972, then edited continuously until its release in 1980—*Mahagonny* at first glance appears out of step, decidedly unrepresentative of its era, a case of recondite obsession fueling a self-fulfilling prophecy of misunderstanding and neglect.

From our current vantage, that judgment seems shortsighted at best, insensitive not only to social and material conditions surrounding the film's genesis but to bracing contradictions informing its aesthetic design. For starters, *Mahagonny* is identified by Smith as a broadly allegorical tale of human liberty and its discontents "translated" into a universal image-language.[3] What appears on-screen, however, is unmistakably site specific and historically resonant, providing viewers with vivid documentation of a loosely knit New York City subculture, resembling a fragmented update of Andy Warhol's *The Chelsea Girls* (1966). Similarly, Smith announced that *Mahagonny* would "introduce a new theoretical basis for films,"[4] yet, regardless of the originality of its approach, the film is at once a culmination of notional principles manifest in Smith's earlier projects and a late, admittedly offbeat example of the minimalist principles undergirding a prominent swath of visual culture in the 1970s. A work of unique demands and exacting requirements for theatrical presentation, it is paradoxically devoted to the metatextual interpretation of a canonical piece of operatic theater; moreover, its insularity does not prevent recognition of a variety of salient cinematic intertexts, from Walther Ruttmann's *Berlin: Die Sinfonie der Großstadt* (1927) to Francis Thompson's *N.Y., N.Y.* (1957). For the purposes of this discussion, then, the aura of crackpot eccentricity surrounding Smith's grand opus cannot vitiate the terms of a sinewy temporal engagement.

I

Until the arrival of a spate of avant-garde New Narrative and essay films in the early 1980s,[5] a crucial, if largely unspoken, desire of American experimental cinema was to operate beyond the bounds of history, forging a realm of creative expression that elided acknowledgment of a shared social past. This aspiration was of course impossible, a supreme fiction, but the chain of reciprocal assertions and disavowals it set in motion became a powerful agent in the revaluation of cinema under the sign of personal imagination. History, the official record of "objective" events, was understood to be complicit with linear narrative—twin forces geared to the regulation, if not total suppression, of subjective perception of the world. Predictably, efforts to circumvent the inscription of a verifiable past acquired their own historical shape, reaching a watershed in the late 1960s as post-Romantic avant-garde lyricism met an oncoming wave of rationalized, antipoetic exercises labeled by P. Adams Sitney as "structural film."[6] In other words, Stan Brakhage encountered Michael Snow at the crossroads of cinematic *presentness,* that galvanizing promise of an autonomous image freed from obligations of verbal language and its baggage of external authority, causality, and closure. The seemingly opposing sides, loosely restated as advocates of metaphoric montage versus advocates of systemic shaping, shared a common goal of bracketing cinema's field of signification in such a way that self-reference, or formal tautology, took precedence over photographic mimesis—hence the manner in which images were recorded and organized was deemed more important than the depiction of social realities. History as it is usually addressed became that which turned the moving picture away from itself.

A corollary to the avant-garde's quest for temporal immediacy is what I have called the "first film/last film" syndrome, a practice related to but somewhat distinct from Sitney's notion of "the absolute film."[7] It is evident in disparate stylistic guises in different historical periods but achieved perhaps its clearest, most concentrated expression during the 1970s. The basic impulse, blending elements of utopian modernism with the despair of cultural marginality, is to make a film that supersedes all previous instances of a given theme or visual approach. In doing so, it positions itself outside the process of historical incorporation, as either the last possible film in a line of development or, alternatively, a film so primordial in method or imagery that no prior work of the same species is conceivable. While a last film tries to calibrate cinema's imaginary posthistory, a first film is engaged in conjuring the

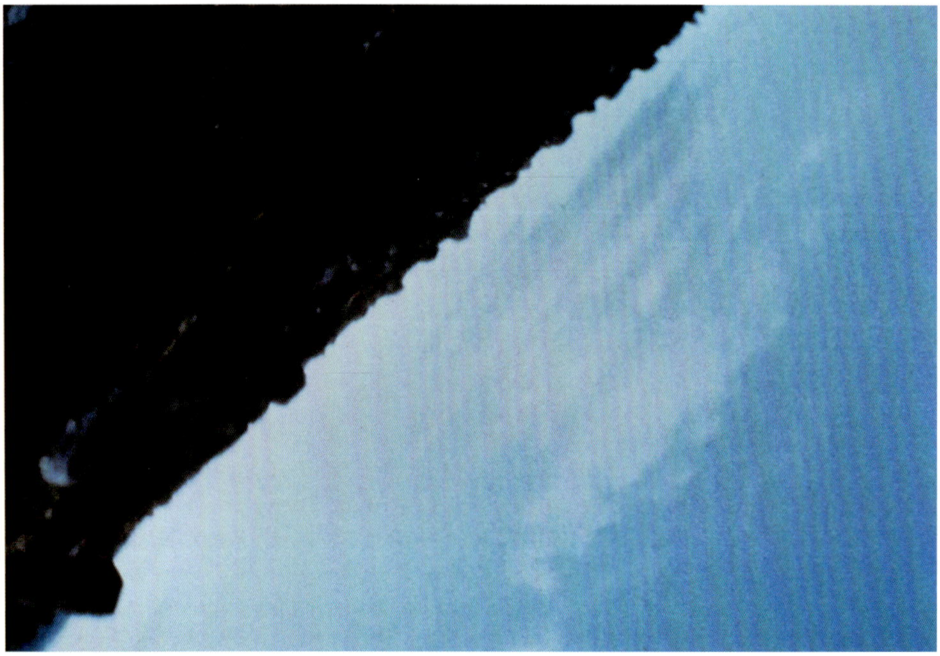

Fig. 1.
Michael Snow (Canadian, b. 1928)
Still from *La région centrale,* 1970–71, 180 min., 16 mm, color, sound

medium's prehistory. In both trajectories, the horizon of "ultimate statement" is often tied to radical applications of standard movie technologies, reminding us of the fragility and circumscribed history of cinema in an increasingly digitalized era.

Michael Snow said of Ernie Gehr's *History* (1970), a movie of film-grain patterns shot with a lensless camera: "At last, the first film!"[8] The same observation could be directed at Tony Conrad's *The Flicker* (1966), Brakhage's *The Text of Light* (1974), or some of Ken Jacobs's double-projector "Nervous System" performances of the late 1970s. Harry Smith's hand-drawn and batiked animations, made between roughly 1946 and 1950, constitute a slightly less reductive version of first film (see pp. 25, 35, 43, 66).[9] The idea of stripping the medium down to its essential properties, using strategies such as etching images directly on film stock or otherwise bypassing photographic processes, intersects Smith's preoccupation with gestures of purification, the alchemy of creating something out of nothing. Indeed, his earliest works—despite bows to Hans Richter and, especially, Oskar Fischinger—are explicitly atavistic in purpose and execution; for instance, the filmmaker helpfully described *Film #1: A Strange Dream* as "the history of the geologic period reduced to orgasm length."[10] His vagueness over dates of completion can be read not just as personal idiosyncrasy but as ambivalence about entering the stream of (codified, evaluative) film history, an anxiety amplified in avant-garde circles of the 1970s by conspicuous trappings of institutional prosperity: expanding governmental and private funding sources; relative stability in nonprofit distribution and exhibition; increased critical coverage in mainstream film and art journals; founding of Anthology Film Archives; publication of Sitney's *Visionary Film,* the first scholarly study of the movement. There is arguably a connection between the tentative promise of cultural viability and the eschatological overtones that shadow both first film and last film, with threats of artistic invisibility or obsolescence taking on heightened urgency with the pressure of added resources and competition.

At the other end of the historical spectrum, as it were, the copious examples of last film offer a clear index of both the decade's rising expectations and, conversely, its hints of imminent collapse. For filmmakers such as Snow and Frampton, perceptions of an unprecedented opening elicited a series of ambitious "final" statements. Attempting to exhaust the possibilities of a predetermined scheme or formal operation, a last film frequently took the form of an encyclopedic survey or an accretion of data. Hence, Snow's *La région centrale* (1970–71) displays the sinuous permutations of computer-controlled nonlinear camera movement (fig. 1); he followed that epic landscape film with a rigorous dissection of the relations between sound and image in *Rameau's Nephew by Diderot (Thanx to Dennis Young) by Wilma Schoen* (1974). Viewers felt at the time that the formal issues addressed by Snow would require no further explication. For his part, Frampton adopted a set of simple numerical formulas in *Zorns Lemma*'s breakneck tour of New York City's signage (fig. 2). He went on to design a gigantic film cycle, the unfinished *Magellan* (1972–84), dedicated to the cinematic friction between movement and stillness. Brakhage, who had stretched the limits of layered superimposition with *The Art of Vision* (1961–65), created what might stand as the avant-garde's ultimate poetic autobiography in his eight-part *Sincerity/Duplicity* (1973–80). Owen Land chimed in with an intricate parody announcing itself as the "last" structural film: *On the Marriage Broker Joke as Cited by Sigmund Freud in "Wit and Its Relation to the Unconscious" or Can the Avant-Garde Artist Be Wholed?* (1977–79). Interestingly, the flow of last film tailed off during the 1980s as stylistic paradigms shifted and public funding for independent films began to decline.

Fig. 2.
Hollis Frampton (American, 1936–84)
Still from *Zorns Lemma*, 1970, 60 min., 16 mm, color, sound

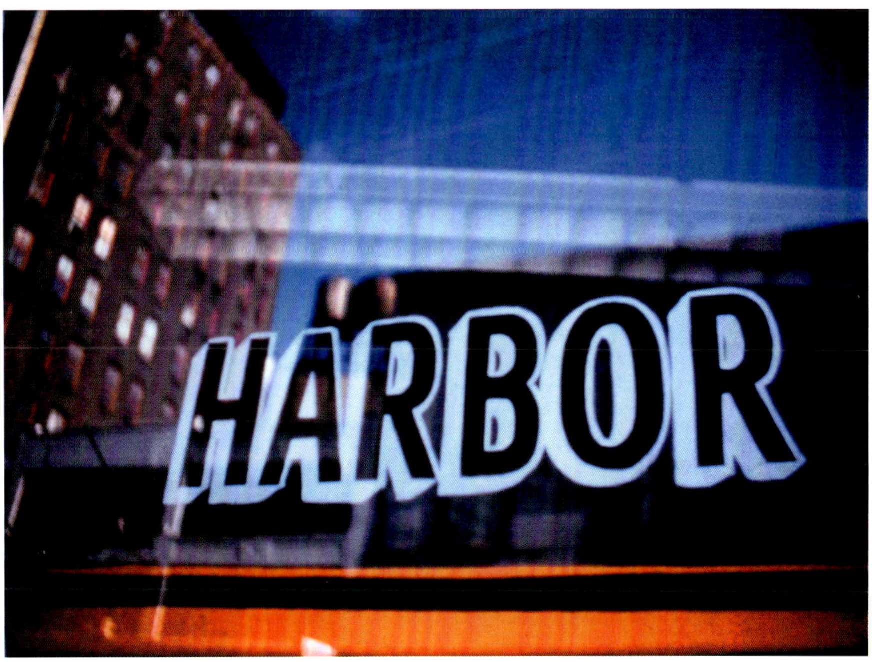

For Sitney, the original conception of *Heaven and Earth Magic* "exemplifies the myth of the absolute film in its expansive form."[11] It is a last film in the sense that is difficult to imagine a work of cutout animation capable of sustaining a more elaborate or replete sequence of visual transformations.[12] *Mahagonny,* a project fantasized by Smith for at least twenty years, merits inclusion in the category of last film on various counts. Formally, the film lays out permutations involving the rhythmic dynamics within a four-screen grid of images. Confirming Smith's declaration that the film would subsume every previous accomplishment in the medium, the long and bumpy course of *Mahagonny*'s production has all the hallmarks of a valediction—or a personal monument boasting an architecture of transient light patterns rather than bricks and mortar. Indeed, architecture is a key visual motif in the film, while the space of its projection may be construed as a sort of foursquare architectural model. Not incidentally, *Mahagonny* can likely claim the final word—the only word?—on nondramatic adaptation of opera.

The scale of Smith's labor- and capital-intensive enterprise required an unusual degree of financial assistance from public and private institutions, as well as help from friends and individual patrons. He solicited funds from at least a half-dozen sources, and although the narrative and budgetary components of different proposals are similar, the documents point to a level of psychological and creative investment in the film's monetary affairs that borders on the symbolic.[13] Quite simply, the treacherous economy mobilized for the film's production was not only instrumental. It was also isomorphic with major themes in Brecht's text, specifically the circulation of money and its malign role in the struggle for human fulfillment; as Brecht's libretto (in Michael Feingold's translation) states,

> In the whole human race
> There is no greater criminal
> Than a man without money.[14]

For Smith, the imagined risks entailed by the *Mahagonny* project mirrored those experienced by characters in the opera, especially the cynical "founders" of the city, for whom "It's easier to get gold out of men than out of rivers!"[15] Establishing the *on-screen* city depended on immersion in the always tricky cultural politics of arts funding. Yet the potential rewards could magically elevate Smith from a life of impoverished obscurity. During an interview in 1993, Lionel Ziprin spoke at length about the filmmaker's paranoid, often self-destructive yet relentless concern with wealthy patronage and entrepreneurial success: "That's all he talked about, was how to make millions."[16]

Sitney argues that Smith's preparations for *Heaven and Earth Magic*—the discovery and cataloging of paper collage elements, the testing of image combinations, and so on—proved nearly as satisfying as the completed film, itself characterized by repeated acts of preparation: "Alchemical texts tend to read like endless recipes of purification, firemaking, etc. The commitment to preliminaries is so strong that in its spiritual interpretation, alchemy becomes the slow perfection of the alchemist; the accent shifts from goals to processes."[17] A similar shift is apparent in the far more complicated plans around *Mahagonny,* except that Smith's focus was on vicissitudes of exchange among social subjects instead of the redemption of individual consciousness through private ritual. That is, just as Brecht and Weill's opera centered on the public repercussions of private moral degradation in a blatantly commodified urban setting, Smith seemed to treat the process of adaptation—despite a mischievous layer of self-parody—as a means of transforming private fetish into marketable commodity. At the same time, as the opera makes clear, the bonding of pleasure and money augurs inevitable disaster in the form of collective, as well as individual, misery. Smith might even have grasped the self-negating consequences of his pursuit as an analog to the last film syndrome. In a letter in support of a grant application, he proclaimed: "You have to live Mahagonny, in fact *be* Mahagonny in order to work on it. Thus it is that it became more convenient and cheaper to set up a cutting [table] where I live than to rent one. I can also arrange things in the room like the city of Mahagonny itself."[18] Just as he turned his living space into a de facto architect's studio, into a blueprint for the *filmic* city he wished to build, he converted practically every social encounter, every piece of correspondence, into a marker of success or failure in an all-consuming system of production.

II

Paracinema—or, in Gene Youngblood's appellation, "expanded cinema"—manifests close historical parallels with objectives and methodologies associated with the avant-garde's "absolutist" tendency. Admittedly, many primal and endgame films take a straightforward approach to the technology of image display, that is, single-screen standard projection with a fixed running time. A provocative group, however, chooses to conjoin ultimate formal statements with alterations to one or several portions of the viewing apparatus, including how theater space is deployed. The most conspicuous strategies involve changing the dimensions or projection properties of the screen or adding performative elements that intervene in the mechanical flow. Among the earliest traces of paracinematic activity were the Vortex Concerts held in San Francisco's Morrison Planetarium between 1957 and 1960, events conducted (with composer Henry Jacobs) by Smith's longtime friend Jordan Belson. Blending music with colored-light projections and snippets from abstract films by Belson, James Whitney, and Hy Hirsh, the concerts immersed the audience in a three-dimensional, semi-improvised multimedia environment in which film neither dominated nor was subjugated to instrumental or vocal rhythms.[19]

Following Fischinger and others, in the 1940s Smith explored the potential for "visual" music—and through it the venerable dream of synthesizing distinct art forms (for which opera has served as the traditional signpost)—by creating a series of abstract paintings, and then short films, cued to recordings by Dizzy Gillespie, Charlie Parker, and Thelonious Monk, an idiom supposedly derived from note-by-note transcription and formal musical analysis (see pp. 26, 195, 198).[20] Although the staggered temporality of movie production militates against direct, immediate synchronicity between music and cinematography, Smith would eventually discover means of transferring other desiderata of performance into the ritual of projection.

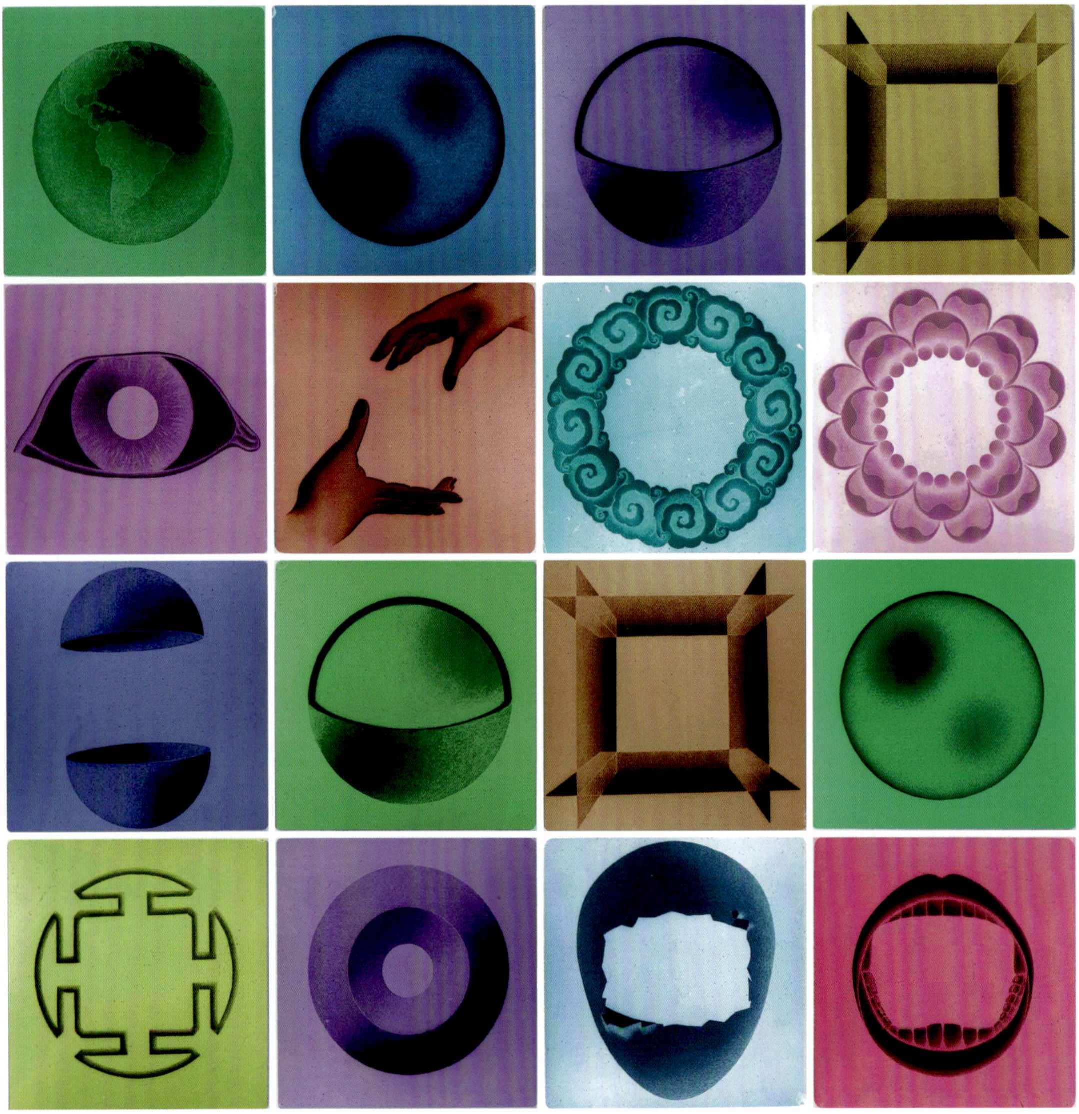

Fig. 3.
Harry Smith
Frame filters for use during the projection of *Film #12: Heaven and Earth Magic*
Harry Smith Archives

In the early 1960s, his original version of *Heaven and Earth Magic* was said to change with each showing according to the varying manipulation of colored gels to tint the film image, slides projected at the borders of the movie screen (fig. 3), and symbolic ornaments hung around the screen.[21] Smith's spontaneous interplay with the movie image frayed viewers' perceptions of textual closure as it deflected film's irreducible status as commercial object. The blurring of distinctions between the time (and space) of a diegetic movie world and that of actual spectators was wielded as a powerful tool in cultural innovations of the late 1960s and 1970s, including disparate metafilmic projects by Warhol, Ken Jacobs, Jack Smith, Paul Sharits, and Tony Conrad. Similar processes of mediumistic expansion were occurring in cutting-edge theater, dance, and sculpture. The sign of avant-garde film's momentary convergence with art world polemics may be Michael Fried's famous denunciation of minimalist sculpture as overly "theatrical," as dependent for its aesthetic impact upon the actions of individual viewers under site-specific conditions.[22] For filmmakers, a logical maneuver was to obliterate the passive, authoritarian model of screen image and viewer by redeploying projection in specially constructed environments or gallery installations that allowed for individualized encounters.

Yet another vector of paracinema saw nonnarrative film clips emerge as a mainstay in rock concert light shows and other "psychedelic" tokens of 1960s counterculture. David E. James elegantly summarizes a fundamental assumption of expanded cinema. "This opening of the optical field, and the conceptual and kinetic liberation of the spectator within it, was often construed as either analogous to or premonitory of some paradigmatic genetic shift" in the manipulation of human consciousness through art.[23] Even if Harry Smith never entirely bought into the counterculture's liberatory rhetoric—his celebration of drug experience as integral to the creative process notwithstanding—his design for the physical spectacle of *Mahagonny* tapped into a sizable vein of efflorescent cultural activity: the string of transformations that begins with Smith's translation of written text into film images continues through the final stage of exhibition, where conventional postures in relation to the moving image are altered not only by the demands of the four-screen grid but by Smith's stipulation that the film be shown on the tops of four interlocked billiard tables enclosed in a boxing ring.[24] Of greater interest than the financial infeasibility of such a setup is its implication that the viewer is invited to move about the projection space in order to engage the image from different angles, in a sense to mirror the trope of circulation governing the film itself. To be sure, Smith extrapolated certain elements of his ideal format from stage directions and settings already inscribed in Brecht's libretto that were, in varying degrees, realized in the opera's initial stage productions (although the figure of the boxer had appeared previously in Smith's oeuvre, in the elevator scene of *Heaven and Earth Magic*).[25] Yet his drive to reconstitute the dynamics of image presentation as a source of ongoing creative energy as well as to take a destabilizing jab at the codified film object is a consistent feature in the jittery terrain of Smith's career.

III

During the years in which Smith designed, shot, and edited *Mahagonny,* the most discussed—if not necessarily most prolific—avant-garde film practice was Sitney's contentious "cinema of structure," an approach, in which "the shape of the whole film is predetermined and simplified, and it is that shape which is the primal impression of the film."[26] This formulation is reminiscent of critical discourse around minimalist painting and sculpture, especially Robert Morris's notion of "unitary forms."[27] In these schemata, whole-part relations were held to best serve the needs of overall shape when expressive, spontaneous, and subjective criteria had been pared away in favor of visual syntax. Principles such as simple repetition, regulated accretion, and logical progression accordingly emerged as ideals of structure. For film, the pursuit of predetermined shape was above all a repudiation of earlier poetic styles that privileged metaphoric montage, complex rhythms, and moment-by-moment articulation of meaning. Significantly, the aesthetic thrust of avant-garde achievement in the 1940s and 1950s had been transposed from models such as dream narrative, postwar urban poetry, jazz, and high-modernist painting—all of which, with the possible exception of poetry, exerted a strong influence on Harry Smith's early work. Brakhage was, of course, the chief theoretical exponent and celebrated master of the avant-garde's expressivist, autobiographical camp. Not unexpectedly, the adoption of formulaic editing and of a reductivist stance toward film's combinatory possibilities, which became commonplace in the 1970s, proved anathema to Brakhage and his colleagues.

By the mid-1960s, Warhol's single-take, fixed-camera portraits had outrageously challenged the avant-garde expressivist doctrine of structure as commensurate with the labyrinthine track of personal imagination. The breach initiated by Warhol soon widened to accommodate a flood of films generated by written scores, logical propositions, mathematical formulas, and so on. Most films in this camp foregrounded techno-perceptual paradoxes inherent in the medium that are usually suppressed or mystified by Hollywood's codes of industrial narrative. From one angle, then, structural films appeared to be invidiously cloaked in a version of the distant, third-person omniscient camera perspective fostered by commercial cinema. Thus, for some detractors, structural film was deemed soulless, a betrayal of humanist precepts. In the context of American culture's reaction to excesses of the 1960s, it countered a post-Romantic lyrical outpouring of subjectivity with a baldly didactic agenda of visual puzzle-solving accompanied by an ironic reverence for mechanized image production. Brakhage's response is captured in a verbal tirade of 1977 aimed at a film by Snow: "It is absolutely preclusive of what to me are the most valuable parts of the process of creativity. That is, that process wherein the maker is called upon to work with what he or she *doesn't* know at every frame's existence,... not as choice of anything that can be taught academically, but as an act of absolute urgency in what, for me, is a kind of trance state."[28] The affront represented by this style was in large measure a disengagement from two intensely personalized stages of film production: a cameraperson's sensuous perceptions of external reality, and an editor's sensuous juxtaposing of recorded images. In effect, the structural imperative bypassed what Brakhage referred to as the primacy of immediate seeing in favor of an anterior moment of rigid conceptualization.

Harry Smith's position in this internecine struggle is typically oblique, contradictory, and symptomatic of even wider philosophical schisms. Smith reports he had written a detailed score for the editing of *Heaven and Earth Magic* more than a decade prior to the start of *Mahagonny.* His explanation for this procedure is, in part, specific to the rigors of large-scale cutout animation, but it also carries echoes of a later rationale invoked by structural filmmakers: "I tried as much as possible to make the whole thing automatic,... to remove things as much as possible from the consciousness or whatever you want to call it so that the manual processes [of editing] could be employed entirely in moving things around."[29] The reference to "automatic" here recalls a surrealist strategy for accessing subversive patterns in the unconscious, but it also reflects an overarching tension in Smith's work—located in extratextual as well as formal arenas—between control and the aleatory, between meticulous precision and the lure of chaotic breakdown. In other words, while he wanted the unfolding of *Heaven and Earth Magic* to resemble the calibrated movement of a mechanical device—not incidentally, machines are arguably the film's paramount motif—he simultaneously composed internal figures as well as external technical features (such as vagaries in projection) that court eruptions of chance events, irrational synapses, the murmur of systemic annihilation.

It was fairly common in the 1970s for structural filmmakers to publicly display notes, charts, and other forms of documentation as adjuncts and guides to the screening experience (figs. 4–6). To my knowledge, Smith never exhibited the extensive scores he wrote for *Mahagonny,* although photographs of portions of those charts (fig. 7; see also p. 2) have been made available since his death. What they suggest to an outsider is an intricately ordered system of horizontal and vertical image relations—that is, pertaining both to a linear axis of the successive shots on a given reel and across adjacent reels and to a spatialized coordination of the images as placed on the four-screen grid at any given moment—whose basic axioms are nonetheless impossible to deduce from a single screening of *Mahagonny,* or even from multiple exposure. Smith's description of his system is as elegant as it is ultimately opaque. Clearly, the numerical rule of "four" or, as Smith maintains, "the three interacting with the four" dictates a variety of structural features, including the image grid.[30] The images themselves have glancing correspondences with classical discourses around the four elements, four seasons, or four humors. Smith, however, ties the quadripartite projection to Marcel Duchamp's *The Bride Stripped Bare by Her Bachelors, Even (The Large Glass)* (fig. 8).[31] Four iconographic shot categories—animation (roughly half the total footage), portraits, nature scenes, and "symbols"—are arranged into a palindrome of twenty-four scenes per reel over a total of twelve reels.[32] Shots vary in duration from a few seconds to several minutes, their lengths synchronized to individual songs in Brecht and Weill's opera or, at times, to melodic changes in a single musical passage. Smith claimed he was matching "appropriate images with music," with those images consisting of "about 250 categories such as eggs breaking, plants growing, rain falling, fire burning, parts of the human body and even scenes of the city,"[33] a claim that is naturally difficult to confirm from the film-text alone.

The point is that although *Mahagonny* consists of a virtual palimpsest of directives, formulas, and mechanisms of "translation," very little of that conceptual baggage is visible on-screen. While other avant-gardists of the period worked from scores, employed palindromes as editing templates, or explored multiscreen articulations, Smith's all-consuming project lacks certain of the demonstrative, gestalt qualities prized by the structural camp. Further, the systemic logic operative in most structural films is geared to an unveiling of cinematic ontology—for instance, the photographic illusion of depth (Gehr's *Serene Velocity*) or the transcendence of language by image (Frampton's *Zorns Lemma*). *Mahagonny* offers neither simple lessons in perception nor intelligible markers of its own fabrication. Indeed, its activating premise, or *pretext,* is a somewhat obscure cultural artifact of a bygone era rather than the ahistorical, quasi-scientific theorems that guided structural film. As I have argued elsewhere, the very best examples of structural film trafficked in,

Page 142

Fig. 4.
Peter Kubelka (Austrian, b. 1934)
Score for his *Arnulf Rainer* (1960), 1958–60, typewriter and pen on DIN A4 paper, 21 × 29.7 cm (8¼ × 11¾ in.), 1
Collection Peter Kubelka

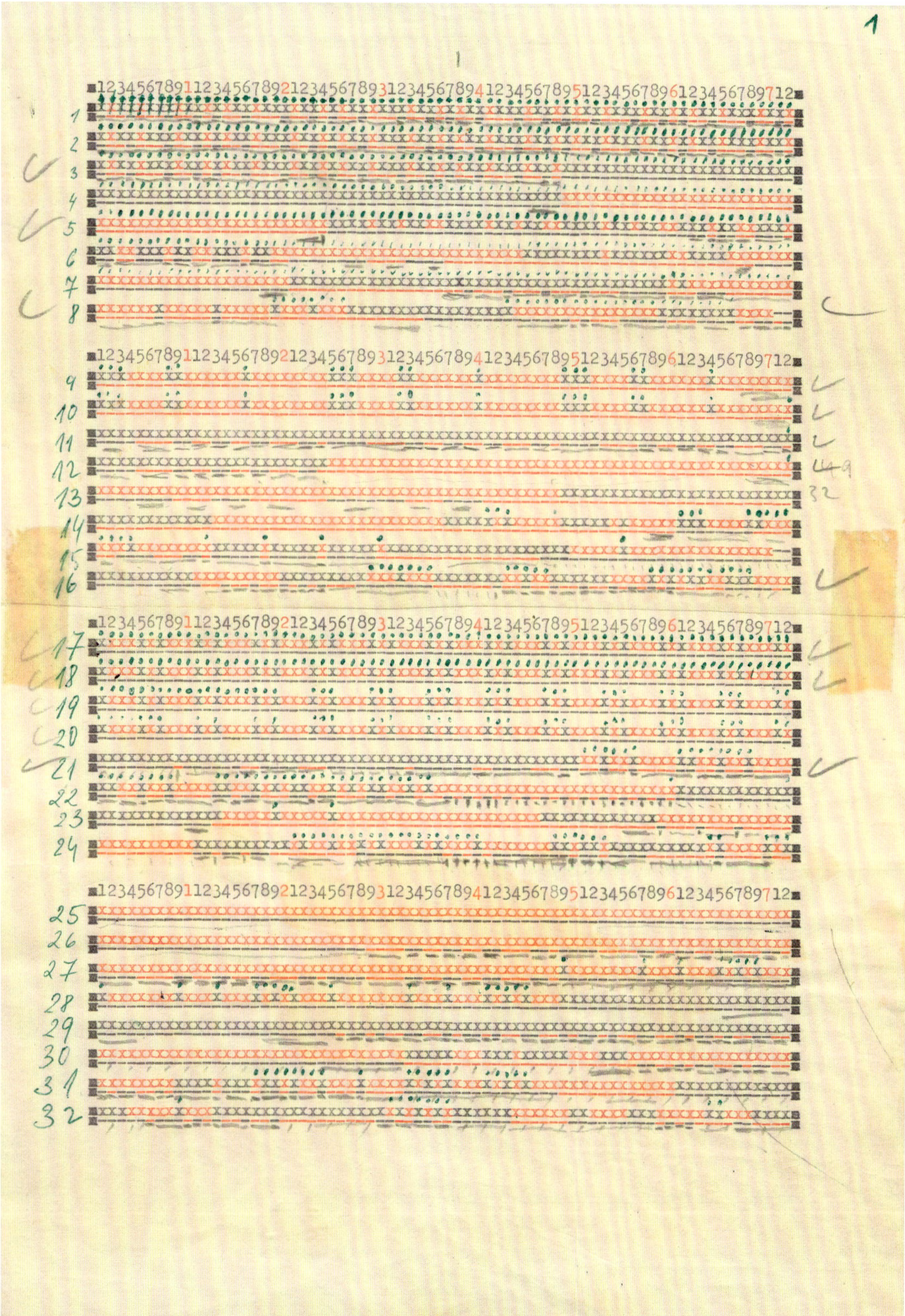

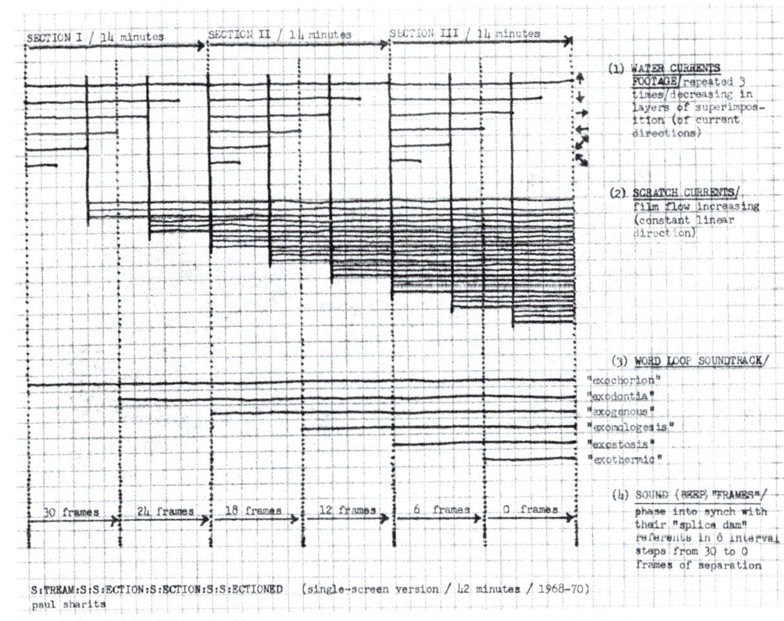

Fig. 5.
Paul Sharits (American, 1943–93)
Chart for his *S:TREAM:S:S:ECTION:S:ECTION:S:S:ECTIONED* (single-screen version, 42 minutes, 1968–70)
From *Film Culture,* no. 65–66 (1978): 28

Fig. 6.
Schematic diagram for Hollis Frampton's *Zorns Lemma* (1970), with annotations by Frampton, ca. 1970, typewriter and pen on paper, 21.6 × 27.9 cm (8½ × 11 in.)
New York, Anthology Film Archives

Fig. 7.
Harry Smith
Chart for the editing and organization of a portion of his *Mahagonny* (1970–80), ca. 1980, pen on paper, 21.6 × 35.6 cm (8½ × 14 in.)
Harry Smith Archives

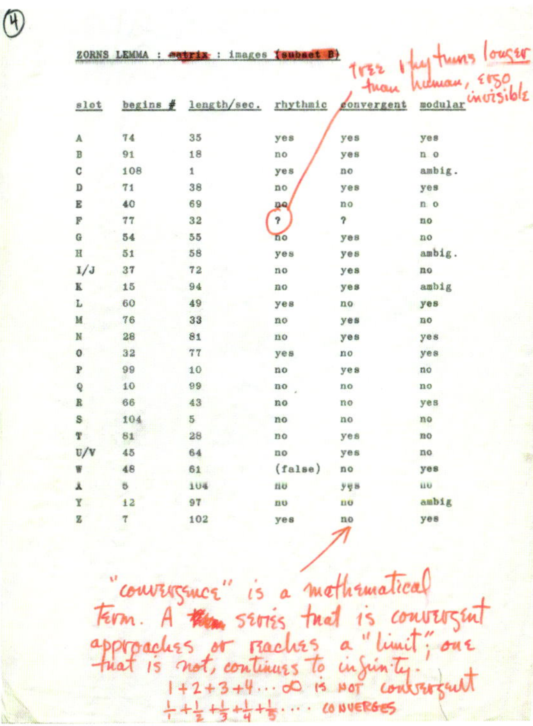

(4)

ZORNS LEMMA : ~~matrix~~ : images ~~(subset B)~~

TREE rhythms longer than human, ergo invisible

slot	begins #	length/sec.	rhythmic	convergent	modular
A	74	35	yes	yes	yes
B	91	18	no	yes	n o
C	108	1	yes	no	ambig.
D	71	38	no	yes	yes
E	40	69	no	no	n o
F	77	32	?	?	no
G	54	55	no	yes	no
H	51	58	yes	yes	ambig.
I/J	37	72	no	yes	no
K	15	94	no	yes	ambig
L	60	49	yes	no	yes
M	76	33	no	yes	no
N	28	81	no	yes	yes
O	32	77	yes	no	yes
P	99	10	no	yes	no
Q	10	99	no	no	no
R	66	43	no	no	yes
S	104	5	no	no	no
T	81	28	no	yes	no
U/V	45	64	no	yes	no
W	48	61	(false)	no	yes
X	5	104	no	yes	no
Y	12	97	no	no	ambig
Z	7	102	yes	no	yes

"convergence" is a mathematical term. A ~~then~~ series that is convergent approaches or reaches a "limit"; one that is not, continues to infinity.
$1+2+3+4 \ldots \infty$ is NOT convergent
$\frac{1}{1}+\frac{1}{2}+\frac{1}{3}+\frac{1}{4}+\frac{1}{5} \ldots$ CONVERGES

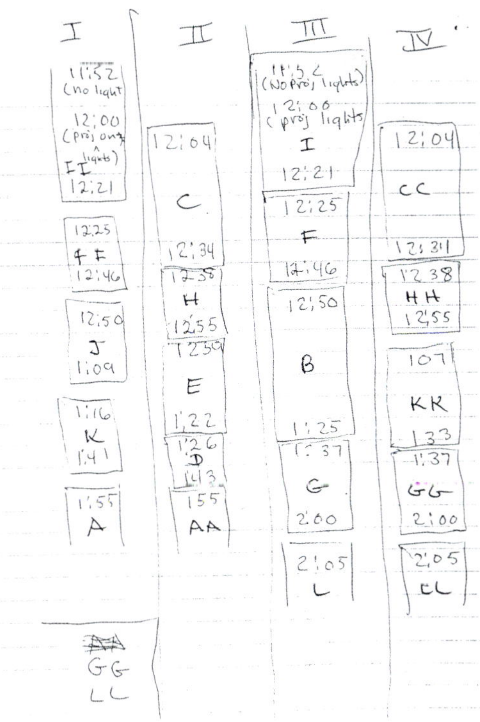

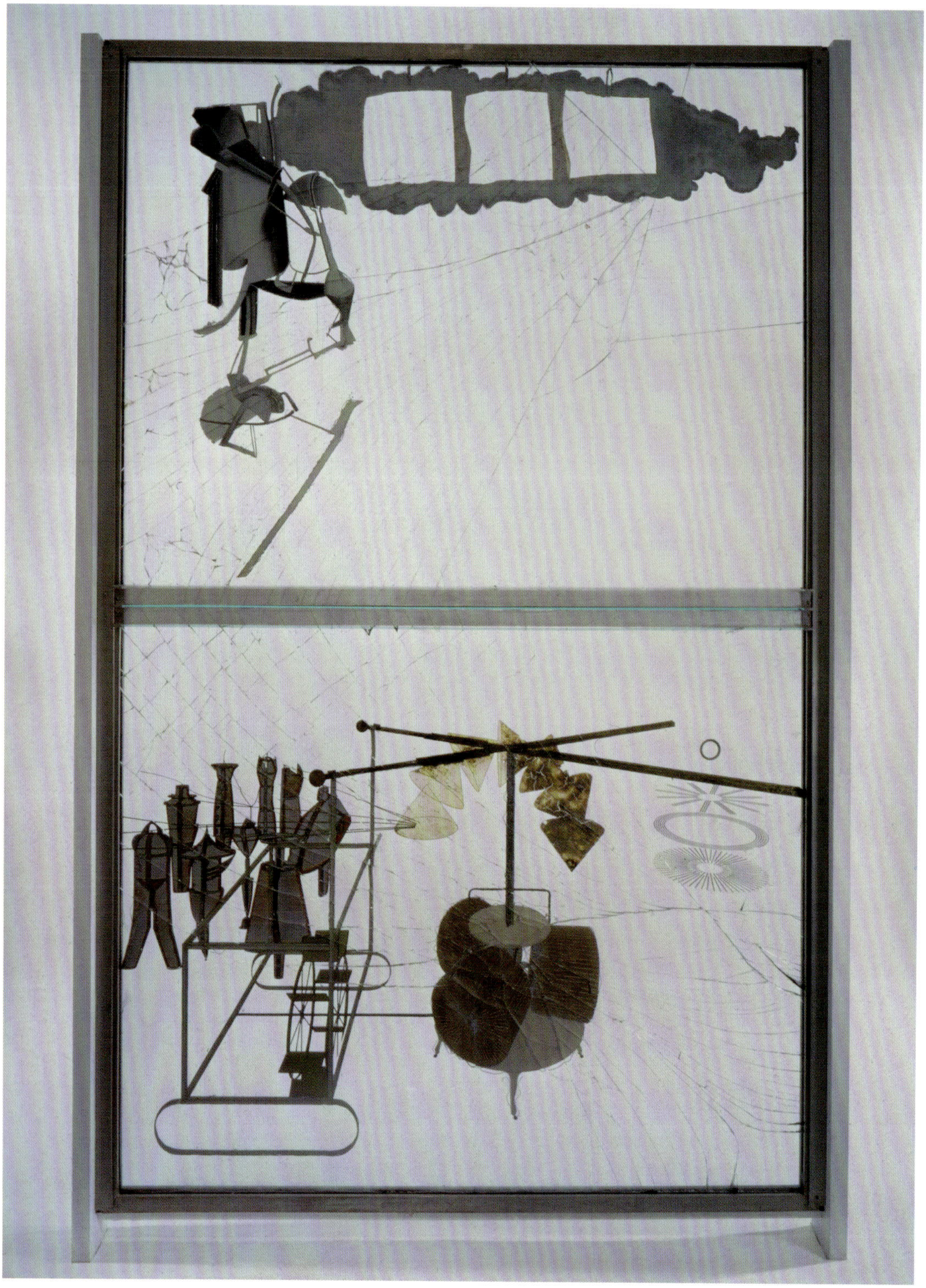

among other issues, problems of realist representation and subcultural coding that exceeded ostensibly narrow programs of reflexivity or demystification.[34] In Smith's case, it might be more accurate to assess the results of his remarkable preproduction exertions as a program of remystification, an emblem of conspicuous impenetrability.

IV

With characteristic prescience, Manny Farber once described Snow's *Wavelength* (1967) (fig. 9), the embodiment of the structural film ethos, as "a straightforward document of a room in which a dozen businesses have lived and gone bankrupt."[35] Although it has gone largely unnoticed, a sizable portion of films constructed from preexisting schemata treat urban space as a field of investigation uniquely receptive to the play of mechanical signifiers. Needless to say, the trope of city as machine is rooted in nineteenth-century literature and painting but finds perhaps its most potent expression in the European city symphonies of the 1920s and 1930s, Ruttmann's *Berlin*, Ralph Steiner's *The City* (1939), and, especially, Dziga Vertov's *Man with a Movie Camera* (1929). In these films, a social ecology of speed, fragmentation, rhythmic density, and diversity are inscribed and celebrated under the aegis of modern cinema's industrial apparatus. To cite but a single analogy, the practice of montage matches the urban subject's fragmentary impressions of chaotic street life. For obvious reasons, city symphonies often focus on public pathways and other sites in which human movement is juxtaposed with mechanized vehicular traffic, creating opportunities for comparison or rhyming of figures in motion through devices such as camera undercranking or superimposition.

The legacy of formalist studies of the urban landscape was extended by the postwar American avant-garde, one vector in a vibrant artistic subculture intent on the reclamation, both real and symbolic, of faltering commercial zones in New York and other cities. By the late 1950s, Brakhage, Shirley Clarke, Marie Menken, Hillary Harris, and, in a more mainstream register, Francis Thompson were transforming familiar monuments and routine street scenes into graphic melodies of color and line. In Clarke's *Bridges-Go-Round* (1958) (fig. 10), sporting a jazz sound track by Teo Macero, shots of isolated details from the Manhattan Bridge—cables, struts, railings, towers—are edited into kinetic sequences rendered increasingly abstract with the aid of colored gels and bipacked superimpositions. The period in which Smith finished shooting *Mahagonny* witnessed yet another round of filmic anatomies of New York City, this time in the guise of minimalist protocols that remapped city space as cinema's tautological counterpart. Along with Snow, Frampton, and Gehr, Barry Gerson, Standish Lawder, Bill Brand, David Rimmer, and Chantal Akerman all made memorable contributions to a growing body of *nouveau* city symphonies.

Once again, Smith's film joined its avant-garde cohort from a skewed angle, in tune with several prominent urbanist themes but diverging in important respects. Like *Zorns Lemma* and Akerman's *News from Home* (1977), *Mahagonny* takes the form of a cross-sectional *tour,* bracketing together an array of New York sights: Central Park and Times Square, soaring architectural interiors and cramped apartments, art world luminaries and anonymous pedestrians (fig. 11).

Fig. 8.
Marcel Duchamp (French, 1887–1968)
The Bride Stripped Bare by Her Bachelors, Even (The Large Glass), 1915–23, oil, varnish, lead foil, lead wire, and dust on two glass panels, 277.5 × 175.9 cm (109¼ × 69¼ in.)
Philadelphia, Philadelphia Museum of Art

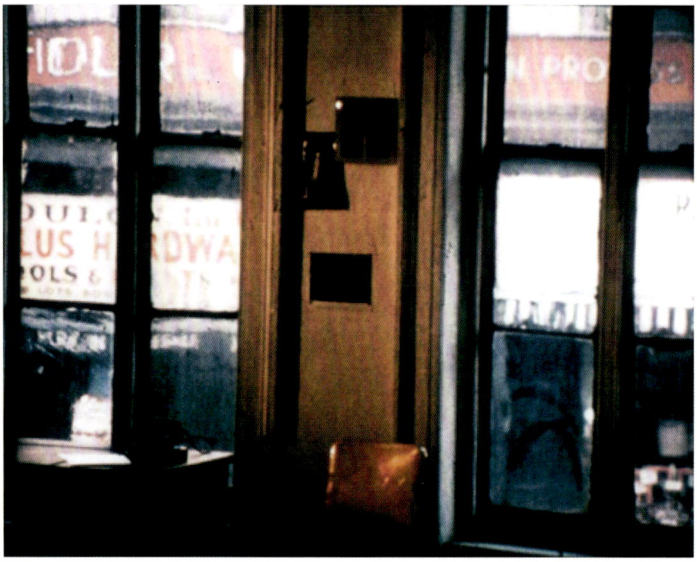

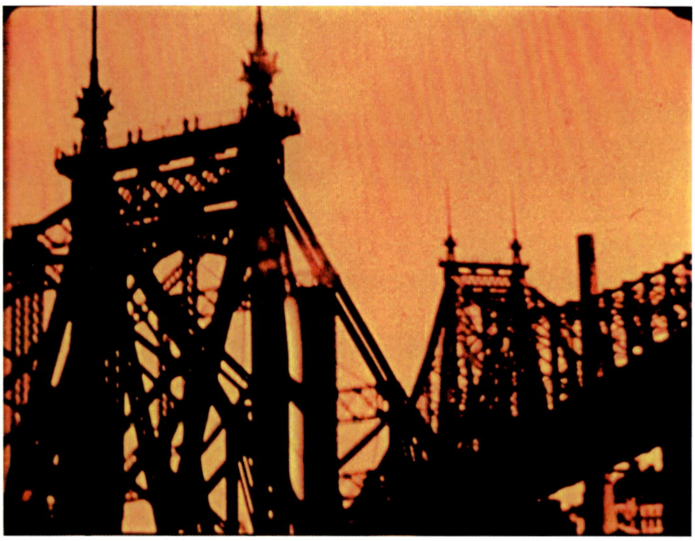

Fig. 9.
Michael Snow (Canadian, b. 1928)
Still from *Wavelength,* 1966–67, 45 min., 16 mm, color, sound

Fig. 10.
Shirley Clarke (American, 1919–97)
Still from *Bridges-Go-Round,* 1958, 7 min., 16 mm, color, sound

Fig. 11.
Harry Smith
Stills from *Film #18: Mahagonny,* 1970–80 (restored, 2002), 141 min., 35 mm, color, sound

Unlike related modes such as the *diary* (Jonas Mekas's *In Between: 1964–8* [1978]), *microcosm* (Rimmer's *Real Italian Pizza* [1971]), and *essay* (Yvonne Rainer's *Journeys from Berlin/1971* [1980]), the *tour* is implicitly linked to an itemized catalog or inventory of activities.[36] In a manner coextensive with the use of lockstep superimposition in Gehr's *Still* (1971) (fig. 12), the combination of fast motion and bilateral mirroring of identical shots in *Mahagonny* distorts natural rhythms of street and sidewalk traffic, suggesting a regime in which time is out of joint (fig. 13). The four-screen grid is itself a device whose structured display of simultaneous yet disparate urban scenes offers a sort of topographic anthology of public versus private domains. Moreover, the patterned exchange of image categories across screen quadrants underscores the function of the grid as a net or web—a character in Brecht's

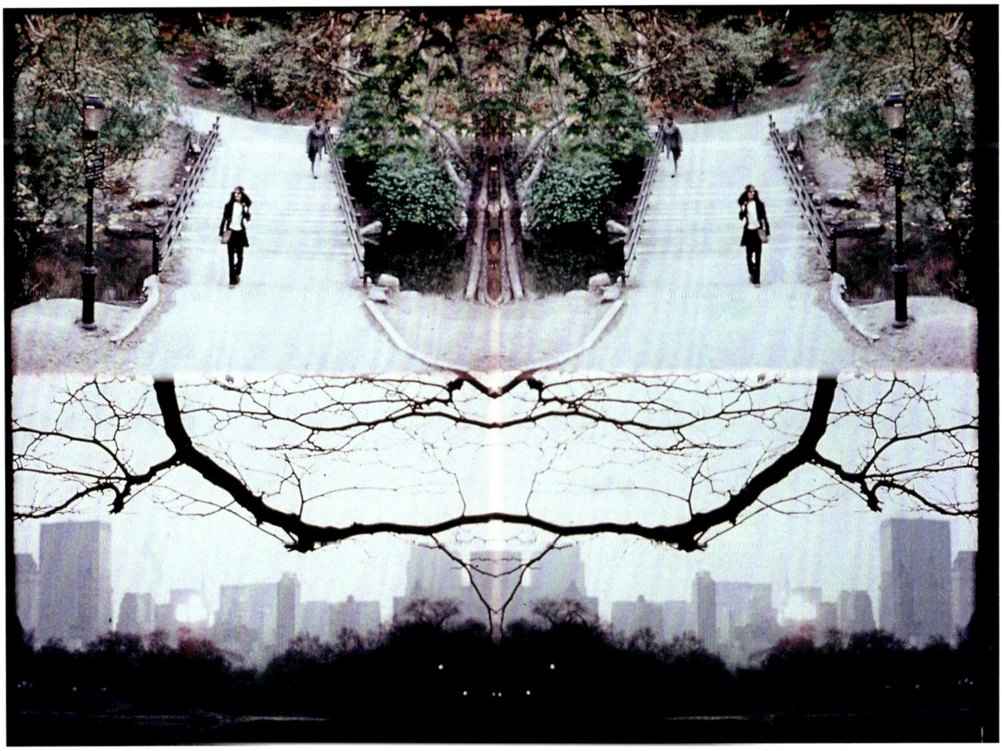

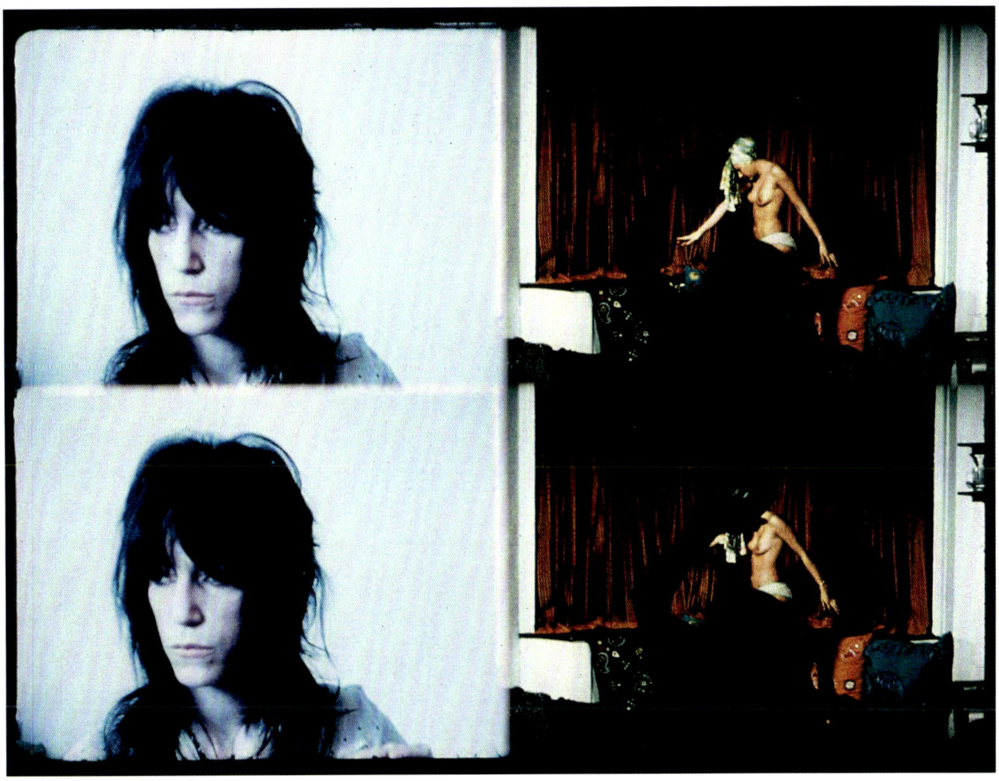

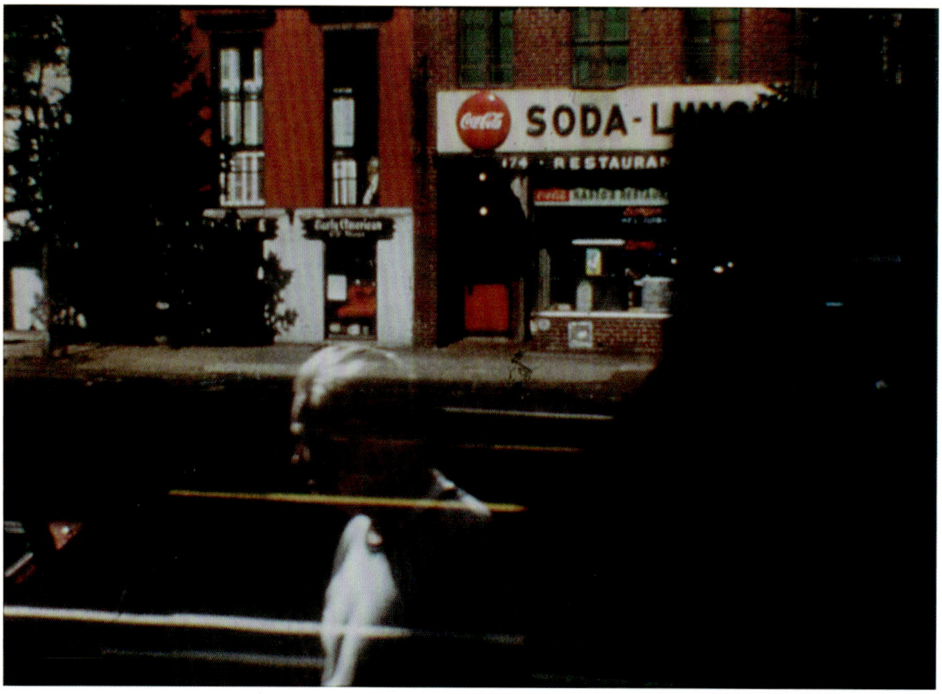
Coca-Cola

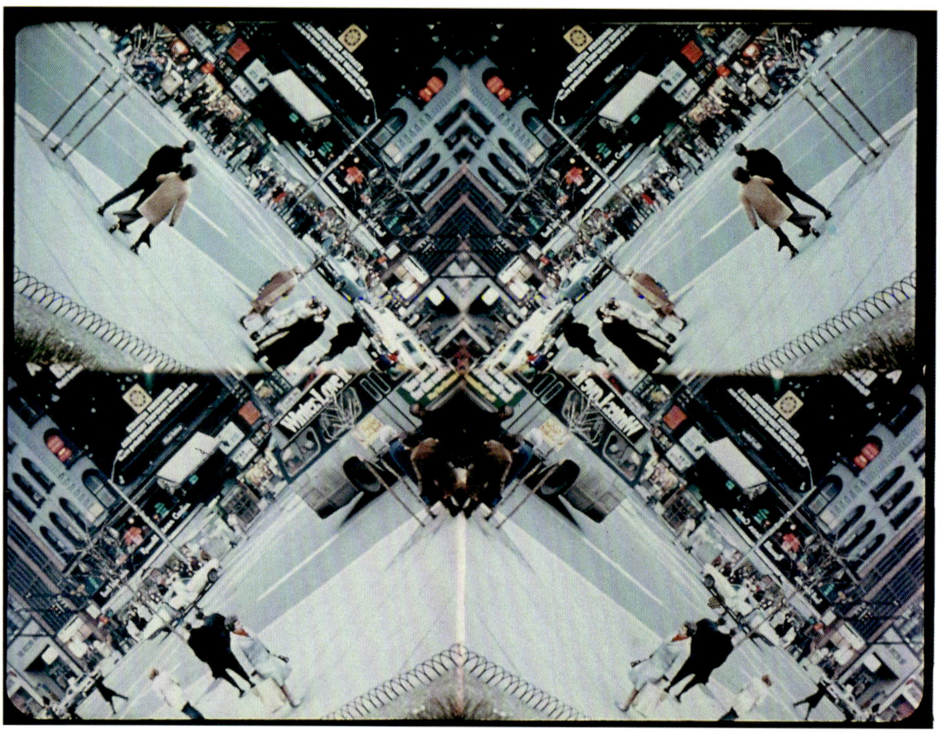

opening scene says that "Mahagonny" means "spiderweb"[37]—for collecting and redistributing excess urban energies, a system for the circulation of represented objects and human desires. In the opera, according to Smith, the triad of pleasures pulsating across the city are sex, money, and whiskey,[38] each of which finds its way into the film's iconography (as do various incarnations of the web motif, including string figures). As in the fantasy city Smith's film was meant to illustrate, stable symmetries and rhythms established in early sections of *Mahagonny* gradually collapse as the grid is permeated by irregular image configurations.

The city under Smith's scrutiny could scarcely be other than it is: New York City in the 1970s. Like Brecht and Weill's Mahagonny in the aftermath of catastrophe, it existed in America's popular imagination as a place where "Anything goes!"[39] Although it fell somewhat short of the decadence and political breakdown that beset Weimar Berlin, New York was by mid-decade immersed in a deep fiscal crisis, its budget governed by a shadowy board of bankers and money managers—the Municipal Assistance Corporation—following the city's brush with outright bankruptcy. A widespread obsession with monetary concerns was ballasted by the conspicuous consumption of sex and drugs: the era's headlines are sprinkled with references to Al Goldstein's *Screw* magazine, the sex club Plato's Retreat, and a cresting wave of cocaine abuse. In Martin Scorsese's *Taxi Driver* (1976), an influential urban threnody released a year before the Summer of Sam, the war-scarred protagonist intones, "This city here is like an open sewer." Nonetheless, despite the fact that a number of *Mahagonny*'s scenes took place in the Chelsea Hotel, a hotbed of bohemian license where Smith resided during most of the film's production, New York's enveloping social climate is inscribed in *Mahagonny* via only indirect references; documentation of the filmmaker's friends and favorite haunts is not exactly congruent with the objectifying thrust of social documentaries.

Smith's bifurcated vision of the allegorical identity of the city in *Mahagonny* is hinted at by Lionel Ziprin: "So here I saw Berlin right in front of my eyes, all over again on 7th Street. Berlin 1930."[40] Indeed, Smith's New York in the 1970s was intended as an anthropological resiting of Brecht and Weill's fictitious Mahagonny, which itself was both a stand-in for inflationary Berlin in the 1920s and a mordant projection of America's boomtown, "anything goes" urban mythology. But it is as well a resiting of the ordered city of Ruttmann's film into the decadent world of Brecht and Weill. Unlike their opera, whose initial staging in Leipzig in 1930 prompted a swirl of critical controversy, Ruttmann's *Berlin* was released to general acclaim. Both *Berlin* and Smith's *Mahagonny* rely on an arsenal of techniques that render individuals as abstract visual patterns (fig. 14), their status as broad social types sealed by tropes of clockwork editing. Both films develop the conceit of a "musical" city whose ambient sound is replaced by an external score; Edmund Meisel, the composer for Sergei Eisenstein's *Battleship Potemkin* (1925), wrote the music for *Berlin*.[41] In contrast to Brecht and Weill's pessimistic warnings about the commodification of human appetites, Ruttmann's film (and its score) valorizes the flow of neatly ordered rhythms, saving its disapproval for intermittent outbursts of disruptive emotion (for example, a street fight and a deftly encapsulated suicide). Within the precinct of the opera's newly founded Mahagonny, reciprocal

Fig. 12.
Ernie Gehr (American, b. 1941)
Still from *Still*, 1971, 54½ min., 16 mm, color, sound

Fig. 13.
Harry Smith
Still from *Film #18: Mahagonny*, 1970–80 (restored, 2002), 141 min., 35 mm, color, sound

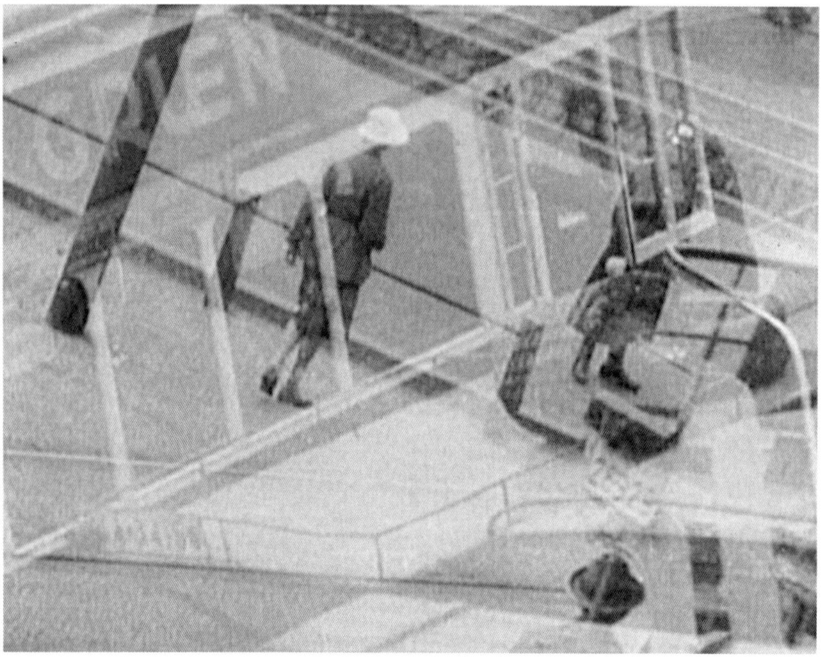

Fig. 14.
Walther Ruttmann (German, 1887–1941)
Still from *Berlin: Die Symphonie der Großstadt,* 1927, 65 min., 35 mm, black and white, silent

affirmations of earthly paradise and living hell temper any prospects for unalloyed social regulation.

During the writing and production of the operatic *Mahagonny,* Brecht's infatuation with the raw opportunism and mystery of American cities had begun to sour as his political views took a leftward turn. Richard Ruland observes that despite admiration for what he imagined as a looser regime of social constraint, Brecht would soon regard America as "the center of the capitalist world where all the evils of the system exist in grotesque and exaggerated form."[42] Weill was not in complete agreement with his collaborator's judgment that the shameless materialism and moral corruption portrayed in the opera was a direct, exclusive consequence of the laws of capitalism: "Mahagonny, like Sodom and Gomorrah, falls on account of the crimes, the licentiousness and the general confusion of its inhabitants."[43] Undoubtedly, Smith was drawn to the opera by a volatile mixture of aesthetic appeals and private obsessions; therefore, it is slightly tricky to extrapolate from the film his interpretation of Brecht and Weill's social beliefs. It is perhaps not far-fetched, however, to contend that the filmed *Mahagonny* might be more sympathetic to the universalizing sympathies of Weill, albeit devoid of his sappy moral opprobrium. Smith's work in this sense is suitably ambivalent, luxuriating in the visual possibilities of props evoking a lust for drugs, alcohol, money, or sex. Yet there are also undercurrents of anxiety, boredom, and disgust.

The city Smith conjures is a realm of leisure, not a pleasure palace of upper-class affluence but rather a dispiriting zone of unproductive, if often hectic, labor—unproductive, that is, except for the agency of representation. Brecht's concept of epic theater, developed at roughly the same period as his creative interactions with Weill, proceeds from a commitment to work out "scenes where people adopt attitudes of such a sort that the social laws under which they are acting spring into sight."[44] The vast compendium of rules adopted by Smith for the invention of his hybridized city symphony—part well-oiled machine, part retrograde human anatomy—in the end reveals very little about universal, or even local, determinants of collective behavior. His rules abide as spectral evidence of the inevitability of regulation, of an autonomous function the on-screen manifestation of which can only gesture at a deeper, more complex mystery—which is also the mystery of its creator's sensibility. That said, it is surely ironic that the esoteric fate of *Mahagonny*, from our vantage, is to serve as an exemplar of so many eclectic concerns within the sect of avant-garde film of the 1970s.

Notes

1. Paul Arthur submitted this essay in May 2004 for publication in this volume. The current version incorporates a number of minor editorial changes permitted by the author's executor but not seen by Arthur himself before his death on 25 March 2008.
2. Smith, this volume, 119. Note that the quotations in Arthur's original manuscript were from the transcription of Harry Smith's talk published as Harry Smith, "Queens Museum, November 11, 1978," *Cinemanews*, no. 78-6/79-1 (1979): 3–5, 27. The editors have chosen to update Arthur's citations of Smith's talk to match the new transcription published in this volume, 115–24.
3. Harry Smith to the Committee on Poetry, New York City, typescript grant application, ca. 1973, Harry Smith Archives: "the story is simple and widespread; the joyous gathering together of a great number of people, their breaking of the rules of liberty and love, and consequent fall into oblivion" (p. i); "In its final form the film will be a series of scenes...all designed to translate the opera into a universal script based on the similarities of life and aspiration in all humans" (p. ii), reprinted in this volume, 272–73.

   Allen Ginsberg was the founder of the Committee on Poetry, which he started in 1964, formally incorporated in 1966, and remained involved with until his death in 1997. It is a literary grant-giving organization that assists artists in the completion of literary work, in the actualization of special projects such as a publication or a performance, by providing working residencies at the foundation's farm, and by giving emergency grants-in-aid.
4. Smith to the Committee on Poetry (note 3), iii; see this volume, 273.
5. On the genres of New Narrative and essay films, see Paul Arthur, "The Resurgence of History and the Avant-Garde Essay Film," in idem, *A Line of Sight: American Avant-Garde Film since 1965* (Minneapolis: Univ. of Minnesota Press, 2005), 65–68.
6. P. Adams Sitney, *Visionary Film: The American Avant-Garde, 1943–2000*, 3rd ed. (New York: Oxford Univ. Press, 2002), 347–71.
7. See Sitney, *Visionary Film* (note 6), 224, 231–35, 258, 265. I discuss the first film/last film syndrome in Arthur, "The Resurgence of History" (note 5), 63–65.
8. Cited in "Gehr, Ernie," *Film-Makers' Cooperative Catalogue*, no. 7 (1989): 188.
9. For descriptions of Smith's early films, see Sitney, *Visionary Film* (note 6), 238–46.
10. Sitney, *Visionary Film* (note 6), 235.
11. Sitney, *Visionary Film* (note 6), 249.

12. An indication of the film's definitive power is the way it has been appropriated and simultaneously disowned by several later ambitious cutout animation films, namely, Larry Jordan's feature-length *Sophie's Place* (1986) and Lewis Klahr's *The Pharaoh's Belt* (1993).
13. In an email sent to me on 9 July 2003, Rani Singh lists a number of benefactors of Smith's film, including the New York State Council for the Arts, New York City Department of Cultural Affairs, Solomon Guggenheim Foundation, American Film Institute, and Foundation for the Study of Consciousness. Smith also received assistance from Stan Brakhage and Shirley Clarke, among other filmmakers. My thanks to Singh and the Harry Smith Archives for making available a selection of Smith's grant applications and supporting documents.
14. Bertolt Brecht, *Rise and Fall of the City of Mahagonny,* trans. Michael Feingold, in idem, *Collected Plays, Volume 2,* ed. Ralph Manheim and John Willett (New York: Vintage, 1977), 135.
15. Brecht, *Rise and Fall* (note 14), 88.
16. Lionel Ziprin, "Lionel Ziprin—May and June 1993," interview by Paola Igliori, compiled with previous interview by Clayton Patterson with K. K., in Paola Igliori, ed., *American Magus Harry Smith: A Modern Alchemist* (New York: Inanout, 1996), 53.
17. Sitney, *Visionary Film* (note 6), 256.
18. Harry Smith to Andy Berler (Creative Artists Public Service Program [CAPS]), 22 December 1975, 1, Harry Smith Archives; reprinted in this volume, 274–75.
19. For details regarding the Vortex series, see Gene Youngblood, *Expanded Cinema* (New York: E. P. Dutton, 1970), 388–91; and Scott MacDonald, "Jordan Belson (and Collaborator Stephen Beck)," in idem, *A Critical Cinema 3: Interviews with Independent Filmmakers* (Berkeley: Univ. of California Press, 1998), 66, 71–76. An important source of early writings on expanded cinema is the issue of the *Tulane Drama Review* published in autumn 1966 that was devoted to film and theater; see especially Stan Vanderbeek, "'Culture: Intercom' and Expanded Cinema: A Proposal and Manifesto," *Tulane Drama Review* 11, no. 1 (1966): 38–48.
20. Sitney, *Visionary Film* (note 6), 241, 243.
21. Mekas talks about the effects Smith created during screenings in Jonas Mekas, "Jonas Mekas—10 July 1993," interview by Paola Igliori, in Paola Igliori, ed., *American Magus Harry Smith: A Modern Alchemist* (New York: Inanout, 1996), 80.
22. Michael Fried, "Art and Objecthood," in Gregory Battcock, ed., *Minimal Art: A Critical Anthology* (New York: E. P. Dutton, 1968), 125.
23. David E. James, *Allegories of Cinema: American Film in the Sixties* (Princeton: Princeton Univ. Press, 1989), 134.
24. Smith, this volume, 119.
25. For a description of the stage design and of Caspar Neher's provocative slide projections for the production of the *Mahagonny Songspiel* at the Deutsche Kammermusikfest in Baden-Baden in 1927, see John Fuegi, *Brecht and Company: Sex, Politics, and the Making of the Modern Drama* (New York: Grove, 1994), 187–89.
26. Sitney, *Visionary Film* (note 6), 348.
27. Cited in Fried, "Art and Objecthood" (note 22), 119. I analyze discursive parallels between Sitney's account of structural film and theories of minimal art in Paul

Arthur, "Structural Film: Revisions, New Versions, and the Artifact," *Millennium Film Journal,* no. 2 (1978): 5–13; and Paul Arthur, "Structural Film: Revisions, New Versions, and the Artifact—Part Two," *Millennium Film Journal,* no. 4/5 (1979): 122–34.

28. Stan Brakhage, "Brakhage Uncensored," *Cinemanews,* no. 78-6/79-1 (1979): 15 (emphasis added). This is a transcription of a portion of a question-and-answer session with Brakhage after a screening of his films *The Domain of the Moment* (1977) and *The Governor* (1977) at the Millennium Film Workshop, New York City, 4 November 1977. The film in question is Snow's *La région centrale.*
29. Cited in Sitney, *Visionary Film* (note 6), 255.
30. Harry Smith, "P. Adams Sitney—NYC [*Mahagonny,* 1977]," interview by P. Adams Sitney, in idem, *Think of the Self Speaking: Harry Smith—Selected Interviews,* ed. Rani Singh (Seattle: Elbow/Cityful, 1999), 103. This was first published as Harry Smith, "Harry Smith Interview," interview by P. Adams Sitney, *Film Culture,* no. 37 (1965): 4–13. It is hard at times to know what to make of Smith's numerological assertions; Brecht's libretto contains nineteen scenes and four is a number that barely surfaces in the text or the distribution of roles.
31. Smith, "P. Adams Sitney" (note 30), 104.
32. Smith, "P. Adams Sitney" (note 30), 106–7.
33. Smith to the Committee on Poetry (note 3), ii; see this volume, 272.
34. Paul Arthur, "The Last of the Last Machine? Avant-Garde Film since 1966," *Millennium Film Journal,* no. 16/17/18 (1986–87): 77–81.
35. Manny Farber, *Movies* (New York: Hillstone, 1971), 250.
36. For more extensive discussion of postwar urban idioms, see Paul Arthur, "The Redemption of the City," in idem, *A Line of Sight: American Avant-Garde Film since 1965* (Minneapolis: Univ. of Minnesota Press, 2005), 45–60.
37. Brecht, *Rise and Fall* (note 14), 88.
38. Smith, "P. Adams Sitney" (note 30), 104.
39. Brecht, *Rise and Fall* (note 14), 114.
40. Ziprin, "Lionel Ziprin" (note 16), 55.
41. Initial screenings of *Berlin* were accompanied by live orchestral performances of Meisel's score, since lost, and the film was initially distributed with sheet music for that score. Meisel's most prominent association was with the Expressionist theater director Erwin Piscator, and his work in the early 1920s included writing incidental music for pieces by Brecht.
42. Richard Ruland, "The American Plays of Bertolt Brecht," *American Quarterly* 15 (1963): 381; cited in Patty Lee Parmalee, *Brecht's America* (Columbus, Ohio: published for Miami University by the Ohio State Univ. Press, 1981), 4.
43. Cited in David Drew, "The History of Mahagonny," *Musical Times,* January 1963, 20.
44. Bertolt Brecht, "On the Use of Music in an Epic Theatre," in idem, *Brecht on Theater: The Development of an Aesthetic,* ed. and trans. John Willett (New York: Hill & Wang, 1964), 86.

STEPHEN HINTON

MUSICAL VISIONS OF URBANITY: *Mahagonny* as Conceived by Kurt Weill and Bertolt Brecht and by Harry Smith

Interviewed in 1936, just over a year after coming to the United States, Kurt Weill reflected on his reputation in his homeland: "In Germany I'm known as a Kulturbolshevist; my music is un-German, un-Aryan. They call it asphalt-music, because it smacks of the city, which is to me a great compliment."[1] In the preceding decade, the city had indeed held an irresistible fascination for many creative artists. For Weill, as for many of his contemporaries, among them Bertolt Brecht, it was a fascination that was double-edged. The city stood for many things, positive and negative, real and imaginary, utopian and dystopian.[2] Nor did Weill's departure from Germany do much to diminish that fascination: the works he produced in the United States between 1935 and 1950, during his so-called American period, also include what the Nazis derogatorily called "asphalt-music."

Weill's first expressly urban piece was his cantata *Der neue Orpheus* (text by Yvan Goll, 1925; The new Orpheus), a work he considered pathbreaking in his evolution as a composer.[3] Here the city serves as the site for a surreal recasting of the Orpheus myth, located somewhere between heaven and hell. The "new Orpheus" is just a regular guy, a democratic "Musikant" (naive musician) whose job it is to furnish music of various kinds for various occasions. He is by turns piano pedagogue, variety artist, circus clown, director of veterans' sing-alongs, emaciated organist, conductor of Gustav Mahler's works at subscription concerts, and accompanist on the "Qualenklavier" (agony piano) in suburban movie theaters. If there is a single point of origin for Weill's topically motivated eclecticism, this is it.

In the one-act opera *Der Zar läßt sich photographieren* (*The Czar Has His Photograph Taken*), written with Georg Kaiser in 1927, the city is specified as Paris. It is the place where the eponymous czar fails in his attempt to appear both normal and up-to-date—that is, urbane. Traditional absolutism and modern democracy do not mix, the piece seems to be saying, despite any appearances to the contrary. The musical idioms associated with the czar are correspondingly incongruous. High-voltage operatic *espressivo* meets—or rather, clashes with—the tango.

The ironically titled *Happy End* (1929), a play by Elisabeth Hauptmann with lyrics by Brecht and music by Weill, brings to the stage a mix of another kind: organized crime and the Salvation Army. Set in Chicago, the piece ends with the canonization of the saints of capitalism, John Pierpont Morgan, Henry Ford, and John D. Rockefeller, as the city's gangsters join forces with its street peddlers of religion to battle the evils perpetrated by capitalism against the common man.

Another example of Weill's varied production of "asphalt-music" is the collection of six songs and choruses called *Das Berliner Requiem* (*Berlin Requiem*), written with Brecht in 1928 for radio broadcast. Pervaded by antimilitaristic sentiments, its content, according to the composer, "undoubtedly corresponds with the feelings and views of the broadest strata of the population. An attempt has been made to express what the contemporary city dweller has to say about the phenomenon of death."[4]

In Weill and Brecht's *Die sieben Todsünden* (1933; *The Seven Deadly Sins*), a secular parable of exile, various American cities (including, of course, Los Angeles) represent the urban "temptations" that threaten personal and artistic integrity. In Weill's American opera *Street Scene* (1946), with lyrics by Langston Hughes and dialogue by Elmer Rice, the city is New York, a symbol of cultural mixing as well as a locus of "love and passion and greed and death."[5] Weill saw the tenement of its theme song, "Lonely House," in symbolic terms, as "a prison for the human spirit" (a comment that recalls his earlier fascination with the Lamentations of Jeremiah, with their opening line, "How doth the city sit solitary, that was full of people!").[6]

As this survey might suggest, all Weill's city pieces amount to essays on the human condition, viewed from various perspectives, a condition at once formed and endangered by the modern city. Weill's Mahagonny project with Brecht, then, is just one among several of his visions of urbanity. The phrase "Mahagonny project" refers to two works: the twenty-or-so-minute *Mahagonny Songspiel,* written in response to a commission from an avant-garde music festival in 1927, and the full-length operatic version, *Aufstieg und Fall der Stadt Mahagonny* (*Rise and Fall of the City of Mahagonny*), which grew out of the *Songspiel* and received its tumultuous premiere nearly three years later, in March 1930. Harry Smith's decadelong *Mahagonny* project, begun some forty years later, is something quite separate, of course. But after focusing on Weill and Brecht's two pieces, I will venture a few observations on the connections between Smith's film and the opera that he used as its sound track. Parallels emerge.

Not only did the years between the conception of the *Songspiel* and the premiere of the opera critically define the careers of the two collaborators but the Mahagonny project marked both the beginning and the end of their partnership, if not literally, then at least spiritually. In fact, it was during the realization of the opera version that their working relationship came to grief, with Brecht proclaiming the death of opera and reportedly denouncing Weill as a phony Richard Strauss (whatever that might be in the Brechtian lexicon, as if Strauss were not phony enough for him already).[7] For this reason, it is potentially misleading to talk of the full-length work as exhibiting their collective vision. Chiefly because of Brecht's politics in general and because of his writings about the piece in particular, *Aufstieg und Fall der Stadt Mahagonny* has often been described as a Marxist opera (although Harry Smith, among others, certainly had his doubts about this). Weill's commentaries tell a somewhat different story,[8] as does the music, which is, after all, what Smith wanted us to listen to, not to the foreign-language text.[9] To say that there were differences in the collaborators' shifting conceptions is to risk stating the obvious about the nature of the differences, which remains a topic of controversy.[10]

Brecht's idea for a "Mahagonny-Opera" can be traced back to a diary entry from 1924 in which he mentions it in connection with "Mar," short for Marianne Zoff, the opera singer who was his wife at the time.[11] And there has survived a draft outline entitled "Auf nach Mahagonny" (Off to Mahagonny), predating Brecht's initial encounter with Weill in 1927, that describes a cabaret diva called Irma who parodies contemporary hit tunes.[12] One of the songs of the Mahagonny project recycles the title of this outline (providing, coincidentally, the opening words of the *Songspiel*). In any event, it was with the fulfillment of the commission for a *Kurzoper* (short opera) for the Baden-Baden festival in 1927 that Weill's partnership with Brecht really took off—a partnership that has been much commented on, though often with little basis in demonstrable fact.

Songspiel, Weill and Brecht's designation for the new mixed genre of Weill's settings, was no doubt meant as a provocation. The label punningly conflates old and new: the German tradition of "singspiel" and the modern American "song." Unlike the vernacular singspiel, comprising vocal arias, duets, and ensembles interspersed with spoken dialogue, the *Songspiel* consists of a sequence of vocal numbers in song form interspersed with instrumental interludes. The interludes accompany the scene shifts, yet they have more than an incidental function. Over his career, Weill would extensively, though not exclusively or uniformly, employ his so-called *Songstil* (song style). Song form and song style are not synonymous, however. The binary forms of the popular American song are new to his musical theater works with Brecht; the features of the style itself are not (its dance rhythms having been introduced in earlier works). Insofar as the composite noun *Songspiel* can also be understood as a "playing with songs," it implies that the new form's distance from both the singspiel and the song is equally great. The new coinage was more than just a neutral designation to describe a sequence of pieces largely in song form, as it later became. Rather, in 1927 it must have come across as a willful corruption of the German tradition of opera begun with works such as Wolfgang Amadeus Mozart's *Entfuhrung aus dem Serail* (1782; *The Abduction from the Seraglio*) and *Die Zauberflöte* (1791; *The Magic Flute*). Weill himself had supplied the context for this in 1925. "Singspiele," he had written, had begun as "small, harmless pieces whose significance would transcend that of a mere operetta" and in Mozart's hands would become "the foundation stone of 'German' opera."[13]

But it is to another classic of German opera that Weill specifically alludes in the music: Carl Maria von Weber's *Der Freischütz* (1821; The marksman), technically also a singspiel. In 1926, echoing the opinion of his teacher Ferruccio Busoni, Weill had put Weber at the top of the list of those composers whose "huge facility" connected them to Mozart.[14] A year later, in the opening "Mahagonny-Song" of the *Songspiel,* titled "Auf nach Mahagonny," Weill invoked Weber's "Chor der Brautjungfern" (Bridesmaids' chorus) at the words "schöner, grüner Mond von Alabama" (beautiful, green moon of Alabama). How campily surreal! In Weber's opera, the bridesmaids of the rural community celebrate their chaste bride, Agathe. In the *Songspiel,* the men await their "Weiberfleisch" (female flesh): the girls from the city of Mahagonny.

The American song part of the punning *Songspiel* equation literally precedes the singspiel part: at their first entrance, to fox-trot accompaniment, the male singers deliver their exhortation "Auf nach Mahagonny!" This opening line, as Jürgen

Schebera has noted, alludes to something very different from Weber's chorus: it can be heard as a reference to "Komm nach Mahagonne" (Come to Mahagonne), an "African shimmy" by hit-tune composer Leopold Krauss-Elka with lyrics by the chanson writer O. A. Alberts, a recording of which, in an instrumental arrangement, had been circulating since the early 1920s.[15] Although there are no musical parallels between the two numbers, beyond the fact that both are dance tunes incorporating fox-trot rhythms, there are textual ones. Where "Komm nach Mahagonne" stutteringly repeats the "Zieh-" of "Spiel mit der Zi-Zi-Zi- / Zi-Ziehharmonika" (Play on the . . . concertina) in a kind of poetic word painting (the instrument is being pulled out, not pushed in), Brecht copies the device, to even less innocent effect, by repeating the first syllable of "Zivilis," a play on "Syphilis" and "Zivilisation" (ex. 1). Of which will the men be "dort geheilt" (cured there), as the words claim? (The line

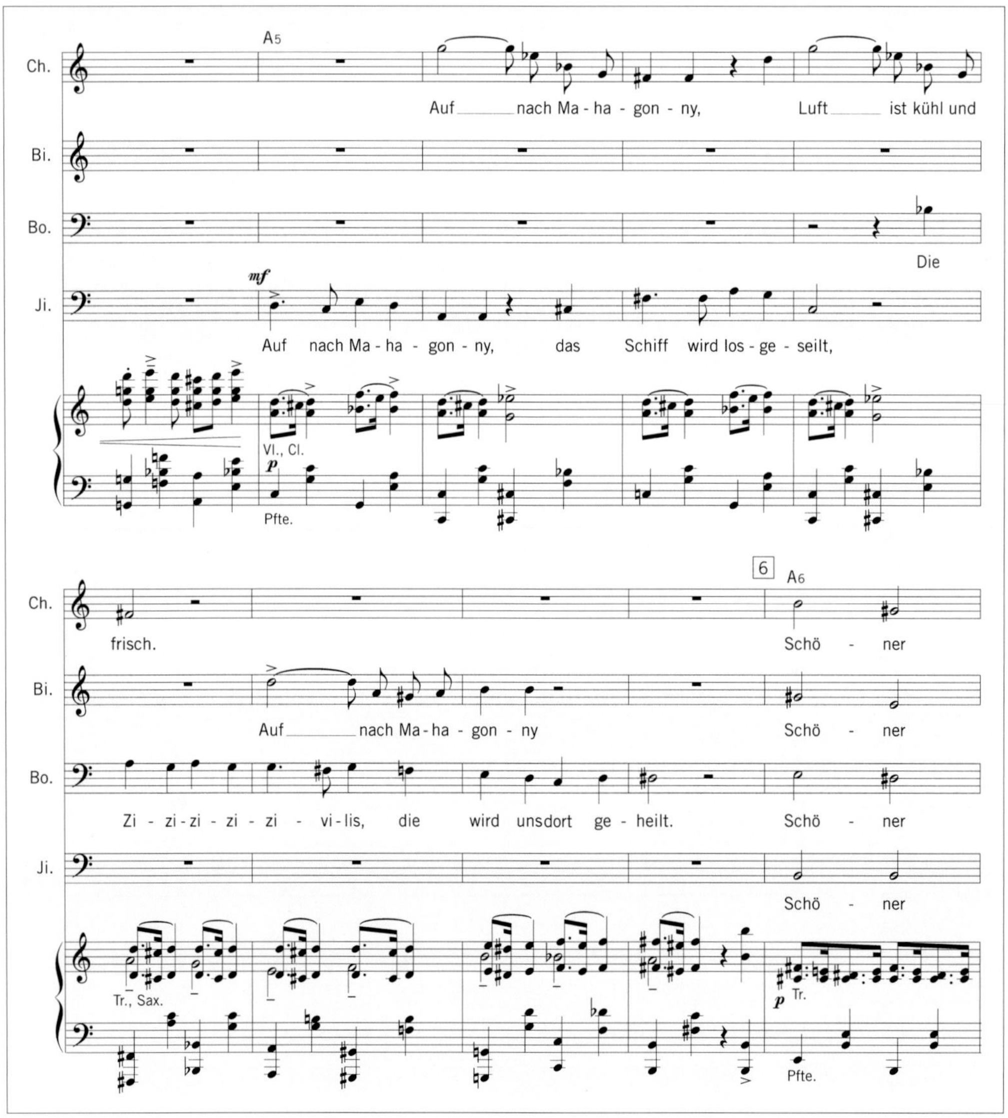

Example 1. Kurt Weill and Bertolt Brecht, *Mahagonny Songspiel*, 1927, "Auf nach Mahagonny"

surely had a particular poignancy at the premiere, given that Baden-Baden was then, as now, a famous spa town.) Brecht transformed the utopian "Mahagonne" of Krauss-Elka's hit into the rather different "Mahagonny" of the poetry collection from which (apart from the finale) the texts of the *Songspiel* were taken, his *Hauspostille* (1927; *Manual of Piety,* 1966). All the more reason, then, especially in the context provided by the commission and its first performance, to hear the first number as a veritable clash of musical cultures—a mixed genre, indeed. This portion of the *Songspiel* was transplanted pretty much wholesale into the opera.

At the concluding words of the *Songspiel* ("Mahagonny ist nur ein erfundenes Wort") (ex. 2), the dotted rhythm that had accommodated the text "Auf nach" (see ex. 1, mm. 2, 3, 7) disappears, while the fox-trot rhythm originally preceding it becomes part of the instrumental texture (see ex. 2, last system). Weill complicates

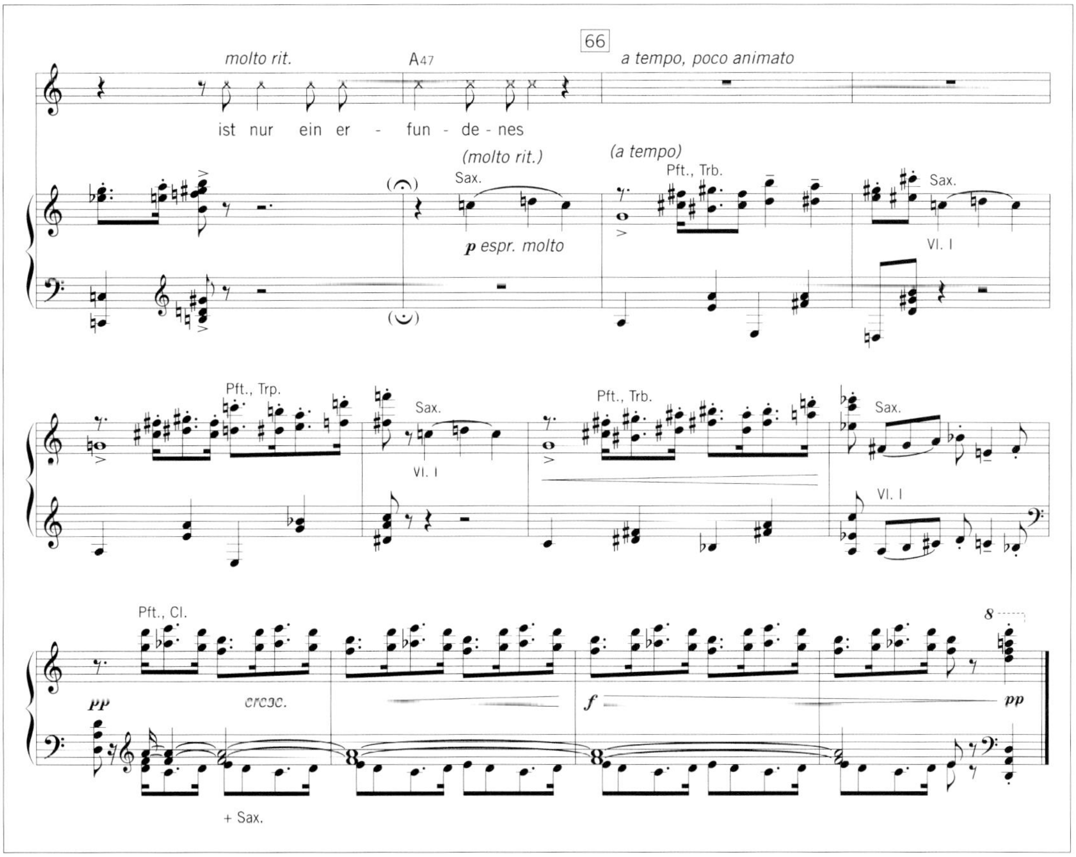

Example 2.
Kurt Weill and Bertolt Brecht, *Mahagonny Songspiel,* 1927, Finale: "Dieses ganze Mahagonny"

the opposition of illusion and reality. Mahagonny, symbolized musically by the popular dance idiom, is textually qualified as an illusion: it is "only a made-up word." Turning into a repeating rhythmic figure, an ostinato, the dotted rhythm (also a feature of Weber's bridesmaids' chorus) swells to forte and then dies away, into nothing. It is a throwaway gesture, both verbally and musically. By extension, *Mahagonny*—the piece—is made up. The *Songspiel*'s end itself, then, illustrates the sense of "playing with songs."

Expecting dissension, customarily expressed by German theatergoers through loud whistling, Brecht had furnished the members of the cast for the *Songspiel*'s premiere with their own whistles, so they could respond in kind, which they apparently did.[16] The *Songspiel,* like the opera after it, thrives on playing the invoked cultural worlds—art and kitsch, high and low, old and new—off against each other. And it does so more tersely, and more pointedly, than any of Weill's earlier one-act operas. This suggests a new connotation of Weill's term *Zwischengattung,* usually (and perhaps misleadingly) translated as "mixed genre": the sense, that is, of the work not so much blending or synthesizing its various ingredients as combining them through juxtaposition. Shaken, perhaps, but not stirred. Weill not only skillfully parodies various idioms and styles; he does so with a heavy dose of irony, as humorous as it is critical. That is the point of the term *Songspiel,* a knowingly sardonic twist on the tradition of German opera with a surreal injection of Americanisms.

Allusions to traditional opera, especially German opera, multiply in the full-length *Aufstieg und Fall der Stadt Mahagonny.* Mozart's *Zauberflöte* is in there; so is Ludwig van Beethoven's *Fidelio* (1805–14) and Richard Wagner's *Tristan und Isolde* (1865); Giuseppe Verdi's *Il trovatore* (1853; The troubadour) can also be detected.[17] And the surreal Americanisms remain, as does the finale, with God coming to Mahagonny "Mitten im Whisky" (Amid the whisky). But much has changed. Writing for an opera house for a full evening's entertainment required quite different measures. The *Mahagonny Songspiel*'s basic idea was not so much coarsened as, of necessity, radically revised. Weill admitted as much when, in a letter to his publisher, he stated: "Almost everything added to the Baden-Baden version is written in a perfectly strict, thoroughly responsible style," that is, *not* in the song style.[18] He was referring to the neoclassical turn taken by a number of his compositions, not just the *Mahagonny* opera.

But it would be wrong to talk about this shift merely in terms of personal style. Serving a dramaturgical purpose in the full-length work, the neoclassical elements (often derived from compositions predating the classical period in music) play a significant or, rather, a *signifying* role in the musical parable of the rise and fall of the city. As Mahagonny emerges, both the timeless topics of academic counterpoint and the compound melodic style of Johann Sebastian Bach—Weill's neoclassical elements—act as a foil to the *couleur locale* provided by the rhythms and sounds of the fox-trot, tango, and other contemporary dance music (fig. 1). The opening scene of the arrival onstage of the fugitives from justice and the founding of the city is accompanied in the opening orchestral prelude by music written in an austere linear counterpoint, a musical style symbolic of flight, perhaps, but also of

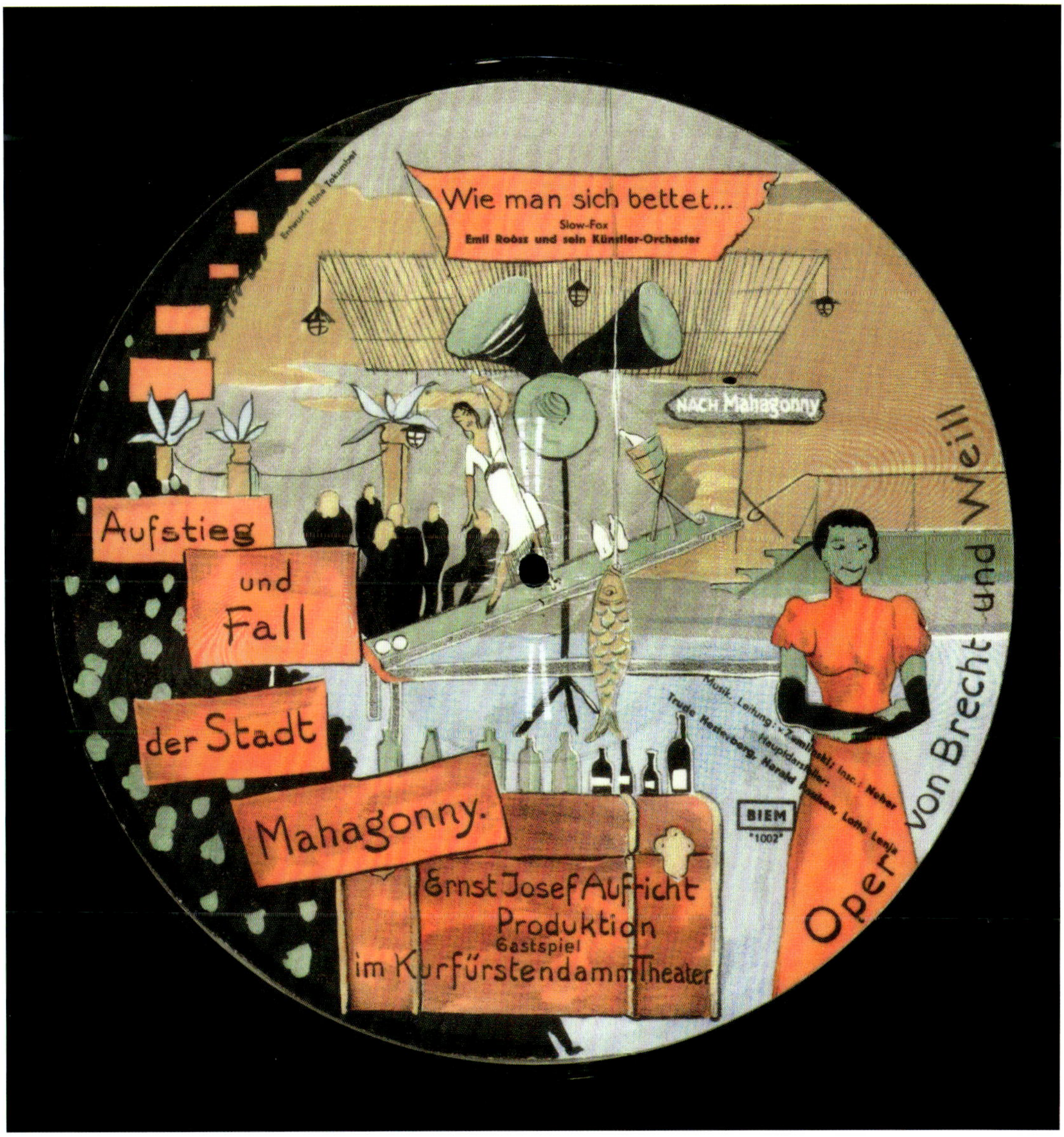

Fig. 1.
Side of a picture record featuring a fox-trot arrangement of "Wie man sich bettet" from Kurt Weill and Bertolt Brecht's *Aufstieg und Fall der Stadt Mahagonny*
Designed by Nina Tokumbet and issued by the theater producer Ernst Josef Aufricht to promote his production of the opera at the Theater am Kurfürstendamm, Berlin, 1931

unadulterated craftsmanship. Then bit by bit, it is contaminated by the trappings of modern civilization, epitomized by the textures of dance music, including offbeat vamping and the dotted fox-trot rhythm (ex. 3, mm. 4–10). At the end of act 1, the hurricane—the threatening force of nature—comes and goes as a topically laden fugue (ex. 4). Here the fugue functions more as polyphonic technique than an exhibition of textbook form; the style sounds quoted, with bold, defamiliarizing instrumentation for brass. The topical associations are complicated, at once chaos and law: the law of nature.

The love duet between Jenny Hill and Jimmy Mahoney, "Sieh jene Kraniche"—the so-called Cranes' Duet—is one of Weill's finest neobaroque compositions. It owes its composition and insertion into the opera at a late stage to a

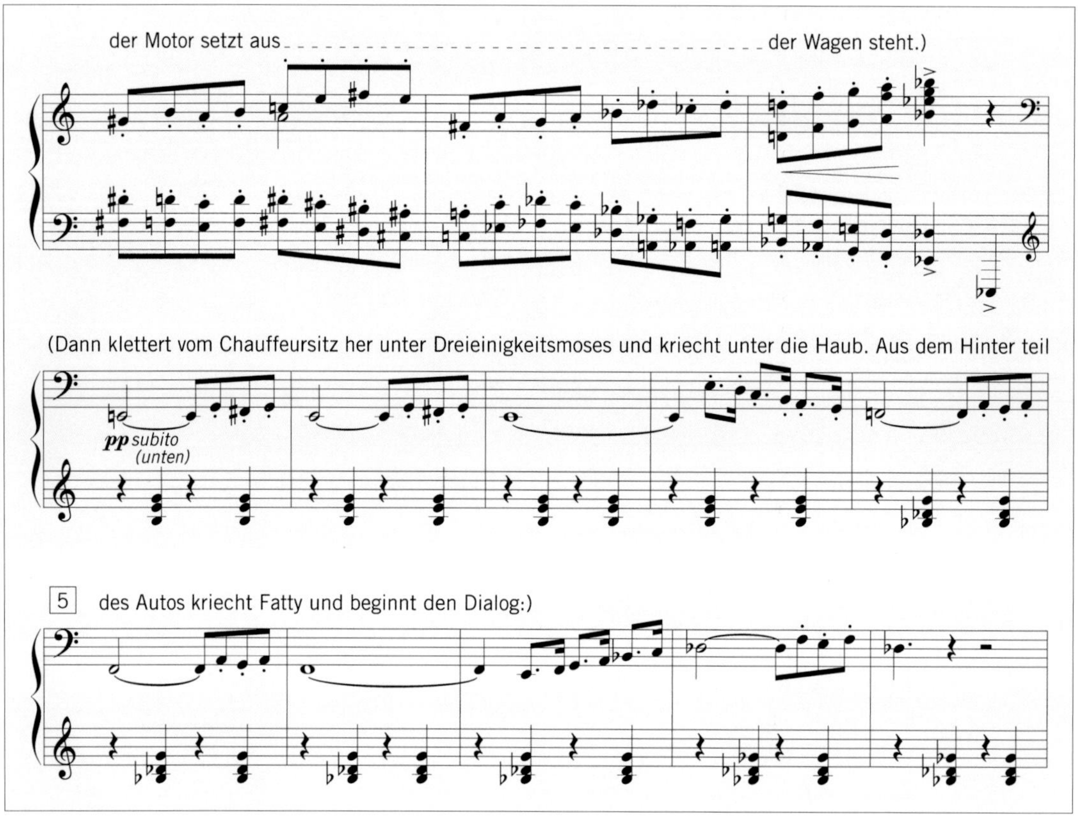
der Motor setzt aus
der Wagen steht.)
(Dann klettert vom Chauffeursitz her unter Dreieinigkeitsmoses und kriecht unter die Haub. Aus dem Hinter teil
pp subito
(unten)
5
des Autos kriecht Fatty und beginnt den Dialog:)

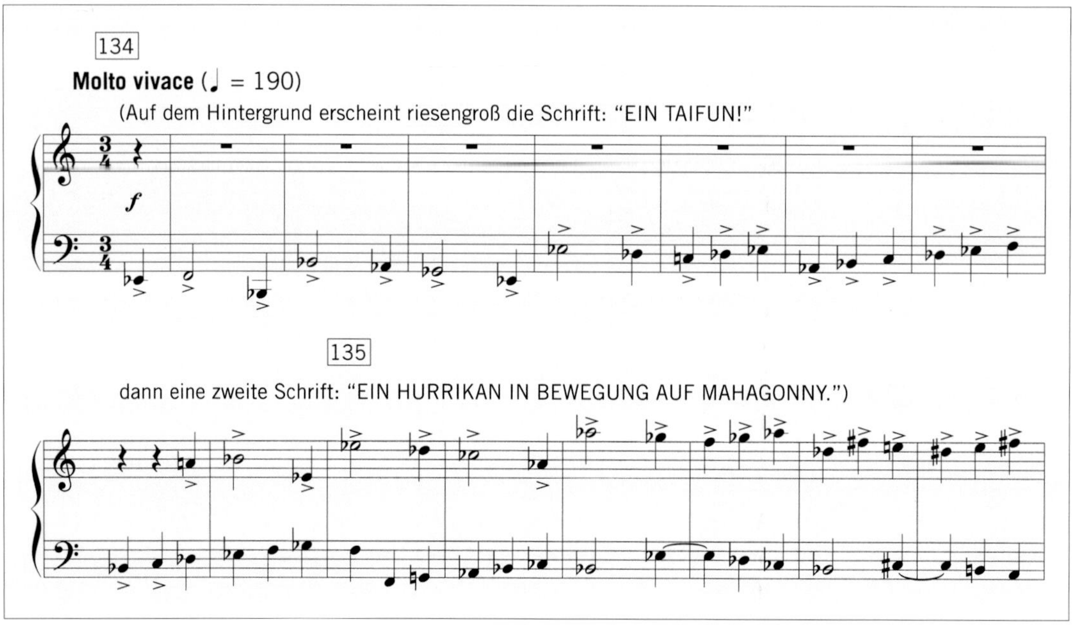
134
Molto vivace (♩ = 190)
(Auf dem Hintergrund erscheint riesengroß die Schrift: "EIN TAIFUN!"
f
135
dann eine zweite Schrift: "EIN HURRIKAN IN BEWEGUNG AUF MAHAGONNY.")

complaint by Weill's publisher, Emil Hertzka. A few months after the premiere of the *Songspiel,* he wrote to Weill, "What emerges from your outline is a new style of opera, yet one that nonetheless signifies merely a sequence of scenes, admittedly sometimes quite gripping and original ones, that can form a new type of 'opera-revue.'... boxing, murder, homicide, drunkenness, and the like predominate, and that could be difficult to bear for a whole evening."[19] Weill responded with a plan to "shift the love plot between Jimmy and Jenny more into the foreground."[20] The imagery of birds in flight in Brecht's text—a parody of verses in canto 5 of Dante Alighieri's *Purgatorio*[21]—finds its musical equivalent in the gorgeous cantilenas of the duet, a musical image of nature's timeless order, an order disturbed elsewhere in the opera by the all-too-human interventions of life in the city.[22]

Based on the musical symbolism of Weill's score, one could make a case for interpreting the opera as more ecological than Marxist in import. Cities in Weill's artistic imagination are expressions of the human spirit, at once vital and debasing, necessary but in many ways ephemeral, the focal point of hope but also of life-threatening corruption. Weill's own description of the opera's plot highlights the centrality of the urban theme within his "parable of contemporary life":

> Two men and a woman, fleeing from the police, get stuck in a desolate area. They decide to found a city in which men coming from the Gold Coast will have their needs satisfied. In the "paradise city" that emerges, people lead a tranquil, idyllic life. In the long run, however, such a life cannot satisfy the men from the Gold Coast. Dissatisfaction prevails. Prices go down. On the night a typhoon approaches the city, Jim Mahoney invents the new law of the city. The law is: "You may do everything." The typhoon changes course. People continue to live according to the new laws. The city flourishes. Needs increase—and with them, prices. You may do everything—provided you can pay for it. Jim Mahoney himself is condemned to death when he runs out of money. His execution gives rise to a huge demonstration against the inflation that heralds the city's demise.
>
> That is the story of the city of Mahagonny. It is represented in a loose juxtaposition of "genre scenes of the twentieth century." It is a parable of contemporary life. The main character of the piece is the city. It emerges from people's needs, and it is people's needs that bring about the city's rise and fall. But we show the individual phases of the city's history only through their effect on the people. Just as people's needs influence the city's development, so in turn the city's development changes people's attitudes. Hence, all the opera's songs are an expression of the masses, even where they are performed by the individual as spokesman of the masses. The group of founders at the beginning confronts the groups of new arrivals. At the end of the first act, the supporters of the new law struggle against its opponents. The fate of the individual is portrayed only in passing, where it exemplifies the fate of the city.
>
> Looking for psychological or contemporary relevance beyond this basic idea would be wrong.

Example 3.
Kurt Weill and Bertolt Brecht, *Aufstieg und Fall der Stadt Mahagonny,* 1930, act 1, instrumental prelude to no. 1: "Halloh, wir müssen weiter"

Example 4.
Kurt Weill and Bertolt Brecht, *Aufstieg und Fall der Stadt Mahagonny,* 1930, act 1, instrumental fugue in no. 10: "Ein Taifun"

> The name "Mahagonny" connotes merely the name of a city. It was chosen for timbral (phonetic) reasons. The city's geographical location is immaterial.[23]

Weill also seems to be warning against allegorical readings—against being too specific in interpreting the piece. He wanted it to have relevance beyond the time of its conception, however much it necessarily reflects that time. (At any rate, it certainly had relevance for Harry Smith some forty years later.)

Weill's breakup with Brecht was elicited, in part at least, by the age-old quarrel between poet and composer. "What principally appealed to me about this subject matter," Weill wrote in notes he published before Brecht retaliated with his own, "was the fact that [Mahagonny] offered me the best possibilities for realizing my musical and formal intentions in the field of opera."[24] More specifically, "The subject matter of the opera *Aufstieg und Fall der Stadt Mahagonny* made possible a *structure based purely on musical laws.*"[25] For the composer, that meant the restitution of the number opera: "dividing the plot or action into distinct numbers and placing greater dramaturgic importance on musical form."[26] Weill's aim, as he expressed it in December 1929, was "a form of opera founded on musical principles."[27] Those musical principles involve not merely a return to the structure of the number opera as a reaction against the uninterrupted flow of the Wagnerian *Gesamtkunstwerk* (total artwork) but also, as I have suggested, a juxtaposition of musical styles whose symbolic import tells its own story about the human condition, about the individual and the masses, about love in the city, about the corruption of nature by so-called civilization, about human values in general—a story more universal in its lyric way than the didactic Marxist parable that Brecht wanted the piece to be. The fate of the individual exemplifying the fate of the city, as the composer defined his vision of the opera, is expressed in purely musical terms, as he understands them; in both realms, sociological and musical, that fate has to do with the clash of laws, the new with the old. Weill's is a vision of contemporary urbanity complicated, then, by his neoclassical aesthetic—an attempt to balance the new with the old, tradition and modernity, responsibility and freedom, order and anarchy, and so forth.

To say that Harry Smith's film is based on the 1956 recording of Weill and Brecht's epic opera is, on one level, to state the obvious.[28] Yet it is also to acknowledge that the film has little to do with Brecht's injection of literature into opera—"Literarisierung," as he called it. The didactic projected titles essential to Brecht's epic theater and to the original production of the opera are missing from the film.[29] Smith's use of the split screen, with juxtaposed images, some more abstract than others, amounting to a highly suggestive montage or collage, some elements urban, some not, can be seen as a visual analogy to Weill's juxtaposition of musical symbols. There seems to be no evidence for Smith having intended such an analogy. Yet his own descriptions of the film serve to corroborate this impression—one that also suggested itself to me when I saw the film for the first time, before reading what Smith had to say.

More generally, Smith seems to take Weill's score as the pretext for what might be seen as the musicalization of visual art, juxtaposing vertical and horizontal elements to create the optical equivalent of harmony and counterpoint. In his own description of the film, which appears in the opening credits, Smith refers to "contrapuntal images": "A Mathematical analysis of Duchamp's 'La Mariée mise à nu par ses célibataires, même' expressed in terms of Kurt Weill's score for 'Aufstieg Und Fall der Stadt Mahagonny' with contrapuntal images (not necessarily in order) derived from Brecht's libretto for the latter work." And in an interview with P. Adams Sitney, he speaks not only of "counterpoint" but also of "rhythmic patterns":

> Four screens are to be used, and rhythmic patterns will occur between the length of the scenes. The general form of twenty-four interlocked shots is the same, backwards and forwards. Individuals in the audience will have their attention directed to one particular part of the counterpoint at each minute. Peter Kubelka wanted to open it in Vienna: "You can use my castle and my Steenbeck [that is, projector]!" But I was afraid they'd understand German there. The whole point of *Mahagonny* is to translate not the story, which is trivial—it's handled much better in *Happy End*—but to translate Brecht's indecision. For you must understand that although a lot of people think that Brecht was a Communist, it wasn't exactly that way. He was caught in the middle, where he either had to jump along with the Nazis or he had to jump along with the Communists.[30]

Smith was explicit that his "photography has not been directed toward making a 'realistic' version of the opera, but rather toward the translating, as nearly as I can, images of the German text into universal, or near universal, symbols and synchronizing the appropriate images with music."[31] He further specified,

> These images consist of about 250 categories such as eggs breaking, plants growing, rain falling, fire burning, parts of the human body and even scenes of the city. About half the footage consists of animation of one sort or another. The animation is based mostly on the fundamental symbols found in all art such as the circle or dots. The emotional connotations of objects moving toward, past, or away from the spectator, or things suddenly forming or dissolving, have also been utilized.
>
> This method has been followed in order that the final film will be just as intelligible to the Zulu, the Eskimo, or the Australian Aborigine, as to people of any other cultural background or age.[32]

Whereas Weill's musical symbols supply a commentary that dovetails with the opera's plot, the relationship of Smith's images to the overall structure of the opera seems casual at best. However much individual images, especially the "scenes of the city," fit with the story of Mahagonny's rise and fall, the musicalization of the film's visual register through symbolic counterpoints tends to follow its own logic. To analyze any musical number in relation to those images, then, is to underscore the relative autonomy of the multifarious visual juxtapositions from the opera sound track, an autonomy that obtains as much between the images themselves as between the visual and other dimensions of the work. To single out, for example, the "Cranes'

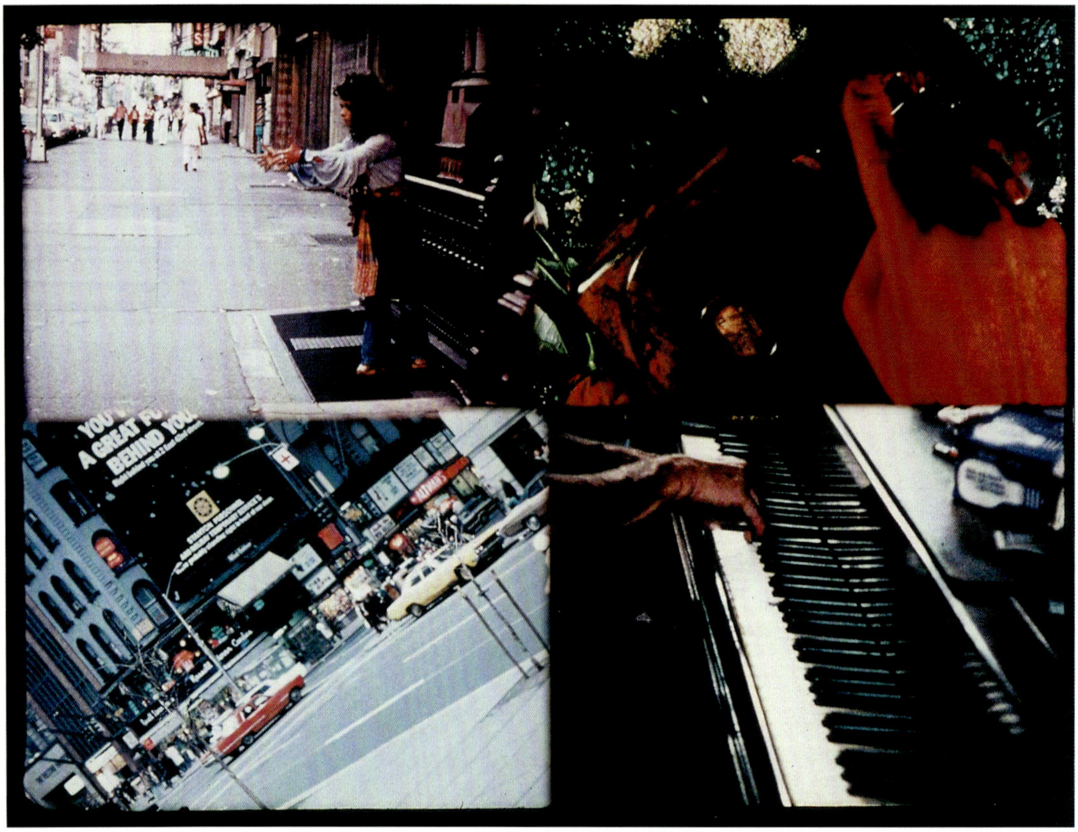

Fig. 2.
Harry Smith
Still from the opening of the "Cranes' Duet" in *Film #18: Mahagonny,* 1970–80 (restored, 2002), 141 min., 35 mm, color, sound

Duet" is to illustrate this general point rather than say anything specific about the visual and musical counterpoints during this five-minute segment of the film. As in other segments, the beginning of the number is not articulated in any obvious visual way.[33] At this point, as in the previous number, the projection is split into four discrete frames, each with a different content that changes every few seconds, though not exactly simultaneously with the content of the other three. The content includes here, as elsewhere, nature scenes from New York City's Central Park, populated street scenes from the city, artificial and real flowers, and abstract moving lines. At the beginning of the duet (fig. 2), in the top left-hand frame, a woman is standing above an air vent next to a New York subway station. In the top right-hand frame, there is a dirty red telephone being covered with roses. Directly below are the arms of a performing pianist. To the left is Times Square. The frames that follow include a Con Edison emergency vehicle (a response to the telephone?), a building with "law offices," a man wearing a headband, a collage of guitars and other objects that include a bottle and a cocktail glass with two slices of lemon decorating the rim. The woman above the air vent begins to perform dance movements to passersby, but then is replaced by a shot of moving orange spheres. The brief insert of an osculating couple in what looks like an art gallery and their interruption by a third person could be taken as more specifically illustrative of the duet's content about two lovers than the rest of the visual images—or not; there are, after all, similar acts of love elsewhere in the film that bear no direct connection to the immediate context of the opera. (The frame is juxtaposed with a shop window showing a price tag proclaiming "super-value 99¢.") The same could be said of this segment's various nature images, which may or may not resonate with the imagery of Brecht's love poem. If Smith derived his images from the opera, he did so, to apply his own projected-title description, "not necessarily in order." The viewer is invited to attach his or her own significance to the moment of synchronization. That significance is likely to occur on several levels, between image and image as well as between image and music, and least of all, perhaps, between image and text, given the absence of subtitles. As Smith put it, "Individuals in the audience will have their attention directed to one particular part of the counterpoint at each minute."[34]

In many other respects, too, the film is composed according to an aesthetic thoroughly at odds with Weill's own—something that makes the topicality of Weill's asphalt-music to the New York City of the 1970s all the more remarkable. It is hard, if not idle, to say what Weill would have made of Smith's *Mahagonny.* To be sure, it is not the realization of Weill's vision of an opera-film, something he dreamed about for years. It is too undramatic for that, too mathematically abstract, too formalistic, but also too "occult," to use Smith's own description.[35] Nor would Weill's work inspire someone to approvingly describe its symbolic images as "palpitating Rorschach blots" (see pp. 128, 147, 148).[36] The respective "objectivities" of the two works are quite dissimilar. In their basic conception, Smith's juxtapositions of image and music are closer to the more nonrepresentational portions of Walt Disney's *Fantasia* (1940) (perhaps an unacknowledged influence[37]) than to anything Weill ever did or would have done. And yet the essentially un-Brechtian spirit of the film's musical principles—its "rhythmic patterns" and "counterpoint"—is not entirely foreign to some of Weill's own ideas about how the opera should work. *Mahagonny* radicalizes Weill's vision, not so much of urbanity as of music's more or less autonomous role in the piece.

Notes

1. Ralph Winett, "Composer of the Hour: An Interview with Kurt Weill," *Brooklyn Daily Eagle,* 20 December 1936, C12.
2. Georg Simmel, some two decades prior to the Weimar Republic, had already drawn attention to the dehumanizing effects of the big city. For a discussion and contextualization of his classic essay of 1902, "The Metropolis and Mental Life," see Harry Francis Mallgrave's introduction to Otto Wagner, *Modern Architecture: A Guidebook for His Students to This Field of Art* (Santa Monica: Getty Center for the History of Art & the Humanities, 1988), 1–51. In his summary of Simmel's ideas, Mallgrave notes how the "blasé attitude" engendered by the fast pace of city life "led … to a cold and calculating behavior in which people were products to be bought, sold, and manipulated" (11). For a broad range of recent musicological papers dealing with the city in general and Weill's *Mahagonny* in particular, see Peter Csobádi et al., eds., *Mahagonny: Die Stadt als Sujet und Herausforderung des (Musik-)Theaters* (Anif, Austria: Verlag Mueller-Speiser, 2000).
3. In a letter to his parents from late October 1925, Weill wrote, "And I'm pleased to

say—as I discovered with *Der neue Orpheus*—that I am gradually approaching 'my real self,' that my music is becoming much surer, much freer, looser and—simpler." See Kurt Weill, *Briefe an die Familie (1914–1950)*, ed. Lys Symonette and Elmar Juchem (Stuttgart: Verlag J. B. Metzler, 2000), 306. All translations from German into English in this essay are my own.

4. Kurt Weill, "Notiz zum *Berliner Requiem*," *Der deutsche Rundfunk*, 17 May 1929, 613; reprinted in Kurt Weill, *Musik und musikalisches Theater: Gesammelte Schriften; mit einer Auswahl von Gesprächen und Interviews*, ed. Stephen Hinton and Jürgen Schebera, rev. ed. (Mainz: Schott, 2000), 410.
5. Kurt Weill, "Score for a Play," *New York Times*, 5 January 1947, X3.
6. Weill's comment about the prison is cited in Kim H. Kowalke, "Kurt Weill, Modernism, and Popular Culture: *Öffentlichkeit als Stil*," *Modernism/Modernity* 2, no. 1 (1995): 40. The biblical verse is Lamentations 1.1 (King James Version).
7. The "phony Richard Strauss" anecdote originated in the memoirs of the impresario Ernst Josef Aufricht, who produced the 1928 premiere of *Die Dreigroschenoper* (*The Threepenny Opera*) and the 1931 production of *Aufstieg und Fall der Stadt Mahagonny*, both in Berlin. See Ernst Josef Aufricht, *Erzähle, damit du dein Recht erweist* (Berlin: Propyläen, 1966), 126. Brecht proclaimed the death of opera in Bertolt Brecht and Peter Suhrkamp, "Anmerkungen zur Oper *Aufstieg und Fall der Stadt Mahagonny*" (1930), in Bertolt Brecht, *Versuche 4–7, Heft* 2 (Berlin: Gustav Kiepenheuer, 1930), 107–15; reprinted in Bertolt Brecht, *Werke: Große kommentierte Berliner und Frankfurter Ausgabe*, vol. 24, *Schriften 4: Texte zu Stücken*, ed. Werner Hecht et al. (Frankfurt am Main: Suhrkamp, 1991), 74–86, esp. p. 79. An earlier version of these notes appeared as "Zur Soziologie der Oper—Anmerkungen zu *Mahagonny*," *Musik und Gesellschaft* 1, no. 4 (1930): 105–12.
8. See the following commentaries by Weill: "Vorwort zum Regiebuch der Oper *Aufstieg und Fall der Stadt Mahagonny*," *Anbruch, Monatsschrift für moderne Musik* (Vienna) 12, no. 1 (1930): 5–7; "Zur Aufführung der Mahagonny-Oper," *Leipziger neueste Nachrichten und Handels-Zeitung*, 8 March 1930; and "Anmerkungen zu meiner Oper *Mahagonny*," *Die Musik* 22 (1929/30): 440–41. All three texts are reprinted in Weill, *Musik und musikalisches Theater* (note 4), 103–4, 106–9, 102–3.
9. Apropos of a proposed premiere in Austria, Smith remarked, "But I was afraid they'd understand German there. The whole point of *Mahagonny* is to translate not the story... but to translate Brecht's indecision." See Harry Smith, "P. Adams Sitney—NYC [*Mahagonny*, 1977]," interview by P. Adams Sitney, in idem, *Think of the Self Speaking: Harry Smith—Selected Interviews*, ed. Rani Singh (Seattle: Elbow/Cityful, 1999), 109.
10. See Stephen Hinton, "The Concept of Epic Opera: Theoretical Anomalies in the Brecht-Weill Partnership," in Hermann Danuser et al., eds., *Das musikalische Kunstwerk: Geschichte—Ästhetik—Theorie; Festschrift Carl Dahlhaus zum 60. Geburtstag* (Laaber, Germany: Laaber, 1988), 285–94.
11. See Joachim Lucchesi and Ronald K. Shull, *Musik bei Brecht* (Frankfurt am Main: Suhrkamp, 1988), 106 (no. 55).
12. See Albrecht Dümling, *Laßt euch nicht verführen: Brecht und die Musik* (Munich: Kindler, 1985), 144–45.

13. Kurt Weill, "Opern-Rück- und Vorschau," *Der deutsche Rundfunk,* 11 January 1925, 84–85; reprinted in Weill, *Musik und musikalisches Theater* (note 4), 217–18.
14. Kurt Weill, "Carl Maria von Weber: Zum 100. Todestage des Komponisten," *Der deutsche Rundfunk,* 30 May 1926, 1517–18; reprinted in Weill, *Musik und musikalisches Theater* (note 4), 308.
15. See Jürgen Schebera, *Kurt Weill: An Illustrated Life,* trans. Caroline Murphy (New Haven: Yale Univ. Press, 1995), 93; and Andreas Hauff, "Mahagonny... Only a Made-Up Word," trans. Margaret M. Sherry, *Kurt Weill Newsletter* 9, no. 1 (1991): 7–9.
16. Lotte Lenya, interview by Schuyler Chapin, WNET/13 TV, conducted 7 December 1978, broadcast in two parts on 30 January 1979 and 6 February 1979; transcript, MSS 30, Papers of Kurt Weill and Lotte Lenya, Irving S. Gilmore Music Library of Yale University, Series X: Interviews, Subseries X.B: Interviews with Lenya, folder 73, item 4, "Skyline," p. 22: "And there we came, yeah,... box ring... out came those six characters, you know, two girls and four men with a bowler hat, you know. That caused quite a sensation, you know... and Brecht with his intuition, you know, he gave us all little... whistles. He said, 'They will... they will... fight... they will whistle, you know at the end,' which means different in Germany, it means disapproval" (ellipses in original).
17. The more obvious allusions occur in the following places: no. 11 ("Haltet euch aufrecht") recalls the armed men of Mozart's *Zauberflöte;* the introduction to no. 7 ("Gründung der Stadt Mahagonny") recalls Beethoven's *Fidelio* (no. 9, "Abscheulicher"); the middle of no. 1 ("Alle großen Unternehmungen haben ihre Krisen" preceding "Sie soll sein wie ein Netz") alludes to the opening of Wagner's *Tristan und Isolde;* the ostinato in the middle of no. 20 ("Aber dieses ganze Mahagonny") is similar to that in act 4 of Verdi's *Il trovatore.* Such allusions are common in Weill's work, creating a rich context of interpretation for the educated listener.
18. Weill to Hans Heinsheimer (Weill's publisher at Universal Edition), 14 October 1929; published in Kurt Weill, *Briefwechsel mit der Universal Edition,* ed. Nils Grosch (Stuttgart: Verlag J. B. Metzler, 2002), 194.
19. Emil Hertzka (director of Universal Edition) to Weill, 16 December 1927; published in Weill, *Briefwechsel* (note 18), 96.
20. Weill to UE (Hertzka), 27 December 1927; published in Weill, *Briefwechsel* (note 18), 98.
21. For a discussion of the origins of Brecht's text, see Jan Knopf, *Bertolt Brechts "Terzinen über die Liebe"* (Frankfurt am Main: Suhrkamp, 1998).
22. Readings of the duet, which are various, depend on two crucial factors: where it is placed in the opera and whether the text is treated separately or in relation to the music. When sung in the brothel scene of act 2, it is juxtaposed with the "Song von Mandelay." Two forms of "love" are contrasted, along with two musical styles. When sung before Jimmy's execution in act 3, the text may appear more existential. Either way, love and the question of transcendence are the principal themes invoked. Before its being set to music and included in the opera, Brecht's text was published separately, in 1928, as "Die Liebenden." The love of which the text speaks offers the

lovers something to hold on to ("So scheint die Liebe Liebenden ein Halt"), however transient. Yet that transience is also celebrated as unavoidable—that, at least, is what the text tells us. The music, for its part, constitutes a lyric space amid the surrounding squalor of love for sale and rough justice. In the recording of the opera used by Smith (see note 28), the duet is placed in the brothel scene. Smith places it in Central Park.

23. Weill, "Vorwort" (note 8), 103–4.
24. Weill, "Vorwort" (note 8), 103.
25. Weill, "Zur Aufführung" (note 8), 107 (emphasis added).
26. Weill, "Anmerkungen" (note 8), 102. The term *number opera* denotes an opera comprising individual sections, or "numbers," which consist of the arias, duets, ensembles, and recitatives that make up the entire work—as distinct from an opera that is "through-composed" or that has a sense of continuity from its beginning to its end.
27. Kurt Weill, "Aktuelles Theater," *Melos* (Berlin) 8 (1929): 524, 527; reprinted in Weill, *Musik und musikalisches Theater* (note 4), 100.
28. *Aufstieg und Fall der Stadt Mahagonny,* recorded 3–11 November 1956, Lotte Lenya (Jenny Hill), Wilhelm Brückner-Rüggeberg, conductor. Released in March 1958 as Philips L 09 418–20/Columbia Masterworks K3L-243/Columbia KL 5271–KL 5273; re-released as CBS M2K 77341/M2K 37874 (U.S. and Canada). Reissued in 2003 as Sony Classical SM2K 91184, in 2006 as Membran 223250-311, and in 2007 as Line Music (Cantus Classics) 5.00959.
29. Bertolt Brecht, "Anmerkungen zur *Dreigroschenoper*" (1931), in idem, *Versuche 8–10, Heft 3* (Berlin: Gustav Kiepenheuer, 1931), 234–43; reprinted in Brecht, *Werke,* vol. 24 (note 7), 57–68. Brecht refers specifically to the screens on which the titles of the scenes are projected as "a primitive attempt" at what he calls the "Literarisierung des Theaters."
30. Smith, "P. Adams Sitney" (note 9), 109.
31. Harry Smith to the Committee on Poetry, New York City, typescript grant application, ca. 1973, i–ii, Harry Smith Archives. Reprinted in this volume, 272–73.
32. Smith to the Committee on Poetry (note 31), ii; see this volume, 272.
33. Smith stated in his outline that "the film will be a series of scenes of varying lengths synchronized to the time of an entire song, and on occasion, synchronized to the length of a single line of the lyrics, but all designed to translate the opera into a universal script based on the similarities of life and aspiration in all humans"; see Smith to the Committee on Poetry (note 31), ii; see this volume, 272–73. The articulation and length of the synchronizations are hard to determine in individual instances, however, chiefly because of the multiplicity of images projected both simultaneously and sequentially. In light of his statement to Sitney that "Individuals in the audience will have their attention directed to one particular part of the counterpoint at each minute" (quoted above, p. 165) Smith is no doubt expecting the nature of the synchronizations to be a function, at least in part, of reception.
34. Smith, "P. Adams Sitney" (note 9), 109.
35. Smith, "P. Adams Sitney" (note 9), 109: "The original decision was to translate an opera into an occult experience."
36. Dave Kehr, "Turning Music into Math, and Math into Images," review of

Mahagonny, directed by Harry Smith, *New York Times,* Late Edition (East Coast), 13 September 2002, E.1:15.

37. Although it should be noted that in 1937 and 1938, Oskar Fischinger—whom Smith met and to whom Smith dedicated his *Film #5: Circular Tensions* (ca. 1950)—worked briefly on *Fantasia*'s opening sequence, which is set to Bach's Toccata and Fugue in D Minor BWV 565.

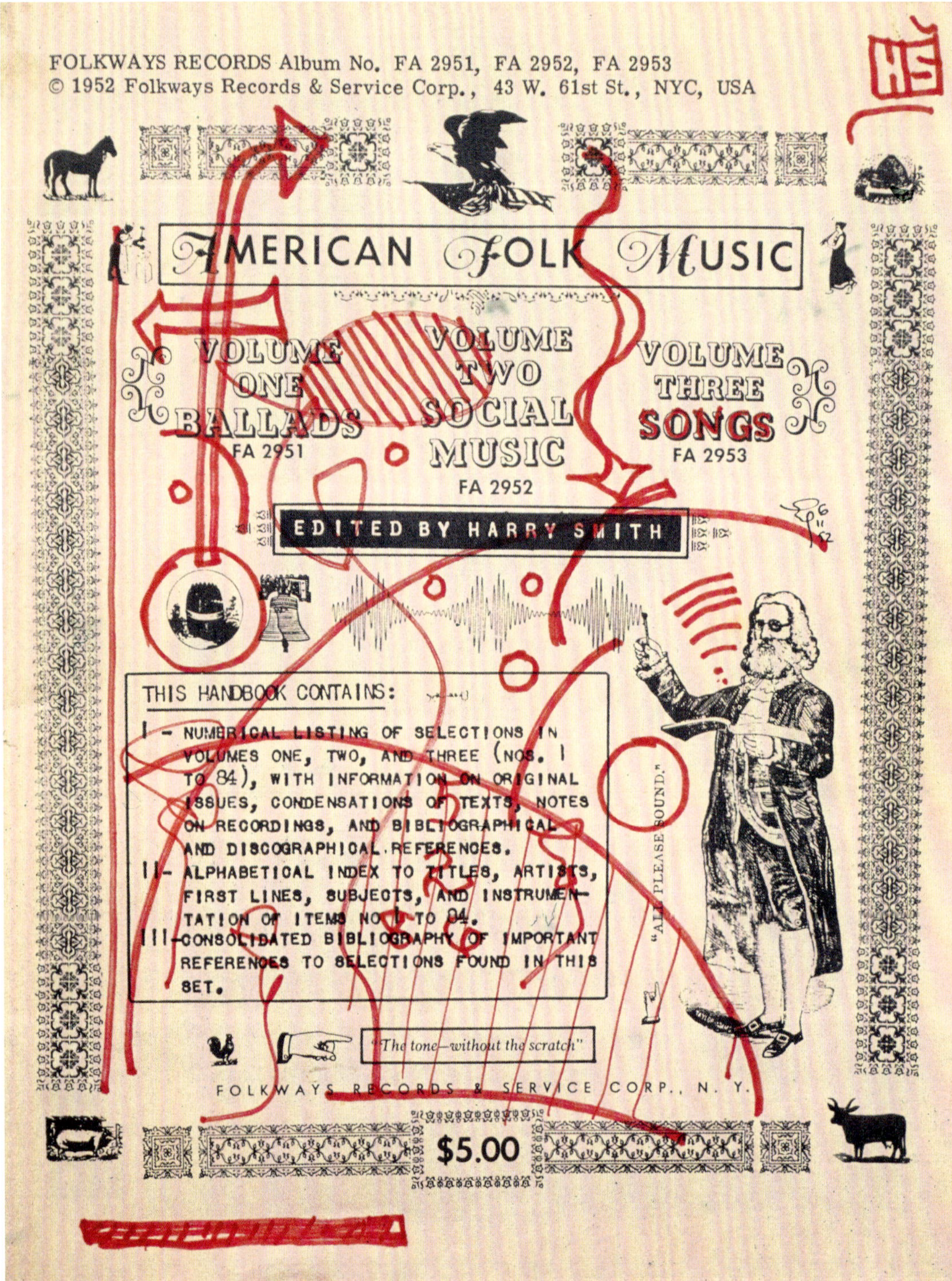
FOLKWAYS RECORDS Album No. FA 2951, FA 2952, FA 2953
© 1952 Folkways Records & Service Corp., 43 W. 61st St., NYC, USA
HS
AMERICAN FOLK MUSIC
VOLUME ONE BALLADS FA 2951
VOLUME TWO SOCIAL MUSIC FA 2952
VOLUME THREE SONGS FA 2953
EDITED BY HARRY SMITH
THIS HANDBOOK CONTAINS:
I - NUMERICAL LISTING OF SELECTIONS IN VOLUMES ONE, TWO, AND THREE (NOS. 1 TO 84), WITH INFORMATION ON ORIGINAL ISSUES, CONDENSATIONS OF TEXTS, NOTES ON RECORDINGS, AND BIBLIOGRAPHICAL AND DISCOGRAPHICAL REFERENCES.
II- ALPHABETICAL INDEX TO TITLES, ARTISTS, FIRST LINES, SUBJECTS, AND INSTRUMENTATION OF ITEMS NO. 1 TO 84.
III-CONSOLIDATED BIBLIOGRAPHY OF IMPORTANT REFERENCES TO SELECTIONS FOUND IN THIS SET.
"ALL PLEASE SOUND."
"The tone—without the scratch"
FOLKWAYS RECORDS & SERVICE CORP., N. Y.
$5.00

PART IV
Anthology of American Folk Music

GREIL MARCUS

UNCLE DAVE MACON: Agent of Satan?

I live in Berkeley, California. Almost every day for twenty five years I've walked up the same steep, winding hill, up a stretch of pavement called Panoramic Way. A few years back, when my fascination with Harry Smith's *Anthology of American Folk Music*—a fascination that began around 1970—was turning into obsession, I began to imagine that Smith had lived on this street.

I knew that Smith was born in 1923 in Portland, Oregon, and grew up in and around Seattle, Washington; that as a teenager he had recorded the ceremonies and chants of the local Indian tribes and in 1940 had begun to collect commercially released blues and country 78 rpm records from the 1920s and 1930s. In 1952, in New York City, when his collection ran into the tens of thousands, he assembled eighty-four sides by mostly forgotten performers as an anthology he at first called simply, or arrogantly, *American Folk Music:* a dubiously legal bootleg of recordings originally issued by Columbia, Victor, Brunswick, and the original Paramount label. Released that year by Folkways Records as three double LPs, the soon-retitled *Anthology of American Folk Music* became the foundation stone of the American folk revival of the late 1950s and the 1960s.

Slowly at first, Smith's set found its way into beatnik enclaves, collegiate bohemias, and the nascent folk scenes in Greenwich Village, Chicago, Philadelphia, Berkeley, and Detroit. By the early 1960s the *Anthology* had become a kind of lingua franca, or a password. For the likes of Roger McGuinn, later of the Byrds, or Jerry Garcia, founder of the Grateful Dead, for folk musicians such as Dave Van Ronk, Eric von Schmidt, and John Fahey, for poet Allen Ginsberg, it was the secret text of a secret country. In 1960, Jon Pankake and others who were part of the folk milieu at the University of Minnesota in Minneapolis initiated a nineteen-year-old Bob Dylan into what Pankake would later call "the brotherhood of the *Anthology*"; the presence of Smith's music in Dylan's has been a template for the presence of that music in the country and the world at large. From then to now, verses, melodies, images, and choruses from the *Anthology* and, most deeply, the *Anthology*'s insistence on an occult, Gothic America of terror and deliverance inside the official America of anxiety and success—as Smith placed murder ballads, explosions of religious ecstasy, moral warnings, and hedonistic revels on the same plane of value and meaning—have been one step behind Dylan's own music, and one step ahead.

As Smith said in 1991, accepting a lifetime achievement Chairman's Merit Award at the ceremonies of the National Academy of Recording Arts and Sciences, some fifty years of experimental filmmaking, jazz painting, shamanistic teaching, and, most of all, dereliction behind him, he had lived to see "America changed by music." He died later that year.

Page 172
Harry Smith
Front cover of handbook, annotated in red ink by Smith, 2 May 1986
From Harry Smith, ed., *Anthology of American Folk Music,* FA 2951–FA 2953 (New York: Folkways Records, 1952)

Page 173
Harry Smith
Book-page border design, 1988
Harry Smith Archives

Six years later, when his *Anthology* was reissued as a six-CD boxed set by Smithsonian Folkways, its uncanny portrayal of the American ethos would unsettle the country all over again. But that event had yet to take place when I began musing about Harry Smith and Panoramic Way. Smith had lived in Berkeley in the mid- to late 1940s; he'd done most of his record collecting there. He had to have lived somewhere, and Panoramic, I decided, looked like where he would have lived.

It's a crumbling old street, with unpredictable, William Morris–inspired Arts and Crafts touches on the brown-shingle and stucco houses—a weird collection of chimneys on one, on another a fountain in the shape of a Gorgon's face sculpted out of a concrete wall, so that water comes out of the mouth, drips down, and, over the decades, has left the Gorgon with a long green beard of moss.

Most of the houses on the downside of the hill are hidden from view. You almost never see anyone out of doors. No sidewalks. Deer and wild turkey in the daytime; raccoon, possums, even coyotes at night. Blackberries, plums, loquats, wild rosemary, and fennel everywhere. Woods and warrens, stone stairways cutting the hill from bottom to top. An always dark pathway shrouded by huge redwoods. The giant curve of a house built by Frank Lloyd Wright. A street where, you could imagine, something odd, seductive, forbidden, or unspeakable was taking place behind every door. Absolute bohemian, absolute pack rat—where else would Harry Smith live if he lived in Berkeley?

I'd read that Smith had lived for a time in the basement apartment of Bertrand H. Bronson, professor of English at Berkeley, ballad scholar, and record collector, so I looked for basement apartments that looked right. I settled on one, in a dramatic house that seemed to have grown out of the ground, surrounded by a wild garden dotted with ceramic monsters and a replica of the Kremlin, just off one of the stone stairways. Then I forgot the whole thing.

A few years later I was in a San Francisco bookstore, doing a reading from a book I'd written that had a chapter on Smith's *Anthology* at its center. Afterward a man with a long white beard came up to me and started talking about Harry Smith, record collecting, a warehouse in Richmond that closed just days before they got the money to buy it out, Jimbo's Bop City nightclub in the Fillmore district, one of its walls covered by Smith's giant bebop mural, a painting of notes, not performers—I couldn't keep up.

I barely caught the man's name, and only because I'd heard it before: Luis Kemnitzer. "That little apartment," he said, "that's where we were, on Panoramic in Berkeley—" "Wait a minute," I said. "Harry Smith lived on Panoramic?" It didn't seem real; Kemnitzer, who died in 2006, began to look like the Panoramic Gorgon. I got up my nerve. "Do you *remember,*" I said to Kemnitzer, who now seemed much older than he had appeared a minute or two before, "what the number of Harry Smith's apartment was?" Kemnitzer looked at me as if I'd asked him if he remembered where he was living now—if he could, you know, find his way home. "Five and a half," he said.

By then it was too late—on Panoramic, much too dark—to look for a number. I could hardly wait for the next morning. And of course there it was: a dull, white door in a gray stucco wall; tiny windows; a cell. Directly across the stone stairway from the house I'd picked out.

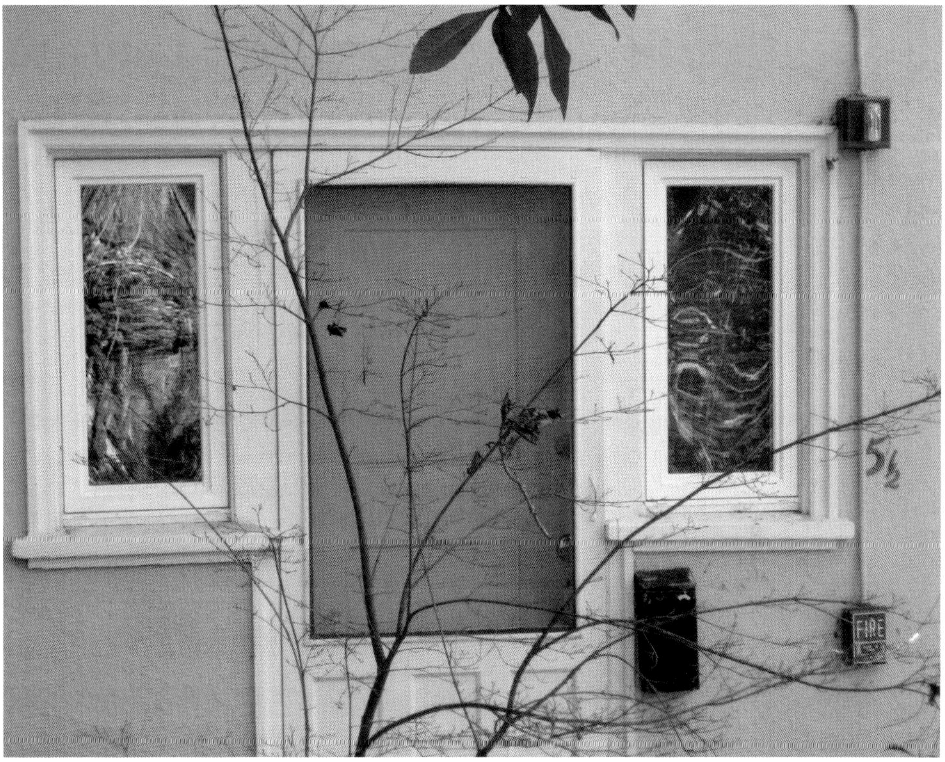

Fig. 1.
Gemma Baumer (American, b. 1995)
Exterior entrance to Harry Smith's apartment, 5½ Panoramic Way, Berkeley, California, 2008

Every day since, as I've walked up Panoramic Hill past Harry Smith's place and then down past it, I've wanted to knock on the door and tell whoever is living there—in eleven years, I've seen no one, typical for Panoramic—who once lived there. Who once lived there, and who surely left behind a ghost, if not a whole crew of them. "WANTED," ran a tiny ad in the September 1946 issue of *The Record Changer* magazine:

> Pre-1940 Race and Hillbilly Vocals
> Bascom Lamar Lunsford, Jilson Setters, Uncle Eck Dunford, Clarence Ashley, Dock Boggs, Grayson and Whitter, Bukka White, Robert Johnson, Roosevelt Graves, Julius Daniels, Rev. D. C. Rice, Lonnie McIntorsh, Tommy McClennan, and many others.
> HARRY E. SMITH
> 5½ Panoramic, Berkeley 4, California

They were still in that little room—they had to be. They sounded like ghosts on their own records, five or ten or twenty years before Harry Smith began looking for them; deprived of their black 78 rpm bodies, they were certain to sound more like ghosts now.

I began to fantasize how I might explain. A few steps from the door of 5½ there's a plaque memorializing Henry Atkins, the designer who created the neighborhood's Orchard Lane stairway in 1909. So I would say, "Hello. I wonder if you know who used to live in your apartment. See that plaque over there? Well, there ought to be a plaque for this man. You see, he did—remarkable things." No, that wasn't going to work. I already sounded as if I were recruiting for a new cult—or, in Pankake's terms, an old one. A better idea: take a copy of the thing. Hold it up. "This is a collection of American music. Just a few years ago," I could say, referring to the London curator Mark Francis, "a man speaking in Paris said that only James Joyce could remotely touch this collection as a key to modern memory. And it all came together right here, in your apartment. I just wanted to let whoever was living here now know that."

After a few weeks this fantasy took a turn and tripped me up. I'd offer the *Anthology,* then walk away, good deed accomplished—but then the person would ask a question. "Sounds interesting," she'd say. "What's it about?"

What is it about? How do you explain—not only to someone who's never heard the *Anthology,* never heard of it, but to yourself, especially if you've been listening to Smith's book of spells for years or decades? An answer came right out of the air: "Dead presidents," I'd say. "Dead dogs, dead children, dead lovers, dead murderers, dead heroes, and how good it is to be alive."

That sounded right the first time I ran it through my head; it sounded ridiculously slick after that. I realized I had no idea what Harry Smith's collection was about. When, in fall 2000, I taught a faculty seminar on the *Anthology,* including what for decades had seemed the apocryphal *Volume 4,* Smith's assemblage of mostly Depression-era recordings, finally released in 2000 on the late John Fahey's Revenant label, I realized I had no idea what it was.

A group of professors—from English, German, Philosophy, Music, History, American Studies, and Art History—sat around a table. Their assignment had been to listen to the CDs; I asked each to pick the song he or she liked most. "The song about the dog," one woman said, referring to Jim Jackson's 1928 "Old Dog Blue." "Why?" I asked. "I don't know," she said, just like any listener. "I played the records when I was doing the dishes, and that one just stuck." There were several votes for "the Cajun songs": for Delma Lachney and Blind Uncle Gaspard's "La Danseuse," Columbus Fruge's "Saut Crapaud," both from 1929, and the Breaux Frères's 1934 "Home Sweet Home," names and titles that in thirty years of listening to the original anthology—but, obviously, not altogether hearing it—I'd never registered.

To these new listeners, these performances—all from the part of the set Smith named *Social Music,* the part that in the 1960s people usually found least appealing—leaped right out. I was disappointed no one mentioned Bascom Lamar Lunsford's 1928 "I Wish I Was a Mole in the Ground," the most seductively unsolvable song I've ever heard, or Richard "Rabbit" Brown's 1927 "James Alley Blues," which I think is the greatest recording ever made. Well, I thought, there's no accounting for taste. And they don't really *know* this stuff—it's not like I got it the first time through. I did mention "James Alley Blues" though. "You mean the one that sounds like Cat Stevens?" someone said. I was horrified. I dropped the subject.

The discussion picked up when I asked each person around the table to name the performance he or she most hated. There was a philosophy professor who, when in later meetings we took up Smith's *Volume 4*, insisted on the instantly unarguable lineage between the Bradley Kincaid of the 1933 "Dog and Gun" and anything by Pat Boone. His first contribution to the session had been to note "the startling echoes of the Stonemans"—in their 1927 "The Mountaineer's Courtship" and 1928 "The Spanish Merchant's Daughter"—"in the later work of the Captain and Tennille." "Hattie Stoneman," responded an art history professor, "ought to be drowned."

An English professor confessed she really couldn't stand the "flatness of the voices"—she meant the Appalachian voices: Clarence Ashley, Dock Boggs, the Carter Family, G. B. Grayson, Charlie Poole, Lunsford. "What's that about?" she said. "What's it for?" "Maybe it's a kind of disinterest," a young music professor said. "Everybody knows these songs, they've heard them all their lives. So they're bored with them." "It's like they don't care if anyone's listening or not," said the first professor. "Maybe that's what I don't like. As if we're not needed." "I don't think that's it," said a German professor, who, it turned out, had grown up in the Kentucky mountains. "It's fatalism. It's powerlessness. It's the belief that nothing you can do will ever change anything, including singing a song. So you're right, in a way—it doesn't matter if you're listening or not. The world won't be different when the song is over no matter how the song is sung, or how many people hear it."

"Uncle Dave Macon isn't like that," someone said of the Grand Ole Opry's favorite uncle. "No," the let's-drown-Hattie-Stoneman professor said. "He's satanic."

I realized I was completely out of my depth—or that Harry Smith's *Anthology of American Folk Music* had opened up onto a country altogether different from any I'd ever found in it. "It's that 'Kill yourself!'" another person said, picking up on the notion, and quickly it seemed as if everyone in the room saw horns coming out of the head of the kindly old banjo player, saw his buck dancer's clogs replaced by cloven hoofs. They were talking about his 1926 "Way Down the Old Plank Road," one of the most celebratory, ecstatic, unburdened shouts America has ever thrown up. Where's the devil?

"Kill yourself!" Uncle Dave Macon yells in the middle of the song, after a verse, taken from "The Cuckoo," about building a scaffold on a mountain just to see the girls pass by, after a commonplace verse about how his wife died on Friday and he got married again on Monday. "Kill yourself!" He meant, it had always seemed obvious to me... actually it was never obvious. He meant, when life is this good it can't get any better so you might as well—kill yourself? Does that follow? Maybe he's saying nothing more than "Scream and shout, knock yourself out," "Shake it, don't break it," or, for that matter, "Love conquers all."

That's not how he sounds, though. He sounds huge, like some pagan god rising over whatever scene he's describing, Dionysus not as master of the revels but as their judge. "Uncle Dave seems much too *satisfied* about the prospect of apocalypse," the agent-of-Satan advocate said. Everyone was nodding, and for a moment I heard it too: Uncle Dave Macon wants you dead. I heard what was really satanic about the moment: when Macon says, "Kill yourself!" it sounds like a good idea—really *fun*. And you can hear the same thing in "Wreck of the Tennessee Gravy Train," which

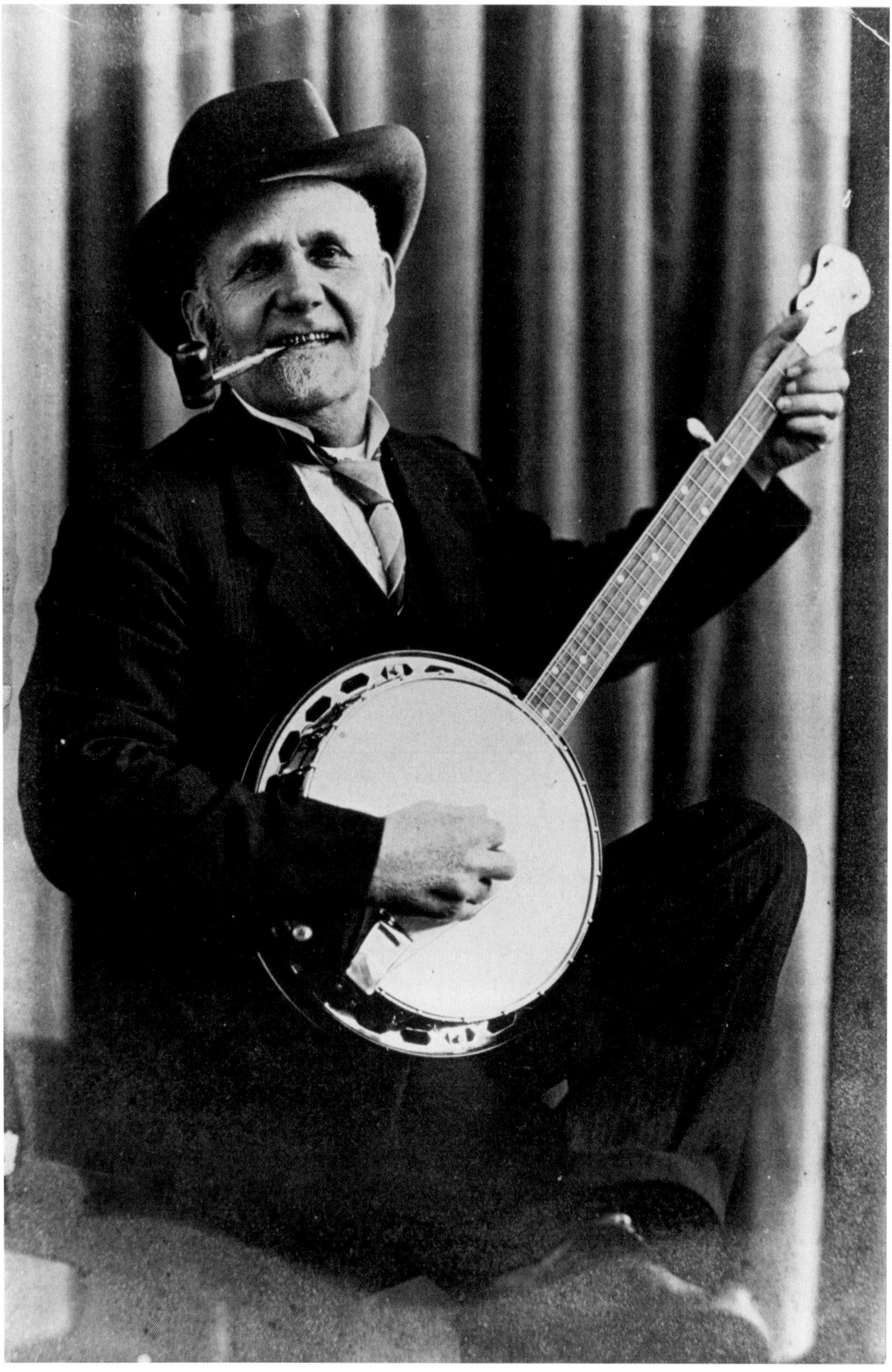

Harry Smith slotted into *Volume 4*. It was 1930, and Macon compressed as much journalistic information as there is in Bob Dylan's "Hurricane" into just over a third of the time, dancing through the financial ruins of his state—the phony bond issue, the collapsed banks, the stolen funds—while crying "Follow me, good people, we're bound for the Promised Land!" over and over. "Kill yourself!"—this is what the devil would sound like singing "Sympathy for the Devil": *correct*.

Hearing Macon this way was like hearing Dylan's onetime sidekick Bob Neuwirth's version of "I Wish I Was a Mole in the Ground." In London in 1999, at the first of a series of Harry Smith tribute concerts put on by the record producer Hal Willner, Neuwirth sang the song's most mysterious line, "I wish I was a lizard in the spring," as "I wish I was a lizard in your spring." Oh. Right. Sure. Obvious.

In most of the vast amount of commentary that greeted the reissue of the *Anthology of American Folk Music* in 1997, the music was taken as a canon, and the performers as exemplars of the folk. Neither of these notions had reached the room we were in. There people were arguing with Uncle Dave Macon, not with whatever tradition he might represent. It was Hattie Stoneman who had to be drowned, not Virginia country white women in general. There was no need to be respectful of a song if you didn't like it.

In 1940 the folklorists Frank and Anne Warner taped the North Carolina singer Frank Proffitt's version of a local Wilkes County ballad called "Tom Dooley," about the nineteenth-century murder of one Laura Foster by her former lover, Tom Dula, and his new lover, Annie Melton. The song traveled, and in 1958 a collegiate trio from Menlo Park, California—my hometown, as it happened, and at that time the most unpretentiously comfortable, cruising-the-strip postwar suburb town imaginable—made the song number one in the country. The whole story is in Robert Cantwell's book about the folk revival, *When We Were Good*—or at least the story up to 1996, when the book was published.

In 2000 Appleseed Recordings released *Nothing Seems Better to Me*, a volume of field recordings made by the Warners, centering on Frank Proffitt. The liner notes for "Tom Dooley" featured a letter from Proffitt, written in 1959. "I got a television set for the kids," he wrote.

> One night I was a-setting looking at some foolishness when three fellers stepped out with guitar and banjer and went to singing Tom Dooly and they clowned and hipswinged. I began to feel sorty sick, like I'd lost a loved one. Tears came to my eyes, yes, I went out and balled on the Ridge, looking toward old Wilkes, land of Tom Dooly.... I looked up across the mountains and said Lord, couldn't they leave me the good memories....
>
> Then Frank Warner wrote, he tells me that some way our song got picked up. The shock was over. I went back to my work. I begin to see the world was bigger than our mountains of Wilkes and Watauga. Folks was brothers, they all liked the plain ways. I begin to pity them that hadn't dozed on the hearthstone.... Life was sharing the different thinking, the different ways. I looked in the mirror of my heart—You haint a boy no longer. Give folks like Frank Warner all you got. Quit thinking of Ridge to Ridge, think of ocean to ocean.

Fig. 2.
Uncle Dave Macon, ca. 1930

This is the classic 1960s account of what folk music is, how it works, what it is for—and how it is seized by the dominant discourse of the time and turned into a soulless commodity. It is the classic account of who the folk are, of how even when everything they have is taken from them, their essential goodness remains. As William Faulkner put it in his appendix to *The Sound and the Fury,* summing up the fate of his characters, naming the black servant Dilsey but at the same time dissolving her into her people, her folk: "They endured."

There wasn't any *they* in the seminar room as the Smith CDs were passed around the table. The all-encompassing piety of Frank Proffitt's letter—a letter which, I have to say, I don't believe for a moment, which reads as if it could have been cooked up by a Popular Front folklorist in 1937, which is just too ideologically correct to be true, even if Proffitt wrote every word—would never have survived the discussion that took place there. It wouldn't have gotten a word in.

I went home and put the *Anthology* on. I had read somewhere that in the 1950s, the photographer and filmmaker Robert Frank would listen to the twenty-first song on the *Social Music* discs, the Memphis Sanctified Singers' 1929 "He Got Better Things for You," over and over, as if there didn't need to be any other music in the world. I'd tried, over the years, to hear something of what he must have heard; I never could. But this day it was all there—as if, again, it had all been obvious.

Smith hadn't credited the singers individually, no doubt because he couldn't find their names. In the supplemental notes to the 1997 reissue written by the Smithsonian Folkways archivist Jeff Place, you find them: Bessie Johnson, leading, followed by Melinda Taylor and Sally Sumler, with Will Shade, of the Memphis Jug Band, on guitar. Johnson starts out deliberately, with small, measured steps. "Kind friends, I want to tell you," she says in a friendly way. Then her almost mannish vibrato deepens; it's getting rougher, harder, with every pace. When she says, "Jesus Christ, my Savior," he's hers, not yours. Her throat seems to shred. With that roughness, and the roughness of the words that follow—"He's got the Holy Ghost and the fire"—right away it's an angry God that's staring you in the face. Uncle Dave Macon, agent of Satan? This is much scarier. But then, as the first verse is ending, the whole performance, the whole world, seems to drop back, to drop down, to almost take it all back, the threat, the rebuke, the condemnation. Every word is made to stand out starkly, right up to the point of the title phrase. "He got better things for you"—the phrase slides off Bessie Johnson's tongue, to disappear in the air, leaving only the suggestion that if you listened all the way into this song, your life would be completely transformed.

The *Anthology of American Folk Music* had been turned upside down and inside out, that was for sure. I was still certain that Rabbit Brown's "James Alley Blues" was the greatest recording ever made, but now another performance I'd never really noticed before, the Alabama Sacred Harp Singers' 1928 "Rocky Road," suddenly stood out. It wasn't a recording, it was a children's crusade. On the *Anthology,* the spiritual "Present Days"—the same group's recording from the same year—has a deep, mature bass, a reedy lead by a man you can see as the town pharmacist, then a farmer or a preacher taking the most expansive moments of the tune, their wives filling out the music. The piece goes on too long: you hear how well they know the number, how complete it is, how finished. It's a professional piece of work. But in "Rocky Road" ten or twenty or a hundred kids seem to be chanting while circle dancing in a field on the edge of a cliff: "Ohhhhhhh—La la / La la / La la la." As if it were something by Little Richard and I was eleven, I didn't hear an English word, or want to. You didn't need to know the language to hear this music; it taught you. Not that it had ever taught me a thing before. You have to be *ready* to accept God, this song was saying; you have to be ready to hear songs.

When you're listening to old records or looking at old photographs, the more beautiful, the more lifelike the sensations they give off, the more difficult it is not to realize that the people you are listening to or seeing are dead. They appeared upon the earth and left it, and it can seem as if their survival in representations is altogether an accident—as if, as the Apocrypha quoted by James Agee at the end of *Let Us Now Praise Famous Men* reads, they in fact "perished, as though they had never been; and are become as though they had never been born." But that's not what the Alabama Sacred Harp Singers sound like on "Rocky Road." Here the persons singing are getting younger and younger with every line. By the end they are just emerging from the womb. Play the song over and over, and you hear them grow up—but only so far. You hear them born again, again and again.

It's impossible to imagine that these people can ever die. That's what they're saying, of course—that's their text. Thousands and thousands of people, over thousands of years, have said exactly the same thing. But they haven't *done* it.

Harry Smith once said that his primary interest in American folk music was the "patterning" that occurred within it. It isn't likely he meant what other record collectors would have meant: the stereotypically male adolescent interest in classification, adding it all up, train-spotting. Sorting it all out by region, period, style, genre, instrumentation, song family, and, most of all, race.

Smith's placement of recordings and performers makes patterns all through his anthologies. Some of these patterns are easy enough to follow, such as the string of murders, assassinations, train wrecks, sinking ships, and plagues that ends his 1952 *Ballads* volume. Some patterns are utterly spectral—you simply intuit that two or three songs that in any formal sense could not be more dissimilar have been placed side by side because they were commissioned by the same god. But in no case is the performer imprisoned by his or her performance—by the expectations the audience might have brought to it. One singer is sly, a con man; another has already gone over to the other side, past death, past any possibility of surprise; a third laughs in the second singer's face.

It's interesting that most of the songs collected on Smith's *Anthology,* and many of those found on his *Volume 4*—the testimony of killers and saints, tales of escape and imprisonment, calls for justice and revenge, visitations of weather and the supernatural, dozens of songs that, overall, leave the listener with a sense of jeopardy, uncertainty, a morbid sense of past and future—had been sung for generations before Smith's recordings were made. But the recordings he chose testify to the ability of certain artists to present themselves as bodies, as will, as desire, as saved, as damned, as love, as hate—as if their singularity removed them from the musical historiographies and economic sociologies where scholars have always labored to maintain them.

In folk music, as it was conventionally understood when Smith did his work, the song sung the singer. The song embodied tradition; the singer's body was simply the vehicle that delivered the song. He or she could not intervene in the song, or in the story or predicament it described. The performance was not an event; when the song played, there was no history. But Smith's work is modernist: the singer sings the song. The singer, to appropriate a line that the actress Louise Brooks liked to quote, offers "a subjective epic composition in which the [artist] begs leave to treat the world according to his point of view. It is only a question, therefore, whether he has a point of view." The people to whom Smith was attracted were themselves modernists: they had a point of view, which they understood as not quite the same as that of anyone else, and Smith helped reveal this. His anthologies are a dramatization of subjectivity—a dramatization of what it might be like to live in a town, or a country, where everyone you meet has a point of view and nobody ever shuts up.

Such a society does not merely decline to ask for a canon, it repels it. Look at the supposed canon-maker. Harry Smith spoke of "the universal hatred" he brought upon himself. He dressed as a tramp and often lived as one. He claimed to be a serial killer. He denied that he had ever had sexual intercourse with another person, and many people who knew him have agreed they could never imagine that he had. Enemies and even friends described him as a cripple, a dope fiend, a freak, a bum. "When I was younger," Smith said in a lonely moment in 1976, speaking to a college student, A. J. Melita, who had called him on the telephone for help with a paper, "I thought that the feelings that went through me were that I would outgrow them, that the anxiety or panic or whatever it is called would disappear. But you sort of suspect it at thirty-five, but when you get to be fifty you definitely know you're stuck with your neuroses, or whatever you want to classify them as: demons, completed ceremonies, any old damn thing."

A canon? What you have behind the anthologies is a man who himself never shut up—a young man in his late twenties in 1952, from the West Coast, now in New York City, who was imposing his oddness, his own status as one who didn't belong and who may not even have wanted to, his own identity as someone unlike anyone else and someone no one else would want to be, on the country itself.

It was his version of the folk process. He would presuppose a nation, a common predicament, a promise and a curse no citizen could escape; he would presuppose a national identity, and then rewrite it. He would rewrite it by whim, by taste—in terms of what he, the editor, as he credited himself, responded to.

No pieties about folk music, about authenticity, about who the folk really are and who they are not, about whose work is respectful of the past and whose exploitive, can survive such a stance—and that may be why Smith's project has proved so fecund, so generative. He suggests to Americans that their culture is in fact *theirs*—which means they can do whatever they like with it.

In the seminar I taught on Harry Smith's anthologies of American folk music, I brought up the notion of the characters in all the performances—the characters named and shaped in the ballads about historical events as well as those characters only implicit and anonymous in the fiddle pieces and calls for deliverance, those representative fictional men and women in the tales told as if they really happened—peopling a town, a community. It was a notion I took from Robert Cantwell's work on the *Anthology*, in his hearing in the voice of the West Virginia slide guitarist Frank Hutchison "a policeman," in that of the North Carolina banjoist Clarence Ashley "a candidate for some local office," in that of the Kentucky banjoist Buell Kazee "a Rotarian." If the songs did indeed make up a town, I asked, what townspeople like roles would those around the table assign the various performers on the anthologies?

This did not go over very well. "Well," someone said finally, "I can see Uncle Dave as the town dentist." "If this is a community," another person said, "it's not one I'd want to be part of." "Of course no one wants to be part of this community," a librarian said after class, frustrated and angry. "All of these people are poor!"

But no one is exactly like anybody else. No one, in fact, is even who he or she was ever supposed to be. No one was supposed to step out from their fellows and stand alone to say what he or she had to say, in the peculiar way he or she had to say it, to thrill those who stand and listen with the notion that they, too, might have a voice, to shame those who stand and listen because they lack the courage to do more than that.

I think it's a great victory—a victory over decades of losing those who did have the courage to speak out in the sociologies of their poverty—that anyone can now hear these men and women, and those they sing about, as singular, as people whose voices no particular set of circumstances could ever ensure would be heard. But once that perspective is gained, it can be reversed without being erased. If we now see the artists Harry Smith found as gazing on a common predicament, each from his or her own perspective, it may be time to return them not to the sociologies that once erased them but to their republic, where each is a moral actor: a citizen.

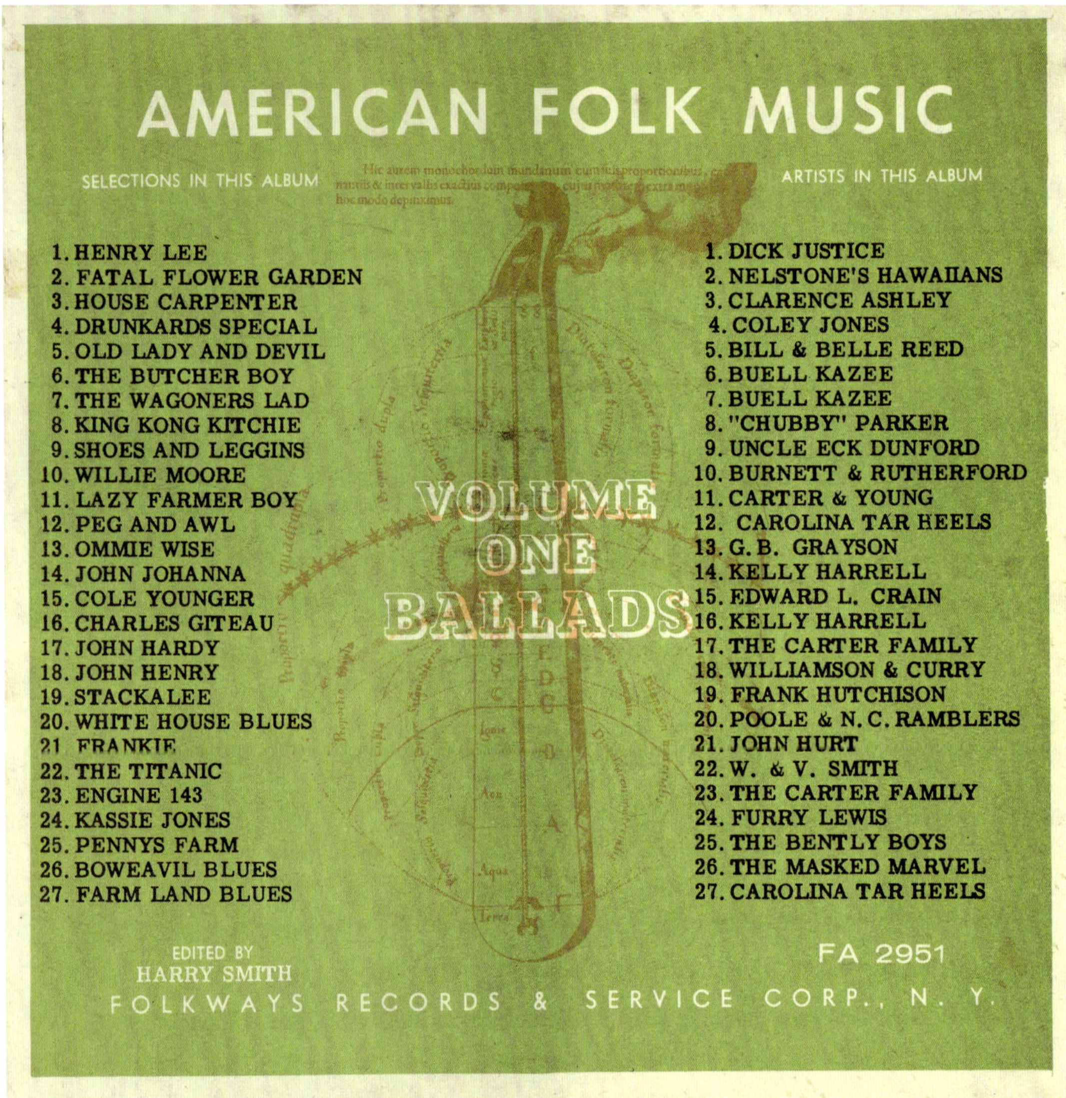
AMERICAN FOLK MUSIC
SELECTIONS IN THIS ALBUM
ARTISTS IN THIS ALBUM
1. HENRY LEE
2. FATAL FLOWER GARDEN
3. HOUSE CARPENTER
4. DRUNKARDS SPECIAL
5. OLD LADY AND DEVIL
6. THE BUTCHER BOY
7. THE WAGONERS LAD
8. KING KONG KITCHIE
9. SHOES AND LEGGINS
10. WILLIE MOORE
11. LAZY FARMER BOY
12. PEG AND AWL
13. OMMIE WISE
14. JOHN JOHANNA
15. COLE YOUNGER
16. CHARLES GITEAU
17. JOHN HARDY
18. JOHN HENRY
19. STACKALEE
20. WHITE HOUSE BLUES
21. FRANKIE
22. THE TITANIC
23. ENGINE 143
24. KASSIE JONES
25. PENNYS FARM
26. BOWEAVIL BLUES
27. FARM LAND BLUES
VOLUME
ONE
BALLADS
1. DICK JUSTICE
2. NELSTONE'S HAWAIIANS
3. CLARENCE ASHLEY
4. COLEY JONES
5. BILL & BELLE REED
6. BUELL KAZEE
7. BUELL KAZEE
8. "CHUBBY" PARKER
9. UNCLE ECK DUNFORD
10. BURNETT & RUTHERFORD
11. CARTER & YOUNG
12. CAROLINA TAR HEELS
13. G. B. GRAYSON
14. KELLY HARRELL
15. EDWARD L. CRAIN
16. KELLY HARRELL
17. THE CARTER FAMILY
18. WILLIAMSON & CURRY
19. FRANK HUTCHISON
20. POOLE & N. C. RAMBLERS
21. JOHN HURT
22. W. & V. SMITH
23. THE CARTER FAMILY
24. FURRY LEWIS
25. THE BENTLY BOYS
26. THE MASKED MARVEL
27. CAROLINA TAR HEELS
EDITED BY
HARRY SMITH
FA 2951
FOLKWAYS RECORDS & SERVICE CORP., N. Y.

ROBERT CANTWELL

"DARKLING I LISTEN": Making Sense of the Folkways *Anthology*

Harry Smith's *Anthology of American Folk Music* is pervaded by darkness: the darkness of recorded sound itself, which mechanically or digitally (and the difference is not immaterial) forges (as in "forgery") the vibrations of instruments and human voices at the same time as it imprisons them in grooves or codes like Ariel in a cloven pine;[1] the historical darkness of music whose origins, provenance, and meaning are obscure or lost; the social and political darkness from within which despised people speak in strange and forbidding, or ingratiating, irritable, or ecstatic voices; the intellectual darkness of caste and race under whose veil secret acts of love have engendered dispositions and powers now visibly abroad in the world. Finally, the *Anthology* labors under a "darke conceit" of allegory,[2] a cloud of obfuscating signs that a confluence of various forces in successive moments—war, economic expansion and collapse, exile, war again, and then an acute recoiling from all that war represents, all that was required to promulgate it—have brought together into a system of signification that perpetually renews itself at the same time as it reincorporates its whole genealogy as a vital element of that renewal.

There is apparently no history as such in the Folkways *Anthology*, then, but a dense throng of stories, reports, complaints, confessions, outcries, choruses, dances, and the rest, all driven by desire and terror, none in the least intelligible relation to any other, save in the few cases of those sung or played by the same artist, none in any systematic relation to the history that, it must be supposed, over two or three generations produced not only the performances themselves but the conditions under which recording machines and performances came together to issue in an inchoate set of recorded performances—or rather the *sounds* of performances. From this body of the music accrues not a history but, perhaps, a kind of alluvial sediment, a sort of cultural bottomland; or, more to the point, an aural iconography that like Renaissance magical iconographies—indeed like Johann Theodor de Bry's celestial monochord, which Smith reproduced on the covers of the three volumes of the *Anthology* (fig. 1; see also p. 228)[3]—salvages from various discarded inventories and lapsed epochs signs, symbols, icons, and images that in their collagelike adhesiveness vibrate with a kind of Masonic inscrutability.

Yet human sounds will not be altogether disconnected from their discursive matter. In this sense, the *Anthology* resembles (but is far from typical of) other collections of folk songs, such as those assembled by Alan and John Avery Lomax, that necessarily embody the moments of their making and the predilections of their collectors. A multitude of historically situated events turn up on the *Anthology*. Two presidents are assassinated, and two murderers executed by hanging. A riverboat dandy shoots his adversary over a poker game, and a betrayed woman shoots her

Fig. 1.
Album cover designed by Harry Smith
From Harry Smith, ed., *Anthology of American Folk Music*, vol. 1, *Ballads*, FA 2951 (New York: Folkways Records, 1952), front

man, in flagrante delicto, through a solid oak door. Two trains crash, the *Titanic* goes down, and several farms fail.[4] Story-songs reference historical and legendary figures such as William McKinley, John Henry, Casey Jones, and Cole Younger, as well as political issues such as worker displacement and convict labor that might tempt us to locate the world of the *Anthology* in or around the end of the nineteenth century.

That is sensible, ethnomusicologically, as much of the body of folk songs commercially recorded for ethnic and regional markets in the brief interval between World War I and the Great Depression—what was then and is now called "old-time music"—had been shaped by the experience, including the popular musical experience, of the late nineteenth century. Much, but not all. Sentimental parlor ballads are conspicuously absent from the *Anthology,* as are, a few stowaways notwithstanding, songs obviously out of the minstrel show. Blues, however, are plentiful, especially blues about misspent lives, ungratified desire, drink, incarceration, overwork, poverty, hunger, infidelity, loneliness, exile, abandonment, and abuse—country blues, for the most part, largely predating the post-1916 northern migrations. And scattered across the *Anthology,* as over the mountain ballad repertoire generally, are materials that, if somewhat altered by their long exile in a far-off land, are quite ancient—medieval, actually, peopled not with steel drivers, hoboes, and bandits but kings, queens, knights, and ladies, given to stabbing themselves and others, or to drowning or strangling over affairs of the heart, or to departing unaccompanied upon splendidly long voyages on ships as, apparently, tests of fidelity. These songs are historical too, I suppose, insofar as they register the imaginative life in relation to which stories of bandits and steel drivers and, perhaps, the drowning of Omie Wise at Deep River, North Carolina, in 1808 or the hanging of the desperado John Hardy in Welch, West Virginia, in 1894 have their meaning.

History is not quite, like balladry, a world of "passion and fury," in Northrop Frye's phrase,[5] and neither history nor romance is as intimate as are myth, fable, and fairy tale with an auxiliary population of animals such as the goose, ox, horse, opossum, rabbit, and catfish who play, in the Folkways *Anthology,* pivotal roles in resolving or failing to resolve some human predicament or to whom, more famously, whole songs are reverently devoted: that well-known couple the mouse and the frog; Clarence Ashley's very British cuckoo bird; Bascom Lamar Lunsford's reclusive mole and lizard; Jim Jackson's ever-loyal blue-tick hound Old Blue. As the human characters in these songs are in regular conversation or some other entanglement with animals, it is perhaps warranted to regard them, anthropologically, as residues of frontier economies or, folklorically, as deposits from African- and Anglo-American song stocks rich in animal fable. Fair enough. But, poetically speaking, these creatures are radioactive: one or two actually talk, or at least exchange knowing looks with their human associates; like the flaming and voluble eagles, doves, bears, lions, and fish of folktale, they are signs of inevitabilities, of fates that are both kinds of habit and a kind of consensus. Mole, lizard, dog, mouse, frog: a humble menagerie, not emblematic of the great faiths, but pressed into service nearer the bottom and closer to the edge of the social body, field, yard, and household spirits that mediate between the human and the natural worlds, vibrating as if bewitched on the boundary between the commonplace and the uncanny. Official religion the

Anthology represents mostly in unofficial form, in a range of vernacular hymns that highlight what for the truly wretched is the central doctrine of faith, the promise of reward in a better world beyond death. Its main theme is release, its setting is social, as Smith made clear, and its emotional tone is joy—which are all as evident in secular dance tunes such as "Sail Away Lady" or Eck Robertson's "Brilliancy Medley" as they are in the ecstasies of the shape-note hymn "Rocky Road" or the sheer pandemonium of "Fifty Miles of Elbow Room."

But, as I have said, the *Anthology* is really an order of sounds, more than of words, which is to say, a babble of voices. Oh, those voices! They are, again, uniformly untutored, rustic, primitive. In the male voices of the *Anthology,* there is occasionally warmth, sensuousness, relaxation—but more frequently the total absence of them. There are cozening and irascible voices, bellowing and officious ones; many are deadpan, dispirited, almost catatonic. Some of the blues and gospel songs sound as if they are being sculpted by chain saws or poured from hoppers, like cement, others seem crafted by dental drills or industrial forges. Mississippi John Hurt sings sweetly, youthfully, with a sense of humor, and Lunsford tenderly, avuncularly, with a suppressed laugh. Uncle Dave Macon sings grandiloquently, like a fifth-term mayor, and Buell Kazee with officious self-importance. Women warble, wail, crackle and cry, or, especially in the shape-note hymns, seem nearly to giggle; there are no sweet-throated, sultry, or seductive voices, no Pre-Raphaelite tresses, no evening gowns, no diamond tiaras.

As we enter this auditory universe, then, every performance becomes a kind of thicket in a synesthetic body of "verdurous glooms and winding mossy ways,"[6] in John Keats's well-known phrase, in this case not only smeared with flickering apparitions like the walls of Altamira but layered with a kind of igneous compound of many musically and lyrically reimagined times and places. Locales such as the East Texas frontier, the Mississippi Delta, the North Georgia hills, the Blue Ridge, the Big Bend Tunnel, Beale Street, or Birmingham are sites of repressed memory or unrealized possibility that cannot otherwise be known; in these locales lives a race of beings—rogues, gamblers and clowns, tramps and vagabonds, drifters, forsaken men, innocent girls, wounded women, a beloved uncle, and a goofy trail-crazed cowboy[7]—whose sudden exposure in the immediacy of their own voices is, and must be, shocking, magical, frightening, and ultimately funny, because they are so precisely and fittingly recognizably unrecognizable. I cannot but picture old Harry, shoulders hunched up, shaking with wheezy laughter—like the young Keats of "Ode to a Nightingale," sick and tired but more worldly and more wise.

From darkness, light. Harry Smith's *Anthology* of "verdurous glooms and winding mossy ways" in fact forcibly recalls the "embalmed darkness" from within which the poet of Keats's "Ode to a Nightingale," listening to the warbling of a night-singing thrush, mythic harbinger of the dawn, synesthetically guesses into existence an invisible but palpable region where incense hangs like moss upon the boughs and moonlight touches the skin with the spring breeze, where space and color exfoliate out of natural music into a "melodious plot / Of beechen green, and shadows numberless." Like Keats's "Ode," Smith's *Anthology* both practices and inspires that visionary conjuring that refuses the intelligible world, with all its habitual distinctions and received truths, only to resurrect it from the borrowed materials of the tactile and auditory body, transforming it from a reflective surface to a vital organic motion, from a reactive to a generative act, its comprehension demanding a prolonged and profoundly inward meditation upon forms and meanings.

Like the *Anthology,* Keats's "Ode" is riddled with darkness, physical and moral. There is first the darkness of the poet's own mind: the heartache and a "drowsy numbness" that "perplexes and retards" his brain, as if, he says, he had just taken opium or swallowed hemlock—that would seem to have sprung from the darkness of despair. The world to him has become a charnel house, "where men sit and hear each other groan," where "youth grows pale, and spectre-thin, and dies," where "but to think is to be full of sorrow/And leaden-eyed despairs." Tuberculosis, which months earlier had killed Keats's brother and which as he wrote was killing him, and a passionate, reciprocated, but unconsummated love for a flighty eighteen-year-old, might account for the young poet's black frame of mind. But another age's "angel-headed hipsters burning for the ancient heavenly connection to the starry dynamo in the machinery of night, / who"—as Allen Ginsberg wrote—"poverty and tatters and hollow-eyed and high sat up smoking in the supernatural darkness of cold-water flats floating across the tops of cities contemplating jazz,"[8] might recognize him as one of their own.

Poetry itself is in a sense always dark—its "viewless wings" can carry him, the poet, through the tactile and auditory flight of a nightingale's song, only into another kind of darkness, that of imagination when it turns self-consumingly away from loneliness and suffering toward its own resources in memory, knowledge, and feeling, to shape what inevitably becomes, the deeper is the heart's dedication to its own fabrications, to its own exile, the "faery lands forlorn" where the poet arrives at the same instant as he awakens to the inescapable isolation of his "sole self." In this sense, the act of listening is like an act of love—absorbed and all-absorbing, envelopingly sensory and ingeniously sensual, an object whose attainment is guaranteed to return us, with an even keener self-awareness and a deeper resignedness, to the very condition from which it offered to deliver us. Clarity and finality, one might think, would be the outcome of such an excursion; instead it is only a deeper and more perfect ambiguity, one that holds at one and the same time, like the music of which it is made, deception and inevitability, hopelessness and necessity: "Was it a vision, or a waking dream?"

Save for "what from heaven is with the breezes blown," if there is light in "Ode to a Nightingale," it is, by an apparent paradox, the light of melodious song and what can sometimes be, under song's influence, an intoxicating excess of happiness—"not through envy of thy happy lot," says the poet, "But being too happy in thine happiness." Where that more glorious existence whose reality music persistently if deceivingly affirms—"the fancy cannot cheat so well / As she is fam'd to do"—may be located is often sufficiently terrestrial that we could plausibly go there, whether with frequent flyer miles or, far more often, metonymically, through associations and with the aid of wine or music, or both, driven by a desire for warmth, for the gratification of appetite, for the light in another's eyes. "O for a beaker full of the warm South," cries the poet, "O, for a draught of vintage!" tasting of "the country green, /

Dance, and Provençal song, and sunburnt mirth!" Keats, like us, and he may be forgiven for it, might be said to be dreaming on the folk—of minstrels and troubadours, country weddings and sunbaked grin-crinkled peasant faces with wine-hazed eyes, though he is perhaps endowed with an at once more discriminating and more sober sense of social actuality when he elects the "viewless wings of Poesy" to get him there. Whatever else this place may be, he seems to know at the outset, it is never anything else but imaginary. "The warm South" is located, unlocatably, in the very process of sense making, which, while it may lead through images, codes, and representations to a verifiable world, produces, by itself, only effigies of its own interiority. It is the process of listening itself that is meaningful, the transitive and immediate knowing of knowing, the dark energy that is as much the issue of the theory that predicts it as of the instrument that detects it, that ultimately renders what is known knowable as a human product. Let us then regard two stanzas of Keats's "Ode to a Nightingale" as a prolegomenon to the act of listening and see whether it reflects our own acts of listening when it comes to something as unexpected as Harry Smith's Folkways *Anthology*.

IV

Away! away! for I will fly to thee,
  Not charioted by Bacchus and his pards,
But on the viewless wings of Poesy,
  Though the dull brain perplexes and retards:
Already with thee! tender is the night,
  And haply the Queen-Moon is on her throne,
    Cluster'd around by all her starry Fays;
      But here there is no light,
  Save what from heaven is with the breezes blown
    Through verdurous glooms and winding mossy ways.

V

I cannot see what flowers are at my feet,
  Nor what soft incense hangs upon the boughs,
But, in embalmed darkness, guess each sweet
  Wherewith the seasonable month endows
The grass, the thicket, and the fruit-tree wild;
  White hawthorn, and pastoral eglantine;
    Fast fading violets cover'd up in leaves;
      And mid-May's eldest child,
  The coming musk-rose, full of dewy wine,
    The murmurous haunt of flies on summer eves.

"Away! away! for I will fly to thee." This threefold call to the act of listening banishes the poet's hideous vision of death and decay, as well as the merely luxurious and stupefying seductions of wine, in favor of the bold cavalier-like declaration that he will deliberately fly away on the conscientiously fabulous, if viewless, wings of Poesy. This is not merely an intellectual activity, and in some sense not an act of mind at all, since "the dull brain perplexes and retards"—but more, it seems, a flight of the spirit out of the confines of thought and the visible world and into the dark interior spaces, the "verdurous glooms and winding mossy ways," of the body itself. The poet has merely to close his eyes ("Already with thee!") and the night is turned flesh, and we are in love with it; Keats has ushered us into what amounts to a love bower, presided over by a matriarchal Queen-Moon and her starry attendants.

The body into which the lover has gained entry is autoerotically the poet's own—as it must be, of course, even, or especially, in an act of love—but one nevertheless enthralled by the music of a night-singing thrush whose mythical ancestress is Philomena (an Athenian princess, her tongue cut out by the brother-in-law who has raped her, transformed into the songbird) and which in any case we already understand to be female, a "light-winged Dryad of the trees." Hence, it is propitious that in this bower of love, there should be no light, other than the light "what from heaven is with the breezes blown" and so on—a light, in other words, that registers its energy on the surface not of the retina but of the skin. It is not, in other words, a merely optical light, that nakedly exposes surfaces, structures, shapes, magnitudes, and proportions, that conceals in order to reveal, dazzles and deceives, but the celestial light of love that creates what it touches. This light opens access to a world not of surfaces but of textures, masses, densities, temperatures, tendencies, and forces, of aroma and color, darkness and brightness, all indicative of a living presence, as they are registered on a tactile spectrum that extends from the skin to that most delicate of tactile organs, the ear.

Though the image of "soft incense" that "hangs upon the boughs," very nearly assuming a botanical or a human anatomic mass, could hardly be more erotic, it is the poet's *musical* imagination that in the space of a few lines restores him, and us, to the world of memory and experience, where he summons into existence a learned inventory of the hawthorn, eglantine, and violets that infuse "The grass, the thicket, and the fruit-tree wild" of Hampstead Heath in the "seasonable month" of mid-May and even bending, it seems, to the smell of "the coming musk-rose," that "murmurous haunt of flies on summer eves," which he audits so closely that we are almost peering into it. Keats knows his flowering plants. Yet the "viewless wings of Poesy" have led the poet not to record this world in any documentary sense but to figure it into existence, virtually creating images, ideas, and objects out of a kind of tactile *aurora borealis* that reaches from the most delicate hairs of the cochlea outward to the skin, the hands, the fingertips, into what music perhaps most centrally arouses, the sensation of purposeful activity, and finally into things and the names of things. This process of creation, evident enough I suppose from the incidental images of the stanza, is clearly linked in the poet's mind to death—for he sees himself laid as if upon a bier with flowers at his feet, swathed in "embalmed darkness"; and yet the process of *listening,* far from a descent into unconsciousness ("To thy high requiem become a sod"), has been instead the unfolding of it, the active sustaining and arousing of consciousness in its fullness and integrity against the forces of dejection and illness that would drag it down.

Keats's hymn to Death, then, is a radical, if ambivalent, turn; his act of listening both restores the world and restores him to it: a poet no longer "half in love with easeful Death," he is ready to consign his "many a mused rhyme" to Death to oblivion. If the act of listening has been a metaphorical kind of dying—or at least a descent into the viscera of perception where the diffusion of self offers relief from pain by effacing the subject of it—listening itself, because it is imaginative, because it springs from memory, invention, and knowledge, and, unlike the mere amnesia of intoxication, invokes what Samuel Coleridge held to be "the living power and prime agent of all human perception, and as a repetition in the finite mind of the eternal act of creation in the infinite I AM," a vital force that, as he famously wrote, "dissolves, diffuses, dissipates, in order to re-create."[9] Keats may, then, at that consummate moment, suppose

> . . . it rich to die,
> To cease upon the midnight with no pain,
> While thou art pouring forth thy soul abroad
> In such an ecstasy!

but it is too late for that. The creative agent is restored, like it or not, to himself—and it is as a resignedly *mortal* being that he sings his paean to the immortal bird, "not born for death," whose voice "was heard / In ancient days by emperor and clown" and has opened windows "on the foam / Of perilous seas, in faery lands forlorn."

That is the phrase: "faery lands forlorn"—it marks the fatal but inevitable slip from imagination to fancy, which for Coleridge was "a mode of memory emancipated from the order of time and space" that receives "all its materials ready made from the law of association";[10] or, as Michel Foucault wrote, from "imagination into voluntary memory, spontaneous attention into reflection, and instinct into rational knowledge,"[11] or, finally, as we might say, from mimesis into agency, culture to ideology.

Is the Folkways *Anthology,* then, an "eternal act of creation" reiterated in each of our acts of listening or a "mode of memory emancipated from the order of time and space?" It is up to us, I suppose—so let us attempt not to calculate, study, reason, figure, or otherwise assemble but, like Keats, to *guess* the Folkways *Anthology* into existence, listen it to life.

Smith, as we have seen, has consciously steered us toward imagination at the expense of fancy—for example, by effacing the racial, historical, occupational, and other distinctions supposed to be proper to the domain of folk song and by which we locate and control it. The *Anthology* is instead, again, an order of human sounds, vocal and instrumental, that—considered apart from the body of scholarship and popular understandings that identified these sounds, that accumulated, collected, and recollected them—are diffuse and obscure in origin, parochial, momentary, in most cases idiosyncratic even within their own milieu and in the various remote settings into which sound recording has carried them, obdurately wondrous, grotesque, curious, queer, amusing, absurd, sometimes ridiculous, sometimes frightening, from time to time sublime. Keats awakens to the forlornness of a momentary vision that turns inevitably to what is "ready made from the law of association"; we wake, I think, to the tooting of Henry "Ragtime Texas" Thomas's panpipes, in laughter.

Since our theme is darkness, however, let us get into the *Anthology*'s dark matter, from which all its distinctive energy is invisibly emanating. Let us recall that as a visual artist Smith worked in a transitional zone between image and afterimage, doodle and drawing, where a neurological anima aroused by its own activity meets itself in the process of creating an intelligible world out of the raw material of perception. Not only was he a master of sensory transliteration—his mural of a Dizzy Gillespie solo at Jimbo's Bop City, preserved only in a few photographs (fig. 2), seems as close to a picture of listening as any visual image could come—but, as in his films, always worked directly in and upon, and not merely through, his medium.

Just what *are* Smith's anthologized voices, then, and what is the medium in which he is working? They are, first of all, the voices of the dead—dead because World War II and all the social and technical forces liberated by it threw a curse of obsolescence over them, from which they were momentarily rescued by the folk revival, only to be buried less than a decade later by the same forces; and dead because buried alive in a kind of cultural fossil fuel, first retailed as a souvenir of time travel to the American past but then, reverting to their material character, collected and stockpiled as war *materiel* and charged with a new regimen of political, cultural, and technical energies; and not only dead but, in a sense, silent, because the recording process stripped them like Philomena of their wagging tongues, so that each is left with only one invariable song.

All this is to say, again, that Harry Smith the folk song anthologist like Harry Smith the filmmaker had his hands directly in the medium, in this case the medium of recorded sound: not, ultimately, a *record* of anything but at best merely an impression or footprint, or a residue, never mind how accurate, faithful, or complete, and as art meaningful photography or the printed word is meaningful in the particular way it transforms what it represents. As a reissue compilation, the Folkways *Anthology* is an accumulation of archaic commercial music originally directed at ethnic and regional markets long since dispersed. Hence, it is first and foremost a gathering. As such, it exposes what formerly could be experienced only in threads and patches as a total design, as a structure of fixed elements whose relationships are narratively as well as architecturally organized. What were many things, in a variety of moments and settings, become one thing, in its own moment and setting. The various signs of an old social ecology were appropriated in the 1920s and 1930s to become signifiers, among other recordings of different types, in the total catalog of early commercial recordings; they are appropriated again in the 1950s to become signifiers of "folk" culture in, among other such collections, Smith's six-LP *Anthology*, itself destined to become a sign of "the folk"; and they are appropriated yet again in the 1960s as a signifier, among other works of art, of the avant-garde and, in 1997, with the Smithsonian Folkways Recordings six-CD reissue, as a sign of cultural preeminence. These many transformations are precisely the "verdurous glooms and winding mossy ways" of layered temporal and social contexts, each of which endows the selections with specific, but different, meanings. Each of the songs had its original life at some distant moment and another life in 1925, or 1952, or 1963, or 1997.

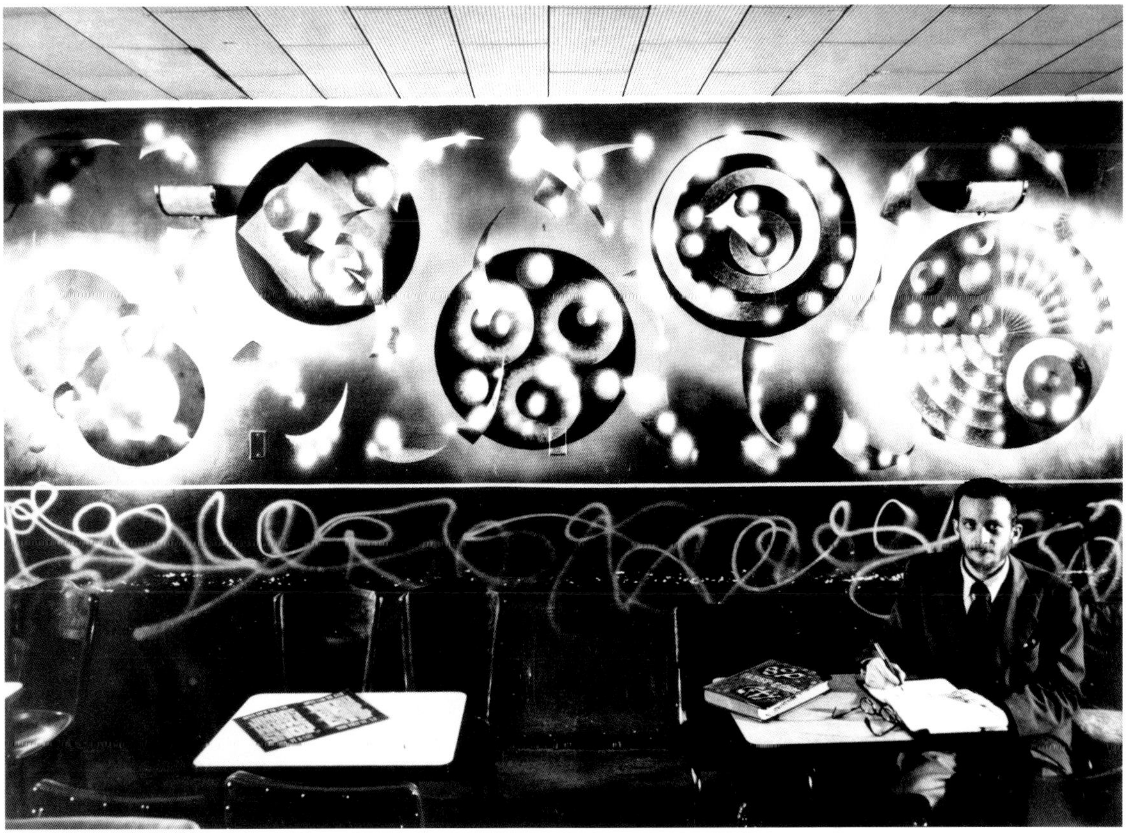

Fig. 2.
Hy Hirsh (American, 1911–61)
Harry Smith with his mural,
Jimbo's Bop City, San
Francisco, ca. 1950

The *Anthology* further transforms technologically, by enunciating its own mediating power: the old *records,* not the old songs, are its subject, whose main interest therefore is that they are old and that they are records. Now all this is a good deal more complicated than it seems. That they are old means that the *Anthology* is, among other things, a salvage and recovery operation. But its constituent set of found objects—more precisely, junk—is not merely an accumulation, already partly accomplished by the U.S. War Department: it is a collection by virtue of which the whole acquires, simply as the outcome of human labor, a value greater than the sum of its parts. Moreover, as an intelligent arrangement of elements, as a recombination, the *Anthology* becomes a kind of hypothesis, an archaeological reconstruction, through which a total way of life might be imagined. At the most superficial level, then, the *Anthology* is a vehicle for the fascination with the antique, with the unknown past brought out of its obscurity and, hence, in a sense radically new and unprecedented, the more curious and quaint as the conditions of its former being are unintelligible and the difficulty of comprehending it according to contemporary usages more daunting.

That they are *records* further complicates their intrigue, for in the first instance the *Anthology,* or Harry Smith, is playing to us a collection of old records of a particular kind in a particular order. He is making designs upon us—but as our primary interest in the medium of the sound recording is the way in which it transforms what it re-presents, we will be conscious of the performances *as records* first and grasp them as performances only as they become transparent as records. But these records do not become transparent, and they never will.

Here is one of the points at which Smith works his extraordinary magic. Speaking now of the vinyl, not the digital, release of the *Anthology,* certain mysteries present themselves: what are, or were, these records? What possible entrepreneurial, scholarly, or other initiative, technical intervention, commercial field, or cultural moment can explain them? On the one hand, like the 78 rpms of fox-trots and light opera that used to gather dust in the Goodwill stores, they seem, misleadingly, to belong to a manifestly earlier stage in the evolution of sound recording, and that is part of what is interesting about them—the scratch, the hiss, and the hurry to the three-minute closing bell, through which, formerly, people had to listen more *for* their music than *to* it. On the other hand, unlike those phonodiscs of fox-trots and operatic selections (typically marketed, as John Szwed points out, more by musical category rather than by individual artist, save in special cases like Enrico Caruso[12]), they do not readily indicate their own history.

On the contrary, the indicators are all hopelessly muddled. Where are we, musically speaking? Not much help from the vocal styles. Some of the voices plausibly emanate from Memphis or Chattanooga, and some from the Kentucky mountains or the cotton mills of the Carolinas. But some just as plausibly might have come from medieval China, as Ralph Rinzler said of "Train on the Island,"[13] or, we might add, from seventeenth-century Senegal or Mozambique. So what is the connection between the material gathering of a heap of forgotten phonodiscs and an accumulation of musical performances? And what has the concentration of performances to do, if anything, with the collection of the "material" performed? The songs (and accompanying instruments) themselves can provide some orientation, since for the most part they belong to identified traditions—but, again, they are doubly removed, not only spun onto the surfaces of inaccessible old 78 rpms (not to put too fine a point on it, it is the *sound* of the old records we have, not the records themselves, unless we happen to be in the Smith collection itself) but also *already* culturally residual at the time the master recordings were made. Like all such collections of "folk" music, then, the old records have become essentially thought experiments, cultural fictions—newer than new, as it were, and older than old. And they lead us, finally, to the *Anthology*'s central mystery: How can *these* performances have found their way to *those* records? Or, better, these records to those performances? Neither question would arise at all were it not for the still deeper question with which Smith has confronted us: *what is a record?*

Smith has placed us roughly where the listeners to Thomas Edison's cylinder phonograph were, phenomenologically speaking, in the early weeks after its public unveiling in December 1877, during which, according to the editor of *Scientific American,* "the machine inquired as to our health, asked how we liked the phonograph, informed us that *it* was very well, and bid us a cordial good night."[14] At succeeding demonstrations of the phonograph, young women fainted, eminent scientific heads proclaimed it a trick of ventriloquism, and a Yale University professor pronounced it a flat-out hoax. What was this machine that could steal the human voice?

That could make absent people present—or was it that it rendered present people absent? That immortalized the human voice but at the same time abolished it? What can one say about a machine that brings the dead back to life but in the same instant buries them again? "Was it a vision, or a waking dream? / . . . Do I wake or sleep?"

Now sound may be a summons, an alert, a stimulus, an incentive, an inspiration, an urge—but in all these cases it is, as Keats's metaphor suggests, necessarily a brush with death, a descent into the "verdurous glooms and winding mossy ways" of the synthetic neurological processes by which we bring coherence and intelligibility to the "blooming, buzzing confusion," in William James's phrase, of the messages of the senses.[15] The same could be said, perhaps, about any of the senses abstracted from the sensory body, since without the interplay of the senses there is no world, or no imagination to complete a world, only its disembodied force, or impress, or reflection; all acts of perception are interpretations, recognitions and misrecognitions but in any case subject creations. Recorded sound, by definition divorced from the spatiotemporal point of its production, in a sense reverses the calculus of recognition, unlike either touch or sight going out of existence just at the point that it is coming into existence, in a sense creating itself just as it undoes itself wholly through our power of inference. As this sound is always revealed by the imagination to be that—a creaky floor, a distant thunderstorm, a Fender Telecaster—so recorded sound, and particularly *musical* sound, which can only make the sound of music, compels the process of listening that is somehow akin either to drowning or to saving oneself from drowning or both, essentially a decision about whether life is worth the effort it takes to live.

All this turns upon the processes of sense making that the obscurity of recorded sound necessitates; like Smith himself, transmuting a solo by Miles Davis or Dizzy Gillespie into a visual pattern of whorls, angles, globes, bubbles, and lights (fig. 3; see also pp. 26, 195), we are confronted with the finally impossible task of making the *Anthology real for us*. It is a fairy land summoned out of the play of memory and sensation whose aim, as in all Smith's work, is to "make sense" of the world as mystery, which is what we call those patterns, processes, and designs in art and in the world that open to perception—and invite, through signs, prolonged contemplation of—the unity of consciousness and its object. It is a process of knowing, an essentially scientific investigation, which, as Bertrand Russell pointed out, historically has been a process of elevating mass and other such notions derived from tactility into an understanding of the nature of the energy that works upon the eye. But unlike the sight-physics of which Russell was speaking,[16] Smith's science is of a Rosicrucian character, dedicated to a description of reality not in terms of orders and relations of magnitude but in registers and hierarchies of human value: not the science of hypothesis, which is never in touch with its object, but the science of revelation, which *is* its object.

My own dull brain "perplexes and retards," but after forty years of listening to the Folkways *Anthology,* its soundscape has begun to fix itself in my imagination as a revelation of the occult iconography with which Harry Smith was so fascinated. There are the animals, of course—a lizard, a mole, a dog, and a bird, all somehow endowed with the gift of speech. I fancy I can see there, too, with an inward eye, a

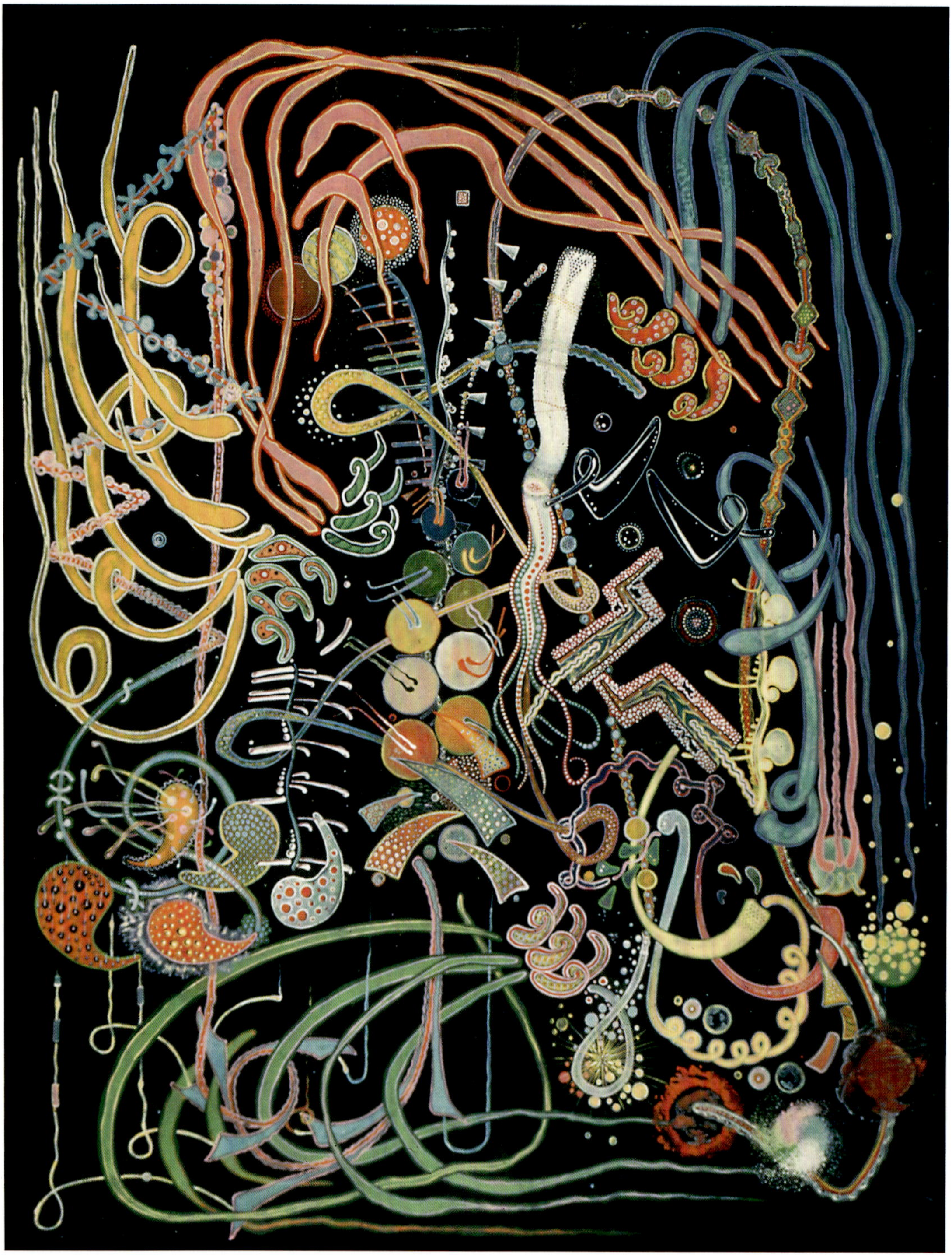

heavenly choir and a blind beggar; a eunuch, perhaps, selling a remedy for impotence; and perhaps a leper, possessed by the voices of spirits and demons. There is a weeping woman, and a man in chains; I think I see a field hand, and a house servant, and, to borrow from William Makepeace Thackeray, "a vagabond with a corked face and a banjo [who] sings a little song, [and] strikes a wild note which sets the whole heart thrilling with happy pity."[17]

But there is also a sturdy farmer with a hoe, and his wife; some hungry, hollow-eyed children; a schoolmaster and a schoolmarm; and a kind of citizen, a businessman, a Mason perhaps, with a round belly and a gold watch. And three young men with blueprints and micrometers: mechanical engineers, out to make a more efficient loom or a stronger bridge. I would say it was a world of this place or that, at some time or another, were it not for Ragtime Texas Thomas, the street singer, who carries his quills—panpipes—in the pocket of his suit jacket and whose two-dollar shoes, in the mud of the riverbank where he's gone a-fishing, leave cloven prints. He is perhaps the spirit who has presided over the central *musical* story of the Folkways *Anthology,* which is the story of two great traditions, African American and Anglo-American, coming together to become one in the crucible of southern vernacular life. A moment's thought will suggest the intense irony of this tale, so subtly told in the sounds of the *Anthology* that it scarcely seems to have been told at all, how its gay, even merry comedy, embodied in such voices as Macon's and Lunsford's, as well as that of Thomas himself, strives bravely against a historical tide of almost incomprehensible suffering to which the music consistently alludes and whose emotional residues it consistently delivers up in fantasy, obsession, resentment, anger, and ecstasy. I do not mean the suffering of slavery and its legacies only, though these are appalling, but also the ugly material and moral consequences of the slave and plantation systems for poor, despised, and disenfranchised whites whose misery and oppression is stridently registered in the *Anthology* in voices strained, stretched, and pinched to the point of comic absurdity.

The *Anthology*'s color blindness, then, is only an aspect of a more comprehensive effacement that yields up an imagined people of no-race, no-time, no-place, a "folk" in the sense that in certain conditional passages of our "unofficial" or unstructured existence we are all "folk," people-as-such prepared by the disarming oddness of the sounds, and by Smith's discontinuous sequencing that tends to defer or subvert any intellectual closure, to project in a nearly Jungian sense our own repressed humanness, with its own debts to pay, onto their tunes, their stories, and their voices. "In that condition of life," as William Wordsworth, speaking not ethnographically but poetically, said of the "humble and rustic life" that he chose for his *Lyrical Ballads,* "the essential passions of the heart find a better soil in which they can attain their maturity, are less under restraint, and speak a plainer and more emphatic language." But he might better have said, *appear* to be—for as he himself well knew, his real subject was ever and always his own spiritual life, and the manner in which, through the "spontaneous overflow of powerful feelings," and the association of "ideas in a state of excitement," poetry wherein "ordinary things should be presented to the mind in an unusual aspect," in a "language really used by men," might reveal "the primary laws of our nature."[18]

Fig. 3.
Harry Smith
Manteca, ca. 1948
Painting of "Manteca," Dizzy Gillespie Orchestra, ca. 1947
Whereabouts unknown

The world of the Folkways *Anthology*, like that of Keats's "Ode to a Nightingale," is one of heartache, forgetfulness, disease, decrepitude, injustice, loneliness, and despair but also of sunshine, laughter, intoxication, joy, and fun. Like Keats's poet, we look longingly away from the charnel house of mid-twentieth-century America, as Smith did, or, as the case may be, from the twenty-first century's crumbling Temple of Mammon, to a dream of the "warm South," of song, dance, and "sunburnt mirth"—but find ourselves transported instead, under the dark spell of the music, into the depths of our own bodies, a region of life-in-death and death-in-life, where, guided by the secret knowledges it is the business of mystical contemplation to summon up, we seem to make a path through our very substance. But the spell, in and by the very act of its enunciation, must ultimately be broken, and our eyes opened; the voices of the *Anthology*, like the nightingale and its song, are after all only visitors from another place—the "faery lands forlorn" from which, as for the poet, only the sound of a living voice, our own, can deliver us. Like the wild heath that lay just up the road from the suburban garden in which Keats composed his poem and to which his harbinger bird ultimately returned, Smith's "old, weird America," as Greil Marcus calls it,[19] though always near at hand, is directly knowable only through transient and irrecoverable experiences we usually associate not with beauty in any conventional sense but with that more jealous apprehension of it that as a kind of revelation glances back at us from what is rude, ugly, frightening, obscure, despised, or merely plain—from what, in a word, we have discovered for ourselves.

If we, like Keats, have been half in love with easeful Death, it is perhaps on account of spatiotemporal change so ruthlessly accelerated that we are as good as continually dying, no sooner consolidating selfhood than packing it up for storage, no longer living *to* music but living *on* it to the point of becoming it, until the very point of selfhood seems to have been lost. Listening to the Folkways *Anthology* we are, like Keats in his "Ode," at once playing at death and playing with it, for the purpose—if the evolution of Keats's meaning can be called a purpose, since it is as much our own as his—of wondering whether we are asleep or awake, seeing or dreaming, and whether it is ever possible to know the difference, or whether it makes any difference that we can or cannot.

Notes

This essay appears, in slightly different form, in Robert Cantwell, *If Beale Street Could Talk: Music, Community, Culture* (Champaign: Univ. of Illinois Press, 2008), 26–41.

1. William Shakespeare, *The Tempest*, ed. Stephen Orgel (Oxford: Clarendon, 1987), I.ii.274–81, 286–93.
2. Edmund Spenser to Sir Walter Raleigh, 23 January 1589; first published in Edmund Spenser, *The Faerie Queene*... (London: printed for William Ponsonbie, 1590), 591.
3. Harry Smith, ed., *Anthology of American Folk Music*, FP 251–FP 253 (New York: Folkways Records, 1952). See also see Robert Cantwell, *When We Were Good: The Folk Revival* (Cambridge: Harvard Univ. Press, 1996), 204; and Frances A. Yeats, *The Rosicrucian Enlightenment* (London: Routledge & Kegan Paul, 1972), 70–72.

4. This phrase and a few others are adapted from Cantwell, *When We Were Good* (note 3), 211–12.
5. Northrop Frye, "Rhetorical Criticism: Theory of Genres," in idem, *The Anatomy of Criticism: Four Essays* (Princeton: Princeton Univ. Press, 1957), 304.
6. All citations of "Ode to a Nightingale" are from John Keats, *The Poetical Works of John Keats*, ed. H. Buxton Forman (London: Humphrey Milford, Oxford Univ. Press, 1920), 230–33.
7. Adapted from Cantwell, *When We Were Good* (note 3), 218.
8. Allen Ginsberg, "Howl," in idem, *Howl and Other Poems* (San Francisco: City Lights, 1959), 9.
9. Samuel Taylor Coleridge, *Biographia Literaria; or, Biographical Sketches of My Literary Life and Opinions*, ed. George Watson, rev. ed. (London: J. M. Dent, 1960), 167.
10. Coleridge, *Biographia Literaria* (note 9), 167.
11. Michel Foucault, *The Order of Things: An Archaeology of the Human Sciences* (London: Tavistock, 1970), 62. Foucault was describing the transformative function of the man-made sign.
12. John Szwed, conversation with the author, fall 2002.
13. Ralph Rinzler, conversation with the author, fall 1986.
14. Robert Conot, *A Streak of Luck* (New York: Seaview, 1979), 107.
15. William James, *The Principles of Psychology* (New York: Henry Holt, 1890; reprint, New York: Dover, 1950), 1:488.
16. Bertrand Russell, *The Analysis of Matter* (London: Routledge, 1927), 163–64.
17. William Makepeace Thackeray, "Charity and Humor," *Harper's New Monthly Magazine*, June 1853, 86.
18. William Wordsworth, "[From] Preface to the Second Edition of Several of the Foregoing Poems, Published with an Additional Volume, under the Title of *Lyrical Ballads*," in M. H. Abrams, gen. ed., *The Norton Anthology of English Literature*, rev. ed. (New York: W. W. Norton, 1968), 2:102, 103.
19. Greil Marcus, "The Old, Weird America," in idem, *Invisible Republic: Bob Dylan's Basement Tapes* (New York: Henry Holt, 1997).

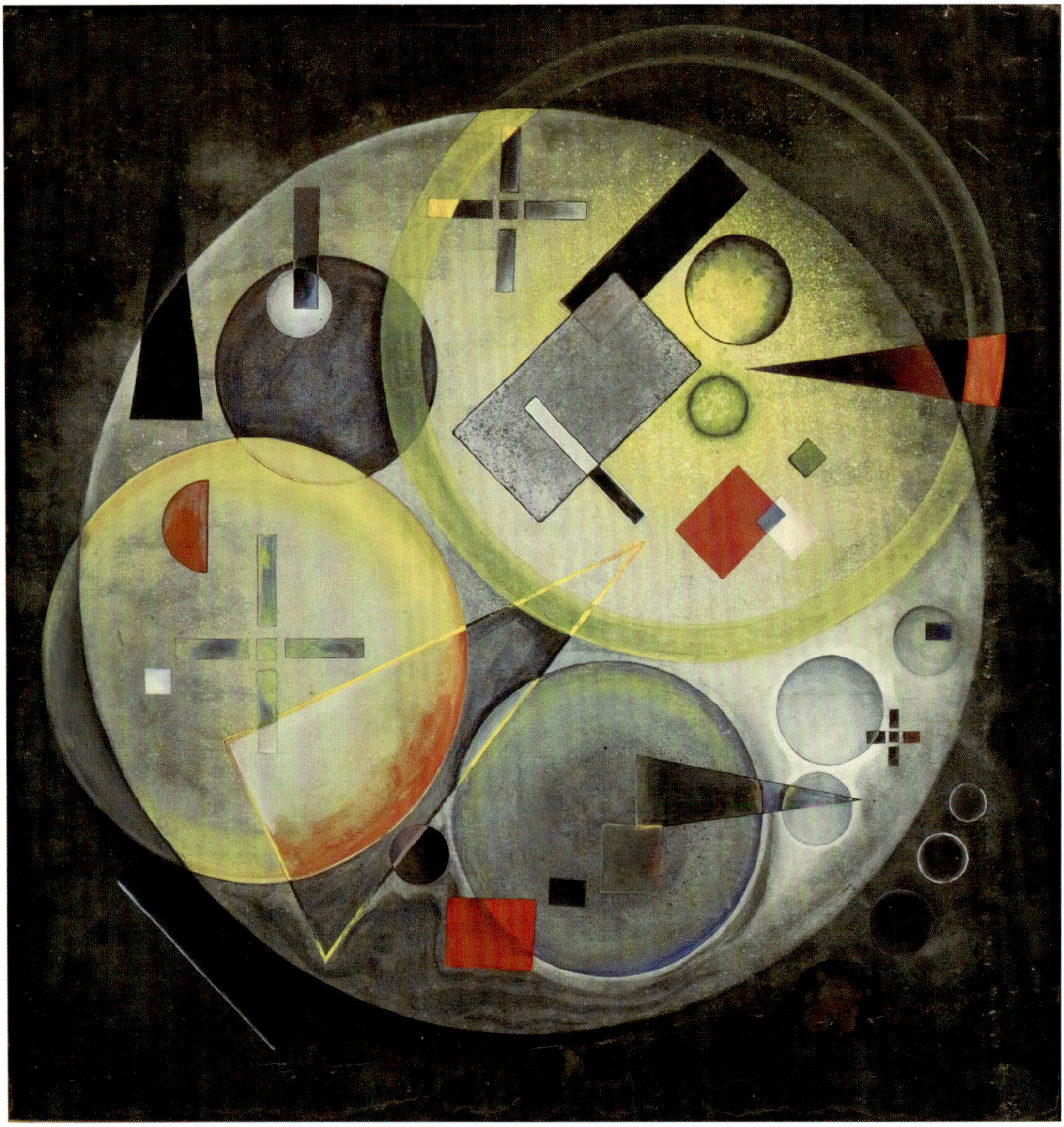

PART V
Collage

THOMAS CROW

FOLK INTO ART: A Phenomenon of Class and Culture in Twentieth-Century America

In summer 1965, Bob Dylan—on the cusp of his transformation from cult folksinger to pop celebrity—challenged an interviewer with the rhetorical question, "Have you ever been in a museum?" He went on to amplify his sudden departure from the immediate topic of his music: "Museums are cemeteries. Paintings should be on the walls of restaurants, in dime stores, in gas stations, in men's rooms. Great paintings should be where people hang out.... Just think how many people would really feel great if they could see a Picasso in their daily diner. It's not the bomb that has to go, man, it's the museums." The vehemence of this outburst suggests he had been brooding on the subject, in particular, on whether a cloistered art can ever be truly Pop, that is, popular and populist. "The only thing where it's happening is on radio and records," he offers by way of contrast. "Music is the only thing that's in tune with what's happening."[1]

Dylan's emergence at the onset of the 1960s coincided almost exactly with the first efforts by Roy Lichtenstein and Andy Warhol in a mode of painting that mimicked the advertisements and comics found "where people hang out." By the mid-1960s, Pop painting had become an international phenomenon, both breaching the walls of the museums and lending the practice of art for the first time a measure of youthful glamour and media excitement. During that same interval, Dylan had functioned within a milieu—the folk music revival with roots in the socialist Left—that looked upon the trappings of fame in a capitalist economy with immense suspicion. When Dylan, shortly before making this pronouncement, first appeared in public with an electrified rock band, the most common and banal charge against him was that he had "sold out."

The Pop artists had heard much the same from the many within the art world who still regarded the Abstract Expressionists, in their troubled pursuit of emotional authenticity, as having established an enduring standard of aesthetic seriousness. But this shared preoccupation, not to say obsession, with "the authentic" had failed to engender any alliance between like-minded artists and musicians—or even much mutual awareness, despite their cheek-by-jowl proximity to one another in lower Manhattan and a strongly shared disdain for bourgeois hypocrisies. One exceptional individual who moved between these divided communities was the young John Cohen, equally important as a Yale University–trained photographer and as an urban old-time musician. Of the folk music world, he writes, "there was and is almost no concern or appreciation for modern or abstract art there. It always has bothered me, because personally, I have always been deeply involved in those ideas

Page 202
Harry Smith
Untitled, ca. 1950–51, mixed media on board,
59.7 × 60.3 cm
(23½ × 22¾ in.)
Collection Cherry Karou Hulsey

Page 203
Harry Smith
Book-page border design, 1988
Harry Smith Archives

of art. I also realized that among the abstract artists and experimental filmmakers, there was very little interest in folk music. They seemed to see it as lower class."[2]

Cohen arrived in the midst of the downtown New York City art scene during the late 1950s. The absolute dominance of the core Abstract Expressionists had passed, and he himself had turned away from painting toward making photographs documenting the lives of the dispossessed: traditional musicians in Appalachia and the Andes, Gypsies in New Haven, or the congregations of African American churches where his Yale mentor, Herbert Matter (a great friend of Jackson Pollock), had embarked upon an extended project of photography and film.[3] In light of that trajectory, it is not surprising that Cohen became close to Robert Frank, then in the midst of fashioning his epoch-making photography collection, *The Americans* (1958). Nor is it surprising that Frank would be one of the rare artists to share Cohen's enthusiasm for Harry Smith's *Anthology of American Folk Music* (1952), as many of Frank's images seem to document the southern settings and even the makers of the music it contains.

Alongside photography, Cohen was embarking on a parallel career that generated more immediate recognition and influence, at least within the folk music revival. With his partners in the New Lost City Ramblers (formed in 1958 with Mike Seeger and Tom Paley), he sought to recapture and continue the unvarnished vocal timbres and instrumental styles that Smith's collection had brought forward from the Depression era. With these and other colleagues, Cohen went further and sought out the living performers who had made the recordings three decades before. These literal embodiments of authenticity could not have stood further from either the brittle ambience of a New York gallery opening or the mass-produced commercial artifacts mimicked by Pop artists. In that light, it is little wonder that the subculture of art and the subculture of folk failed to make any kind of common cause. But there remain other lines of connection between cultural spheres that exist apart from overt group dynamics and explicit awareness at any given moment.

When the young folk revivalists were fanning out over the southern states in search of authentic musical voices, they were following some of the same paths trodden decades earlier by agents of the most princely family of American art collectors. It was the personal philanthropy of Abby Aldrich Rockefeller, wife of John D. Rockefeller Jr., that set this process in motion. Apprised in the late 1920s of the distress experienced by American artists starved for patronage, she began to buy, from a few struggling downtown galleries, paintings by local artists that she displayed alongside the works of European modernism in her midtown Manhattan mansion. Then, at the urging of her advisers, she embarked upon the now-celebrated Rockefeller collection of vernacular artifacts from the hinterlands of America. Their largely anonymous makers, she was told, were the "American Ancestors" of the needy American modernists. She displayed these finds in an art deco gallery installed in a domestic space, side by side with her German Expressionist prints and sculpture by Henri Matisse.[4]

The story of the founding of the Museum of Modern Art (MoMA) is too well known to require much rehearsal: three women of means—Abby Rockefeller with

Lillie P. Bliss and Mary Quinn Sullivan—resolved to create a museum that would both validate their modernist and avant-garde aesthetic commitments and educate an American public to share them.[5] The appointment of the young, unheralded Wellesley College instructor Alfred H. Barr Jr. to oversee the collection came soon after, in 1929. Ambitious American artists would find Barr frustratingly partial to Europeans at their expense, yet his coolness did not extend to all American art. Across his career, Barr would exhibit enthusiasm for those living artists who lacked the educated, cosmopolitan ambitions of their New York School cohort. Indeed, Barr's longtime assistant Dorothy Miller, in whom he placed enormous trust, had married the man who was then doing most of the groundwork in creating the Rockefeller American folk art collection, the curator and arts administrator Holger Cahill.[6] When Barr went on an extended sabbatical from his duties in 1932, Cahill took his place (at Abby Rockefeller's suggestion) and promptly unleashed what the museum's first president recalled as a "flood of Americana."[7] And one of the first waves in this flood was an exhibition entitled *American Folk Art: The Art of the Common Man in America, 1750–1900*, composed—though without acknowledgment—almost entirely from the Rockefeller holdings.[8]

Cahill went on to direct the Federal Art Project under the New Deal's Works Progress Administration, where he emphasized a broad inclusiveness of artists and regions of the country, beneath the umbrella of emergency government aid.[9] With his departure from MoMA, the museum's mission seemed quickly to resolve itself in favor of self-conscious modernist art in the European tradition (Barr had spent his sabbatical getting back in touch with artists and galleries in Europe). By 1947, the MoMA board had shifted the Rockefeller donations of folk art to the Metropolitan Museum of Art, from which they eventually migrated to the museum named in Abby Rockefeller's honor that opened in 1957 in the restored colonial settlement at Williamsburg, Virginia.[10]

But there are signs that the original linking of European modernism with naive American productions had not been abandoned by either Barr or Rockefeller. In a remarkable letter written in 1933, Barr recommends to his principal patron—surely at her request—a program of summer reading. He begins with books by the famous art dealer Ambroise Vollard on Paul Cézanne and Pierre-Auguste Renoir: basic instruction, it might seem, in the modernist pantheon, though Barr calls them no more than "light and entertaining." In startling juxtaposition to these suggestions, he next recommends that she read Thorstein Veblen's *Theory of the Leisure Class* (1899): "not very easy reading," he acknowledges, but it "is an exciting, witty and clarifying discussion" and "one fundamental book which I think every person interested in modern culture ought to read." He does not expect that his patron will agree with much of it but thinks she will "enjoy it" and "the act of disagreement will, I think, prove valuable."[11]

Among the many fascinating implications of this recommendation is its show of respect for her range of mind and disinterestedness. It follows more items of heavyweight cultural criticism: three works by Lewis Mumford and a recently published volume called *The Liberation of American Literature* (1932) by V. F. Calverton, a lengthy historical survey that reaches from the colonial period to the moment of its writing. On the best hope of American literature, Calverton's conclusions are uncompromisingly socialist: Emerson's and Whitman's nineteenth-century faith in the common man as an individual was admirable but mistaken. "What we need to-day," Calverton argues, "is a return of that faith in the common man, in the mass, but a faith founded upon a collective instead of an individualistic premise. . . . ; our belief must be in him as proletarian collectivist."[12]

Barr was vaunting Calverton's popular front–style Marxism *after* the affair of Diego Rivera's inclusion of Vladimir Ilich Lenin in his Rockefeller Center mural had already blown up in public (during which fracas Abby's son Nelson had defended the artist against the ultimately victorious property managers who wanted the painting effaced). Notions such as Calverton's were also commonplaces of the emerging American avant-garde, which discovered itself within the collective public service of the Federal Art Project and looked to the avowedly socialist (even Stalinist) Mexican muralists as guides to reconciling assertive formal ambition with a political salience and a charismatic public presence.

The work of "Los Tres Grandes"—Rivera, José Clemente Orozco, and David Alfaro Siqueiros—never left behind its fund of folkloric motifs, which signified commitment to the Mexican masses while affording readily accessible points of entry into their heroic national narratives. The removal of Rockefeller's folk art collection to a provincial tourist destination ensured that an equivalent American repertoire of imagery would never enjoy—if ever there were a chance it would—anything like the same sort of prestige. The New York avant-garde of the late 1950s had little in the way of concrete visual markers at its disposal to particularize the democratic vision that it had inherited from the days of the popular front. The hinterland of the nation appeared to be in the exclusive possession of their main antagonists, the midwestern regionalists such as John Steuart Curry and Thomas Hart Benton (Pollock's early training under Benton notwithstanding). Despite some artists half-heartedly enlisting a few Native American motifs, as a group they probably had little recourse but to turn their universalizing aspirations toward abstract gestures on a dominating scale.

One figure slow to be persuaded of the rightness of this path was Alfred Barr, the enthusiast of Veblen, Mumford, and Calverton. Much of the Rockefeller collection of Americana—the weather vanes, decoys, doorstops, cigar store figures, lawn ornaments, oils, watercolors, fracturs, paintings on velvet and on glass, and all the other surviving artifacts of (largely) anonymous visual expression—may have departed New York City for Williamsburg in 1935, but Barr remained on the lookout for comparable practitioners in his own time. In 1942, he had helped precipitate his own dismissal as director by museum president Stephen C. Clark when he stubbornly insisted on exhibiting and publicly praising the wildly decorated shoe shine stand constructed by one Joe Milone (fig. 1) (the existence of which had been called to his attention by the young Louise Nevelson).[13] Despite Clark's appalled incomprehension of his director's determination to install Milone's naive rococo extravagance in

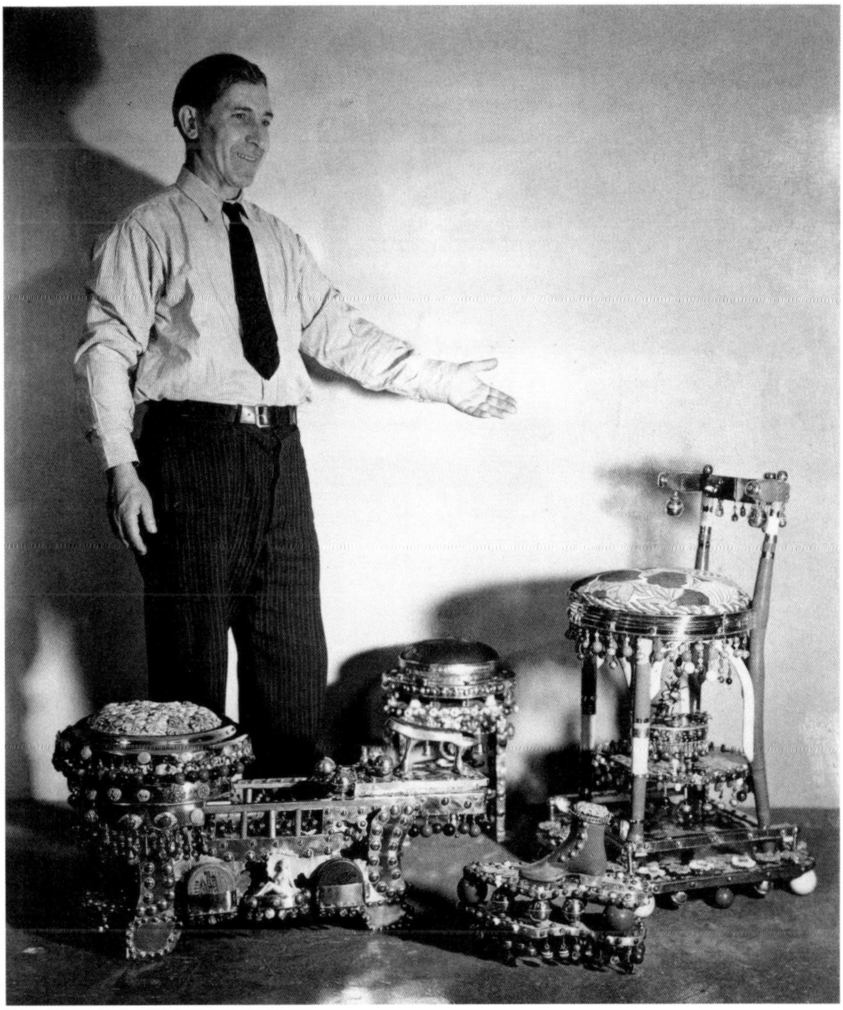

Fig. 1.
Joe Milone and his shoe shine equipment, which was exhibited in *Joe Milone's Shoe Shine Stand,* Museum of Modern Art, New York, 22 December 1942–10 January 1943

the sacred precincts of MoMA, it proved to be an inspired piece of public relations, generating positive commentary throughout the country in newspapers that would normally have paid scant attention to the museum's activities.[14]

Barr was also willing to endure some ridicule—and Clark's further exasperation—by agreeing to the requests of dealer Sidney Janis that he exhibit the self-taught Brooklyn painter Morris Hirshfield. That same year, 1942, he provided the foreword to *They Taught Themselves,* a book written by Janis that celebrated "unknown" American primitive painters. While he confessed that he wished Janis had been less "generously inclusive" in his choices, Barr singled out for praise a small group that included Hirshfield and John Kane, whose self-portrait he declared to be as moving as any he knew (and he bought it for the museum). These artists, he asserted, could "hold their own in the company of their best professionally trained compatriots."[15] His loyalty to Kane remained especially marked. After returning to the chastened museum in 1947—now as its director of museum collections—he raised the artist's name and example in public lectures; and when he

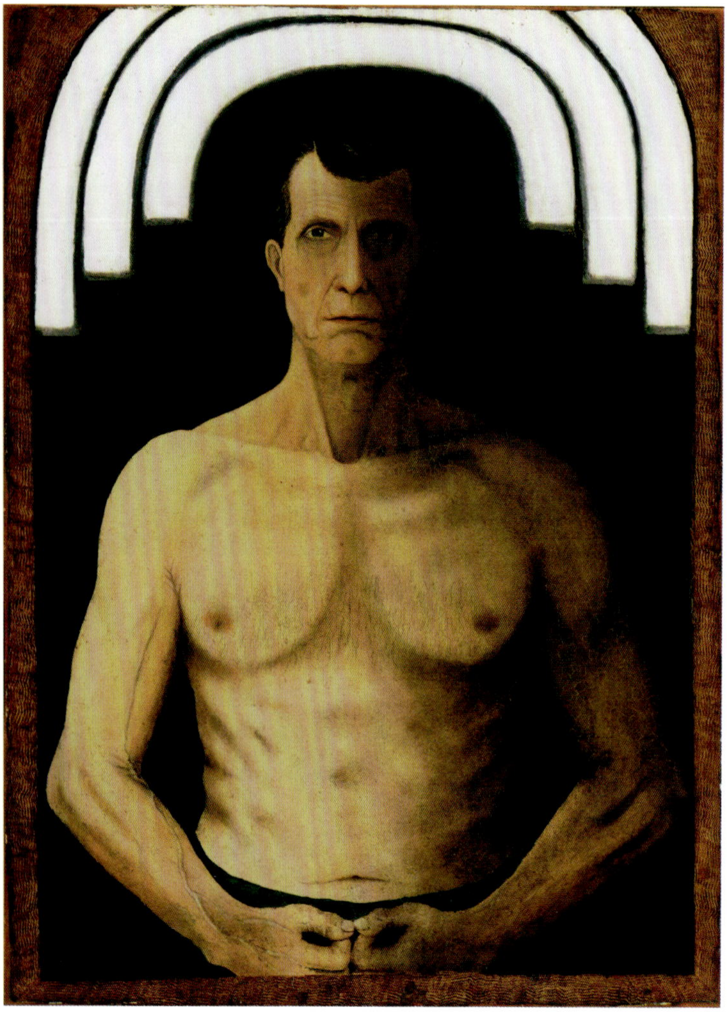

Fig. 2.
John Kane (American, 1860–1934)
Self-Portrait (Arkus 1), 1929, oil on canvas over composition board, 91.8 × 68.9 cm (36⅛ × 27⅛ in.)
New York, Museum of Modern Art

organized a major statement of American art for an exhibition held in 1953 at the Musée national d'art moderne in Paris, he placed Kane's *Self-Portrait* (fig. 2) in an unmissable position at the entrance to the installation.[16]

At that moment, Barr seemed to be fighting a losing battle. Advocates of a grandly universalizing vision, untethered to parochial symbols—as exemplified by the works of Willem de Kooning, Barnett Newman, Clyfford Still, Franz Kline, Mark Rothko, and Jackson Pollock—commanded the heights of critical opinion. Irving Sandler, art historian and self-designated chronicler of the New York School, explicitly sets the two impulses at odds with one another in his recent memoir of the period. "If Harvard-bred WASPs controlled the Museum of Modern Art," he recalls, "ghetto-bred, heterosexual Jews (the sons of immigrants) dominated writing about avant-garde art in the late 1940s and 1950s." His imputation of homosexuality to the MoMA faction points toward certain of Barr's close associates such as Philip Johnson and Lincoln Kirstein: "aspiring cultural aristocrats," Sandler sneers, whose "often 'campish' taste" extended to a "regard for popular culture, embrace of chichi surrealism, and admiration for Rauschenberg and Johns, and, in the sixties, pop art. They would accept art that was low, like folk art and outsider art, or was witty, outré, or exercised a *nostalgie de la boue*."[17]

This rancid outburst, brimming with retrospective resentments, has the virtue at least of reinstating a paradox of taste and social class that received histories of postwar art obscure. Sandler's glaring misrecognition is not to see that Barr, Johnson, and Kirstein (who was Jewish, bisexual, and married) had no need to aspire to a cultural aristocracy: on American terms at least, they were that aristocracy. It was the arrivistes with whom Sandler identifies who could not readily afford to link themselves with folk or outsider forms, much as John Cohen diagnoses the later indifference of his artist friends to the folk music revival that was exploding all around them ("They seemed to see it as lower class").

With historical hindsight, the longer term trends in the visual arts were far more favorable to the inclusive impulses and populist outlook of the "Harvard-bred WASPs." In the wake of the dominance of Abstract Expressionists and their grandly universalizing abstraction in painting, the next generation seemed ineluctably drawn to the shards and discards of commerce in small-town and backstreet America. In 1954, two years after Smith's *Anthology* appeared, Robert Rauschenberg fashioned his first major "combine." Packed with references to his own Southern upbringing, this embrace of the vernacular became, so it seems, the only way he knew to comprehend the sophisticated, urban artist that he had become in light of the provincial and unsophisticated culture that had first made him.[18] The retention of Abstract Expressionist spontaneity as a value in Rauschenberg's work, along with its formal untidiness, was most likely enough in itself to steer Barr away for quite some time.[19] At that juncture, it probably required an avatar who was himself a consummate outsider to manifest the underlying strength of a visual art that embraced vernacular artifacts in the service of a national narrative. The balletomanes Kirstein and Johnson would no doubt have found the recordings in the *Anthology* hard on the ears, in the unlikely event that they were aware of it at all. But had they examined the handbook that accompanied the records, they might well have responded with some enthusiasm.

Entirely designed by Smith and reproduced in a rough-and-ready style by photostatic process, its twenty-eight pages (including cover sheets) are nearly as difficult to summarize as the *Anthology*'s sound world. There is, sequestered in a box on the front cover, a description of expected and straightforward utility: "This handbook contains... numerical listing of selections... with information on original issues, condensations of texts, notes on recordings, and bibliographical and discographical references" (fig. 3). All this is accomplished in a way that answers the demands of an impersonal scholarly discipline. But the visual signals that surround these data transmit layers of complicating signals, as Robert Cantwell has phrased it: "a bricolage of printed ephemera that like junk sculpture incorporates many alien forms, each set off in its own character against all others and against the whole." Cantwell goes on to provide a partial inventory:

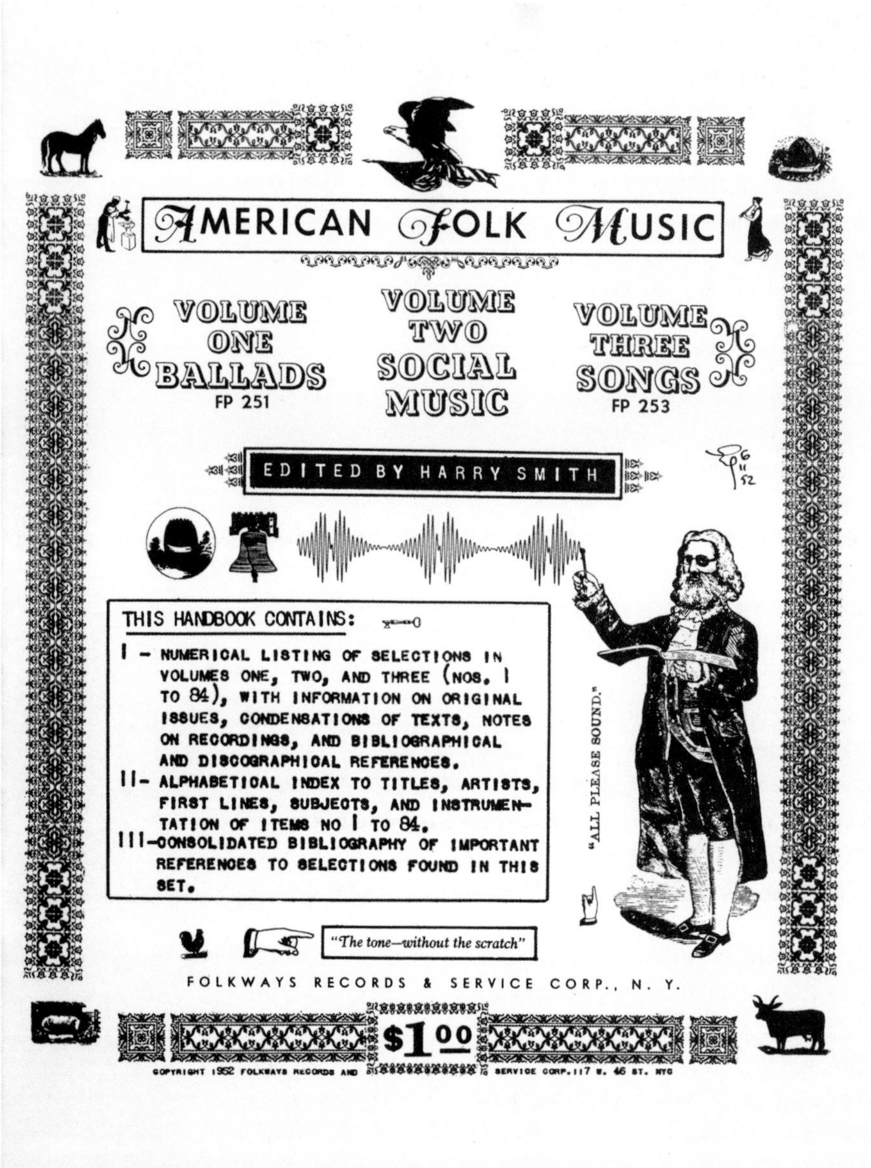

Fig. 3.
Harry Smith
Front cover of handbook
From Harry Smith, ed., *Anthology of American Folk Music*, FP 251–FP 253 (New York: Folkways Records, 1952)

Quaint old printer's devices—the American eagle, a pointing index finger, the bearded figure of an eighteenth-century musicmaster, the liberty bell, a blacksmith, a horse, a pig, an Arcadian piper—festoon its covers: so many of them in fact that the catalogue seems at first to belong in a printshop, not a record collection. This festive abundance of emblems is reiterated inside the handbook by imperfect photographically reduced reproductions of the catalogues and dustjackets of old record companies, which include photos of the performers—the Carolina Tar Heels, Reverend Gates the holiness singer, the Carter Family, Stoneman's Mountaineers, and so on, all from the 1920s—along with old record labels and musical instruments such as the fiddle and banjo as well as the bass drum, clarinet, trumpet, harmonica, jew's-harp, kazoo, mandolin, autoharp, triangle, tambourine, and accordion, all from the mail-order catalogues that used to advertise these instruments for sale.[20]

Such an inventory is revealing enough, but it cannot capture the arresting unity that binds these disparate components and exceeds the handbook's documentary focus on musical performance. Indeed, Smith's devices anticipate procedures that become signature for leading fine artists over the next decade. The photostatic reprocessing to which he subjected his antique advertisements transforms them into uniformly lo-fi, stamped-out silhouettes, much as Warhol's photo-silkscreen technique would later iron out the nuances in his own vernacular sources. The fact that white Appalachian performers such as Stoneman's Mountaineers or the Carter family would thereby appear as dark on the page as the African American Furry Lewis or Gus Cannon and his Jug Stompers was no doubt for Smith a welcome bonus (fig. 4).

An early Warhol disaster painting such as *129 Die in Jet* reinvents the arresting compression with which Smith summarizes the content of each shellac 78 rpm record: the late medieval text of "Fatal Flower Garden" (as recorded by Nelstone's Hawaiians in 1930) becomes "Gaudy woman lures child from playfellows; stabs him as victim dictates message to parents." Similarly telegraphic reports of accidents, disasters, murders, executions, suicides, and two presidential assassinations thread through the first two of the six LP discs and set the tone for the whole of the *Anthology*. Smith could even derive a droll swipe at American racism—"Zoologic miscegeny achieved in mouse frog nuptuals, relatives approve"—from Chubby Parker's 1928 version of the Elizabethan "Froggy Went A-Courting" (titled "King Kong Kitchie Kitchie Ki-Me-O" for the occasion).[21]

As Smith drew his musical material from some of the best-selling recordings of their era, parallelisms with Warhol's *noir* Pop world should come as no great surprise. Both of them had the capacity to recognize the latency within their found materials of the condensed memorability, in both theme and form, that is the hallmark of achieved fine art. And other artists would soon discover for themselves the utility and power of Smith's visual procedures. The handbook's blocks of typewritten, sans serif script (along with terse verbal compression) became a hallmark of the circle of artists who formed themselves around John Cage. In *An Anthology of Chance Operations, Concept Art, Anti Art, Indeterminacy, Plans of Action, Diagrams, Music, Dance Constructions, Improvisation, Meaningless Work, Natural Disasters, Compositions, Mathematics, Essays, Poetry* (1962), the editor La Monte Young and George Maciunas, the Fluxus founder who served as the compendium's designer, aimed for a similarly spare, commonplace typography (fig. 5). And if it conspicuously lacked the Victorian ornamentation of Smith's handbook, that archaistic design vocabulary found its place in the repertoire of Fluxus ephemera generated in such abundance by Maciunas and his collaborators (figs. 6, 7).

Perhaps the most insistent design feature of the handbook's interior pages is the uniform, serial character of each of the ruled blocks that contain data and commentary on individual tracks. Standing out from the folkloric devices and period illustrations is the sequence of bold, black numbers that herald each entry, imposing on

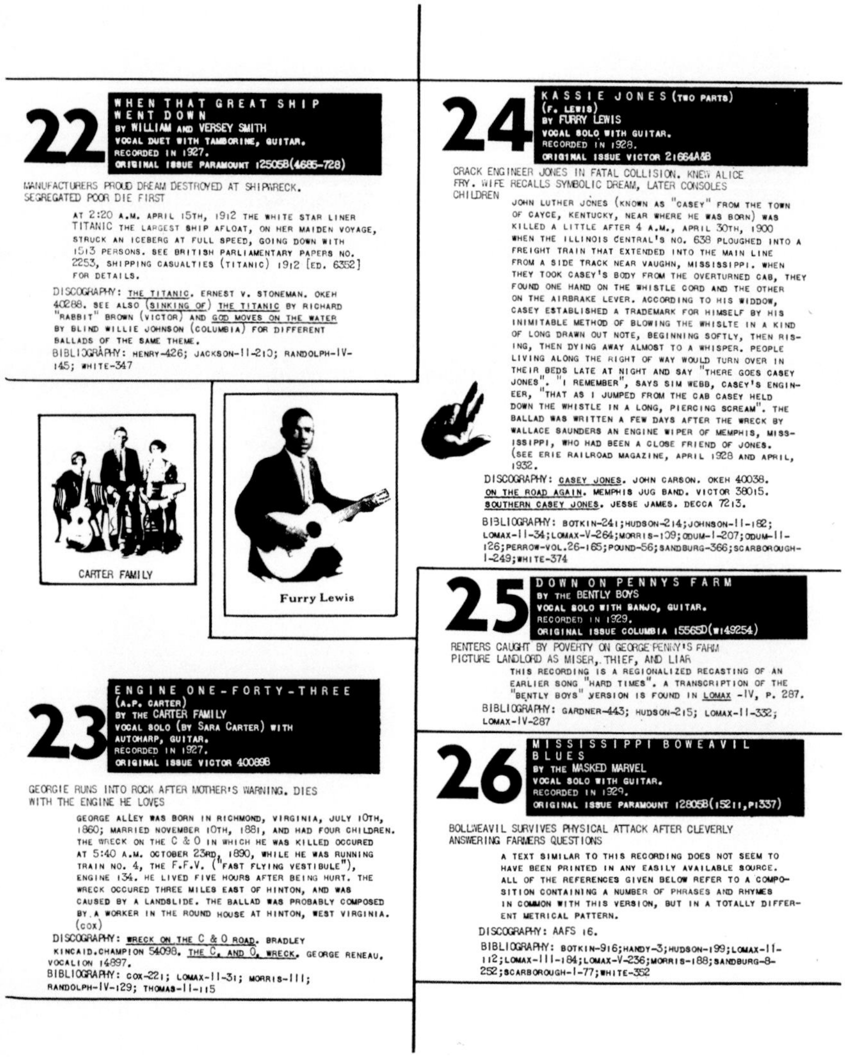

22 WHEN THAT GREAT SHIP WENT DOWN
BY WILLIAM AND VERSEY SMITH
VOCAL DUET WITH TAMBORINE, GUITAR.
RECORDED IN 1927.
ORIGINAL ISSUE PARAMOUNT 12505B(4685-728)

MANUFACTURERS PROUD DREAM DESTROYED AT SHIPWRECK. SEGREGATED POOR DIE FIRST

AT 2:20 A.M. APRIL 15TH, 1912 THE WHITE STAR LINER TITANIC THE LARGEST SHIP AFLOAT, ON HER MAIDEN VOYAGE, STRUCK AN ICEBERG AT FULL SPEED, GOING DOWN WITH 1513 PERSONS. SEE BRITISH PARLIAMENTARY PAPERS NO. 2253, SHIPPING CASUALTIES (TITANIC) 1912 [ED. 6352] FOR DETAILS.

DISCOGRAPHY: THE TITANIC. ERNEST V. STONEMAN. OKEH 40288. SEE ALSO (SINKING OF) THE TITANIC BY RICHARD "RABBIT" BROWN (VICTOR) AND GOD MOVES ON THE WATER BY BLIND WILLIE JOHNSON (COLUMBIA) FOR DIFFERENT BALLADS OF THE SAME THEME.
BIBLIOGRAPHY: HENRY-426; JACKSON-II-210; RANDOLPH-IV-145; WHITE-347

CARTER FAMILY

Furry Lewis

23 ENGINE ONE-FORTY-THREE
(A.P. CARTER)
BY THE CARTER FAMILY
VOCAL SOLO (BY SARA CARTER) WITH AUTOHARP, GUITAR.
RECORDED IN 1927.
ORIGINAL ISSUE VICTOR 40089B

GEORGIE RUNS INTO ROCK AFTER MOTHER'S WARNING. DIES WITH THE ENGINE HE LOVES

GEORGE ALLEY WAS BORN IN RICHMOND, VIRGINIA, JULY 10TH, 1860; MARRIED NOVEMBER 10TH, 1881, AND HAD FOUR CHILDREN. THE WRECK ON THE C & O IN WHICH HE WAS KILLED OCCURED AT 5:40 A.M. OCTOBER 23RD, 1890, WHILE HE WAS RUNNING TRAIN NO. 4, THE F.F.V. ("FAST FLYING VESTIBULE"), ENGINE 134. HE LIVED FIVE HOURS AFTER BEING HURT. THE WRECK OCCURED THREE MILES EAST OF HINTON, AND WAS CAUSED BY A LANDSLIDE. THE BALLAD WAS PROBABLY COMPOSED BY A WORKER IN THE ROUND HOUSE AT HINTON, WEST VIRGINIA. (COX)

DISCOGRAPHY: WRECK ON THE C & O ROAD. BRADLEY KINCAID. CHAMPION 54098. THE C. AND O. WRECK. GEORGE RENEAU. VOCALION 14897.
BIBLIOGRAPHY: COX-221; LOMAX-II-31; MORRIS-111; RANDOLPH-IV-129; THOMAS-II-115

24 KASSIE JONES (TWO PARTS)
(F. LEWIS)
BY FURRY LEWIS
VOCAL SOLO WITH GUITAR.
RECORDED IN 1928.
ORIGINAL ISSUE VICTOR 21664A&B

CRACK ENGINEER JONES IN FATAL COLLISION. KNEW ALICE FRY. WIFE RECALLS SYMBOLIC DREAM, LATER CONSOLES CHILDREN

JOHN LUTHER JONES (KNOWN AS "CASEY" FROM THE TOWN OF CAYCE, KENTUCKY, NEAR WHERE HE WAS BORN) WAS KILLED A LITTLE AFTER 4 A.M., APRIL 30TH, 1900 WHEN THE ILLINOIS CENTRAL'S NO. 638 PLOUGHED INTO A FREIGHT TRAIN THAT EXTENDED INTO THE MAIN LINE FROM A SIDE TRACK NEAR VAUGHN, MISSISSIPPI. WHEN THEY TOOK CASEY'S BODY FROM THE OVERTURNED CAB, THEY FOUND ONE HAND ON THE WHISTLE CORD AND THE OTHER ON THE AIRBRAKE LEVER. ACCORDING TO HIS WIDDOW, CASEY ESTABLISHED A TRADEMARK FOR HIMSELF BY HIS INIMITABLE METHOD OF BLOWING THE WHISLTE IN A KIND OF LONG DRAWN OUT NOTE, BEGINNING SOFTLY, THEN RISING, THEN DYING AWAY ALMOST TO A WHISPER. PEOPLE LIVING ALONG THE RIGHT OF WAY WOULD TURN OVER IN THEIR BEDS LATE AT NIGHT AND SAY "THERE GOES CASEY JONES". "I REMEMBER", SAYS SIM WEBB, CASEY'S ENGINEER, "THAT AS I JUMPED FROM THE CAB CASEY HELD DOWN THE WHISTLE IN A LONG, PIERCING SCREAM". THE BALLAD WAS WRITTEN A FEW DAYS AFTER THE WRECK BY WALLACE SAUNDERS AN ENGINE WIPER OF MEMPHIS, MISSISSIPPI, WHO HAD BEEN A CLOSE FRIEND OF JONES. (SEE ERIE RAILROAD MAGAZINE, APRIL 1928 AND APRIL, 1932.

DISCOGRAPHY: CASEY JONES. JOHN CARSON. OKEH 40038. ON THE ROAD AGAIN. MEMPHIS JUG BAND. VICTOR 38015. SOUTHERN CASEY JONES. JESSE JAMES. DECCA 7213.
BIBLIOGRAPHY: BOTKIN-241; HUDSON-214; JOHNSON-II-182; LOMAX-II-34; LOMAX-V-264; MORRIS-109; ODUM-I-207; ODUM-II-126; PERROW-VOL.26-165; POUND-56; SANDBURG-366; SCARBOROUGH-I-249; WHITE-374

25 DOWN ON PENNYS FARM
BY THE BENTLY BOYS
VOCAL SOLO WITH BANJO, GUITAR.
RECORDED IN 1929.
ORIGINAL ISSUE COLUMBIA 15565D(W149254)

RENTERS CAUGHT BY POVERTY ON GEORGE PENNY'S FARM PICTURE LANDLORD AS MISER, THIEF, AND LIAR

THIS RECORDING IS A REGIONALIZED RECASTING OF AN EARLIER SONG "HARD TIMES". A TRANSCRIPTION OF THE "BENTLY BOYS" VERSION IS FOUND IN LOMAX -IV, P. 287.
BIBLIOGRAPHY: GARDNER-443; HUDSON-215; LOMAX-II-332; LOMAX-IV-287

26 MISSISSIPPI BOWEAVIL BLUES
BY THE MASKED MARVEL
VOCAL SOLO WITH GUITAR.
RECORDED IN 1929.
ORIGINAL ISSUE PARAMOUNT 12805B(15211,P1337)

BOLLWEAVIL SURVIVES PHYSICAL ATTACK AFTER CLEVERLY ANSWERING FARMERS QUESTIONS

A TEXT SIMILAR TO THIS RECORDING DOES NOT SEEM TO HAVE BEEN PRINTED IN ANY EASILY AVAILABLE SOURCE. ALL OF THE REFERENCES GIVEN BELOW REFER TO A COMPOSITION CONTAINING A NUMBER OF PHRASES AND RHYMES IN COMMON WITH THIS VERSION, BUT IN A TOTALLY DIFFERENT METRICAL PATTERN.

DISCOGRAPHY: AAFS 16.
BIBLIOGRAPHY: BOTKIN-916; HANDY-3; HUDSON-199; LOMAX-II-112; LOMAX-III-184; LOMAX-V-236; MORRIS-188; SANDBURG-8-252; SCARBOROUGH-I-77; WHITE-352

Fig. 4.
Harry Smith
Handbook catalog nos. 22–26, for songs at the end of the *Ballads* volume
From Harry Smith, ed., *Anthology of American Folk Music*, FP 251–FP 253 (New York: Folkways Records, 1952)

the wildly complex materials that the *Anthology* comprises an apparently autonomous and arbitrary order of the simplest kind.[22] That sequence of blocky, compartmentalized numerals has its most obvious artistic corollary in the work that Jasper Johns would begin to do a few years after the *Anthology* appeared. His number paintings, as did his flags and targets, manifested a repleteness of surface akin to the two-dimensional objects fashioned by practitioners of folk art in the strict sense of anonymous creativity. The flag of the United States, for example, having begun life as an exercise in textile piecework, gave rise to countless quilts. And its permutations in other utilitarian and ornamental objects—as in the famous flag gate of around 1876 (fig. 8)—is equally endless.

METHODS FOR READING ASYMMETRIES

Asymmetries are poems of which the words, punctuation, typography and spacing on the page are determined by chance operations. In later asymmetries the prolongation or reiteration of certain sounds in words (indicated by special notation) is similarly determined. A number of different, though related, groups of chance operations have been used in producing asymmetries since September 1960. They may be performed by 7 different methods - singly or several poems simultaneously. A basic method underlies the others and is the one to be followed when all or most of the others are ruled out by circumstances.

BASIC METHOD: Blank spaces before, after and between words or parts of words, between lines of words, and before whole poems are rendered as silences equal in duration to the time it wd take to read aloud the words printed anywhere above or below them. A right margin is defined by the end of the word printed farthest to the right and blank spaces in each line extend to that margin. Where more than one line of type might be placed between lines, two or more successive lines of silence are indicated. At least one line of silence occurs before every word beginning at the left margin; one occurs after every period, question mark or exclamation point.*A left-marginal word preceded by a period, etc., is always preceded by at least 2 lines of silence. In some poems these durations of silence are doubled or tripled, as indicated by the spacing. The notation "(---/---)" indicates a prolongation of the sound before the parenthesis; the IPA symbol for the prolonged sound stands in the left margin when the prolongation continues from the line above. Notation such as (-t-t-t-) indicates a reiteration of the last sound. Durations of prolongations and of series of reiterations are measured like those of silences.

Words in emphatic typography (initial capitalization other than that of proper nouns and adjectives derived from them, total capitalization, italics, bold face). or followed by exclamation points, are read quite loudly or shouted. Words within enclosing punctuation (quotation marks, parentheses, brackets) are read quite softly or whispered. Other words are read moderately loudly or moderately softly. Pitch change is regulated by punctuation as in prose. Otherwise, pitches, timbres, speeds and durations are free.

*These statements do not hold true for some of the earlier asymmetries.

OTHER METHODS: When all 7 methods are used, singly or simultaneously, each performer throws a pair of dice for each poem. If he throws a

2 or 4: Words only: He reads the words as in basic method but makes only punctuation pauses and breath pauses at unpunctuated line endings: no long silences. A slight optional prolongation of final sounds of lines is allowed.

3 or 5: Basic Method.

6: Silence only: He is silent as long as it wd take him to read the poem aloud (with space silences) by basic method.

7: Silence, words & tones: He produces on any instrument one continuous (or continually reiterated) tone during each duration notated by a right-marginal space. Tones shd be reiterated only when necessary and then with minimal attack. Pitch of each tone is determined by free choice of any letter in preceding words which is a tone name. Any chromatic or microtonic variant of "a" through "g" may be played in any register; "h" is always "b natural". The same pitch shd not end 2 successive lines: at least a different variant or register shd be used. During whole lines of silence in basic method he is either silent, or, not too often, continues the tone from the line above. If he chooses to play a tone in place of the line of silence before a poem, he chooses a letter from the first line of words. He is silent during left-marginal spaces. He speaks all words by basic method.

8: Tone only: He plays one tone, determined in pitch as in 7, by any letter in the poem, continuously (reiterating with minimal attack when necessary) for as long as it would take him to read the poem aloud (with silences) by basic method.

9 or 11: Tones & silences: Reading poem silently, he plays tones determined as in 7 during right-marginal spaces; is silent during left-marginal spaces & words (duration as read aloud); is silent or prolongs tones from line above throughout whole empty lines, as in 7; empty lines before poem also as in 7.

10 or 12: Words & tones: Reading all words by basic method. he plays tones determined in pitch as in 7 during all durations that would be silent by basic method.

Note that in 7, & 9 or 11, one may begin with a tone of a line's duration; in 8, & 10 or 12, one must begin with a tone.

It would be Johns, early in 1958, who would trigger MoMA, in the persons of Alfred Barr and Dorothy Miller, to revive the institution's repressed origins in the collecting of American folk objects. Miller recalled being summoned in the pelting rain on a Saturday morning in January, Barr asking her over the telephone how soon she could get herself to the gallery; the two of them spent only an hour discussing what to buy: "It wasn't a question of one picture," she said. "We chose four pictures. They were inexpensive and they were just so remarkable."[23] These were *Green Target* (1955), *Target with Four Faces* (1955), an early version of *White Numbers* (1957), and *Flag* (fig. 9) (though the last spent some years under Philip Johnson's proxy ownership before entering the collection proper). No MoMA precedent existed for such a sudden, wholesale acquisition of no less than four works by a young artist then barely known outside his immediate circle of friends. (And the astute Miller bought *Gray Numbers* [1957] for her own collection.)

Barr and Miller acted in an instant, but the recognition behind their action had been patiently built over decades. To account for their response, one needs to look at Johns's various *Flag* and *Target* paintings with eyes honed to discern the virtues of

Fig. 5.
First page of Jackson Mac Low's "Methods from Reading Asymmetries"
From George Brecht et al., *An Anthology of Chance Operations, Concept Art, Anti Art, Indeterminacy, Plans of Action, Diagrams, Music, Dance Constructions, Improvisation, Meaningless Work, Natural Disasters, Compositions, Mathematics, Essays, Poetry*, ed. La Monte Young, designed by George Maciunas (New York: George Maciunas & Jackson Mac Low, 1962), n.p.
Los Angeles, Getty Research Institute

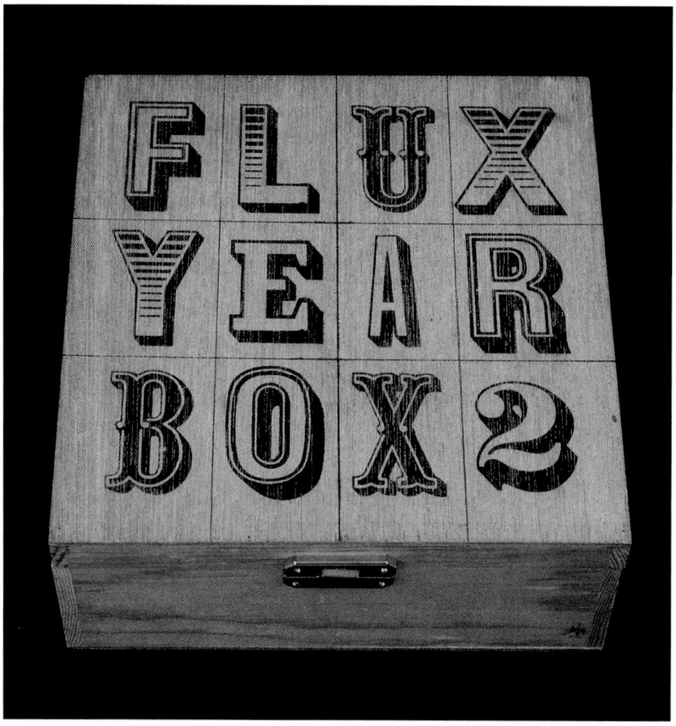

Fig. 6.
Fluxus
Flux Year Box 2, 1966, wooden box, with printed title on lid, containing various printed items and objects, 20.4 × 20.4 × 8.5 cm (8 × 8 × 3⅜ in.)
Los Angeles, Getty Research Institute

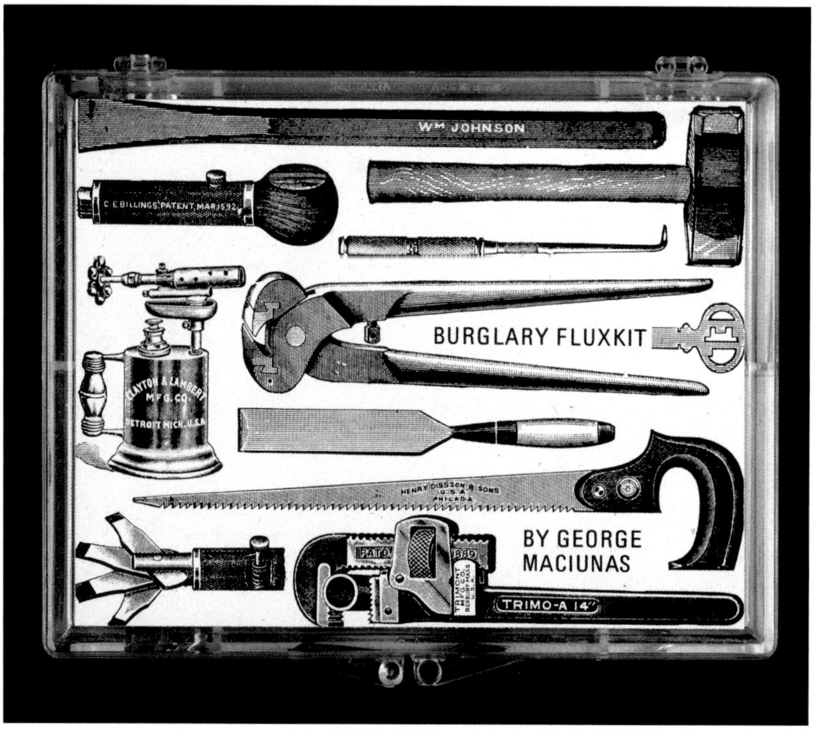

Fig. 7.
George Maciunas (American, 1931–78)
Burglary Fluxkit, 1971, clear plastic box, with printed label on lid, containing eleven keys, 9.2 × 12 × 2.5 cm (3⅝ × 4¾ × 1 in.)
Los Angeles, Getty Research Institute

Fig. 8.
Unidentified artist from Jefferson County, New York (American, late 1800s)
Flag Gate, ca. 1876, paint on wood with iron and brass, 100.3 × 144.8 × 9.5 cm (39½ × 57 × 3¾ in.)
New York, American Folk Art Museum

Fig. 9.
Jasper Johns (American, b. 1930)
Flag, 1954, encaustic, oil, and collage on fabric mounted on plywood, 107.3 × 154 cm (42¼ × 60⅝ in.)
New York, Museum of Modern Art

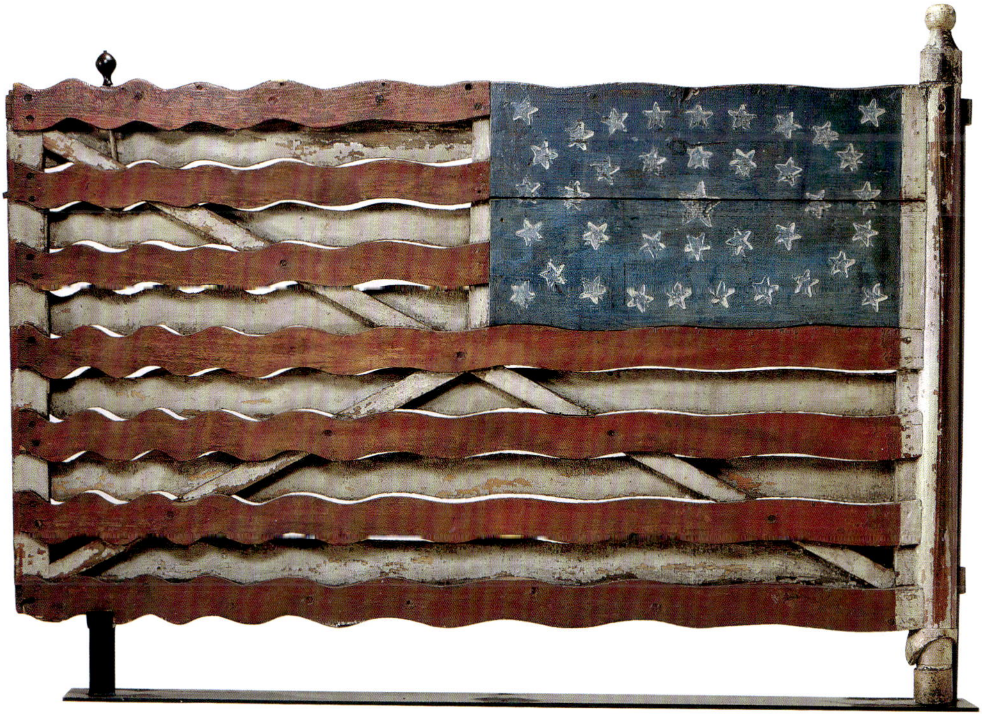

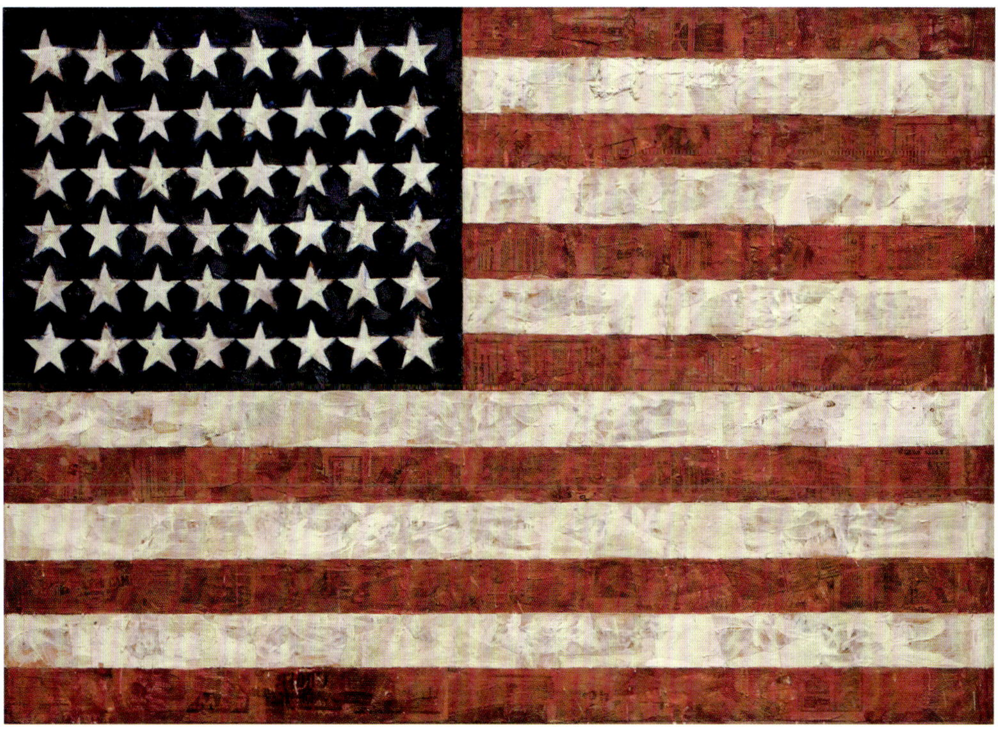

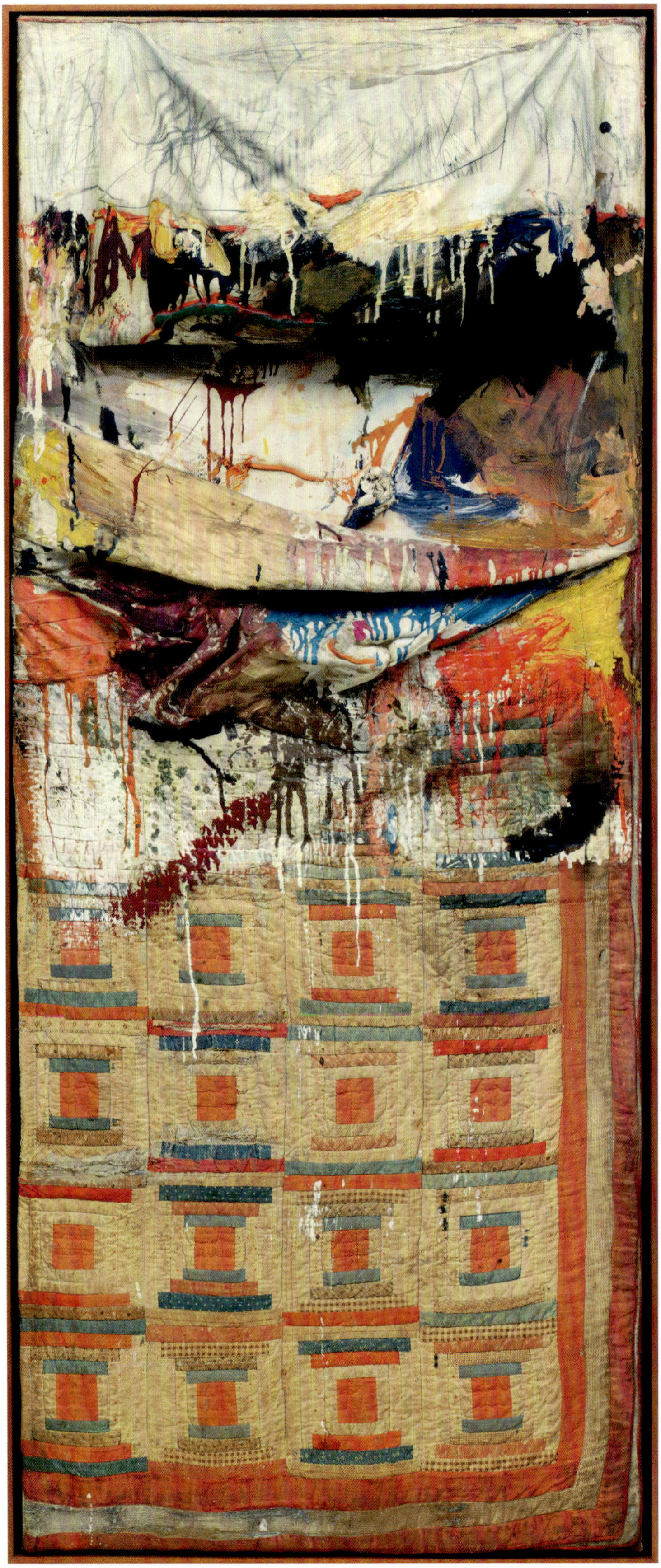

Fig. 10.
Robert Rauschenberg
(American, 1925–2008)
Bed, 1955, combine painting:
oil and pencil on pillow, quilt,
and sheet on wood supports,
191.1 × 80 × 20.3 cm
(75¼ × 31½ × 8 in.)
New York, Museum of
Modern Art

homespun ornaments and the earnest efforts of a John Kane (who made a number of paintings based on the pattern of the American flag, even depicting himself in the act of painting one) but equally alert to any sign that these things and the art of the School of Paris might somehow belong to the same universe. Within that vision, Johns must have seemed a godsend. In contrast to Rauschenberg's combines (fig. 10) (or to minor contenders such as Larry Rivers), Johns's paintings offered the far closer homology to folk forms: to their modesty and restraint; to their tendencies toward symmetry and embellishment of entire surfaces; to their masking of obsessive and private meanings in self-imposed disciplines of work. At the same time, he had self-evidently become an artist of high self-consciousness, whose faux-naïf technique radiated sophistication.

In retrospect, there is a worthwhile analogy to be made between the sealed surfaces of Johns's encaustics of the 1950s and the bottling of folk-performance lightning in the grooves of the commercial, 78 rpm shellac discs out of which Smith's *Anthology* was built—and then its rebottling in the more technologically and socially distinguished microgrooves of the *Anthology*'s LPs issued under the Folkways Records label. Cantwell points out the degree to which the long-playing record was associated in its early days with classical music and enthusiasts for expensive high-fidelity equipment. What Smith's source material had been, he writes, "to the people who originally recorded it, essentially the music of the poor, the isolated, and the uneducated, the *Anthology* reframed as a kind of avant-garde art."[24] Smith made that fact visually manifest in the way he selected and presented the material that went into his handbook.

To the extent that the newer forms of advanced art found their core material in things that already existed in some prior form of organization—inventories, documents, catalogs, newspapers, advertising vehicles—rather than presupposing an always-original act of creative synthesis, the distance between the collecting of art and the making of art had significantly narrowed. There is no reason to think that any of the artists instanced above took any notice of Smith or his *Anthology;* Smith, as an immensely sophisticated artist, had simply applied his manifold creative intelligence to that convergence in advance of its emergence within the recognized realm of fine art. In the process, he hit upon a set of artistic devices that mapped much of the territory that others would discover for themselves a few years down the road.

The two trajectories of collecting—that of folk art and that of folk music—nonetheless remained out of synchrony with one another. The circulation of the *Anthology* prompted its keenest listeners to search out the surviving musicians and their immediate heirs. The clubs, festivals, and college concerts of the early 1960s became suddenly populated with the actual bearers of memory, conjured from the hollers and plantations of the rural American South. The memories carried by many of those performers reached back to the British popular ballads of the seventeenth century, borne to the New World by Scots-Irish immigrants who had bypassed the coastal cities for isolated inland settlements.[25] The young Bob Dylan had assiduously mastered these forms, while the Dylan of 1965 embarked upon his own inspired conception of their continuity. As he later recalled, "My songs, what makes them different is that there's a foundation to them. That's why they're still around.... It's not because they're such great songs. They don't fall into the commercial category. They're not written to be performed by other people. But they're standing on a strong foundation, and subliminally that's what people are hearing. Those old songs are my lexicon and my prayer book."[26]

No such revival or expansive effect lay in store for the self-taught visual artists who were the contemporaries of the *Anthology*'s musicians. In the wake of the Rockefeller folk art collection departing his museum, Barr had engaged in an analogous pursuit of contemporary practitioners who might embody and perpetuate the unselfconscious virtues of their eighteenth- and nineteenth-century forebears. But his efforts on behalf of Kane, Hirschfield, and Milone had made little headway and by the mid-1950s had largely been abandoned. No art world luminary credited the Pop explosion to august folk forebears. The vernacular prototypes sealed inside Johns's encaustic envelopes rapidly ceased to signify anything beyond a generic realm of the commonplace. As Johns's laconic emblems catalyzed a wave of art based on the heraldic totems of contemporary commerce, their folk genealogy passed into near invisibility.

But an adequate art history of Pop is under no obligation to reproduce institutional forms of blindness and misrecognition. Dylan railed, in the outburst with which this essay began, against a kind of bad faith, whereby the modern art museum sought to refurbish itself with a glamour from the streets to which it was not entitled. But what he failed entirely to recognize was that the aspirational cachet of Pop art can itself radiate a form of power that obliterates museum walls. His own aggrieved consciousness of visual art would have been heightened by recent musical events in Great Britain, where in spring 1965 he had toured and sat in with local rock musicians. The Who were at that moment undergoing a publicity makeover, whereby their canny manager was seeking to distinguish his powerful emerging group by identifying them with the visual markers of Pop art. Drummer Keith Moon appears in contemporary publicity photographs wearing T-shirts emblazoned with Jasper Johns–style targets. Leader Pete Townshend, for his part, adopted a jacket tailored from the Union Jack in a trademark and indirect homage to Johns's famous encaustic paintings of the American national symbol.[27] "The Who are linking their image with what they call pop-art," reported the music weekly *Melody Maker* just after Dylan's departure. "They describe their current chart success, 'Anyway, Anyhow, Anywhere,' as 'the first pop-art single.'"[28]

Johns (with Barr's crucial assistance) had thus unintentionally forged a point of productive contact between popular art and popular music that the dedicated collectors of each art form had never realized in the past (and few works of Pop art from the later 1960s can stand comparison to the album cover of *The Who Sell Out* [1967]). Dylan envied the ways in which the British bands had managed to achieve wide popular success with versions of vernacular American music transmuted by evident intellectual self-consciousness. That feeling drove his own successful drive to achieve the same thing himself, indeed to go them one better. In the process, he altered the entire landscape of popular entertainment such that succeeding cohorts of artists found that what it meant to be Pop had become a decisively different affair than what it had been for the artists of the 1960s. Such delayed effects and subterranean bindings of the visual arts with popular music can be as elusive as they are in many ways decisive, opaque even to those who are direct parties to these interactions. That would be to say, except for such a conspicuous exception as Harry Smith, for whom the two art forms never ceased to run on parallel tracks.

Notes

1. See Bob Dylan, interview by Nora Ephron and Susan Edmiston, shortly after 28 August 1965; reprinted in Bob Dylan, *Bob Dylan, the Essential Interviews,* ed. Jonathan Cott (New York: Wenner, 2006), 54.
2. John Cohen, descriptive text published in the liner notes to *Harry Smith's Anthology of American Folk Music, Volume Four,* RVN 211 (Austin: Revenant/Harry Smith Archives, 2000), 37–38.
3. John Cohen, interviews by Thomas Crow, July and August 2006. See also John Cohen, *There Is No Eye: John Cohen Photographs* (New York: PowerHouse, 2001).
4. Bernice Kert, *Abby Aldrich Rockefeller: The Woman in the Family* (New York: Random House, 1993), 296–99, 322–27.
5. The standard histories include the account by the museum's first president, A. Conger Goodyear, *The Museum of Modern Art: The First Ten Years* (New York: n.p., 1943); Russell Lynes, *Good Old Modern: An Intimate Portrait of the Museum of Modern Art* (New York: Atheneum, 1973); and Alice Goldfarb Marquis, *Alfred H. Barr Jr.: Missionary for the Modern* (Chicago: Contemporary Books, 1989).
6. On Miller, see Lynn Zelevansky, "Dorothy Miller's 'Americans,' 1942–63," in *The Museum of Modern Art at Mid-Century: At Home and Abroad* (New York: Museum of Modern Art, 1994), 67–69. On Cahill and Rockefeller, see Kert, *Abby Aldrich Rockefeller* (note 4), 322–24.
7. See Goodyear, *The Museum of Modern Art* (note 5), 41.
8. See *American Folk Art: The Art of the Common Man in America, 1750–1900,* exh. cat. (New York: Museum of Modern Art, 1932).
9. In 1938, while still in his government position, Cahill came back to MoMA to help Miller organize the American section of a major exhibition that paired a group of self-taught American artists with a number of their European counterparts; see Holger Cahill et al., *Masters of Popular Painting: Modern Primitives of Europe and America* (New York: Museum of Modern Art, 1938).
10. Fourteen items were transferred to the Metropolitan Museum but later retrieved by Abby's husband and sent to Colonial Williamsburg; see Lynes, *Good Old Modern* (note 5), 290; and Marquis, *Alfred H. Barr Jr.* (note 5), 246. They joined an earlier donation of Americana, comprising 251 pieces, that had been placed on display in Colonial Williamsburg in 1935 and given permanently by 1940; see *American Folk Art: A Collection of Paintings and Sculpture Produced by Little-Known and Anonymous American Artists of the Eighteenth and Nineteenth Centuries; the Gift of Mrs. John D. Rockefeller, Jr. to Colonial Williamsburg, Incorporated, on Exhibition at the Ludwell-Paradise House,* exh. cat. (Williamsburg, Va.: Colonial Williamsburg,

1940). When the museum bearing Abby Rockefeller's name opened in 1957, it held a total of 434 folk art objects from her personal collection.

11. Quoted in Kert, *Abby Aldrich Rockefeller* (note 4), 340–41.
12. V. F. Calverton, *The Liberation of American Literature* (New York: Charles Scribner's Sons, 1932), 480.
13. See Marquis, *Alfred H. Barr Jr.* (note 5), 201–2.
14. The abundant press clippings regarding Milone and this exhibition have been collected in a scrapbook in the archives of the Museum of Modern Art; see Department of Public Information Records, I (reel #15; frame #708 ff.), Museum of Modern Art Archives, New York.
15. Alfred H. Barr Jr., "Foreword," in Sidney Janis, *They Taught Themselves: American Primitive Painters of the 20th Century* (New York: Dial, 1942), xx.
16. See *12 peintres et sculpteurs américains contemporains,* exh. cat. (Paris: Musée National d'art Moderne, 1953); and Marquis, *Alfred H. Barr Jr.* (note 5), 239–40.
17. See Irving Sandler, *A Sweeper-Up after Artists: A Memoir* (London: Thames & Hudson, 2003), 179–80; see also p. 125, where Sandler mentions, among others, the gay composers Aaron Copland, John Cage, and Virgil Thomson as close associates of Barr.
18. For more on this aspect of Rauschenberg's work, see Thomas Crow, "Southern Boys Go to Europe: Rauschenberg, Twombly and Johns in the 1950s," in Stephanie Barron and Lynn Zelevansky, eds., *Jasper Johns to Jeff Koons: Four Decades of Art from the Broad Collections* (Los Angeles: Los Angeles County Museum of Art, 2001), 44–61.
19. In 1959, for example, Leo Castelli apparently had a donor in the wings ready to give Rauschenberg's *Magician* (1959) to the museum collection, but Barr dithered long enough for the would-be benefactor to withdraw. See Calvin Tomkins, *Off the Wall: Robert Rauschenberg and the Art World of Our Time* (Garden City, N.Y.: Doubleday, 1980), 61–62; and Marquis, *Alfred H. Barr Jr.* (note 5), 246.
20. Robert Cantwell, *When We Were Good: The Folk Revival* (Cambridge: Harvard Univ. Press, 1996), 194–95.
21. See Harry Smith, ed., *Anthology of American Folk Music,* FP 251–FP 253 (New York: Folkways Records, 1952), handbook cat. no. 8.
22. Cantwell, *When We Were Good* (note 20), 198–99, makes a similar observation.
23. See Zelevansky, "Dorothy Miller's 'Americans'" (note 6), 80; see also Lynes, *Good Old Modern* (note 5), 299.
24. Cantwell, *When We Were Good* (note 20), 190 (italics added).
25. The literature on this pattern of settlement is vast; for the most comprehensive account, see David Hackett Fischer, *Albion's Seed: Four British Folkways in America* (New York: Oxford Univ. Press, 1989). Clinton Heylin, in his invaluable *Dylan's Daemon Lover: The Tangled Tale of a 450-Year Old Pop Ballad* (London: Helter Skelter, 1999), 104–15 and passim, provides a capsule description of the phenomenon as it bears on the transmission to the New World of the ballad "The House Carpenter" (cf. Smith, ed., *Anthology* [note 21], no. 3).
26. John Pareles, "Pop/Jazz: A Wiser Voice Blowin' in the Autumn Wind," *New York Times,* 28 September 1997; reprinted in Dylan, *Bob Dylan* (note 1), 396. In these

later remarks on this theme, Dylan understandably expands his range of examples to include African American blues and sacred music as well as early commercial country-and-western songs. This renders the restriction of his examples in the interviews of 1965 to the British ballad tradition all the more striking, as he was conversant with all these genres at the earliest stages of his career.

27. On the transformations of this motif, see David Mellor, *The Sixties Art Scene in London*, exh. cat. (London: Phaidon, 1993), 119–26.

28. "Every So Often, a Group Is Poised on the Brink of a Breakthrough. Word Has It It's . . . The Who," *Melody Maker*, 5 June 1965, 7. Townshend was quoted the next month declaring: "We stand for pop-art clothes, pop-art music and pop-art behaviour. This is what everybody seems to forget—we don't change off stage. We live pop-art"; see Nick Jones, "Well, What Is Pop Art?" *Melody Maker*, 3 July 1965, 11.

STEPHEN FREDMAN

FORMS OF VISIONARY COLLAGE: Harry Smith and the Poets

"The Problem of Rhythm in Relation to Thought"

As a latecomer to the works of Harry Smith, I have felt compelled to look at his output as a whole in an effort to understand its central principles and to see where it might be located in the landscape of the arts of the twentieth century. The largest and most expansive ambit in which to situate Smith's artistic endeavors is that of collage, for nearly everything he did—from filmmaking to painting to collecting to the *Anthology of American Folk Music*—is composed not in a narrative sequence but by juxtaposition. Although here I can consider only certain of its aspects, Smith's relationship to collage is multifaceted and its implications are profound. To make some of these implications evident, I have chosen to compare Smith to three poets who were his contemporaries: Allen Ginsberg (1926–97), Robert Duncan (1919–88), and Jack Spicer (1925–65). Not only was Smith acquainted with each of these poets but, more significantly, he shared with them a commitment to the West Coast collage and assemblage aesthetic that mingles the avant-garde with the occult, the vernacular with the cosmological.[1] A comparison of his artistic activities—which extended to publishing poetry only once, as far as we know[2]—with the productions of these notable poets suggests ways in which Smith made the technique of collage his own, as well as reasons why collage was for him not only an aesthetic but also an existential issue.

First, I would like to envision the sorts of internal questions that might drive an inquisitive and original mind such as Smith's to take an existential turn toward collage. For instance, imagine asking yourself, in all seriousness, what does it take to make life appear meaningful moment by moment? Say you are not content with just getting by day-to-day or with entering into the splashy events projected by the news media as a constantly consuming narrative. Or what if you engage in years of study in order to master one or more fields of knowledge but find that no intellectual discipline provides a strong enough purchase on how things happen that you would want to remain within its embrace? Or what if, with even more desperation, you find that no religion or philosophy or science or esoteric system seems capable of tagging all the reality hurtling at you from every direction? Then you might, like Harry Smith, try to create your own skeleton key to unlock how things make sense. Smith believed this key consisted not of concepts but of tuning into an underlying rhythm discernible in the way things happen. Focusing his attention on momentary conjunctions rather than on fixed ideas, he began to view life as a constantly evolving collage composition. Most of us look at reality on the alert for familiar patterns, ignoring as meaningless anything that does not settle into a recognizable construct, but Smith looked at every event, every coincidence of objects, as obeying or maybe creating a certain rhythm; from this perspective nothing that occurs can be discarded or ignored because it all participates in the ongoing composition of meaning. This is why, as many people remarked in near-reverential tones, Smith was never bored: "no matter where he was and whatever space he found himself he made it gigantic. . . . He always found the treasures of the world absolutely under his feet. Heard things and saw things and tasted things that nobody ever had before. If you were with Harry you could discover something new every moment and it was in complete disguise."[3]

For Smith was always making art. Because his art practice relied on his understanding of how meaning happens, he was constantly engaged in it, forever building collections—bringing things into startling new relationships—and by so doing making explicit his notion that reality is composed of meaningful, if unanticipated, conjunctions. As one of his students put it, "Harry was always into the process. The one thing that he said to me that I particularly remember was the most important thing about reality is the relationship of objects. And he said that what makes everything real is the fact that things are ordered in the present status. In other words, things are set beside themselves and that is what makes reality. Reality is made up of just the placement of objects."[4] Smith not only collected things, he placed them in suggestive contexts that would allow them to call attention to themselves by virtue of what was around them, thus turning a collection into a work of art. Many people have noted that the *Anthology of American Folk Music* (1952) is a very peculiar kind of collection, ordered not by any simple method of classification but as an assemblage in which songs call out to one another along multiple axes of meaning. Smith himself admits to this mode of composition: "The whole *Anthology* was a collage. I thought of it as an art object."[5] To have practiced standard classification in keeping with the disciplines of folklore or ethnomusicology would have meant acceding to a preestablished order, rather than engaging in the active pursuit of meaningful patterns—the foremost concern of his every waking (and probably dreaming) hour.

In viewing composition as a boundless process, in which nothing that occurs is exterior to the artistic activity, Smith carried forward the avant-garde collage enterprise spearheaded by people such as Gertrude Stein, Hans Arp, and Marcel Duchamp. These precursors had opened the way to conceiving of collage as not merely an artistic form but a way of life. In *Composition as Explanation* (1926), for instance, Stein gave a classic formulation of the central idea behind such collage composition: "The composition is the thing seen by every one living in the living they are doing, they are the composing of the composition that at the time they are living is the composition of the time in which they are living."[6] If the artist recognizes reality as a constant collage activity, then he or she can signal that recognition by employing a collage method that foregrounds the compositional activity occurring constantly in the modern world. Across the gamut of his endeavors, Smith's method involves a number of processes that conduce to an understanding of and participation in "the composition of the time in which [he is] living." These processes include perspicacious collecting, diligent study, striking insight into hitherto unnoticed relationships, and, finally, a surrender to the arbitrariness of the moment.

One of Smith's students describes this methodology as an intertwining of purpose and chance: "he would just concentrate and study and work and go haywire, drive himself crazy, getting everything in exactly the right order and then he would just give it a kick and say 'that's it.' But he knew when he kicked it that he'd chosen the right moment and however it fell was going to be right."[7]

Like Duchamp, whose accidentally cracked *The Bride Stripped Bare by Her Bachelors, Even (The Large Glass)* (1915–23) (see p. 144) he keenly admired,[8] Smith had a Dadaist's trust that the carefully prepared work of art achieves final realization only through a chance operation. But unlike Duchamp's acolyte John Cage, whose compositional methods of chance and indeterminacy reflected a philosophical commitment to letting be, Smith joins the great bebop improvisers (whose procedures he charts note by note in some of his paintings [see pp. 26, 195, 198]) in insisting that an inherent rhythm to the way things happen can be found, although it can be apprehended only by the most rigorous, vigilant attention. In his notes to *The Kiowa Peyote Meeting,* issued by Folkways Records in 1973, Smith lauds an ascetic rigor he finds in the singers and contends that their philosophical asceticism brings them to an appreciation of the rhythmic nature of life: "I particularly hope that examples of the Kiowa approach to things will give an insight into how one people has dealt with the problem of rhythm in relation to thought."[9] The desire to relate rhythm and thought has been around in Western philosophy at least since Pythagoras combined mathematics, music, and asceticism, and it reached its zenith in the works of Plato. Smith himself invoked the Platonic tradition by reproducing on the *Anthology*'s three LP covers the image of the divine monochord—in which the Ptolemaic universe is related mathematically to musical intervals—from a treatise by the Renaissance Neoplatonist Robert Fludd (fig. 1; see also p. 186).[10] It should not be surprising, then, that in 1962 Smith calls upon Plato's example to explain how high his hopes had been for the *Anthology:* "I felt social changes would result from it. I'd been reading from Plato's *Republic.* He's jabbering on about music, how you have to be careful about changing the music because it might upset or destroy the government. Everybody gets out of step"—which was exactly what Smith was hoping for.[11] He affirms this statement when accepting the lifetime achievement Chairman's Merit Award from the National Academy of Recording Arts and Sciences in 1991: "I'm glad to say my dreams came true, that I saw America changed through music."[12]

The relationship between rhythm and thought stands at the heart of Smith's conception of the universe. As the poet and biochemist Harvey Bialy testifies, Smith "had the uncanny ability to understand the basic connections between things that were seemingly completely disparate and the forces and dynamics and magnetic interactions and terrestrial activities and geomagnetic polarizations... that made culture, that made music, that made art, that made all of the things that are timeless in human culture."[13] For Bialy, this ability to capture the relationship between rhythm and thought and to envisage the ways this relationship structures the artifacts of human culture made Smith "an extraordinary being that comes along maybe once in a hundred years or in a thousand years. Harry is a genius on the order of Da Vinci."[14] Despite this ringing endorsement, Smith's achievement is not easy to evaluate. Although claims like Bialy's are common from Smith's intimates,

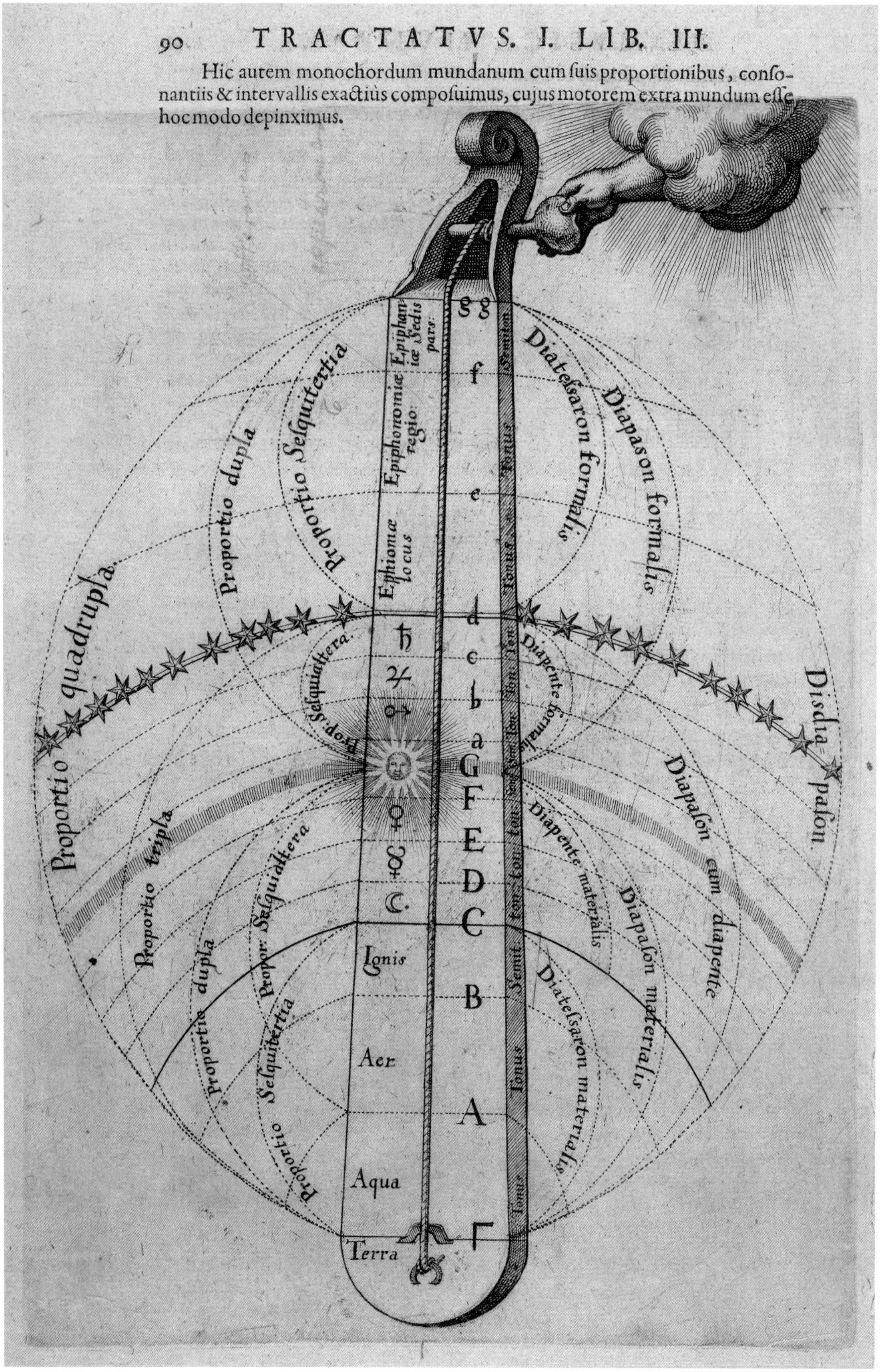

90 TRACTATVS. I. LIB. III.

Hic autem monochordum mundanum cum suis proportionibus, consonantiis & intervallis exactiùs composuimus, cujus motorem extra mundum esse hoc modo depinximus.

the same people (and others) offer testimony that paints Smith as a self-absorbed crackpot, an angry drunk, or a charlatan. It is difficult for one who never met him to evaluate Smith because his creativity and his philosophical principles seem to have been most in evidence during performances he staged for individuals or small groups of people—shows that might be visual (his films and paintings and collections) but might also be aural (his records and tapes spanned a huge variety of sound worlds) or strictly verbal (as transcriptions of his interviews make apparent). The interviews collected in *Think of the Self Speaking* (1999) give a glimpse of his performative persona, which is an amalgamation of pedant, scholar, raconteur, trickster, and madman. One way to measure the public effect of Smith's work without firsthand experience of the man is to note the cultural developments for which he was an important inspiration: the folk music revival and the subsequent rise of rock and roll; central aspects of visionary filmmaking; the concert light show; facets of modern alchemical magic; and creative and intuitive impulses in countless individuals.

One of the most nuanced attempts to gauge Smith and his achievement can be found in *Think of the Self Speaking*'s introduction, in which Allen Ginsberg tells Hal Willner about his long and eventful friendship with Smith, striking a balance between admiration for Smith's work and exasperation at his personal habits. In the midst of recounting an evening at Smith's apartment, during which he was plied with marijuana and then shown a number of Smith's early films, Ginsberg comments appreciatively on the subtly interpenetrating rhythms in those works:

> What he had done was set... certain ones of them, short ones, to "Misterioso."... I saw that his point was that the actual frames moved in relation to the music—he had been calculating the frames to the Monk music. In addition, he had a theory that the time of movement would be a cross current of... certain kinds of brain waves, the average heartbeat pattern, certain biological rhythms..., and he was animating his collages and setting the time according to archetypal body rhythms. His references to this were certain drumming patterns of the Australian Aborigines [and] Zulu music.[15]

Notwithstanding his awe at the technical range and the rhythmic subtlety of Smith's radical genius, Ginsberg reports being afraid to enter Smith's apartment:

> He had no source [of income] but he was a genius, like the painter Albert Pinkham Ryder. I got to be scared of going up there because he'd get me tremblingly high on grass and show me these amazing movies. I'd be totally awed and intimidated by the universality of his genius in music and painting.... But he'd always hit me up for money, if he could capture me, get me up there and hypnotize me with his films.[16]

Although he generously gave substantial support, both financial and otherwise, to Smith over the years, Ginsberg makes palpable the pressure Smith placed on the people in his life. In the largest sense, this might be called a pressure for

Fig. 1.
Johann Theodor de Bry (Franco-Flemish, 1561–1623)
Mundane monochord (also known as the celestial monochord or the divine monochord)
From Robert Fludd, *Utriusque Cosmi Maioris Scilicet et Minoris Metaphysica, Physica atque Technica Historia*, vol. 1, *De Macrocosmi Historia in Duos Tractatus Divisa* (Oppenheim: aere Johan-Theodori de Bry, typis Hieronymi Galleri, 1617), tract. 1, bk. 3, p. 90

acknowledgment: Smith wanted his talent acknowledged so that he would be given enough money to fund his ambitious projects (and, incidentally, to stay alive); he wanted his solutions to "the problem of rhythm in relation to thought" acknowledged as signal innovations in modern art and scholarship; and he wanted people he knew to acknowledge the creative possibilities inherent moment by moment in their own lives. The pressure for acknowledgment made Smith a difficult person to be around, and yet such demands (and the discomfort they provoke) are not atypical for some of the most creative personalities in the modern world.

"To Have the Serpent Intertwined in Their Eyeballs"

Smith and Ginsberg were friends for over thirty years. At certain periods, Smith lived with Ginsberg for months at a time (fig. 2), causing the poet so many headaches that he was greatly relieved to secure Smith a sinecure as shaman-in-residence at the Naropa Institute in Boulder, Colorado, which lasted three years, until Smith's death in 1991.[17] Given that Smith and Ginsberg inhabited substantially the same world, I find it remarkable how much they diverge aesthetically while remaining within the ambit of collage. Ginsberg's poetry strikes a reader most forcibly by the nakedness of its address, issuing a plea for compassion and for mutual recognition of our desiring loneliness. Although Smith's art, like Ginsberg's, arises from a maverick sensibility planted in direct opposition to an entire range of social institutions, Smith maintains, unlike Ginsberg, a remarkable impersonality. Emulating his masters William Blake and Walt Whitman, Ginsberg yearns for the visionary role; he succeeds, however, as a courageously generous poet of the

Fig. 2.
Brian Graham (Canadian, b. 1951)
Allen Ginsberg and Harry Smith cook at Ginsberg's apartment, 1986

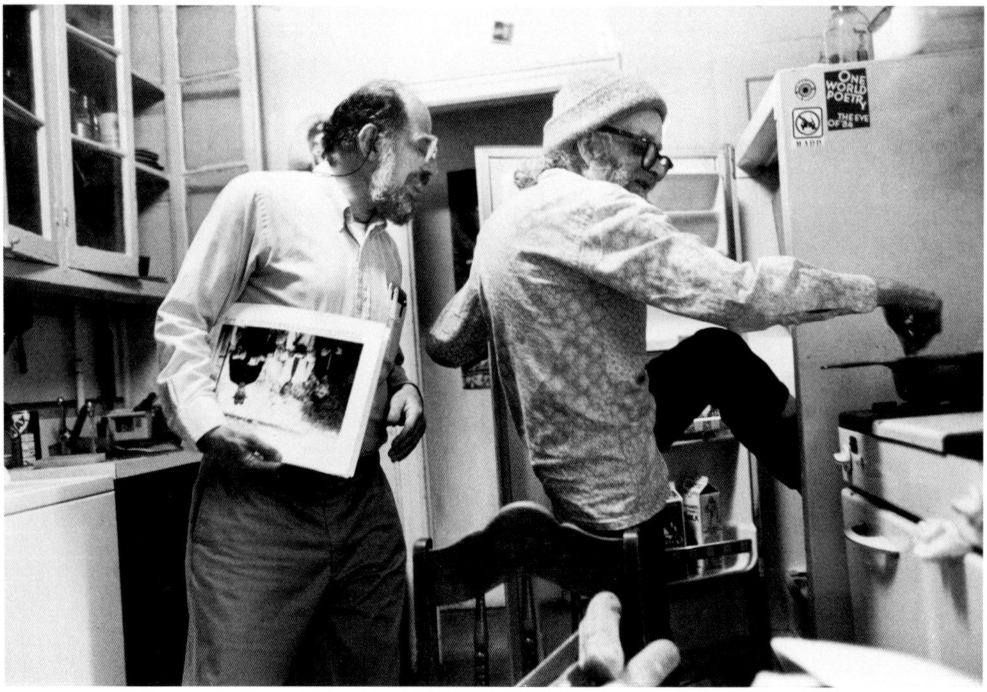

personal. Smith, by contrast, is a legitimate visionary, whose disdain for the personality can be found not only in the absence of biographical references in his art but also in the lies he tells about himself, in the tricks he plays so assiduously to hold others at a distance, and in his utter disregard for physical and emotional well-being, whether his own or that of others.

In their use of collage techniques, both Smith and Ginsberg erase distinctions between life and art but in radically different ways. Ginsberg's collage method is summed up by his aphorism, "First thought, best thought," which advocates a spontaneous, wildly associative, and unrevised poetry that is an inheritor to the surrealist doctrine of automatic writing and a companion to Jack Kerouac's "spontaneous bop prosody."[18] By contrast, Smith asserts that, since the universe itself already employs the principle of spontaneous juxtaposition, his job is to study in great detail the conjunctions that actually occur in reality and to submit the meaning he finds there to laborious compositional techniques. Although in general terms their aesthetic predilections hark back to Dada and surrealism, Ginsberg and Smith maintain what might be thought of as an inverse or complementary relationship with respect to the personal. A notorious example of this complementarity can be seen in their drug use: where Ginsberg took drugs to explore and transcend personal demons and to seek cosmic revelations, Smith ingested substances to construct a working environment for deliberately calibrated explorations of objects and forces at work in the world.

In the poem "Journal Night Thoughts" (1961–64), Ginsberg stages a vivid confrontation between Smith and himself.[19] Illustrative of Ginsberg's stream-of-consciousness collage technique, the poem reveals how drugs inevitably drew him toward his own psychological fixations. It narrates an evening devoted to marijuana that Ginsberg spent in Smith's unnerving company; during the night, the poet recalls a variety of earlier drug sessions and muses upon the outrageous images in Smith's vast repertoire of cultural oddities. Nearly four years after writing the poem, Ginsberg added a commentary along the right margin, identifying Smith as his visitor and specifying the drugs whose effects he recalls during the poem: yagé (ayahuasca), psilocybin, LSD, nitrous oxide, and mescaline. The drugs signify entire contexts that Ginsberg draws into the assemblage, for, as Marcus Boon argues, different kinds of drugs affect writing in different ways.[20] The poem begins with Ginsberg already intoxicated and staring into Smith's hypnotic gaze, which registers so strongly as a "pressure" that it propels hallucinations that hover around the transfixing eye into which the poet peers:

> In bed on my green purple pink
>   yellow orange bolivian blanket,
> the clock tick, my back against the wall
> —staring into black circled eyes magician
>   man's bearded glance & story
> the kitchen spun in a wheel of vertigo,
> the eye in the center of the moving
>   mandala—the

eye in the hand
the eye in the asshole
serpent eating or
    vomiting its tail
—the blank air a solid wall revolving
    around my retina.[21]

Ginsberg finds Smith both fascinating and scary, as the citations from *Think of the Self Speaking* attest. Here, the "magician / man's bearded glance" magnetizes Ginsberg's attention while Smith feeds the poet's vertigo on macabre stories in which the iconography of the serpent figures prominently. Ginsberg illustrates "Journal Night Thoughts" with a drawing by Smith, *Southern Cult Composite: The Staten Island Massacre* (fig. 3), that incorporates motifs from the poem, such as hands with eyes in their palms and intertwined rattlesnakes. As the poem riffs through visions from Ginsberg's past, alternating between the beatific and the horrific, the poet returns to his vertiginous conversation with Smith and to the central image of the serpent. Smith sparks hallucinations by regaling the poet with tales of Natchez sun ceremonies and the Spiro Mounds, an eight-hundred-year-old Southern Cult site in Oklahoma—what Ginsberg calls in his marginal commentary "*Smith's Anthropological Gossip*":

Fig. 3.
Harry Smith
Southern Cult Composite: The Staten Island Massacre, 1984, ink, pencil, charcoal on paper, 51 × 38 cm (20⅛ × 15 in.)
Harry Smith Archives

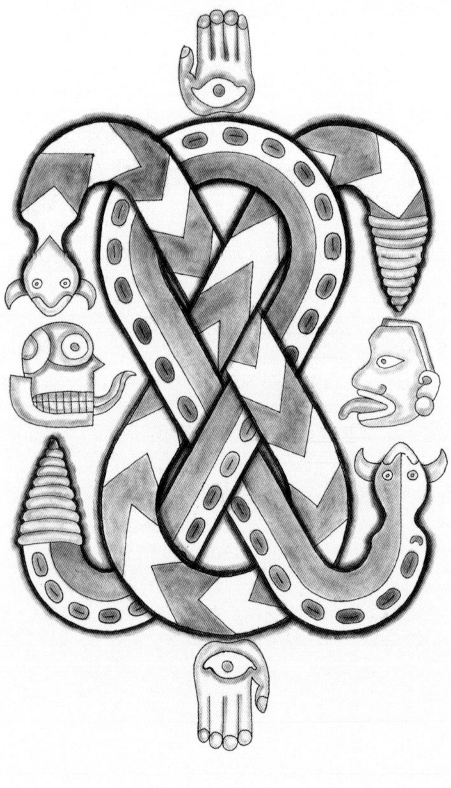

Natchez, he was saying with his head one side
of the center of the wheel
of Vertigo—
burned babies in the blaze of a fiery house
sending them back to the Sun—
They drank a black elixir, and threw it up
To have the serpent intertwined
in their eyeballs—
One man was born with genitals all over
his body—there were 15,000,000
Indians in North America then—
The mushroom image in the Spiro Mound.[22]

The content that seems especially to fascinate Ginsberg in Smith's bizarre stories is the phallic imagery: the serpent in the eyeballs, the genitals all over the body (fifteen million it seems, because of the way the line breaks), and the mushroom in the mound. This phallic imagery unites the physical genitals with transgressive social rituals and ecstatic mystical experiences. These images lead up to one taken directly from Smith's animated collage *Film #12: Heaven and Earth Magic* (ca. 1957–62), a print of which Ginsberg had recently purchased because Smith was desperately short of funds:[23]

Here is the Homunculus wavering in the brain,
the aggregate of ignorant patterns
looking like Denny Dimwit
The genitals are larger than the head.[24]

Notwithstanding the interest he shared with Ginsberg in the phallic qualities of the alchemical homunculus (the "little man" whose creation involved the use of human sperm) (fig. 4), Smith would never have considered him an "aggregate of ignorant patterns," for such occult patterns were exactly what Smith sought to

Fig. 4.
Harry Smith
Still from *Film #12: Heaven and Earth Magic,* ca. 1957–62, 66 min., 16 mm, black and white, sound

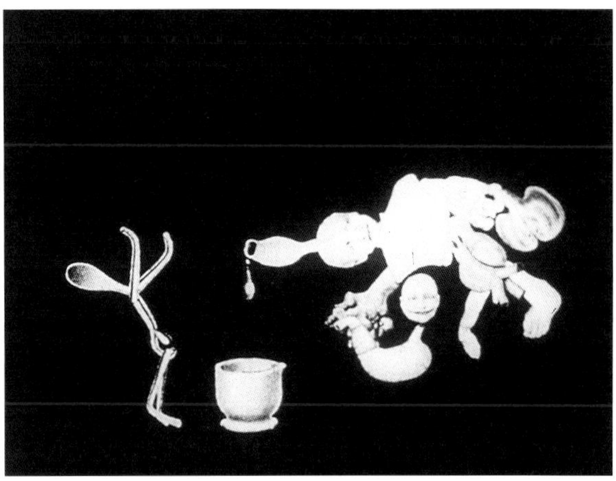

know. Subsequent to noting the phallic apotheosis induced by Smith's anthropological gossip, Ginsberg returns in the poem to narrating apocalyptic drug scenes, accompanied by paranoid statements such as "I dreamt I had to destroy the human / universe to be Messiah."[25] After a further string of remembered drug visions, Ginsberg falls back finally into the embrace of two lifelong obsessions: mother and sex. Although he has tolerated a parade of visions that tested his mental equanimity, the glimpse of "my mother's skull not yet white" is the one threatening vision to which he shouts, "GO / BACK!" Significantly, the poem's final scene follows immediately on this command: a compensatory depiction, in loving detail, of an episode of happy sex, in which, he reports, "I come in the ass of my beloved."[26] Despite the allure of Smith's gleefully sinister lore about American Indians and despite the poet's apocalyptic hallucinations, Ginsberg's primary interlocutors—mother and sex—emerge forcefully, joined together at the end of the poem as they must incessantly have been in his mind. No matter how far Ginsberg ranges in the subject matter of his collage poetry, he is more like his master Walt Whitman than Harry Smith in centering his visionary flights on an individual self, its desires and aversions.

Grand Collage

If Ginsberg's poetry evokes the visionary but finally sides with the personal, another poet among Smith's contemporaries, Robert Duncan, occupies a position midway between Smith and Ginsberg on the continuum of visionary to personal. When Smith lived in Berkeley in the late 1940s, the Berkeley Poetry Renaissance, whose primary figures were Duncan, Jack Spicer, and Robin Blaser, was in full swing. During that time, Smith and Duncan traveled in a larger circle of filmmakers, poets, and painters in Berkeley and San Francisco, and there is evidence that by 1948 they had met.[27] Comparison of Duncan and Smith hinges on the fact that they, like other artists in the wider circle, subscribed wholeheartedly to the signature West Coast aesthetic that mingles the avant-garde and the esoteric—an aesthetic in which collage and assemblage have been major elements. Convinced that an occult discipline can deepen artistic experimentation, both endeavor to set aside the ego by regarding the artist as a medium rather than an originator: in Smith's formulation, "My movies are made by God; I am just the medium for them."[28] By contrast, the two part company dramatically on the matter of personal psychology and individual experience, which Duncan explores assiduously with the aid of Freudian psychology but Smith approaches only by physiological means—for example, by using drugs for psychological derangement and by calibrating his films to various biorhythms. Although they differ with respect to psychology, the most salient similarity between Smith and Duncan is that both were brought up in theosophical families; this early training in magical thinking supplied their work its lifelong direction.[29] The theosophical belief that there is a secret key to the universe hidden in the scriptures and arts of every society sets each of them on an inexorable quest to ascertain connections and correspondences among the images of the world's cultures.

In *The H. D. Book*, his inquiry into the sources of his own conception of poetry, Duncan considers the influence of theosophical notions both on modern writers (especially H. D., Ezra Pound, and D. H. Lawrence) and on the domestic world of his family. He recalls as a child hearing voices whisper in the other room:

> And in the inner chamber, the adults, talking on, wove for me in my childish overhearing, Egypt, a land of spells and secret knowledge, a background drift of things close to dreaming—spirit communications, reincarnation memories, clairvoyant journeys into a realm of astral phantasy where all times and places were seen in a new light, of Plato's illustrations of the nature of the soul's life, of most real Osiris and Isis, of lost Atlantis and Lemuria.[30]

This hypnagogic overhearing helped invoke an overheated imagination in the young Duncan, who developed the habit of looking for hidden connections among the multifarious phenomena before him. Later, this would enable him to claim that the founder of the Theosophical Society, Helena Petrovna Blavatsky, evinced in the incredible hodgepodge of her writings an intuitive understanding of how the esoteric and the avant-garde might work together. "In the mess of astrology, alchemy, numerology, magic orders, neo-Platonic, kabbalistic and Vedic systems combined, confused, and explained, queered evolution and wishful geology, transposed heads," Blavatsky discovered, Duncan says, "the collagist's art."[31] The elements of collage he discerns in Blavatsky (who for her own part insisted that her works were "revealed to her in the Astral Records"[32]) include a "charged fascination"[33] with the material being composed, an obedience to unknown but compelling feelings, and a new respect for discarded phenomena. Speaking of her two books, he avers that "*Isis Unveiled* and *The Secret Doctrine,* midden heaps that they are of unreasonable sources, are midden heaps where, beyond the dictates of reason, as in the collagist's art, from what has been disregarded or fallen into disregard, genres are mixed, exchanges are made, mutations begun from scraps and excerpts from different pictures... to form the figures of a new composition."[34] Taking on and eventually refining this compositional method, Duncan advances toward his mature poetics, which he comes to call *grand collage*—a kind of mystical art of assemblage, in which the poet sees hidden correspondences among disparate sources, claiming no originality for his art other than in the finding and arranging of the materials. More than a poetic method, grand collage offers Duncan an overarching principle of the imagination: "in this realm of men's languages," he states, grand collage produces "a poetry of all poetries."[35]

As with any sort of collage, the "materials" of the poem have equal standing with the form in which it is composed. Duncan's grand collage, which is a kind of metacollage, draws on a particular stratum of materials, consisting of the most highly charged artifacts of any society and every era; from these, he can construct "a poetry of all poetries." Like Blavatsky's books, but much more artfully and self-consciously, Duncan's poems are "midden heaps," in which "genres are mixed" and materials are extracted not only from acknowledged masterpieces but from "disregarded" or "unreasonable sources," providing "the figures of a new composition" that remains constantly in process. In the 1950s and 1960s, Duncan began two open-ended series of collage poems, "Structure of Rime" and "*Passages,*" which wind through the books he published in the last thirty years of his life.[36] The ultimate subject of Duncan's "poetry of all poetries," as of the many varieties of Smith's assemblages, is humanity writ large—that is, a vision of the totality of human possibilities: "Mankind that does not come to an end... has become for me the central theme—a Man of all men, multiphasic, beyond what we can know but central, as we are immediate realities of Man, to what we are. This was the Adam in whom all the species have their identity. In the traditions of the Jewish Kabbala this Adam falls apart into the lives of all men—his identity hidden in our identities"[37]—as if this Adam were the true human being and each of us a tiny homunculus. Such a collage art, based on a notion of nested levels of reality, carries the implicit conviction that *anything* human beings are capable of doing or thinking or saying must be accounted for in the larger picture of what we are, which is ultimately one species among many. Taking seriously this larger view of what constitutes the grand collage of life forms, Duncan proposes the need for a "symposium of the whole":[38]

> If I seek to picture Man in his multiplicity for myself, and in that multiplicity to imagine a composition in which goods and evils belong to the order of things..., it is because I feel the world as creation and what is happening as a drama, the processes of the actual world as the deepest drama. The stars, the dark depths of space beyond, and the light streaming from the sun, speak to us; the earth, the waves and winds, the twittering of birds and the glances of animals, speak to us. The fall of a rock, the shifting of sands can be read and, in one way of reading, the story of the earth is revealed, in another way of reading, elusive apprehensions of our own inner fate or identity in process emerge.[39]

Smith, too, seems to "feel the world as creation and what is happening as a drama, the processes of the actual world as the deepest drama," and this apprehension underlies, for instance, his superimposed films and his ambient audio recordings, in which he composes visual or auditory patterns in a collage drama beyond individual volition. Recognizing the centrality of collage to his artistic practice, Smith describes the *Anthology of American Folk Music* as a collage;[40] like his purely collage film *Heaven and Earth Magic,* the *Anthology* is one of his most fully realized projects. Notions of collage similar to Duncan's also figure prominently in Smith's conversation, which often takes the form of reading the world in order to find "elusive apprehensions of... inner fate" and to watch an "identity in process emerge." This sort of collagist's "reading" appears in interviews he gives, during which Smith bounds from topic to topic without transition. He builds an "identity in process" by repeated jump-cuts that confront his interlocutor like a series of dares, as if to say, "I dare you to keep up with the leaps of my mind. I dare you to pretend to have expert knowledge in the entire range of the topics I draw together. I dare you to maintain your equanimity and not be confounded by my outrageousness." Forming a clear picture of Smith and his achievement is so difficult because he conducts himself like Proteus or Taliesin, eluding the grasp of pursuers and interlocutors by continually shifting shape, a trickster first and foremost. Even the self-deprecatory tone audible in recorded conversations with him sounds like a dodge, as though he were daring his audience *not* to recognize that he has a universal mind.

Smith's parry-and-thrust attitude joins a range of his stylistic attributes, which might be summed up as a blending of the vernacular and the cosmological. On the one hand, many of the objects Smith collects—folk music, string figures, paper airplanes, Ukrainian painted eggs, Seminole patchwork patterns—are funky, down-home, and homegrown, and his penchant for an extravagant cobbling together of rejected materials and for speaking like a teller of tall tales reflects those interests. On the other hand, Smith has a fastidious, meticulous, alchemical side, which accounts for his spending years engaged in cataloging and calibrating the elements of a project; this side of his style produces paintings and films that are symmetrical or otherwise geometric, numerological, and diagrammatic. What the vernacular and the cosmological have in common is a preference for use value over aesthetic value. Smith's art seeks not to excite critical admiration or appeal to canons of taste but rather to be efficacious, to make something happen. In that sense, the work is purely iconic, rather than expressive: it does not make a statement—whether in the form of artistic commentary or political commitment or personal revelation—but rather invites participation. Speaking of his Kiowa peyote recordings, for instance, Smith makes the point that his collecting is all done for iconic purposes:

> When I was in Oklahoma I realized that it was possible to perform some kind of saturated study of something. It just happened that it was with recordings, although I went there to make films.... The Seminole project grew out of that, but I didn't record their music. Then the egg business grew out of the Seminole stuff.... The problems that I'd set myself on have to do with correlating music into some kind of a visual thing, into some kind of a diagram. It was much simpler to skip the music entirely and study diagrams that had already been made.... I'm sure that if you could collect sufficient patchwork quilts from the same people who made the records, like Uncle Dave Macon or Sara Carter's houses, you could figure out just about anything you can from the music. Everything could be figured out regarding their judgment in relation to certain intellectual processes.[41]

In his films, paintings, collections, and conversations, Smith ties iconic elements together to create previously unsuspected examples in the mode of Duncan's grand collage. For his part, Duncan employs grand collage in many periods of his life, with the "*Passages*" series as his most sustained effort in that genre. These poems join Duncan with Smith not just by way of their mutual interest in collage techniques but also through their research in hermetic philosophy and magic, their shamanistic pursuits, their fascination with American Indian lore, their metaphorizing of filmic projection, their depiction of dream landscapes, and their construction of the artist's room as a cave of alchemical creativity. By discussing one poem from Duncan's "*Passages*" series, "The Architecture, *Passages* 9," dated 6 June 1964, I can suggest how the preoccupations he shares with Smith are woven throughout that sequence. "The Architecture" registers elements of the Victorian house in San Francisco's Mission district that Duncan shared for many years with the painter Jess

(Burgess Collins, 1923–2004). Duncan had a long-standing engagement with architecture: "My father had been an architect and, until he died, when I was sixteen, I had been preparing to enter that world. Ideas of architecture still continue in my art today as a poet."[42] The poem begins with a prose quotation from Gustav Stickley's book *Craftsman Homes* (1909):

> ". . . it must have recesses. There is a great charm in a room
> broken up in plan, where that slight feeling of mystery is given
> to it which arises when you cannot see the whole room from any
> one place . . when there is always something around the corner"[43]

For Duncan, the design of the house mirrors the design of the poem. They cannot be laid out in a rationalized, comprehensive fashion but, as an assemblage, must be approached piecemeal and from a variety of angles; both must maintain a sense of incipience, as though "there is always something around the corner." Smith likewise transformed each of the rooms he occupied during his life into a charged, mysterious space, in which the conjunction of objects signified incipient metaphorical relationships. The musician and photographer John Cohen describes one such space, Smith's room at the Chelsea Hotel in 1968:

> A visit to his room is a somewhat mystifying experience, for what appears on first impression as orderly piles of books and objects is actually a storehouse for cross-disciplinary investigations of visual, anthropological, and musical phenomena. The closet is filled with women's dresses from the Florida Seminole Indians. One corner of the room, marked with a "Keep Off" sign, is filled with Ukrainian Easter eggs; on the bureau are stacks of mounted string figures; behind the table is a movie camera alongside portfolios of his paintings and graphic work. In another corner is a clay model of an imaginary landscape which is re-created from a dream. On the walls hang empty frames from which the pictures have been ripped out. . . . Small file cabinets of index cards are distributed between the stacks of research books. Each book becomes more exotic by its juxtaposition with other such books—Mayan codices beside Eskimo anthropology studies, under a collection of Peyote ceremonial paintings, et cetera, et cetera.[44]

Duncan's poem "The Architecture" maps out how an artist's living space such as his own or Smith's instantiates the grand collage and becomes a charged locus for the making of art. The house on 20th Street was both a work of assemblage in its own right and a breeding ground for the interpenetrating poetic and visual oeuvres that Duncan and Jess created (fig. 5). In a retrospective catalog entitled *Jess: A Grand Collage 1951–1993*, Michael Auping asserts that "the association between Jess and Duncan is itself a collage that extends beyond Duncan's poetry or Jess's art to an interactive collage encompassing the house they inhabited, itself symbolic of the products of their combined imaginations."[45] The house not only held Duncan's extensive library and classical record collection and Jess's studio but was packed with works of art on every surface imaginable; Jess even made cutouts in one wall to carry fragments of a stained-glass window patterned with poppies that had been broken before they moved in. Many of the art pieces on display inside the house consisted of the assemblages ("Assemblies") (fig. 6) and elaborate black-and-white collages ("Paste-Ups") that form two of the main series pursued by Jess for many years.[46] The presence of these objects drew attention to the dizzyingly elaborate collage composition that obtained throughout the Victorian house with an Arts and Crafts interior. Describing Jess's working environment in the 1990s, Auping characterizes the house and studio as "a warehouse of surplus imagination and a dense accumulation of symbolic fragments that are continually being added to and collaged together as a constant reinvention of a self."[47]

In "The Architecture," after the extract from Stickley, Duncan presents himself as looking out "from the window-shelter" (an important element of Stickley's Craftsman design) while listening to Bertolt Brecht and Kurt Weill's opera *Aufstieg und Fall der Stadt Mahagonny* (1930; *Rise and Fall of the City of Mahagonny*)—the basis, coincidentally, of one of Smith's major cinematic projects.[48] From his vantage point in the window seat, Duncan sees a series of symbolic objects with which Smith would have felt right at home:

> . . . the bookcases the glimmering titles arrayd keys
> Hesiod • Heraklitus • *The Secret Books of the Egyptian Gnostics* . . .
> . . . .
> *La Révélation d'Hermès Trismégiste*
> *Plutarch's Morals: Theosophical Essays*
> *Avicenna*
> *The Zohar*
> *The Aurora*[49]

These "keys" comprise a selection of esoteric texts from the theosophical tradition in which Duncan and Smith were raised. The texts—which he presents himself as "reading while the music playd / curld up among the ornamental cushions"[50]—proffer correspondences between different levels of reality and thus model for Duncan the metaphorical connections he explores in his poetry. He intercuts the evocation of a theosophical reading scene with quotations from Stickley, thereby drawing attention to symbolic elements in Arts and Crafts architecture. By one passage he quotes, for instance, Duncan hints at an occult significance to the staircase:

> "the staircase, instead of being hidden away in a small hall or
> treated as a necessary evil, made one of the most beautiful and
> prominent features of the room because it forms a link between
> the social part of the house and the upper regions" . . .[51]

If we take the phrase "upper regions" in a metaphysical sense, then the excerpt discloses an architecture in which a staircase becomes a Jacob's Ladder, a shamanic device for climbing out of the mundane realm and into the visionary.

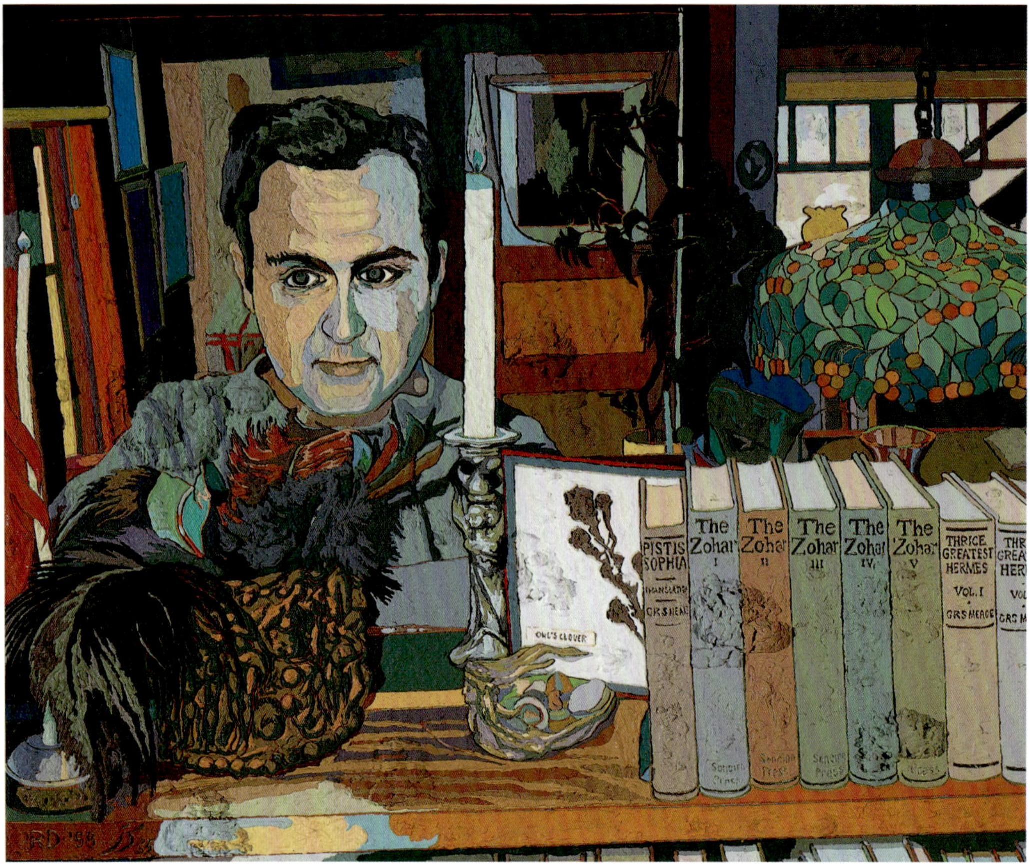
OWL'S CLOVER
PISTIS SOPHIA
The Zohar I
The Zohar II
The Zohar III
The Zohar IV
The Zohar V
THRICE GREATEST HERMES VOL. I

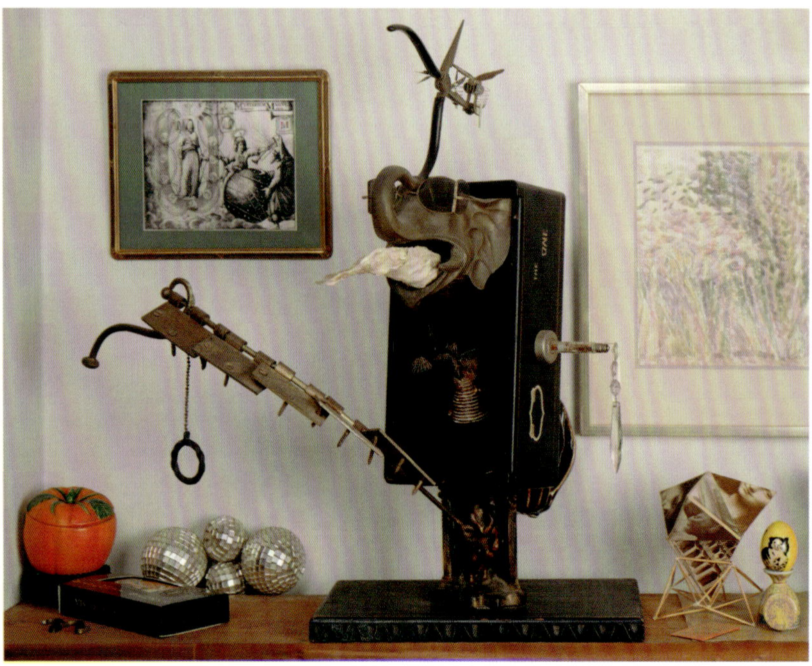

Like Smith, who made extensive sound recordings of American Indian ceremonies as a teenager, Duncan had been fascinated by shamanism as early as 1939, when he undertook an ambitious project in prose poetry that he called "Toward the Shaman."[52] Alluding in "The Architecture" to the visionary world of the American Indians, he includes in the closing section two quotations from the ethnologist Truman Michelson's *The Owl Sacred Pack of the Fox Indians* (1921). They report conversations between Owl and his shamans regarding a medicine kit Owl gives to human beings. In the first, Owl says of the pack,

> " *'You are to make it,' I told you in the past. I do*
> *not suppose you recognize me. 'Owl' is what I am*
> *calld. This is how I am.*"[53]

At this point, Duncan's collage poem has an implied narrative: through his reading the poet has climbed the mystical stairs and had a shamanistic encounter with the Owl spirit. Not coincidentally, the owl is Duncan's chosen totem animal, emblematic of the visual disability that kept his eyes from focusing simultaneously on a given object and earned him the epithet "owl-eyed."[54] In the context of this poem, recognizing Owl constitutes self-recognition: "*I do not suppose you recognize me,*" queries Owl; "Oh, yes I do!" Duncan might well reply. After 1955, when he wrote the poem "An Owl Is an Only Bird of Poetry,"[55] Duncan's house began to fill with owl images sent by friends, so that the owl became not only an uncannily strange but also a most familiar presence. The owl's paradoxical familiarity and strangeness symbolize a tension maintained throughout the "*Passages*" series between the domestic and the visionary. Moreover, in "The Architecture," the act of reading stands on the threshold between these two realms as a necessary creative process for bridging them. The concluding section of the poem portrays the liminal process of reading as a form of projection both cinematic and psychological. "The Architecture" ends with an image of the printed page as a movie screen upon which lamplight shines, pulling him into the narrative:

> *Phantastes, At the Back of the North Wind,*
> *The Princess and the Goblin,*
> *The Princess and Curdie,* *Lilith*
> the lamplight warm upon the page where I •
> romance • in which lost, reading •
>
> " *You will often tell the story. If you do that you*
> *will be able to marry those you love. You will fear*
> *me. If I even see you, you will die.*"

..."which belong to the inner and individual part of the family life."[56]

In these three final passages, Duncan pastes together the domestic scene of the poet reading, the shamanic vision of Owl, and the final clause of the sentence

Fig. 5.
Jess (American, 1923–2004)
The Enamord Mage, Translation #6, 1965, oil on canvas mounted on wood, 62.2 × 76.2 cm (24½ × 30 in.)
San Francisco, de Young Museum

Fig. 6.
Jess (American, 1923–2004)
A Letter Box for Hellgate, 1961, assemblage, height: 63.5 cm (25 in.), in Jess's home, ca. 1983
Collection Odyssia Skouras

from Stickley about the staircase as a link between the "social part" and the "upper regions." The juxtapositions make evident Duncan's profound attachment to the personal and the psychological, which accounts for his placement between Smith and Ginsberg along the continuum of visionary to personal I have been constructing. In addition, by presenting the vision of Owl as a projection on the white screen of a page, Duncan equates the "romance" of reading—a domestic pleasure that occurs in a safe, cozy, enveloping space—with the romance of film. Like Smith, Duncan believes in the visionary potential of film, which accounts for his lasting friendships with underground filmmakers such as Stan Brakhage, Kenneth Anger, Larry Jordan, James Broughton, and Bruce Conner. As it does for these filmmakers, for Duncan the domestic world becomes the ground from which oneiric flights to higher realms take off. Film's oneiric quality has been remarked upon from its beginnings; this quality is made explicit in one of the works that inspired postwar avant-garde filmmakers: Hans Richter's *Dreams That Money Can Buy* (1947). By means of its dream sequences designed by Man Ray, Max Ernst, Marcel Duchamp, Fernand Léger, Alexander Calder, and himself, Richter brought art installations directly into modern film. With its central conceit of an analyst figure who sells dream visions to neurotic patients, the film is a reflection on the interplay of cinema, dreams, and psychoanalysis that fascinated and inspired Duncan. In his working method, Smith too explores and exploits the oneiric quality of film: not only does he claim that for years during the composing of *Heaven and Earth Magic* he would waken himself after a few hours of sleep and transfer to film what had transpired in his dreams but he also states that the most effective way to enter fully into his monumental *Film #18: Mahagonny* (ca. 1970–80) is to fall asleep while viewing it.[57]

Reflecting on his home with Jess as a place of permission that allows for a concatenation of the romance of oneiric reading, the shamanistic flight, and "the inner and individual part of the family life," Duncan affirms, "The household Jess and I made I have seen as a lone holding in an alien forest-world, as a campfire about which we gathered in an era of cold and night—a made-up thing in which participating we have had the medium of a life together."[58] For gay partners making a home during the Cold War, the world outside held much that was bitter and benighted. Beyond the unmistakable dangers posed by a frightening mundane reality, though, an encounter with extraordinary beings such as Owl or his shaman would be fraught with danger for anyone: "*If I even see you,*" the shaman says, "*you will die.*"[59] Against such a threat, Duncan raises the shield of the domestic to keep him from losing his identity. Ultimately, however, he knows that danger can never be banished from the psyche, for the encounter with Thanatos (Death) is a central reality of the Freudian world that haunts Duncan's poetry. The danger that what you see may kill you must also belong to "the inner and individual part of the family life." For the most part, Smith eschewed "family life," giving the impression that, for all his burrowing like a pack rat into the rooms in which he resided, he possessed no sense of the domestic whatsoever. Having no interest in cultivating that protective sense of warmth that Duncan figures as "a campfire about which we gathered in an era of cold and night," Smith left himself continually exposed to winds from the outside.

"The Big Lie of the Personal"

At the end of the continuum of visionary to personal farthest from Ginsberg dwells Jack Spicer, a poet who despised the intrusion of the personal into art and who claimed that his poetry was dictated to him from "outside."[60] Like Duncan, Spicer was born in California and was a central figure in the Berkeley Poetry Renaissance of the late 1940s and of the San Francisco Renaissance of the 1950s and 1960s. In a career that spanned merely twenty years, Spicer wrote the influential serial poems brought together as *The Collected Books of Jack Spicer* (1975) and developed a striking theory of poetic composition. Within his poetic oeuvre, Spicer's obsession with American folk music runs as a leitmotif. Inveterate collectors, Spicer and Smith combed Bay Area record stores together, and in 1949 Smith appeared on Spicer's "Most Educational Folk-Song Program West of the Pecos," which aired over the new Pacifica radio station KPFA.[61] Like Smith, Spicer eagerly sought to alter the mental states of his friends, as illustrated by his making them drunk ahead of appearing on his broadcast in hopes of inducing them to sing bawdy improvised verses for old folk songs over the air—thus confirming his contention that an "authentic" folk song remains alive.[62] Kevin Killian, Spicer's biographer, points out that Spicer's penchant for folk song parody harks back to his days with Allan Sherman at Fairfax High School in Los Angeles. Sherman created the long-running television game show *I've Got a Secret* in the 1950s, and in the 1960s he released LPs of updated folk songs and parodies, beginning with the Jewish-humor inflected *My Son, the Folksinger* (1962) and culminating in the hit "Hello Muddah, Hello Fadduh! (A Letter from Camp)" from *My Son, the Nut* (1963).[63] Rather than create "ethnic" versions of popular folk songs, though, Spicer appropriates folk material in his poetry as a means of effacing the poet's ego—which is his aesthetic goal. Like Duncan and Smith, Spicer counters the notion of genius and originality by claiming that he is a conduit rather than a creator. Unlike Duncan, who sees himself as a "derivative" poet occupying an interpersonal "field" of poetry, Spicer believes that his poetry is a form of dictation from "beyond." In a theory that likely would satisfy Smith, Spicer conceives of the poet's primary job as pushing the personality aside to allow what is "outside" to speak through.[64]

In the course of four lectures he gave in Vancouver and Berkeley in 1965, the year of his death, Spicer develops a set of analogies to illustrate a theory of impersonal poetry to which he subscribes. He begins by recounting the famous story of the genesis of William Butler Yeats's *A Vision.* As Spicer tells it, riding on a train between San Bernardino and Los Angeles in 1918, Yeats found his new wife falling into a trance and beginning to channel voices. Yeats "finally decided he'd ask a question or two of the spooks as Georgie was in her trance. And he asked a rather good question. He asked, 'What are you here for?' And the spooks replied, 'We're here to give metaphors for your poetry.'"[65] A second analogy that Spicer develops for an impersonal poetry involves Jean Cocteau's film *Orphée* (1950), in which a modern poet, Orphée, receives and publishes under his own name poems dictated over the car radio by a dead poet.[66] Finally, to emphasize that the source of an authentic poem is completely from the outside, Spicer characterizes his poetry as being written by Martians.[67] These three analogies for a poetics of dictation help

Spicer advocate a wholly impersonal visionary art and place him at the opposite end of the spectrum from the emotionally vulnerable art of Ginsberg. Cognizant of this difference, Ginsberg speaks of their interaction:

> He was friendly toward me, but held a different vision of poetry. I think he had a thing that has nothing to do with Ego, messages come through the radio stations of the mind, so to speak, whereas I was thinking of the spontaneous mind. . . . But at any rate I think he thought that my own method was much too involved with personal statement and ego: it's a legitimate objection.[68]

While admitting a conflict in their stances toward the personal, Ginsberg does not feel that their collage methods of composition are "actually very different in operation: as a practical matter of composition"[69] they both bring obsessive interests into poems marked by unanticipated juxtapositions. Although Spicer would disagree that their methods are similar, he does admit the inevitability of leaving his own signature on a poem. Unlike Blavatsky, he does not claim that words and images in his writing are unknown to him, but he does feel the need to explain the apparent paradox that poems dictated from the outside still sound recognizably like Jack Spicer. In a way that might have intrigued Harry Smith, he imagines art as occurring inside a memory theater, within which the spirit of the poem (which comes from the outside) arranges all the words and knowledge the poet has gathered like so much "furniture." Once the furniture has been collected, the poet cedes the space to what is from the outside: "given the cooperation between the host poet and the visitor—the thing from outside—the more things you have in the room the better if you can handle them in such a way that you don't impose your will on what is coming through." Most poets, however, "can't resist, if they have all of these benches and chairs in the room, not to arrange them themselves instead of letting them be arranged by whatever is the source of the poem."[70]

The theory that the source of the poem arrives from elsewhere to arrange a series of objects bears a remarkable similarity to the compositional principle at work in Smith's collections and artworks. Both artists hold that each particular moment generates a distinct arrangement, a unique patterning, its own collage, which links composition to divination as the age-old attempt to read the moment's imprint upon an array of objects. Divination appealed strongly to Smith and Spicer, particularly in the form of the reading of tarot cards. Smith produced an entire deck of irregularly shaped cards (fig. 7);[71] Spicer outlined a book to write entitled "Understanding Tarot Cards: A Short Manual on the Use of Tarot Cards for Predicting the Future and Clarifying the Past." In Spicer's outline, a section of the book called "The Poetry of Chance" would offer a quasiscientific explanation for the efficacy of tarot divination "in terms of the difference between randomness and nonsense in statistical theory." More important, Spicer advocates an approach to the cards that ties divination to collage: his promised description of the deck would stress "strongly the fact that the individual card has no meaning solely in itself but only in relation to the cards around it and its position in the layout—exact analogy to words in a poem."[72] Like the poetics of dictation, tarot reading gives meaning to

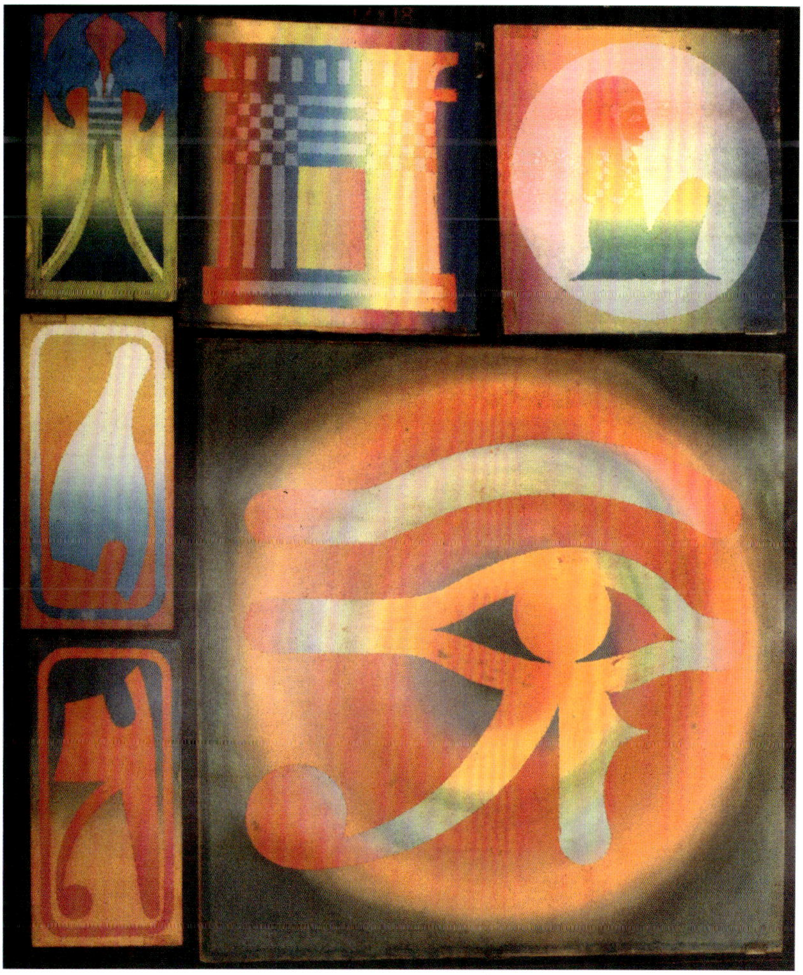

Fig. 7.
Harry Smith
Tarot card, ca. 1980s
Whereabouts unknown

a series of objects by virtue of their arrangement at a particular moment. For Spicer, words in a poem and poems in a book acquire meaning by a serial rather than a narrative or thematic arrangement. As with Smith, pattern is paramount.

The poetics of dictation leads Spicer to write a collage poetry quite different from Duncan's grand collage. If the grand collage describes a "poetry of all poetries," Spicer's poetry resembles a collection of real objects such as those Smith assembles. In his first serial book, *After Lorca* (1957), Spicer presents a set of poems purportedly by Federico García Lorca as "real objects." These objects consist of the following: translations and transformations of poems by Lorca, poems by Spicer posing as translations by Lorca, letters to Lorca, and an introduction written by the already dead poet.[73] The apocryphal quality of this book might intrigue Smith, as would the instructions for turning collections of objects into works of art in one of the letters to Lorca:

Dear Lorca,

I would like to make poems out of real objects. The lemon to be a lemon

> that the reader could cut or squeeze or taste—a real lemon like a newspaper in a collage is a real newspaper. I would like the moon in my poems to be a real moon, one which could be suddenly covered with a cloud that has nothing to do with the poem—a moon utterly independent of images. The imagination pictures the real. I would like to point to the real, disclose it, to make a poem that has no sound in it but the pointing of a finger....
>
> Things do not connect; they correspond. That is what makes it possible for a poet to translate real objects, to bring them across language as easily as he can bring them across time.... —every place and every time has a real object to *correspond* with your real object—that lemon may become this lemon, or it may even become this piece of seaweed, or this particular color of gray in this ocean. One does not need to imagine that lemon; one needs to discover it.[74]

The concepts in this "letter" resonate remarkably well with many of Smith's principles. At base, both Spicer and Smith employ an alchemical logic, believing they can affect the world by manipulating correspondences. They counsel artists to avoid what Spicer calls "the big lie of the personal"[75] and to engage objects found in the actual world, thereby making patterns and correspondences visible. In a Smith-like tone of oracular contrariety, Spicer claims in the letter to create a work of art that corresponds to the gesture of disclosing the meaningful nature of what occurs moment by moment. Imbibing alcohol in quantities similar to the quantities of drugs and alcohol ingested by Smith, Spicer likewise invites a derangement that will make his collagist's art attentive to what comes from outside human control. Neither places any stock in the imagination. The goal is to reveal correspondences among objects while performing a Zen disappearing act, in which the finger that points out the patterns that make up the real can vanish—leaving only the quivering lemon.

In the post–World War II period of heroic personal expression in the arts—dominated by gesture and confession and the aching desire to concoct a personality—these two difficult, learned, hermetic figures move in a direction counter to many of their peers. Rather than project an identity, they seek to so hone their creative capacities as to disappear wholly into their work and leave other people in a position of seeing more. This ego-dissolving stance is one pole of the continuum of visionary to personal that characterizes the West Coast collage aesthetic, with its unique intertwining of the avant-garde and the occult. The multifarious oeuvre of Harry Smith provides a signal reference point for the large range of stances within this aesthetic: Smith's similarities to and differences from Ginsberg, Duncan, and Spicer illuminate not only some of the ways in which the personal and the visionary have interacted in West Coast collage art but also how collage moves beyond the status of a formal principle and becomes a means of conducting life. Inheriting collage from modernism, West Coast artists of the 1950s and 1960s inflected it in ways both personal and visionary that led to new forms of lifestyle experimentation. Like John Cage—whose upbringing and first work were on the West Coast—Smith brought the anarchic and mystical qualities of West Coast culture into his highly original and influential collage projects. The standard critical bias toward the East Coast as cultural fountainhead has obscured the impact of these West Coast aesthetic innovations on the arts as well as on the explosive social movements of the 1960s and 1970s whose residual effects remain with us today. The restless, anarchic, polymathic creativity of Harry Smith in turning collage into a principle of life represents much that is innovative in the arts in California at midcentury and, beyond that, much that characterizes the social revolution spawned by this aesthetics.[76]

Notes

1. See Michael Duncan and Kristine McKenna, *Semina Culture: Wallace Berman and His Circle,* exh. cat. (New York: D.A.P./Distributed Art Publishers, 2005), for an extensive investigation of the collage aesthetic of the California artists and poets surrounding Wallace Berman, of whom Robert Duncan was one. My chapter in that text—Stephen Fredman, "Surrealism Meets Kabbalah: Wallace Berman and the Semina Poets," 40–48—extends a number of the arguments of the present essay.
2. The only published poems by Smith I have seen were the two printed posthumously as Harry Smith, "'(Think of the Self Speaking),'" *Film Culture,* no. 76 (1992): 8–11. The poems are apparently dated "10-4-76" and "10-7-77"; on the contents page for the issue, the editors of *Film Culture* note that the poems have "been set from Smith's original manuscript given us some years ago. We have taken the liberty of correcting a few obvious misspellings, but we have left most of the manuscript intact." Philip Smith has shown me a manuscript of poems Harry Smith wrote about tarot cards, "Evensongs of Exstasy" (1977). Both Harvey Bialy and Allen Ginsberg remember Smith writing poetry, and Rani Singh says that Smith published poems in "obscure East Village magazines"; see Harvey Bialy, "Harvey Bialy, 9 October 1995," interview by Paola Igliori, in Paola Igliori, ed., *American Magus Harry Smith: A Modern Alchemist* (New York: Inanout, 1996), 207; Allen Ginsberg, "Introduction," interview by Hal Willner, in Harry Smith, *Think of the Self Speaking: Harry Smith—Selected Interviews,* ed. Rani Singh (Seattle: Elbow/Cityful, 1999), 4; and Rani Singh, email message to Michelle Bonnice, 17 September 2008.
3. Bialy, "Harvey Bialy" (note 2), 197.
4. Henry Jones, "Henry Jones, 26 October 1995," interview by Paola Igliori, in Paola Igliori, ed., *American Magus Harry Smith: A Modern Alchemist* (New York: Inanout, 1996), 209.
5. Harry Smith, "John Cohen—Chelsea Hotel, NYC [*Sing Out!* Volume 19, No. 1, 1969]," interview by John Cohen, in idem, *Think of the Self Speaking: Harry Smith—Selected Interviews,* ed. Rani Singh (Seattle: Elbow/Cityful, 1999), 81.
6. Gertrude Stein, *Composition as Explanation* (London: Hogarth, 1926), 13.
7. Jones, "Henry Jones" (note 4), 210.
8. Lionel Ziprin remembers that Smith moved to New York City in part to meet Marcel Duchamp; see Lionel Ziprin, "Lionel Ziprin—May and June 1993," interview by Paola Igliori, compiled with previous interview by Clayton Patterson with K. K., in Paola Igliori, ed., *American Magus Harry Smith: A Modern Alchemist* (New York: Inanout, 1996), 39. Smith's film *Mahagonny* has in its opening credits this statement: "A Mathematical analysis of Duchamp's 'La Mariée mise à nu par ses célibataires, même' expressed in terms of Kurt Weill's score for 'Aufstieg Und Fall der Stadt Mahagonny' with contrapuntal images (not necessarily in order) derived from

Brecht's libretto for the latter work"; and Smith says in Harry Smith, "P. Adams Sitney—NYC [Mahagonny, 1977]," in idem, *Think of the Self Speaking: Harry Smith—Selected Interviews,* ed. Rani Singh (Seattle: Elbow/Cityful, 1999), 104: "In *Mahagonny,* four different images are being projected at once, more or less as a commentary on Duchamp's *Large Glass.*" Smith's *Film #12: Heaven and Earth Magic* was included in a show inspired by Duchamp's *The Large Glass;* see Marc Le Bot et al., *Le macchine celibi/The Bachelor Machines,* ed. Jean Clair and Harald Szeemann, exh. cat. (New York: Rizzoli, 1975), 5, 214.

9. Harry Smith, "The Kiowa Peyote Meeting," in Paola Igliori, ed., *American Magus Harry Smith: A Modern Alchemist* (New York: Inanout, 1996), 164.
10. See Harry Smith, ed., *Anthology of American Folk Music,* FP 251–FP 253 (New York: Folkways Records, 1952). Robert Cantwell discusses the *Anthology* as a "memory theater" built on the model of Fludd's mnemonic library for encouraging thought, knowledge, and rhetoric; see Robert Cantwell, *When We Were Good: The Folk Revival* (Cambridge: Harvard Univ. Press, 1996), 204–6.

    The explanation offered by Fludd above the image itself (see fig. 1) may be translated as follows: "We have coordinated this monochord of the world with its [spatial] proportions, [musical] harmonies, and [scalar] intervals, the mover of which we represent here as now being out of this world" (trans. Michele Ciaccio).
11. Smith, "John Cohen" (note 5), 83.
12. See Ed Sanders, descriptive text published in Harry Smith, ed., *Harry Smith's Anthology of American Folk Music, Volume Four,* RVN 211 (Austin: Revenant/Harry Smith Archives, 2000), 30.
13. Bialy, "Harvey Bialy" (note 2), 196.
14. Bialy, "Harvey Bialy" (note 2), 197.
15. Ginsberg, "Introduction" (note 2), 3 (brackets in original). "Misterioso" (1948) is a song by the jazz musician Thelonious Monk.
16. Ginsberg, "Introduction" (note 2), 4 (brackets in original).
17. Ginsberg, "Introduction" (note 2), 8–11.
18. See Ginsberg's 1958 review of Kerouac's *The Dharma Bums* for a defense of this method and a citation of Kerouac's "Essentials of Spontaneous Prose," in Allen Ginsberg, *Deliberate Prose: Selected Essays, 1952–1995* (New York: HarperCollins, 2000), 342–48. For more on Ginsberg's collage method, see Allen Ginsberg, "'First Thought, Best Thought,'" in idem, *Composed on the Tongue,* ed. Donald Allen (Bolinas, Calif.: Grey Fox, 1980), 106–17.
19. Allen Ginsberg, "Journal Night Thoughts," in idem, *Collected Poems 1947–1980* (New York: Harper & Row, 1984), 267–71.
20. Marcus Boon, *The Road of Excess: A History of Writers on Drugs* (Cambridge: Harvard Univ. Press, 2002).
21. Ginsberg, "Journal Night Thoughts" (note 19), 267.
22. Ginsberg, "Journal Night Thoughts" (note 19), 269.
23. Ginsberg, "Introduction" (note 2), 4.
24. Ginsberg, "Journal Night Thoughts" (note 19), 269.
25. Ginsberg, "Journal Night Thoughts" (note 19), 270.
26. Ginsberg, "Journal Night Thoughts" (note 19), 271.

27. Luis Kemnitzer, like Smith an inveterate record collector, told me in April 2001 at the Getty Research Institute's symposium on Harry Smith that he remembers being in the same room with Duncan and Smith in spring or summer 1948. (For more of Kemnitzer's reminiscences, see Luis Kemnitzer, "West Coast Record Collector," in *A Booklet of Essays, Appreciations, and Annotations Pertaining to the "Anthology of American Folk Music" Edited by Harry Smith,* SFW 40090 [Washington, D.C.: Smithsonian Folkways Recordings, 1997], 29–31.) In a recent biographical sketch of Smith, Ed Sanders also mentions a letter a friend of Smith's wrote to Duncan urging him to meet Smith; see Sanders, descriptive text (note 12), 9.
28. See the drawing by Harry Smith reproduced in Paola Igliori, ed., *American Magus Harry Smith: A Modern Alchemist* (New York: Inanout, 1996), 2.
29. Harry Smith's family background in theosophy is documented in Darrin Daniel, *Harry Smith: Fragments of a Northwest Life* (Seattle: Elbow, 2000), 11–13. Duncan's can be found in Ekbert Faas, *Young Robert Duncan: Portrait of the Poet as Homosexual in Society* (Santa Barbara, Calif.: Black Sparrow, 1983), 17–29; with further discussion in Peter O'Leary, *Gnostic Contagion: Robert Duncan and the Poetry of Illness* (Middletown, Conn.: Wesleyan Univ. Press, 2002), 74–77.
30. Robert Duncan, "From the *H. D. Book,* Part I: Beginnings, Chapter 5: Occult Matters," *Stony Brook,* no. 1/2 (1968): 5.
31. Duncan, "From the *H. D. Book*" (note 30), 9, 10.
32. Duncan, "From the *H. D. Book*" (note 30), 7.
33. Duncan, "From the *H. D. Book*" (note 30), 9.
34. Duncan, "From the *H. D. Book*" (note 30), 10.
35. Robert Duncan, "Introduction," in idem, *Bending the Bow* (New York: New Directions, 1968), vii.
36. See, for example, Robert Duncan, *Bending the Bow* (New York: New Directions, 1968), Structure of Rime XXII–XXVI: 4, 23, 36–37, 68; *Passages* 1–30: 9–22, 24–35, 40–50, 58–83, 112–32.
37. Robert Duncan, "Man's Fulfillment in Order and Strife," in idem, *Fictive Certainties: Essays* (New York: New Directions, 1985), 115.
38. Robert Duncan, "Rites of Participation," in idem, *A Selected Prose,* ed. Robert J. Bertholf (New York: New Directions, 1995), 98.
39. Duncan, "Man's Fulfillment" (note 37), 121–22.
40. Smith, "John Cohen" (note 5), 81.
41. Smith, "John Cohen" (note 5), 85.
42. Duncan, "Man's Fulfillment" (note 37), 112.
43. Robert Duncan, "The Architecture, *Passages* 9," in idem, *Bending the Bow* (New York: New Directions, 1968), 26; and Gustav Stickley, *Craftsman Homes* (New York: Craftsman Publishing, 1909), 136.
44. Smith, "John Cohen" (note 5), 66–67.
45. Michael Auping, "Jess: A Grand Collage," in Michael Auping, ed., *Jess: A Grand Collage, 1951–1993,* exh. cat. (Buffalo: Buffalo Fine Arts Academy, 1993), 39. For additional discussion of the artistic collaboration between Duncan and Jess, see Ingrid Schaffner, *Jess: To and From the Printed Page,* exh. cat. (New York: Independent Curators International, 2007).

46. Auping, "Jess" (note 45), 47–52. Jess's "Assemblies" date to the 1950s and 1960s, while his "Paste-Ups" first appear in 1951 and continue through at least 1993.
47. Michael Auping, "Introduction," in idem, ed., *Jess: A Grand Collage, 1951–1993*, exh. cat. (Buffalo: Buffalo Fine Arts Academy, 1993), 14–15.
48. Duncan, "The Architecture" (note 43), 26; and P. Adams Sitney, *Visionary Film: The American Avant-Garde* (New York: Oxford Univ. Press, 1974), 300.
49. Duncan, "The Architecture" (note 43), 26–27.
50. Duncan, "The Architecture" (note 43), 27.
51. Duncan, "The Architecture" (note 43), 27. The (slightly modified) quotation is from Stickley, *Craftsman Homes* (note 43), 196.
52. Faas titles the chapter of his biography of Duncan that treats this period "The Shaman Poet"; see Faas, *Young Robert Duncan* (note 29), 81–92. O'Leary uses the figure of the shaman as a central interpretive device, drawing on the scholarship of Mircea Eliade, as part of his exploration of Duncan's poem "My Mother Would Be a Falconress"; see O'Leary, *Gnostic Contagion* (note 29), 130–32, 144–51, 160–67.
53. Duncan, "The Architecture" (note 43), 27. In the original text, a young woman and her uncle "came to a lonely spot" and "saw a man who was naked." This man says to them, "'I instructed you in the past about the sacred pack. "You are to make it," I told you in the past. I do not suppose you recognize me. "Owl" is what I am called,' they were told. 'This is how I am,' they were told. To be sure, they saw an owl." See Truman Michelson, *The Owl Sacred Pack of the Fox Indians*, Smithsonian Institution, Bureau of American Ethnology, Bulletin 72 (Washington, D.C.: Government Printing Office, 1921), 39, 41.
54. Duncan told me about the epithet and the totem in conversations over the years.
55. Robert Duncan, "An Owl Is an Only Bird of Poetry," in Donald M. Allen, ed., *The New American Poetry* (New York: Grove, 1960), 41–44.
56. Duncan, "The Architecture" (note 43), 28. See also Michelson, *The Owl Sacred Pack* (note 53), 65; and Stickley, *Craftsman Homes* (note 43), 196.
57. These points about the oneiric quality of Smith's films were offered to me in email correspondence by Rani Singh, director of the Harry Smith Archives, 2001. See also Harry Smith, "A. J. Melita—Chelsea Hotel, NYC [1976]," interview by A.J. Melita, in idem, *Think of the Self Speaking: Harry Smith—Selected Interviews*, ed. Rani Singh (Seattle: Elbow/Cityful, 1999), 139; and Harry Smith, "P. Adams Sitney—NYC [*Mahagonny*, 1977]," in idem, *Think of the Self Speaking: Harry Smith—Selected Interviews*, ed. Rani Singh (Seattle: Elbow/Cityful, 1999), 106.
58. Robert J. Bertholf, "The Concert: Robert Duncan Writing Out of Painting," in Michael Auping, ed., *Jess: A Grand Collage, 1951–1993*, exh. cat. (Buffalo: Buffalo Fine Arts Academy, 1993), 80.
59. The shaman who carries the sacred pack destroys a Sioux war party, leaving only one survivor, whom he sends home having told him, "'You will often tell the story. If you do that you will be able to marry those you love. You will continue to marry. But you shall fear me. If I even see you, you will then die'"; see Michelson, *Owl Sacred Pack* (note 53), 65.
60. See Robin Blaser's classic essay on Spicer, "The Practice of Outside," in Jack Spicer, *The Collected Books of Jack Spicer*, ed. Robin Blaser (Los Angeles: Black Sparrow,

1975), 271–332. For Spicer's biography, see Lewis Ellingham and Kevin Killian, *Poet Be Like God: Jack Spicer and the San Francisco Renaissance* (Hanover, N.H.: University Press of New England, 1998).

61. For the contacts between Spicer and Smith, see Sanders, descriptive text (note 12), 9; and Kevin Killian, "Jack Spicer's Secret" (paper presented at "The Opening of the Field: A Conference on North American Poetry in the 1960s," University of Maine, 30 June 2000), 4.
62. Jim Herndon to Robin Blaser, n.d.; reprinted in Jack Spicer, *The Collected Books of Jack Spicer,* ed. Robin Blaser (Los Angeles: Black Sparrow, 1975), 375.
63. Killian, "Jack Spicer's Secret" (note 61), 1.
64. These statements derive from lectures Spicer gave in 1965, best referenced in Jack Spicer, *The House That Jack Built: The Collected Lectures of Jack Spicer,* ed. Peter Gizzi (Hanover, N.H.: University Press of New England, 1998). See also the back cover of the reissue of Duncan's *Roots and Branches* (1964; reprint, New York: New Directions, 1969), for example, where he is quoted as saying, "I am not an experimentalist or an inventor, but a derivative poet, drawing my art from the resources given by a generation of masters."
65. Jack Spicer, "Vancouver Lecture 1: Dictation and 'A Textbook of Poetry,'" in idem, *The House That Jack Built: The Collected Lectures of Jack Spicer,* ed. Peter Gizzi (Hanover, N.H.: University Press of New England, 1998), 4–5.
66. Peter Gizzi, "Afterword: Jack Spicer and the Practice of Reading," in Jack Spicer, *The House That Jack Built: The Collected Lectures of Jack Spicer,* ed. Peter Gizzi (Hanover, N.H.: University Press of New England, 1998), 188.
67. Peter Gizzi, "Vancouver Lecture 1: Introduction," in Jack Spicer, *The House That Jack Built: The Collected Lectures of Jack Spicer,* ed. Peter Gizzi (Hanover, N.H.: University Press of New England, 1998), 2–3.
68. Allen Ginsberg, as quoted in Ellingham and Killian, *Poet Be Like God* (note 60), 58.
69. Allen Ginsberg, as quoted in Ellingham and Killian, *Poet Be Like God* (note 60), 58.
70. Spicer, "Vancouver Lecture 1" (note 65), 9.
71. Bill Breeze, "In Memoriam, Harry Smith," in Paola Igliori, ed., *American Magus Harry Smith: A Modern Alchemist* (New York: Inanout, 1996), 9.
72. Jack Spicer, "[A Plan for a Book on Tarot]," ed. Robin Blaser and John Granger, *boundary* 2 6, no. 1 (1977): 27.
73. Clayton Eshleman, "The Lorca Working," *boundary* 2 6, no. 1 (1977): 31–49, identifies the instances where Spicer's translations from Lorca become partially or wholly compositions of his own. In addition, Eshleman sees Spicer's serial poems as forms of collage: "a collage is a kind of serial poem" (47).
74. Jack Spicer, *After Lorca,* in idem, *The Collected Books of Jack Spicer,* ed. Robin Blaser (Los Angeles: Black Sparrow, 1975), 33–34.
75. Spicer, *After Lorca* (note 74), 48.
76. See Richard Cándida Smith, *Utopia and Dissent: Art, Poetry, and Politics in California* (Berkeley: Univ. of California Press, 1995), for a convincing treatment of the thesis that the innovations of the assemblage and collage artists and poets of postwar California were instrumental in creating the basis for the broader countercultural movement of the 1960s and 1970s.

SELECTED DOCUMENTS

Apex Cannery,
Anacortes, Washington,
February 10, 1942

Dear Bill:

"Clean Up Day" will be held next Saturday, the fourteenth, at the Smoke-house on the Swinamish Reservation. I have writen to Rod Hardies urging him to get a group together and come up, and I wish that if he comes up at all that you would come along and help me with my recording equipment.

Please write and let me know whither or not you will be able to come.

Sincerly,

Harry E. Smith

Harry Smith to Bill Holm, 10 February 1942

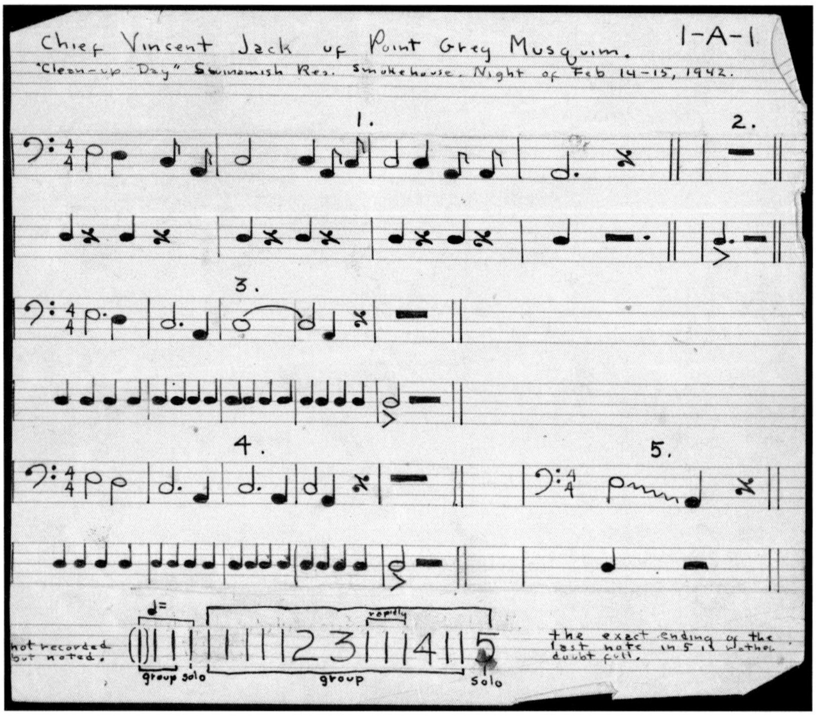

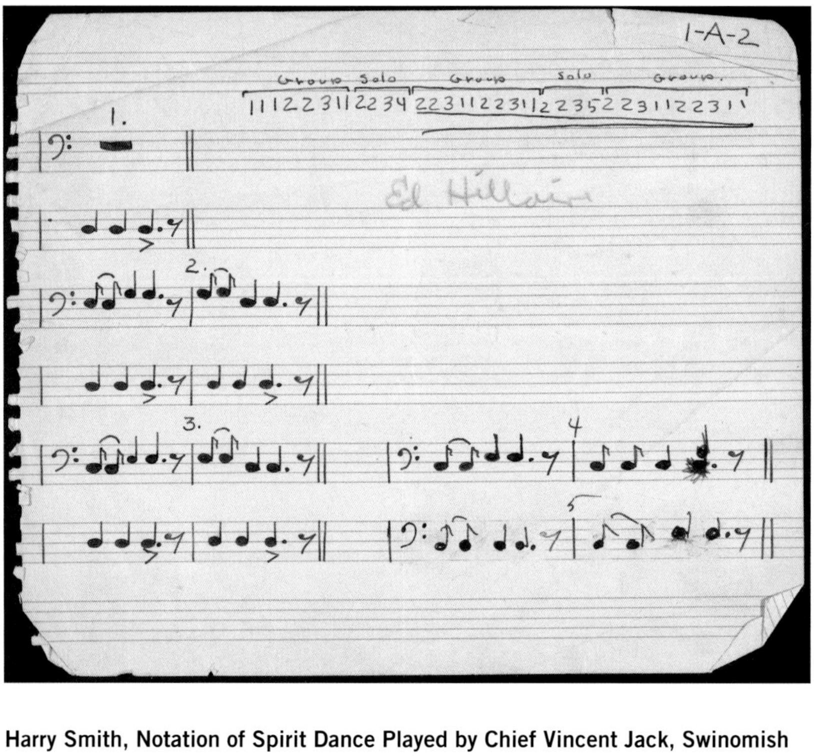

Harry Smith, Notation of Spirit Dance Played by Chief Vincent Jack, Swinomish Smokehouse, Swinomish Indian Reservation, Washington, 14–15 February 1942

THE SAN FRANCISCO MUSEUM OF ART

ART IN CINEMA - Series III
October 24, 1947

ALLEGRETTO........................Oskar Fischinger
COMPOSITION IN BLUE...............Oskar Fischinger

FLAT HATTING......................John Hubley and Phil Eastman
PLASTICS..........................Jim Davis
*NUMBER FIVE (FAST TRACK).........Harry Smith
*HORROR DREAM.....................Sidney Peterson, Hy Hirsh
(Intermission 10 minutes)
THE DREAM OF A RAREBIT FIEND......Edwin S. Porter
THE NAVIGATOR.....................Buster Keaton, Donald Crisp

*premiere showing

PROGRAM NOTES

ALLEGRETTO and COMPOSITION IN BLUE (German, 1931) Mr. Fischinger's latest film is still delayed in the processing studios, and meanwhile he has sent us some of his earlier works. Although many of you have already seen them on previous programs, they do not easily lose their delightfully gay and dynamic verve. Mr. Fischinger has been a pioneer in this field, and these two films are among his earliest. (Running time 10 minutes. Loaned by Mr. Fischinger)

FLAT HATTING (American, 1946) By John Hubley and Phil Eastman; produced by United Productions of America. A naval training short that uses animation in a wholly different and unique manner. Besides the amazing excellence of the design, the message --which is a point of pure psychology--is conveyed in such simple terms that it becomes immediately clear to the most negative spectator. (Time 6 min. Loaned through the courtesy of Mr. Hubley)

PLASTICS (American, 1946-7) Designed and photographed by Jim Davis. This is simply an uncontrolled series of designs resulting from photographing Mr. Davis unusually interesting work with various kinds of plastic materials. Mr. Davis tells us that this film has opened up to him the possibilities of utilizing the material for more controlled abstract films, rather than using the medium only as a way of displaying his plastic work. At present he is making further cinematic experiments which, he says,"begin where this leaves off". (Time 8 min. Courtesy of Mr. Davis)

FILM NUMBER FIVE (FAST TRACK) (American, 1947) by Harry Smith. (The color films originally scheduled for this program have not yet been returned from the processing plant where 16mm reductions are being made from the 35mm originals. These films will be shown on a later program.) Although the images of NUMBER FIVE are closely synchronized with sound, they are to be viewed as a purely visual sequence with themes and rhythms for the eye, completely independent of the musical score which augments what is on the screen, without determining its direction or commenting upon it. (Time 10 min. Loaned by Harry Smith)

HORROR DREAM (American, 1947) by Sidney Peterson and Hy Hirsh. Choreography designed and performed by Marian Van Tuyl and her dance group; musical score composed especially for the dance by John Cage. Test situations such as examinations, performances, etc. commonly produce certain types of dreams. In HORROR DREAM the process has been inverted and the dream has produced a dance representing the hazards of a performance. Intimate use of the camera, deliberately resorted to in order to escape the obvious limitations of a performance in a theatre has resulted in a film that is not a faithful record of a stage performance. The translation into a new medium develops new patterns and meanings, where film, movement, and sound synthesize into a revolutionary kind of choreography. The musical score, composed for the dance by John Cage, was produced in a specially equipped sound studio from the noises made by buzzers, irons, cymbals dippd in hot water and a piano "prepared" with iron bars and cotton batting. The bizarre score resulting, implements Mr. Cage's theory that anything that makes a noise can be used to make music. (Time 10 minutes. Loaned through the courtesy of Mr. Peterson)

THE DREAM OF A RAREBIT FIEND and THE NAVIGATOR: Please refer to the accompanying notes of Miss Iris Barry of the Museum of Modern Art. (Note: We are not showing HIGH AND DIZZY)

The music for PLASTICS, DREAM OF A RAREBIT FIEND,
and THE NAVIGATOR has been selected by Paul Velguth.

PLEASE DO NOT SMOKE IN THE AUDITORIUM.

Art in Cinema, Series 3, Program Notes, 24 October 1947

Courtesy Pacific Film Archive Library and Film Study Center, University of California, Berkeley Art Museum and Pacific Film Archive. Reprinted by permission of Barbara Stauffacher Solomon

THE ART IN CINEMA SOCIETY OF THE SAN FRANCISCO MUSEUM OF ART PRESENTS

art in cinema series four

The Art in Cinema Society of the San Francisco Museum of Art Presents

ART IN CINEMA - SERIES FOUR

September 24th, 1948

(NOTE: Tonight's program will be without several films originally scheduled and announced, one of them being the RACCONTO DA UN AFFRESCO of Luciano Emmer and Enrico Gras. This film, as well as one other by Emmer and Gras on Hieronymus Bosch, has been mysteriously withheld by the Italian consulate in Canada without explanation. It is a circumstance beyond our control. When these films are again available, they will be shown at a special Art in Cinema program, free to you as subscribers to this present series. An announcement will be forthcoming."

MOTION PAINTING ONE..............Oskar Fischinger
THE UNCOMFORTABLE MAN............Kent Munson & Theodore Huff
PRIMITIVE VISUAL RHYTHM..........Harry Smith
CLINIC OF STUMBLE................Peterson, Marian van Tuyl
H2O..............................Ralph Steiner

(Intermission)

SYMPHONIE DIAGONALE..............Viking Eggeling
FILMSTUDIE.......................Hans Richter
VORMITTAKSPUK....................Hans Richter
EVERYTHING TURNS!................Hans Richter
THE PAWN SHOP....................Charles Chaplin

MOTION PAINTING ONE by Oskar Fischinger, 1946-49. Complying with numerous requests after last week's program, this latest film of Mr. Fischinger's will again be shown.

THE UNCOMFORTABLE MAN. An experimental film by Kent Munson and Theodore Huff, New York, 1947-48. This is the study of a young man in a city. Searching for his identity, he stands in the path of Light and becomes one with shadow players. But alas, on entering a film, you must be sure that you identify yourself with the right character! Endlessly frustrated, he retires from the world in his underground room. Consumed by the underlying anarchism of the age, his personality splits and he ignores Life until he develops consolatory complexes to compensate for the gaps and pressures of the misfit. (Program note by Theodore Huff)

PRIMITIVE VISUAL RHYTHM by Harry Smith, Berkeley, 1947-48. Mr. Smith provides the following note: "The squares, circles and triangles of the non-objective painting have no compositional or directly emotional significance in the sense that objects in a realistic picture do. They merely indicate the general nature of the space surrounding the form, leaving it to the observer to supply a specific and personalized meaning. For this reason, the non-objective painting, by its lack of directional intertensioning, is perpetually new.

Unfortunately, motion, by giving specific action, completely destroys the possibility of the spectator constructing his own experience from the material presented, and substitutes abstract reality of the generalized emotion that is the basis of non-objective art. It is possible, however, by limiting movement to the most simple kinds, and presenting only one form at a time, to construct a truly non-objective motion sequence.

The forms used in this film have been limited to two classifications: a circle (or circles) moving across the field of vision, and a stationary circle segmenting itself on its own axis. These two simple actions are arranged in a slowly accelerating rhythmic series, with angular movements and highly saturated colors in the body of the film, replacing and being replaced by oblique movement and a grayed spectrum at the beginning and end of the work." (Harry Smith)

H2O by Ralph Steiner, New York, 1929. A visual study of water composed in terms of cinematic form and rhythm. (Museum of Modern Art Film Library)

Art in Cinema, Series 4, Program Notes, 24 September 1948

Courtesy Pacific Film Archive Library and Film Study Center, University of California, Berkeley Art Museum and Pacific Film Archive. Reprinted by permission of Barbara Stauffacher Solomon

THE SAN FRANCISCO MUSEUM OF ART PRESENTS

ART IN CINEMA

SIXTH SERIES

A survey of the most important new directions in experimental film-making, together with some epic avant-garde films of the past.

FRIDAY, MAY 5

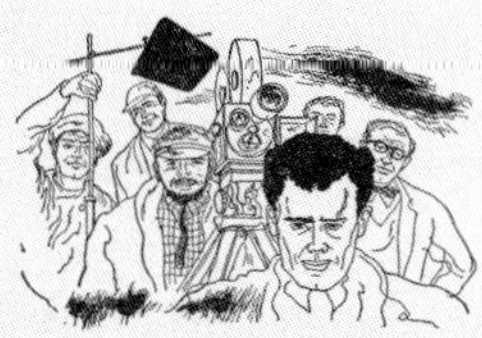

1. OCTOBER *(TEN DAYS THAT SHOOK THE WORLD)* By SERGEI EISENSTEIN. Here are developed the great Russian director's theories of film form in a most concentrated and volcanic masterpiece. **2. COLOR AND LIGHT; REFLECTIONS No. 8; JERSEY FALL, SEQUENCE No. 1, By James Davis.** This famous artist in plastics who produced the film, **Light Reflections** (winner of an award at the Belgium International Film Festival) will present his three new short films in person, and deliver a unique demonstration of their method of production. **3. SODA JERK,** an early one-reeler with **Buster Keaton.**

FRIDAY, MAY 12

1. FIVE INSTRUMENTS WITH OPTICAL SOLO. The film **by Harry Smith,** will serve as the sixth instrument in a be-bop jam session to consist of an expert group in person, on the piano, cornet, valve-trombone, bass and drums. This is the first presentation anywhere, of a performance in which the optical images will be tried, not as visualization of the music, but as a basis for its departure. **2. DESTINY *(DER MUDE TOD)* By Fritz Lang.** The legend of Death and the Maiden in one of the most ambitious of early German epics. **3. BE GONE DULL CARE By Norman McLaren.** The recent work of this eminent Canadian film artist. **4. EYES HAVE IT,** an early one-reeler with **Ben Turpin.**

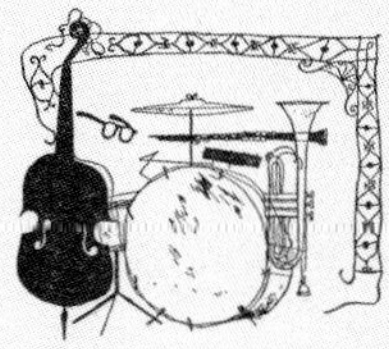

FRIDAY, MAY 19

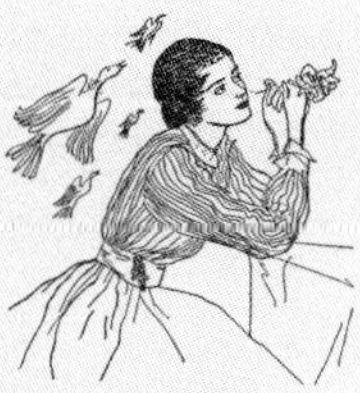

1. WEST WIND *(VINDEN FRAN VASTER)* By Arne Sucksdorff. The beautifully realized poetry of this young Swedish director's camera finds a sympathetic theme in a legend of Lapland. (At the time of this printing we are negotiating for an additional film by Sucksdorff). **2. RAGAMUFFIN.** Produced by Films Polski; written and directed by **W. Hos.** A remarkable Polish essay of a child's poignant dream and reality. **3. THE PRIVATE LIFE OF A CAT. Alexander Hammid's** famous documentary, the subject matter of which has restricted its general showing. **4. TOCCATA MANHATTA** and **ROUND TRIP IN MODERN ART By Robert Bruce Rogers.** Two short experiments in optical music. **5. DRIFTERS, By John Grierson.** The film that created the foundation for British documentary. **6. LOOPS By Norman McLaren.** A portion of his experimental reel submitted last year to the Edinburgh Film Festival. **7. DO NOT DISTURB, By L. Moholy-Nagy.** A film based on the theme of jealousy. **8. VAMPYRE,** a remarkable study of this creature by France's renowned **Jean Painleve.**

FRIDAY, MAY 26

1. THE QUIET ONE. Written by **James Agee** and directed by **Sidney Meyers.** First showing locally of this important and much-discussed new achievement in American film history. **2. FANTASY FOR GIRL AND ORCHESTRA By Dick Ham,** with Shirley Winters and the orchestra of Phil Moore. Experiment in fitting images to preconceived sound track. **3. DIMINISHED IRIS,** an experimental dance film **by Josephine Booth. 4. UNTITLED FILM by Charles Maddux. 5. COLOR FRAGMENTS By Elwood Decker.** Part of a work-in-progress. **6. A SHORT PROGRAM OF REJECTED TELEVISION SPOTS.** These rejected commercial spots **(by John Whitney, Denver Sutton, Frank Stauffacher, Dorsey Alexander, Charles Maddux, Keith Monroe, and others)** display a wonderful dynamic visual vitality that is, unfortunately (and apparently) years ahead of its time. **7. JAIL BAIT,** an early one-reeler with **Buster Keaton.**

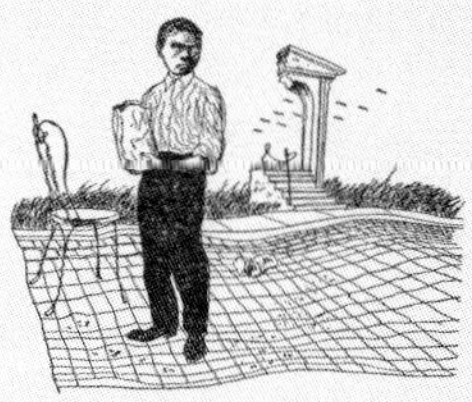

NOTE: The films have been drawn from a wide variety of sources, from the Museum of Modern Art Film Library, from various other distributors, and from the individual artists themselves. We ask your indulgence when programs must be altered due to circumstances beyond our control—shipping failures, poor quality of prints, etc. The series is organized on the same basis as previous series: Non-profit, non-commercial, with admission by series subscription only. Due to previous seating difficulties, seats at this sixth series will be reserved.

Art in Cinema is collaborating with the University Extension, University of California, in presenting an additional series of films at Wheeler Auditorium, May 2, May 23, June 8 and June 20, to consist of some of most outstanding films already shown at the San Francisco Showings in past series. For details, see the University Extension bulletin.

(TEAR HERE)

ORDER BLANK
Sixth Series

TO: ART IN CINEMA SOCIETY
San Francisco Museum of Art
Civic Center, San Francisco

☐ Museum Member
☐ Public
(CHECK ONE)

Please send me________series tickets at $3.60 each (series) including tax ($2.40 for Museum Members) for the series of 4 nights of ART IN CINEMA film series, May 5 through May 26, at 8:00 P.M. Friday evenings.

NAME:____________________ ADDRESS:____________________

TOTAL AMOUNT ENCLOSED____________________

(Make check or money order payable to the San Franciso Museum of Art, and enclose stamped, self-addressed envelope for return of tickets.)

Art in Cinema, Series 6, Program Announcement, Spring 1950

Courtesy Pacific Film Archive Library and Film Study Center, University of California, Berkeley Art Museum and Pacific Film Archive. Reprinted by permission of Barbara Stauffacher Solomon

Harry Smith to Hilla Rebay, 4 April 1950

COPY

1636 Buchanan Street
San Francisco, Cal.
April 4, 1950

Dear Miss Rebay,

I was certainly glad to get your letter yesterday, for when I did not hear from you I was afraid that my paintings had not reached you or that you had not liked them, but instead you were in Europe teaching and discovering. I hope that your trip was in every way successful.

I cannot state precisely how much the film I visualize would cost, as there has been no investigation in this field before. I must solve certain problems in order to approach the final goal. The slides that I sent you represent the solution of most questions to be answered as far [as] the actual drawing is concerned; I can now compose third dimensionally free-hand and almost as quickly as I can two dimensionally.

By great luck the funds have been provided to solve this one other, most important, problem. The museum here is giving me a small amount of money for rental of my films; (see ad enclosed) not much, but it together with the fifteen dollars from yourself will be enough to make a special film for them to show next month. It will have no forms in it, just carefully composed rhythmic and spectral sequence for the musicians to improvise on. This film will very easily answer the questions concerning the plane on which a color will appear when appearing for only a second or less between other different colors. It is most important that this question be settled at the first, because in composing colored moving forms in three dimensional space all factors affecting the precise plane of the form must be controlled in order to keep out unwanted forces in the three dimensional inbetween space.

If you feel that there is a possibility of money being available to continue these investigations, what I would like to do first of all is make a series of perhaps three hundred or so double thirty-five millimeter slides designed to be projected at a rate much slower than an ordinary motion picture but still rapidly enough to give the impression of motion. I have worked out a method of slightly rebuilding a standard model of slide projector in such a way that very beautiful results can be got with much less complicated equipment than would be required for films at regular speed, although, of course, that is the next step I will take.

The ideal plan for me to follow would be for me to be able to devote my time for the next few months to working with this simpler system and with it solve all technical problems [p. 2] connected with this new medium. As I mentioned when I saw you, I am going to come to New York at about the end of June. This would make it possible for me to learn from you exactly your feelings as to the many compositional problems to be decided in the third dimension for the final film.

The reason that I don't come to New York right away is that Dizzy Gillespie, the band leader who made the records I use with my paintings is going to be in town about the first of next month and I think he quite probably will be interested in using my film with his band at concerts, dances, etc. This would do much to make non-objectivity known to a very large number of people who not only are in need of its spiritual influence, but who are at the same time much less prejudiced in their thinking than are many of those who come in contact with the so-called "art" world.

The projection system that I want to use requires that spectators wear lightweight and inexpensive polaroid glasses (in frames similar to sun glasses) to assure that light vibrating on the right plane for each eye gets to that eye only. This system is the most perfect in that it gives exquisite clarity of form and color, and is not indistinct as are some earlier three-dimensional systems. The wearing of glasses, instead of being cumbersome, makes the spectator feel as if he is on an adventure, and causes him to look at the forms with greater penetration and perception.

To do what I have outlined above would require buying a special projector and having it partly rebuilt, getting film, colors, etc., etc., and sufficient money to make it possible for me to devote all my time for three months to actual work.

I believe that five hundred dollars would cover all expenses. For this you would get the slides I will make and you will also own a projector powerful enough for auditorium use and suitable for ordinary thirty-five millimeter slides as well as my special ones. Just because this projector costs less than a regular motion picture machine, do not think that it is in any way inferior or unsuitable for public showing, as it will be very, very beautiful as well as educational.

Jordan Belson recently gave me some books and reproductions you had sent to him. I am studying the two Kandinsky books very carefully. I also particularly enjoyed the catalogue of your exhibition and the comments in the hostess reports. The mimeographed sheet "New Age" by yourself is also very valuable. If I could get a few more copies of this I would appreciate it very much as I know lots of people I would like to give them to.

[p. 3] I hope you are rested from your trip and that you are in good health.

Best wishes,

signed Harry Smith

Hilla von Rebay Foundation Archive. M0007. Solomon R. Guggenheim Museum Archives, New York, N.Y.

Hilla Rebay to Harry Smith, 8 May 1950

May 8th, 1950

Mr. Harry Smith
1636 Buchanan Street
San Francisco, California

Dear Mr. Smith:

I hope you will be able now to make this film you wrote about, which should cost about $150.

I am sending you for the next 6 months $50. a month. The first $150. you use for the film making and the next $150. you use for another one. So you receive now every month $50. to go on with your work, and I am trying also, later on, to get you $150. for that little machine and the little paintings that you sent for it.

Please be a little patient as we are in the middle of a great deal of important work.

Sincerely yours,

Hilla Rebay

HR:g

Hilla von Rebay Foundation Archive. M0007. Solomon R. Guggenheim Museum Archives, New York, N.Y.

Harry Smith to Hilla Rebay, 17 June 1950

COPY

1636 Buchanan St.
San Francisco Calif.
June 17th 1950

Dear Miss Rebay –

I am now sending you the films I promised last month, so that, when you have time, you can look at them and tell me of changes and improvements possible in my next work. I have taken longer to get these to you than I expected because with the money you sent this month I remade parts of "Interwoven" to follow out your suggestion of having movement originate within the screen rather than moving across it. This one simple change (that seems so obvious and natural now that I learned of it) improves the film many hundred percent. Also I was delayed because I had wanted to make duplicate prints of these for you to keep, if you wanted them, but by the time I made the changes mentioned above, I was out of raw film to print on. Naturally your comments are much more valuable to me than having the films here, so I am sending you my master prints at this time with the hope I can get them back soon. I would not ask you to return even these, if it was not for the interesting developments. I outline below.

Since I showed my films at the museum here using live musicians improvising from the images rather than from a score, the musicians who gather nightly in the back room of a cafe near here, to play for their own amusement, after they have their regular jobs, have asked me to bring my projector to their "Jam Session" several times, because now everyone wants to try playing while looking at the film. I am sending you some photographs taken at the museum of the musicians, who played there, and who are the most advanced here. These people are now intuitively creating a new kind of music that will not be accepted by the public probably for 50 years. They are all really poor, sometimes hungry, because they would rather express what they call "soul" in their playing than hurt themselves by changing it to fit the backward standards of todays listners. As you probably know, all the popular musical developments of the last hundred years (spirituals, ragtime, jazz, Blues, "Boogie Woogie", Swing, Be Bop etc) were made by intuitive, but uneducated, genuses (sic) who died without getting any money or recognition because they were leaders and ahead of their time by fifty or seventy five years. All of the types of music I list above are worthless because of their vulgarity and striving for effect. But now, due to the same forces that gave birth to real art after five thousand years of objective attempts, a great change, unsuspected, to the world is about to occur in music. This is too complex to discuss here, but I hope to be nearer to you soon and will then describe the evidence I have. But to return to musicians – Stanley Willis, a piano player (wearing an Indian hat in the photographs) saw my music diagrams about a year and a half ago and told other musicians about them. Those in the photo group all got very interested in my work at that time and most of them had played with the films long before the museum showing. Hardly any of these people can read music and many have trouble even reading and writing English, but for these very reasons they are often in unknowing contact [p. 2] with the true sources of creativity. None of them had ever heard of modern painting but they all appreciated it at once. The trombone player (seated far right), for example, pointed out many remarkable things I myself had not noticed in your "Royally" the very first time I showed it to him. Last month I luckily borrowed a tape recorder and made records of about thirty different performances of musicians following the films. By comparing these tapes with each other and with the films it has been possible to make a start toward an investigation of intuitive creation. By investigating these observable forces which effect man, but which are scorned by pedantic science, it will be possible for us soon to realize the final stages of man's development. It is not impossible that your Institute of Light is the "Fire" spoken of in the Bible (and in Leonardo's prophesies) as heralding Armageddon and the beginning of the new world. I am using part of each day on these investigations and one of my most useful tools has been comparison of individual reactions to the films, which is why I ask you to return them as soon as it is convenient for you to do so. The ones I need are the color films on the large reel. I have several copies of the black and white one on the small reel, so you can keep it now if you want it for your files. I will make prints of any of the color ones you want a little later, but right now I can not do so, as I must live totally on the 65 dollars a month I get from you, as time is short and I can't waste it bothering with trying to get money. I eat only two meals a day now, but drink lots of water and eat nothing with white flower or sugar in it, so I save money and I hope improve my health at the same time.

Now about the films – the titles on them were added for the museum audience. Originally they were not titled and I still feel that giving specific titles is destructive because it tensions them to specific emotions, and for these particular films are as out of place as a chemest (sic) naming his experiments according to the colour they produce, rather than the purpose. But, for an audience as at the museum who represent as really stupid element who are prejidiced (sic) against accepting <u>anything</u> unless they are first told what it is, titles are of some value.

To me, the soul is expressed in the relations that exists between the rhythm of the physical world and the rhythm of the spiritual world. In wordly life the limits imposed by the material state keep us from comprehending the ultimate physical unit or the ultimate spiritual unit, however our intuitive preception of the ever changing relation between the two clarifies them both. My films so far have been examinations of these forces.

My <u>first film</u> made in 1946 and called on the Reel "A Strange Dream" shows what I feel are the links between mans body and the rest of the physical world.

The rhythm of man is the rhythm of his heart. The rhythm of his heart is the rhythm of the Day. The rhythm of the Day is the rhythm of the earth. The rhythm of the earth is the rhythm of the rock. The rhythm of the rock is the rhythm of the molecule. The rhythm of the molecule is the rhythm of the atom and so on to the ultimately physically describable unit. The integration of all these [p. 3] physical levels illustrated step by step is shown in this first film.

The <u>Second</u> <u>Film</u> (1946–1948) called on the reel "Message from the Sun" is an investigation of the rhythmic organization of mans (sic) mind. Just as the atom is a small model of the solar system, in that both consist of a central force with circling points around it, the mind of man is miniature of a greater mind. This is part of what the Bible means by saying that God made man in his own image.

This film is like the diary of the earths path around the sun during the two years I worked on it. I feel that certain forces effecting us originate in the sun. It is possible to partially explore these by comparison of creativity among musicians playing, unconciously, (sic) at different angles to the sun, and also at night when the forces must pass through the earth and be changed in quality for that reason. In making this film I suppressed sensory impulses from my body, as much as possible, and tried to record actual daily changes in the brain. The film divides itself into two general sections. This is partly due to my being able to induce a more perfect trance state as time went on, but is perhaps also because the suns changing position in the Galaxy changes the strength of energy coming from other sections of the universe.

In the film the stationary circle with three squares inside it represents the brain. Change in position of these squares are due to forces from outside the material world. The forces are represented by moving circles. Changes in color of the squares are due to messages from the material senses. The moving circles of four sizes and colors that precede the first statements of the brain symbol correspond to values of thought of four possible kinds. Identification of red, green, blue, and yellow with sections of a circle is the most important mental image known. The Tibetan Mandala is a nearly perfect diagram of this sort which is why it orders the mind so perfectly. It is less accurate than the film, however, because colors are not actual parts of the circle but are on a coincident plane whose exact relation shifts depending on the use – reasoning, memory, preception, intuition. This shows how the motion picture can illustrate facts known earlier but not visible except through movement.

Please remember that these films were not made for entertainment but for exploration and instruction. All the motions across the screen in the second one are unfortunate, but make the clearest two dimensional diagram of what is happening. In a three dimensional film on this same subject I will make someday, the forms will move out of infinity toward the spectator. Also remember that these films are made of up visual percussions in strict time like music, and must be thought of by the mental sequences that integrates strongly rhythmic auditory sensations, for example, and not the ones used for stationary art. Some people who see my movies for the first time say that they move too fast, but this is because they are using the wrong parts of their Brain.

The third film "Circular Tensions" and fourth film "Interwoven" and the Black & White one are imperfect attempts to use the [p. 4]discoveries discribed (sic) above. Also in the box are two samples of the original film in two stages of completion.

The rhythm of my films will automatically synchronize with any music having the same general speed. They are best silent, however.

The films should be projected at standard silent speed (16 frames a second) on as large a screen as possible.

I hope that this letter has not been too long and complex, but I wanted to tell you the best I could what I have been doing. A lot of my ideas are, I know, incorrect and will be changed later, but I have tried to say truthfully what I feel now.

I have also made about a hundred studies for a three dimensional film since I wrote you, but will not be able to do more on this particular project until I have projection equipment. Also I must learn your opinion on certain points before I go on with this. I am going to make every effort to move to your city next month, but unless a miracle happens I wont, (sic) as I am several hundred dollars short of what I need.

Please be carefull (sic) of your health, Miss Rebay, also of traffic, as the city is a dangerous place, and your life is of much greater value to us than even you suspect.

My friends and I pray for you every day.

Respectfully

Harry Smith

Hilla von Rebay Foundation Archive. M0007. Solomon R. Guggenheim Museum Archives, New York, N.Y.

Typographical errors and the "(sic)"s in the archival typescript are preserved in this transcription

Folkways
RECORDS & SERVICE CORP.
165 WEST
46 STREET
N. Y. C. 36
JUdson 6-7260

May 7 '64

Mr. Harry Smith
Hotel Earle
New York, N.Y.

To Whom it May Concern:

I am in receipt of 10 (ten) tapes #'s as follows; 19/2, 17/2,23/1,17/3,16/1,14/1,14/2,18/1,12/3,13/2, of American Indian material that I have recorded for Moses Asch of Folkways Records.

These tapes are part of the series that I have recorded in Oklahoma for Moses Asch.

I have in my possession a tape machine loaned from Vaseco Inc., 2301 Classen Blvd., Oklahoma City 6, Okla.and belonging to them.

I have received $20.00 in cash from Moses Asch yesterday (May 6th.) and have today (May 7th.) received a further $10.00 in cash as an advance for recordings and issuance of these tapes, in addition to previous money advanced to me.

I am going to edit and return to Moses Asch of Folkways Records the edited tapes for issuance of 10 (ten) or more long-playing records of Indian material that I have recorded in Oklahoma.

I owe to Moses Asch 2 (two) paintings of American Indians that I have at the Hotel Earle, New York City, for him.

Harry E. Smith
300½ 75th St. N.Y. 21, N.Y.

Harry Smith - Hotel Earle, N.Y.C.

Harry Smith, 7 May 1964

Vaseco Inc.
Visual and Sound Equipment Co.
TELEPHONE JAckson 5-3513 • 2301 CLASSEN BLVD. • OKLAHOMA CITY 6, OKLAHOMA

May 20,1964

Mr. Moses Asch,Director,
Folkways Records and Service Co,
165 W. 46th st,
New York,N.Y.

Dear Mr. Asch:

Thank you very much for your letter of May 18th explaining the situation with regard to Mr. Harry Smith.

First let me say there is no kind of insurance that will protect against infidelity,we found this out a long time ago.

Secondly,we recognize the fact that you are a producer and generally entitled to wholesale discounts,however we are not a wholesaler,but strictly a retailer and rental concern.The machine we let Mr. Smith have was a late model Wollensak,and to make the unit more adaptable to the type of work Mr. Smith was supposed to be using this for,we put a brand new $65.00 microphone with it,in addition to the mike that was normally supplied. I think you will find out that this is a very good price on this equipment,and not as you say some "fictitious" retail price.We supplied tape at $2.50 per roll,which normally sells for $3.50

Our invoice is enclosed for the amount previosly mentioned including the other items he took with him.

Sincerly yours,

W G Maxwell

Wgm/lc

wgm/lc

CC: Van Gray

W. G. Maxwell to Moses Asch, 20 May 1964

Courtesy Ralph Rinzler Folklife Archives and Collections, Smithsonian Institution, Washington, D.C.

Jonas Mekas, "The Magic Cinema of Harry Smith," 18 March 1965

Does Harry Smith really exist? Is he a black or a white magician? Who will be the next victim of Harry Smith? What horrors is he preparing, and for whom?

For years Harry Smith has been a black and ominous legend and a source of strange rumors. Some even said that he had left this planet long ago—the last alchemist of the Western world, the last magician.

Then one day, last summer, a year ago, Harry Smith gave up the darkness and appeared in the open. He was still full of evil, hate, small curses, and sneers, but he came out. We began looking into him, peeking into Harry Smith. And we were surprised to find, behind the beard and the curses, a sweet, humorous, and completely harmless man. We found that his little curses were only a protective wall, not an attack on others. The black magic was suddenly gone.

But not entirely.

Soon we discovered where Harry Smith's true magic was. Last Monday, at the Cinematheque, the audience gave Harry Smith a huge ovation. For three hours Harry Smith was pouring across the screen the most beautiful images conceivable. Here was a magician of images, of motion, of rhythms, of color. One of the greatest magicians of cinema alive.

For 30 years Harry Smith worked on these movies, secretly, like an alchemist, and he worked out his own formulas and mixtures to produce these fantastic images. You can watch them for pure color enjoyment; you can watch them for motion—Harry Smith films never stop moving; or you can watch them for hidden and symbolic meanings, alchemic signs. There are more levels in Harry Smith's work than in any other film animator I know. Animated cinema—all those Czechs, Poles, and Yugoslavs, and Pintoffs, and Bosustovs, and Hubleys are nothing but makers of cute cartoons. Harry Smith is the only serious film animator working in cinema today. His untitled work on alchemy and the creation of the world (none of Harry Smith's movies have titles) will remain one of the masterpieces of the animated cinema. But even his smaller works are marked by the same masterful and never-failing sense of movement—the most magic quality of Harry Smith's work.

Harry Smith respects his friendship with Fischinger and the Whitney brothers. But Fischinger has given up cinema years ago; and the Whitney brothers got involved in pure technical virtuosity and op art. Harry Smith remained the enfant terrible of the group and continued working and producing new work.

Not all his work is pleasant and happy. Some of it tastes of horror. But it is always a total expression of a unique personality, a unique world, both evil and kind—open, lyrical, and paranoiac.

I have to confess that very often I pity Andrew Sarris, my good friend—and I pity all other theorists of the auteur cinema who remain blind to some of the greatest film authors alive. Something is completely wrong with our movie theatre system, with our distribution of works of art—that's where the trouble lies. The balance must be restored. There should be three or four theatres on Times Square playing *Normal Love,* Brakhage, Markopoulos, Harry Smith, Ken Jacobs, Anger. I hope somebody will do something about it—like our honorable foundations, before the devil takes them. As it is now, the

New York (and world) motion picture theatre scene stinks; it is so overrun by one type of cinema that it's no wonder at all that our critics know nothing about the best motion pictures of our times. That's the situation of American film criticism and film distribution, A.D. 1965.

Originally published in Jonas Mekas, Movie Journal, Village Voice, *18 March 1965, 23; reprinted in Jonas Mekas,* Movie Journal: The Rise of the New American Cinema, 1959–1971 *(New York: Macmillan, 1972), 181–82.*

Jonas Mekas, "God Helps Harry Smith, Because He Helps Himself," 3 June 1971

For more than a year now, Harry Smith has been shooting what he himself calls his most important film to date, *Mahagonny*, based on Brecht and Weill. I keep seeing him dragging tripods, cameras, and rolls of film. Whenever I don't see Harry with a tripod, it means only one thing: Harry is out of production money. Harry Smith has faithfully remained with the tradition of the underground, working day by day, week by week, as the money comes. Where does it come from? Nobody knows. He simply trusts that it will come. The other day, he said, somebody sneaked $300 into his mail box, to continue the film work. But now, he said, he needs much more, maybe $2000, because he's ready to begin editing, needs a work print. So he said, pass the message to the people. Which I am doing here, because I consider Harry Smith one of the four or five greatest living film-makers. Plus, Harry is a genius.

A couple of months ago, Harry stopped in to visit me. He called me, he said he had to talk to me. Here are bits from our taped conversation.

Harry Smith: (about his new film) In addition to having like a political import, it will also be very complicated. It has 1,300 cuts in it, at least in the script that I've worked out. Because some of the scenes are like quarter-seconds, and some are ten minutes long. Right now, I need $200—to continue....

Jonas Mekas: How far will the $200 push you?

HS: It will get me another 1,000 feet of film. Plus the developing.

JM: And then, what?

HS: Then I'll come back and I'll ask for another $200. So if there is any way of raising money quickly, like on a loan basis....

JM: I think I know someone. I may need two or three days to hustle it. I know I couldn't get it for myself, but I think I may get it for you. I can't do it right now, I am too harassed.... But I figure something could be done.

HS: As I say, $200 would pay for 1,000 feet, and $400 would pay for 2,000 feet, and so forth. I think I'll have to shoot two-to-one. But there are important scenes that are missing. Because the reason for this process of like dividing a song maybe one picture for one word, or one line of the poem to one picture, or one song for one picture, is that I want to make the film intelligible for the Eskimos or the Australian aborigines, and so forth. I derived great pleasure from Eskimo poetry, you know, that's my line. It's like anthropology. In a sense I want to give them something back. So I took Brecht's poem "Mahagonny" and I tried to translate it to ideographs that are universally known. The film isn't going to be shown very much commercially, because I'm making a special screen for it, of tornoff newspapers so that the whole thing looks like a collage, a two-and-a-quarter-hour collage. So that any time that you can... I wouldn't bother you about this, except that I think the world is in peril and I'm trying to do something now other than the mere artistic thing. I'm trying to make something that combines a political message with the highest artistry that I'm capable of. This is by far the most complicated and expensive and everything-else film that I ever made. I assume it's going to be the most complicated and artistic underground film ever made... see... and the process has got to be speeded up because both Barry Miles and Allen Ginsberg seem to think the serious political situation is going to be beginning next summer and I want to have the film completed by then. So that I don't have nearly as much time as I thought I did. Now, I have living money, and I suppose, I have little money coming in from the Co-op. I am $1,400 behind in the rent, you know, at the hotel. That sort of thing. But any money given for the film is used only on the film. It can be a loan. I'll pay it back, you see. One thing that can be done, an interesting idea maybe, is for you to buy prints of the film at different stages of development, in other words, when the rushes are completed, buy a set of the rushes. Then, when the first cut is made, buy a set of that....

JM: Great idea. The only thing is where to get money for it?

HS: There is no money. I mean, the depression is in....

JM: Two hundred dollars, that I can get somewhere for you. I have a friend, he just came from Cincinnati, a newcomer, we can borrow $200 from him. We'll have to work on him, both of us.

HS: I don't need it right today. You understand, it has been costing about $150 a day to shoot. I think this film is going to cost around $30,000. These people, Film Planning Associates, they were way off on all the figures.

JM: Who are they?

HS: Somebody that I gave $300 to figure out how much the whole was going to cost, because this is the first time I have used all these things like A and B prints and careful cutting to the sound track—and I must say it was a great advantage to use your cutting room upstairs. So, in other words, production can go on and, as I say, if you can get $400—do that; or if you can get $600—do that.

JM: That's too much. Two hundred, that's what I hope for.

HS: Yeh, that would carry things for another 1000 feet.... Well, as I told you before, I think I'm the third best film producer in the country. I think Andy Warhol is the best. Kenneth Anger is the second best. And now I've decided I'm the third best. There was a question in my mind whether Brakhage or myself was third best. But I now think I am.... I don't want to stop, as long as I can still get pictures of trees with leaves on them. Otherwise, I have to, you know, rent a car and go to South Carolina, and I don't want to waste money doing that.... It's a shame to ask you for money this way...

JM: I don't talk about money, you know. Because I don't have any. But I'm willing to hustle for people I believe in.

HS: Well... in other words... well, you know... it's like playing marbles...

P.S. That's where our conversation ended in February. To bring you up to date: we managed to swindle $200 from Steve, after buying him five drinks at the Chelsea Hotel bar. Harry managed to shoot his leaves. I have no idea how he did it, because in February, when I looked at the trees, all I could see were some brown shrivels hanging on the branches. But Harry is a magician, I know he made them look like leaves. The other day I bumped into Harry and he had ten rolls of film in his lap: ten rolls of cherry blossoms, he said. Day by day, with the help of all good people, Harry Smith, one of the very, very few underground filmmakers left on this planet, an underground filmmaker as an Old Master, keeps pushing ahead, roll by roll. I remember someone once asked Harry how come he likes his own films, he always comes to see them. He answered: "I like my films because I didn't make them: God made them."

Harry Smith to Committee on Poetry, ca. 1973

APPLICATION FOR A GRANT IN AID FROM THE COMMITTEE ON POETRY INC., P.O. BOX 582, STUYVESANT STATION, NEW YORK CITY 10009.

APPLIED FOR BY HARRY SMITH, HOTEL CHELSEA, 222 W 23RD STREET, NEW YORK CITY 10011

(COMM.
C. R.)

IN CAMPAM.

For more than 2 1/2 years I have been working on the photography for a film version of Kurt Weil and Bertolt Brecht's magnum opus, "Rise and Fall of the City of Mahagonny," a parody of life in America.

QUIDAM PRECES NEGLIGUNT.

I selected "Mahagonny" as a vehicle for two reasons. First, because despite the complexity of repetition in the 21 songs in the opera, there are sections that approximate the sounds of both those muscial cultures that select melody as their fundamental trait and those which use rhythm as the point for development. Second, because the story is simple and widespread; the joyous gathering together of a great number of people, their breaking of the rules of liberty and love, and consequent fall into oblivion.

AUTOR ROSAM SUAM DONAT VIRGINI.

My photography has not been directed toward making a "realistic" version of the opera, but rather toward the translating, as nearly as I can, images of the German [p. ii] text into universal, or near universal, symbols and synchronizing the appropriate images with music.

DISCESSUS VIRGINI LUCIFERAE.

These images consist of about 250 categories such as eggs breaking, plants growing, rain falling, fire burning, parts of the human body and even scenes of the city. About half the footage consists of animation of one sort or another. The animation is based mostly on the fundamental symbols found in all art such as the circle or dots. The emotional connotations of objects moving toward, past, or away from the spectator, or things suddenly forming or dissolving, have also been utilized.

POTUS.

This method has been followed in order that the final film will be just as intelligible to the Zulu, the Eskimo, or the Australian Aborigine, as to people of any other cultural background or age.

INTERLUDIUM

In its final form the film will be a series of scenes of varying lengths synchronized to the time of an entire song, and on occasion, synchronized to the length of a single line of the lyrics, but all designed to translate the opera into a universal script based on the similarities of life and aspiration in all humans. As far as I know, the attempt to make a film for all people [p. iii] whether they be Papuans or New Yorkers, has not been so far attempted. It is by far the most complex of the 20 or so films I have made in the last 30 years; and my hope is that it will not only be successful, but will introduce a new theoretical basis for films and through the use of world wide symbols, help to bring all people of the Earth closer together.

MIRA CUPIDINUS LAETITIA.

The photography, more than 11 hours of raw material, was completed in July; and since then a slight start made at the editing. This start has been to separate those photographs which will not be used at all from about five hours of usable footage that the final shots will be selected from.

LIBERATUR VINCULIS.

The film now has to be cut down according to the principles, outlined earlier, to 2 1/2 hours – the length of the Weill-Brecht opera. Naturally this is the most complex and critical step in the production and will take a number of months – perhaps a year.

DONANTUR A SENE.

At this time I am not asking the Committee on Poetry for a grant sufficient to cover the completion of the film, but merely to continue the work. I estimate that 1500 dollars would cover three months and 5000 dollars [p. iv] six months of the process – the six month sum being greater per month because I would be able to employ more complex methods immediately, rather than waiting until later.

Sincerely,

AUTOR DORMIT CUM ATLANTE & SENE CUSTODE TURRIS.

Harry Smith

Harry Smith to Andy Berler, 22 December 1975

December 22, 1975.

Andy Berler,
C A P S [Creative Artists Public Service]
250 West 57th Street,
N Y C

Dear Andy:

I am writing you this rather informal progress report for two reasons. First because though I have tried to convince you by word and deed that I was suffering from what my doctor enigmatically calls a "severe psychic discompensation", you have been adament in your refusal to accept the fact that I was perhaps loco. I now may prove it to you. Secondly, because even among the laity there is an ever increasing interest in the literature of the mentally deranged in which genre I am always ready, nay, eager, to be a Master, I am, alas, myself a maniac.

There is admitedly a connection between art and madness whether it be a severe case of the latter, or a scarcely noticable but telltale super-accuracy of the brush or pen. I have always used my God-given gift of mental disease as perhaps the most valuable componant of my work. In point of fact, the whole film on the merits of which I was awarded the CAPS grant was made during a period of particularly severe derangement.

When I drunkenly told you as I accepted the first check how unlikely it was that I would follow the budget, I little suspected just how far my barque would drift from its appointed mooring. How the money was actually spent can be learnt from the bills, etc. that accompany this report. As the sort of film I make is "improvised" according to the dictates of a diseased brain I can never tell which direction its going to jump any more than I can tell what I am going to dream of a week from next Thursday.

Mahagonny is particularly difficult. You have to live Mahagonny, in fact be Mahagonny in order to work on it. Thus it is that it became more convienient and cheaper to set up a cutting where I live than to rent one. I can also arrange things in the room like the city of Mahagonny itself. Money that was alloted to raw stock, etc., for achieving certain effects by the use of filters, was used to study more about movement and personality in relation to emotion insofar as they affected the rhythmic cutting technique I am using. As the tedious task of analizing [p. 2] the sound track and translating its several thousand cuels into "universal" symbols proceeded it was necessary to make an extensive study of Weil's musical accomplishments before and after "Mahagonny" and especially to increase available information on non-European religion and art. Thus a number of books and records had to be obtained and people rewarded to impart information. This on top of paying the Hotel, a psychyatrist, etc.

As to the film itself; it is proceeding very nicely. The problems involved in turning the opera into "One" Big Ceremony (for that is what it is), and at the same time preserving the meaning and flavour of Brecht's libretto is not easy. The sound track has been analized, to almost its final form, a preliminary cutting of the film made and the final one charted.

The completion of the film will undoubtedly be later than the deadline originally agreed upon. I was drunk and sick most of the time before I went to the Hospital in August and September and am still weak. None the less, I will thanks to CAPS, soon finish a film that has taken all of my resources for the last seven years.

I estimate the cost of completing the film to be 8500 dollars;

Optical reprinting of two tableau of the film	1000
Titles (including special lettering and filming)	1500
Print of fully cut film	1000
Tinting print	1000
Internegative of tinted print	1500
Transferring Magnetic Film to optical track	1500
Composite print of image and sound	1000
	8500

This is slightly above the budget, but where there's a will there's a way, I guess. You must remember that I spend all of my income on one thing or another directly connected with making Mahagonny by my living through the birth and death of Mahagonny myself (more detailed information concerning the general method of approach to and theoretical [p. 3] background of the film can be found in the original application).

I enclose a letter from my psychiatrist and general advisor in things medical to attest that I no longer drink and am Good, etc. etc. etc. The doctor himself is a little balmy, dating the letter January 3, 1976 and, in a spasm of garbled syntax, seemingly makes CAPS responsable for my drunkeness "of twenty years standing". There is no doubt that the CAPS grant percipitated a drinking anf eating frenzy unparalelled in my recent history; a frenzy terminated only when I was strapped in a bed with a twenty % chance of living, a raving manic suffering for two weeks from halucinitory dolours that rival those Senate-president Schreber deliniates so skillfully in his "Memoirs of My Nervous Illness". So that if CAPS did nothing else it saved my life by frightening me so thoroughly that I no longer have the bad, bad desire for fire water.

Now I can proceed serenely, but sternly, on with Mahagonny producing a film that will make CAPS and all the millions of people who will see it during 1976 and the next few hundred years, thoughtful, edified, and pleased.

Sincerely yours,

Harry E. Smith
222 West 23rd Street, NYC

HS/mg

Typographical errors in the original are preserved in this transcription

SELECTED BIBLIOGRAPHY

Berge, Carol. "Dialogue without Words: The Work of Harry Smith." *Film Culture,* no. 37 (1965): 2–4.

A Booklet of Essays, Appreciations, and Annotations Pertaining to the "Anthology of American Folk Music" edited by Harry Smith. Reissue liner notes. SFW40090. Washington, D.C.: Smithsonian Folkways Recordings, 1997.

Brown, Mick. "Life in the Far-out Lane." *Daily Telegraph* (London), 19 June 1999, A6.

Cantwell, Robert. "The Ghost in the CD." Review of *Harry Smith's Anthology of American Folk Music, Volume Four* (Revenant). *Village Voice,* 8 August 2000, 65–66, 71.

———. *When We Were Good: The Folk Revival.* Cambridge: Harvard Univ. Press, 1996.

Carroll, Noël. "Mind, Medium and Metaphor in Harry Smith's *Heaven and Earth Magic.*" *Film Quarterly* 31, no. 2 (1977–78): 37–44.

Cohen, John. "Stringing Along: Harry Smith Figures." *Ganzfeld* 4 (2005): 33–41.

Daniel, Darrin. *Harry Smith: Fragments of a Northwest Life.* Seattle: Elbow, 2000.

Dollar, Steve. "An *Anthology* Grows, and a Folk Hero Lives." *Wall Street Journal,* 4 October 2000, A24.

Filene, Benjamin. "O Brother, What Next? Making Sense of the Folk Fad." *Southern Cultures* 10, no. 2 (2004): 50–69.

Frankel, David. "Old Folk." *Artforum,* January 1998, 21–22.

Fricke, David. "America's Greatest Hits." Review of the reissue of the *Anthology of American Folk Music,* edited by Harry Smith (Smithsonian Folkways Recordings, 1997). *Rolling Stone,* 18 September 1997, 101–2.

Gahr, David, and Robert Shelton. *The Face of Folk Music.* New York: Citadel, 1968.

Gascard, Lorettann Devlin. "Motion Painting: 'Abstract' Animation as an Art Form." *Leonardo* 16, no. 4 (1983): 293–97.

Gates, David. "The Roots of Rock." *Newsweek,* 2 June 1997, 72–73, 76.

Gehr, Richard. "Making the Cut." Music. *Village Voice,* 30 November 1999, 130.

Ginsberg, Allen. "Harry Smith—300 ½ E. 75 St. N.Y.C." In idem, *Journals: Early Fifties, Early Sixties,* ed. Gordon Ball, 185–86. New York: Grove, 1978.

———. *Snapshot Poetics: A Photographic Memoir of the Beat Era.* San Francisco: Chronicle, 1993.

Graham, Brian. *Brian Graham: Absurdity Is King: Twilight of the Beats.* Exh. cat. Lisbon: Casa Fernando Pessoa, 2005.

Gschwandtner, Sabrina. "A Brief History of String." *Cabinet,* no. 23 (2006): 38–41.

Harry Smith's Anthology of American Folk Music, Volume Four. Liner notes. RVN 211. Austin: Revenant/Harry Smith Archives, 2000.

The Heavenly Tree Grows Downward: Selected Works by Harry Smith, Philip Taaffe, Fred Tomaselli. Exh. cat. New York: James Cohan Gallery, 2002.

Hinckley, David. "Perfecting the Self: Harry Smith." *Daily News* (New York), 15 October 1999, 39.

Hoberman, J. "Animators from Hell." *Premiere,* April 1991, 38–39.

Igliori, Paola, ed. *American Magus Harry Smith: A Modern Alchemist.* New York: Inanout, 1996. Includes recollections of Harry Smith by Moe Asch, Jordan Belson, Harvey Bialy, Bill Breeze, Khem Caigan, Robert Frank, Debbie Freeman, Allen Ginsberg, Joe Gross, Paola Igliori, Henry Jones, Kasoundra Kasoundra, Jonas Mekas, Rosebud (Rosemarie Feliu-Pettet), Rani Singh, Jim Wasserman, and Lionel Ziprin.

"Injuneer." Interesting People. *American Magazine,* March 1943, 118.

Kelman, Ken. "Death and Trancefiguration." *Film Culture,* no. 34 (1964): 51–53.

Lukach, Joan M. *Hilla Rebay: In Search of the Spirit in Art.* New York: George Braziller, 1983.

MacDonald, Scott. *Art in Cinema: Documents toward a History of the Film Society.* Philadelphia: Temple University Press, 2006.

———. "Jordan Belson (and Collaborator Stephen Beck)." In idem, *A Critical Cinema 3: Interviews with Independent Filmmakers,* 64–92. Berkeley: Univ. of California Press, 1998.

Mancini, JoAnne Marie. "Messin' with the Furniture Man": Early Country Music, Regional Culture, and the Search for an Anthological Modernism." *American Literary History* 16 (2004): 208–37.

Manvell, Roger, ed. *Experiment in the Film.* London: Grey Walls, 1949.

Marcus, Greil. *Invisible Republic: Bob Dylan's Basement Tapes.* New York: Henry Holt, 1997.

———. *Mystery Train: Images of America in Rock 'n' Roll Music.* New York: E. P. Dutton, 1975.

Mekas, Jonas. *Movie Journal: The Rise of the New American Cinema, 1959–1971.* New York: Macmillan, 1972.

Noguez, Dominique. "Les quatre mille farces du diable: Le cinema d'Harry Smith." In idem, *Éloge du cinéma expérimental: Définitions, jalons, perspectives,* 96–99. Paris: Éditions Paris Expérimental, 1999. First edition published by the Musée national d'art moderne, Centre Georges Pompidou, in 1979.

Perl, Jed. *New Art City: Manhattan at Mid-Century.* New York: Knopf, 2005.

Renan, Sheldon. *An Introduction to the American Underground Film.* New York: Dutton, 1967.

Sargeant, Jack. "'Eyeball Head Poem': The Animated Worlds of Harry Smith." In idem, *Naked Lens: Beat Cinema,* 91–100. Expanded ed. London: Creation, 2001. First edition, 1997.

Sexton, Jamie. "Alchemical Transformations: The Abstract Films of Harry Smith." *Senses of Cinema* 36 (2005), http://archive.sensesofcinema.com/contents/05/36/harry_smith.html (accessed 4 June 2009).

Singh, Rani. "Harry Smith." *Film Culture,* no. 76 (1992): 13–19.

———. "The Last Day in the Life of Harry Smith." *Film Culture,* no. 76 (1992): 20–21.

Sitney, P. Adams. "Absolute Animation." In idem, *Visionary Film: The American Avant-Garde, 1943–2000,* 231–67. 3rd ed. New York: Oxford Univ. Press, 2002. First edition, 1974; the second edition, 1979.

———. "Animating the Absolute: Harry Smith." *Artforum,* May 1972, 60–71.

Skinner, Katherine. "'Must Be Born Again': Resurrecting the *Anthology of American Folk Music.*" *Popular Music* 25 (2006): 57–75.

"Smith, Harry." *Film-Makers' Cooperative Catalogue,* no. 3 (1965): 57–58. The entire catalog was appended to *Film Culture,* no. 37 (1965).

Smith, Harry. Handbook to the *Anthology of American Folk Music.* FP 251–FP 253. New York: Folkways Records, 1952. Facsimile included in the reissue of the *Anthology of American Folk Music* (Smithsonian Folkways Recordings, 1997).

———. "Harry Smith Interview." Interview by Arthur Cantrill. *Cantrills Filmnotes* (Melbourne), no. 19 (1974): 6–13.

———. "Harry Smith Interview." Interview by P. Adams Sitney. *Film Culture,* no. 37 (1965): 4–13 (with John Palmer's series of photographs of Harry Smith). Reprinted in P. Adams Sitney, ed., *"Film Culture" Reader* (New York: Praeger, 1970), 260–76; in P. Adams Sitney, ed., *The Avant-Garde Film: A Reader of Theory and Criticism* (New York: New York Univ. Press, 1978), 87–102; and as "P. Adams Sitney—NYC [*Film Culture,* no. 37, 1965]," in Harry Smith, *Think of the Self Speaking: Harry Smith—Selected Interviews,* ed. Rani Singh (Seattle: Elbow/Cityful, 1999), 44–64.

———. "Harry Smith Interviewed, January 5th and January 15th, 1972, New York City." Interview by Mary Hill. *Film Culture,* no. 76 (1992): 1–7. Reprinted as "Mary Hill—NYC [1972—*Film Culture,* no. 76, 1992]," in Harry Smith, *Think of the Self Speaking: Harry Smith—Selected Interviews,* ed. Rani Singh (Seattle: Elbow/Cityful, 1999), 166–79.

———. "John Cohen—Chelsea Hotel, NYC [*Sing Out!* Volume 19, No. 1, 1969]." Interview by John Cohen. In idem, *Think of the Self Speaking: Harry Smith—Selected Interviews,* ed. Rani Singh, 66–100. Seattle: Elbow/Cityful, 1999. Expanded version of Harry Smith, "A Rare Interview with Harry Smith," *Sing Out!* 19, no. 1 (1969): 2–11, 41; no. 2 (1969): 22–28.

———. Liner notes for *The Kiowa Peyote Meeting.* FE 4601. New York: Folkways Records, 1973. Excerpt printed in Paola Igliori, ed., *American Magus Harry Smith: A Modern Alchemist* (New York: Inanout, 1996), 162–67.

———. "On *Mahagonny.*" Interview by P. Adams Sitney. In P. Adams Sitney, ed., *The Avant-Garde Film: A Reader of Theory and Criticism* (New York: New York Univ. Press, 1978), 103–9. Reprinted as "P. Adams Sitney—NYC [*Mahagonny,* 1977]," in Harry Smith, *Think of the Self Speaking: Harry Smith—Selected Interviews,* ed. Rani Singh (Seattle: Elbow/Cityful, 1999), 102–10.

———. "A Rare Interview with Harry Smith." Interview by John Cohen. *Sing Out!* 19, no. 1 (1969): 2–11, 41; no. 2 (1969): 22–28. Reprinted in facsimile in Paola Igliori, ed., *American Magus Harry Smith: A Modern Alchemist* (New York: Inanout, 1996), 125–36, 138–44.

———. *Think of the Self Speaking: Harry Smith—Selected Interviews.* Edited by Rani Singh. Seattle: Elbow/Cityful, 1999. Includes interviews of Harry Smith by Dawn Michelle Baude, John Cohen, Mary Hill, Gary Kenton, A. J. Melita, and P. Adams Sitney, along with an interview of Allen Ginsberg by Hal Willner.

Smith, Philip. "The Art of Memory." *Wire,* June 2000, 25–27.

———. "Harry Smith." In Eric Olsen, Paul Verna, and Carlo Wolff, *The Encyclopedia of Record Producers,* 740–41. New York: Billboard, 1999.

Sons et lumières: Une histoire du son dans l'art du XXe siècle. Exh. cat. Paris: Centre Pompidou, 2004.

Turner, Florence. *At the Chelsea.* London: Hamish Hamilton, 1986.

Visual Music: Synaesthesia in Art and Music since 1900. Exh. cat. London: Thames & Hudson, 2005.

Ward, Geoff. "Going Fishing: Harry Smith, the *Anthology of American Folk Music,* and the Fan." In idem, *The Writing of America: Literature and Cultural Identity from the Puritans to the Present,* 136–57. Cambridge: Polity, 2002.

Wasserman, James. *Art and Symbols of the Occult: Images of Power and Wisdom.* Rochester, Vt.: Destiny, 1993.

Weisbard, Eric. "The Folk Slingers." *Village Voice,* 13 January 1998, 71–74.

BIOGRAPHICAL NOTES ON THE CONTRIBUTORS

PAUL ARTHUR was professor of English and film studies at Montclair State University in New Jersey. Well known for his writings about the aesthetics and politics of avant-garde cinema, film noir, and documentaries, he was a contributing editor to *Film Comment*, associate editor of *Cineaste*, and coeditor of *Millennium Film Journal*. He was also a filmmaker, with fifteen shorts and one feature to his credit, and, in the mid-1980s, served on the boards of the Collective for Living Cinema and the Film-Makers' Cooperative. His study *A Line of Sight: American Avant-Garde Film since 1965* appeared in 2005.

ROBERT CANTWELL is Townsend Ludington Professor of American Studies at the University of North Carolina, Chapel Hill. He is the author of *Ethnomimesis: Folklife and the Representation of Culture* (1993), *When We Were Good: The Folk Revival* (1996), and *If Beale Street Could Talk: Music, Community, Culture* (2008). His first book, *Bluegrass Breakdown: The Making of the Old Southern Sound* (1984), won the ASCAP Deems Taylor Award.

THOMAS CROW is Rosalie Solow Professor of Modern Art at the Institute of Fine Arts at New York University and served as director of the Getty Research Institute from 2000 to 2007. He is a contributing editor to *Artforum* and writes frequently on contemporary art and cultural issues. Since his award-winning first book, *Painters and Public Life in Eighteenth-Century Paris* (1985), he has published several volumes on the art of the later twentieth century, including *The Rise of the Sixties: American and European Art in the Era of Dissent* (1996) and *The Intelligence of Art* (1999), as well as major essays on Gordon Matta-Clark (2003), Robert Smithson (2004), Robert Rauschenberg (2005), and Jasper Johns (2008).

STEPHEN FREDMAN is professor of English at the University of Notre Dame. His research interests range across twentieth-century and contemporary American poetry and poetics, prose poetry, translation theory, and issues of Judaism within the modern era. He has published three books of criticism, including *Poet's Prose: The Crisis in American Verse* (1983), which was nominated for a Pulitzer Prize, and *A Menorah for Athena: Charles Reznikoff and the Jewish Dilemmas of Objectivist Poetry* (2001), which was nominated for the Koret Jewish Book Award. He is also the editor of *A Concise Companion to Twentieth-Century American Poetry* (2005).

STEPHEN HINTON is professor of music and senior associate dean for humanities and arts at Stanford University. He has contributed widely to scholarship on modern German music and cultural history, with a particular focus on Kurt Weill. He is the author of *The Idea of Gebrauchsmusik* (1989) and the editor of *Kurt Weill: The Threepenny Opera* (1990), published in the Cambridge Opera Handbooks series, and Kurt Weill, *Musik und Theater: Gesammelte Schriften* (with Jürgen Schebera, 1990; rev. ed., 2000), and has served as the editor of *Beethoven Forum*. His current book project is entitled *Weill's Musical Theater: Stages of Reform*.

GREIL MARCUS is the author of *The Shape of Things to Come: Prophecy and the American Voice* (2006), *The Old, Weird America: The World of Bob Dylan's Basement Tapes* (1997), and *Lipstick Traces: A Secret History of the Twentieth Century* (1989), among other books. He is as well the editor of *The Rose and the Briar: Death, Love and Liberty in the American Ballad* (with Sean Wilentz, 2005) and of *A New Literary History of America* (with Werner Sollors, 2009). In recent years, he has taught at the University of California, Berkeley; Princeton University; The New School; and the University of Minnesota.

ANNETTE MICHELSON is professor emeritus of cinema studies at New York University. She has published widely on topics ranging from the work of early Soviet filmmakers and the films of Andy Warhol to the minimalist sculpture of Robert Morris. She is a founding editor of the journal *October*, which has been a powerful voice in contemporary debates surrounding art criticism, politics, and aesthetics since 1976. In 2003, *Camera Obscura, Camera Lucida*, a volume of essays by some of the many scholars influenced by her unique contributions to art and film criticism, was published in her honor.

WILLIAM MORITZ was a film historian, author, poet, educator, and filmmaker. An expert on animation, experimental film, and visual music, he was the author of over one hundred essays and articles as well as the critical biography *Optical Poetry: The Life and Work of Oskar Fischinger* (2004). He was professor of film at the California Institute of the Arts and lectured and presented experimental film programs at museums, festivals, conferences, and universities worldwide. The recipient of a Lifetime Achievement Award for his work in visual music from the Royal Academy of the Netherlands in 1993, he was a founder of the Center for Visual Music.

ANDREW PERCHUK is deputy director of the Getty Research Institute. He was formerly a curator at the Alternative Museum in New York City, for which he organized exhibitions such as *Maureen Connor: Discrete Objects* (1995) and an installation on Malcolm X featuring the collective X-Prz (1993). He has coedited two other volumes, *The Masculine Masquerade* (with Helaine Posner, 1996) and *Allan Kaprow—Art as Life* (with Eva Meyer-Hermann and Stephanie Rosenthal, 2008), and is a frequent contributor to journals that publish on contemporary art. He is currently organizing a major exhibition on postwar art in Los Angeles that will be presented at the J. Paul Getty Museum in 2011 as part of the initiative *Pacific Standard Time: Art in L.A. 1945–1980*.

RANI SINGH is senior research associate in the Department of Architecture and Contemporary Art at the Getty Research Institute. At present she is coordinating the documentation of the visual arts in Los Angeles since 1945 as part of the Research Institute's "Modern Art in Los Angeles" project; she is also associate curator of a major exhibition on postwar art in Los Angeles that will be presented at the J. Paul Getty Museum in 2011 as part of the initiative *Pacific Standard Time: Art in L.A. 1945–1980*. She was Harry Smith's assistant from 1988 until his death in 1991, and since 1991 she has been the director of the Harry Smith Archives. Her film *The Old Weird America: Harry Smith's "Anthology of American Folk Music"* appeared in 2007.

P. ADAMS SITNEY is professor of visual arts at the Lewis Center for the Arts at Princeton University. A founder of Anthology Film Archives in New York City, where he first met Harry Smith in 1964, he is the author of *Visionary Film: The American Avant-Garde* (1974, 2nd ed. 1979, 3rd ed. 2002), the first major history of post–World War II avant-garde filmmaking in the United States. He is also the author of *Modernist Montage: The Obscurity of Vision in Cinema and Literature* (1990), *Vital Crises in Italian Cinema: Iconography, Stylistics, Politics* (1995), and *Eyes Upside Down: Visionary Filmmakers and the Heritage of Emerson* (2008).

ILLUSTRATION CREDITS

Unless otherwise noted, all works by Harry Smith are © Harry Smith Archives and are reproduced in this volume by permission. The following sources have also granted permission to reproduce images in this volume:

viii Courtesy Allen Ginsberg Estate
2 Photo: Scott A. Feero. Courtesy Harry Smith Archives
14, 52 © Allen Ginsberg Estate
17, 22, 195 Courtesy Harry Smith Archives
20, FIG. 4 Photo: Bill Holm
20, FIG. 5 Courtesy of the Samish Indian Nation
21 Courtesy Bret Lunsford
25, FIG. 9 Photo: Lew Tyrell. Courtesy The *DownBeat* Archive.
32, 172, 186, 212, 214 Reproduced by permission of the Center for Folklife and Cultural Heritage, Smithsonian Institution, Washington, D.C.
40; 146, FIG. 10 Courtesy Anthology Film Archives
47, FIG. 22 Research Library, Getty Research Institute (1378-552)
48, FIG. 25 Research Library, Getty Research Institute (1378-360)
53 Photo: Peter Cole
77 Reproduced by permission of Little Brown & Company, an imprint of Lippincott Williams & Wilkins
78 Research Library, Getty Research Institute (84-S968)
95 Reproduced by permission of the publisher
97, 98 Courtesy Cornell University, Carl A. Kroch Library, Division of Rare & Manuscript Collections, RJ101.S37
99 Courtesy Cambridge University Library, Hunter.c.87.34.a
114 © Friedl Kubelka. Photo: Friedl Kubelka/ Fotocollection Ôsterreichische Filmmuseum/ The Austrian Film Museum, Vienna
134; 146, FIG. 9 © Michael Snow. Reproduced by permission
135; 143, FIG. 6 © Hollis Frampton Estate, courtesy Anthology Film Archives
142 Courtesy Peter Kubelka
143, FIG. 5 © The Paul Sharits Estate, courtesy Anthology Film Archives
144 © 2008 Artists Rights Society (ARS), New York/ADAGP, Paris/Succession Marcel Duchamp. Photo: The Philadelphia Museum of Art/Art Resource, New York
148 Courtesy Ernie Gehr
158, 159, 162 Musical notation: Don Giller, New York City
161 Collection of Dr. Jürgen Schebera, Berlin
177 Photo: © Gemma Baumer
180 Courtesy Charles Wolfe Collection
209; 217, FIG. 9; 218 Digital Image © The Museum of Modern Art/Licensed by SCALA/Art Resource, New York
210 © The Estate of John Kane, courtesy Galerie St. Etienne, New York. Digital Image © The Museum of Modern Art/Licensed by SCALA/Art Resource, New York
215 © The Estate of Jackson Mac Low. Photo: Research Library, Getty Research Institute (94-B19099)
216, FIG. 6 Research Library, Getty Research Institute (890164, Box 167)
216, FIG. 7 © The Estate of George Maciunas, courtesy Billie Maciunas. Photo: Research Library, Getty Research Institute (890164, Box 192)
217, FIG. 8 *Flag Gate,* Artist unidentified, Jefferson County, New York, c. 1876, Paint on wood with iron and brass, 39½ × 57 × 3¾ in. Collection of the American Folk Art Museum, New York, Gift of Herbert Waide Hemphill, Jr., 1962.1.1. Photo by Gavin Ashworth
228 Research Library, Getty Research Institute (1378-183)
230 From *Brian Graham: Absurdity Is King: Twilight of the Beats,* exh. cat. (Lisbon: Casa Fernando Pessoa, 2005), 27. Reproduced by permission
240, FIG. 5 Jess (Burgess Franklin Collins), 1923–2004, *The Enamord Mage: Translation #6,* 1965, oil on canvas mounted on wood, 62.2 × 76.2 cm (24½ × 30 in.). Fine Arts Museums of San Francisco, Foundation Purchase, Gift of a grateful Board of Trustees in honor of Harry S. Parker III, Director of the Fine Arts Museums of San Francisco, 1987–2005, 2005.87. Copyright © 2009 by the Jess Collins Trust and used by permission. Photo: Fine Arts Museums of San Francisco
240, FIG. 6 Copyright © 2009 by the Jess Collins Trust and used by permission. Photo: Benjamin Blackwell, Alameda, California

INDEX

Illustrations are indicated by page numbers in italic.

Titles in the ISSUES & DEBATES series and other books based on events and programs of the Getty Research Institute

The Issues & Debates series makes available scholarship produced by the programs and staff of the Getty Research Institute in collaboration with scholars and institutions worldwide. The volumes in this series are usually inspired by the Research Institute's conferences, workshops, and lecture series, which draw from the extensive archival, rare books, and artistic holdings of the Research Institute or bear upon its annual research themes.

IN PRINT

Bernard Picart and the First Global Vision of Religion
Edited by Lynn Hunt, Margaret Jacob, and Wijnand Mijnhardt
ISBN 978 0 89236 968 3 (paper)

The Fragment: An Incomplete History
Edited by William Tronzo
ISBN 978-0-89236-926-3 (hardcover)

Ephemeral Bodies: Wax Sculpture and the Human Figure
Edited by Roberta Panzanelli
ISBN 978-0-89236-877-8 (hardcover)

The Life and the Work: Art and Biography
Edited by Charles G. Salas
ISBN 978-0-89236-823-5 (hardcover)

Rethinking Boucher
Edited by Melissa Hyde and Mark Ledbury
ISBN 978-0-89236-825-9 (paper)

Late Thoughts: Reflections on Artists and Composers at Work
Edited by Karen Painter and Thomas Crow
ISBN 978-0-89236-813-6 (paper)

Seeing Rothko
Edited by Glenn Phillips and Thomas Crow
ISBN 978-0-89236-734-4 (paper)

Situating El Lissitzky: Vitebsk, Berlin, Moscow
Edited by Nancy Perloff and Brian Reed
ISBN 978-0-89236-677-4 (paper)

Representing the Passions: Histories, Bodies, Visions
Edited by Richard Meyer
ISBN 978-0-89236-676-7 (paper)

The Archaeology of Colonialism
Edited by Claire L. Lyons and John K. Papadopoulos
ISBN 978-0-89236-635-4 (paper)

Looking for Los Angeles: Architecture, Film, Photography, and the Urban Landscape
Edited by Charles G. Salas and Michael S. Roth
ISBN 978-0-89236-616-3 (paper)

Disturbing Remains: Memory, History, and Crisis in the Twentieth Century
Edited by Michael S. Roth and Charles G. Salas
ISBN 978-0-89236-538-8 (paper)

Nietzsche and "An Architecture of Our Minds"
Edited by Alexandre Kostka and Irving Wohlfarth
ISBN 978-0-89236-485-5 (paper)

Dosso's Fate: Painting and Court Culture in Renaissance Italy
Edited by Luisa Ciammitti, Steven F. Ostrow, and Salvatore Settis
ISBN 978-0-89236-505-0 (paper)

Censorship and Silencing: Practices of Cultural Regulation
Edited by Robert C. Post
ISBN 978-0-89236-484-8 (paper)

Otto Wagner: Reflections on the Raiment of Modernity
Edited by Harry Francis Mallgrave
ISBN 978-0-89236-258-5 (hardcover)
ISBN 978-0-89236-257-8 (paper)

American Icons: Transatlantic Perspectives on Eighteenth- and Nineteenth-Century American Art
Edited by Thomas W. Gaehtgens and Heinz Ickstadt
ISBN 978-0-89236-247-9 (paper)

Art in History/History in Art: Studies in Seventeenth-Century Dutch Culture
Edited by David Freedberg and Jan de Vries
ISBN 978-0-89236-200-4 (paper)

IN PREPARATION

Cultural Identity and the Peoples of the Ancient Mediterranean
Edited by Erich S. Gruen
ISBN 978-0-89236-969-0 (paper)

Designed by Stuart Smith
Production coordinated by Suzanne Watson
Type composed by Diane Franco in Minion and Trade Gothic
Printed in China through Asia Pacific Offset, Inc., on Gold East Matte

Issues & Debates
Series designed by Stuart Smith